THE GREAT TRANSFORMATION OF
MUSICAL TASTE

Grounded in knowledge of thousands of programs, this book examines how musical life in London, Paris, Leipzig, Vienna, Boston, and
other cities underwent a fundamental transformation in relationship
with movements in European political life. William Weber traces how
musical taste evolved in European concert programs from 1750 to 1875,
as separate worlds arose around classical music and popular songs. In
1780 a typical program accommodated a variety of tastes through a
patterned "miscellany" of genres, held together by diplomatic musicians. This framework began weakening around 1800 as new kinds of
music appeared, from string quartets to quadrilles to ballads, which
could not easily coexist on the same programs. Utopian ideas and
extravagant experiments influenced programming as ideological bat-
tles were fought over who should govern musical taste. More than a
hundred illustrations or transcriptions of programs enable readers to
follow Weber's analysis in detail.

William Weber is Professor Emeritus of History at California State
University, Long Beach.

THE GREAT TRANSFORMATION OF MUSICAL TASTE

Concert Programming from Haydn to Brahms

WILLIAM WEBER

John Michael Cooper
Denton, Texas
12 November 2012

CAMBRIDGE
UNIVERSITY PRESS

CAMBRIDGE UNIVERSITY PRESS
Cambridge, New York, Melbourne, Madrid, Cape Town, Singapore,
São Paulo, Delhi, Dubai, Tokyo

Cambridge University Press
32 Avenue of the Americas, New York, NY 10013-2473, USA

www.cambridge.org
Information on this title: www.cambridge.org/9780521124232

First published 2008
Third printing 2009
This digitally printed version 2009

A catalog record for this publication is available from the British Library

Library of Congress Cataloging in Publication data
Weber, William, 1940–
The great transformation of musical taste : concert programming from Haydn to Brahms /
William Weber.
p.   cm.
Includes bibliographical references (p.   ) and index.
ISBN-13 : 978-0-521-88260-6 (hardback)
1. Concerts – Europe – History – 19th century.   2. Concerts – Europe – History – 18th century.
3. Music – Social aspects – History – 19th century.   4. Music – Social aspects – History –
18th century.   I. Title.
ML240.W43   2008
780.78–dc22   2007037290

ISBN 978-0-521-88260-6 Hardback
ISBN 978-0-521-12423-2 Paperback

To Linda

Contents

Illustrations follow page xvi

Illustrations of concert programs

C. ORCHESTRAL AND PROMENADE CONCERTS

11. Abonnenten-Concerte (Subscription Concerts), Gewandhaus, 15 February 1787: Stadtgeschichtliches Museum, Leipzig.
12. Philharmonic Society, Hanover Square Rooms, London, 1 May 1826: CPH/RCM.
13. University Musical Festival, Holywell Music Room, Oxford, 16 June 1832: CPH/RCM.
14. Concert Spirituel, Saal der Musikfreunde, Vienna, 10 March 1833: Universität der Musik und Darstellende Kunst.
15. Allgemeine Deutsche Musikverein, Königliches Theater, Hannover, 24 May 1876: Deutsche Staatsbibliothek, Berlin.
16. Promenade Concert, Royal Lyceum Theatre, London, 26–29 December 1838: British Library.
17. Johann Strauss, the Younger, Centralhalle, Leipzig, 11 October 1852: Stadtbibliothek.
18. Germania Musical Society, City Hall, Worcester, Mass., 5 June 1849: American Antiquarian Society.

D. VOCAL-MUSIC CONCERTS

19. Breakfast Concert, Villa Gardens, Bath, 25 April 1787: British Library.
20. Miss Helen Davis, Boylston Hall, Boston, 15 May 1822: Huntington Library.
21. Mr. Shaw, Hull, 1834: John Johnson Collection, Bodleian Library.
22. Singspiel-Halle (Salon Variété), Hôtel de Saxe, Leipzig, 4 December 1866: Stadtgeschichtliches Museum.
23. *Café-Concert*, Casino de Paris, February 1868: Bibliothèque Nationale de France.
24. Jacques Blumenthal, Dudley Gallery, Egyptian Hall, Piccadilly, London, 25 June 1857: CPH/RCM.
25. Mme Ronzi, née Scalese, Salle Herz, Paris, 3 May 1869: Bibliothèque Nationale de France.
26. *Potpourris sur les motifs d'Opéras favoris pour le Piano*, by Henri Cramer, c. 1860–1870: Getty Research Institute.

Transcriptions of concert programs

Ideally, a concert program is reconstructed from both a printed program and reports in periodicals. But periodical coverage was limited before 1840, and even after that reviewers usually did not mention all pieces performed. Printed programs have therefore been the principal resource for this study, especially for concerts offering a large number of pieces. The transcriptions identify pieces as closely as can be established. Note the following indicators:

- [?]: uncertain item, e.g., [?Pietro Alessandro] Guglielmi
- Quotation marks in title: text on the printed program
- †: composer deceased
- Dashes (–): known intermission.
- Parentheses: name of performer, e.g., (Joseph Joachim)
- *Italics*: composer also performer

EXAMPLES OF PROGRAMS

Acknowledgments

The book emerged from a grant made by the Leverhulme Trust to the Royal College of Music in 2002 for the collection of concert programs and my visit to the college that year. I am particularly indebted to Dame Janet Ritterman, director of the Royal College of Music, and to Paul Banks, director of the Centre for Performance History. I would also like to thank members of staff for their support – Oliver Davies, Paul Collen, Janet Hilton, Peter Horton, Neil Mackie, and Ian Curror.

I began doing research on this project earlier in my career, aided by fellowships from the National Endowment for the Humanities, the Rockefeller Foundation, and the Fulbright-Hayes Program. I benefited greatly from residencies at the École des Hautes Études en Sciences Sociales, Max Planck Historical Institute, Huntington Library, and William Andrews Clark Memorial Library at UCLA, and finally a grant by the Music & Letters Trust. My colleagues at California State University assisted me greatly, as did the inter-library loan staff. I wish also to thank the staff of the British Library, Bodleian Library, Bibliothèque National, Bibliothèque de l'Opéra, Musée de l'Histoire de la Ville de Paris, Leipzig Stadtgeschichtliches Museum, Leipzig Stadtbibliothek, University of Göttingen Library, Deutsche Staatsbibliothek, Oesterreichische Nationalbibliothek, Gesellschaft der Musikfreunde and Stadtbibliothek in Vienna, Boston Public Library, and Harvard Musical Association Library.

I wish to express my debt for comments and criticism to Mark Evan Bonds, Michael Broyles, Dexter Edge, Katharine Ellis, Joël-Marie Fauquet, Robert Fink, James Garratt, Matthew Gelbart, Christopher Gibbs, Dana Gooley, David Gramit, Kenneth Hamilton, David Wyn Jones, Annette Landgraf, Simon McVeigh, Mary Anne Morrow, Nancy Newman, Michel Noiray, Hilary Poriss, Derek Scott, Rita Steblin, Mark Swed, Patrick Taïeb, and Beverly Wilcox. Victoria Cooper and Rebecca Jones have aided me with their high professionalism. I owe particular gratitude to Linda Clark, my wife, for extensive editorial comments and deep support for the project.

Introduction

Designing a concert program necessarily involves a set of compromises among publics, musicians, tastes, and, by extension, social forces. Because most concerts serve a variety of groups with different tastes, desires, and needs, planning a program is a kind of political process. Musicians and concert administrators learn to negotiate among these groups, seeking ways to satisfy them separately and jointly. But such social accommodation went much deeper in musical life during the eighteenth century than it does today. Fewer concerts then took place, the public was far smaller, and musical life was much more tightly bound and necessarily collegial. Writers liked to talk about the Republic of Music, where disputes occurred comparable to those among monarchs, legislative bodies, and public opinion. Conflict over taste was built into this social system, and some listeners found musical dispute an intellectual pleasure. This dialogue on musical values served as the public forum where musical values were transformed fundamentally during the first half of the nineteenth century.

The guiding principle for designing concert programs in the eighteenth century, often called "miscellany," grew out of longstanding musical traditions. Given the limited number of concerts at that time, musicians and listeners assumed that they would have to accommodate one another in programming, taste, and social behavior – concerts were a collegial undertaking. Whereas we expect a typical orchestral concert to offer three works by great composers, programs around 1780 included between eight to fifteen pieces, a few by deceased composers. On one program one would hear a mix of opera numbers, concertos, instrumental solos, overtures, or symphonies, and possibly a string quartet or a song. There existed no great distinction between serious and casual interest in music; people with a variety of musical needs and tastes came together to hear the same program.

Still, we should not exaggerate the extent of miscellany in eighteenth-century concerts. Songs composed for the salon, tavern, or men's clubs were excluded from most concerts because formal and informal kinds of music-making were thought best kept separate. No hierarchical scheme differentiated these areas of music-making, though the aesthetic status of songs differed significantly in France, Britain, and Germany. Indeed, conventional miscellaneous programming entered into crisis when songs became more numerous in public concerts in the early nineteenth century. By 1830 many new kinds of music appeared in programs – dance music, sentimental ballads, and medleys of opera tunes. That raised serious questions about how diverse a program ought to be musically and socially, producing conflict among sections of the public such as had not occurred during the eighteenth century. An idealistic movement arose with a vision for taste and programming according to "higher" principles than those seen in what was called "salon" music, the latter consisting of opera excerpts and variations on popular opera tunes. Because the old framework of concert life could not maintain order in that new context, musical life began to break apart into separate regions of repertory and taste. During the 1850s a dichotomy between music deemed more serious and that deemed less serious became established, even though the word *popular* was not widely used in this sense outside Britain and North America.[1]

Aggressive composers did much to initiate the transformation of musical culture, seen in W.-A. Mozart's *Le Nozze di Figaro* (1786), Luigi Cherubini's *Médée* (1797), Joseph Haydn's *Schöpfung* (1798), and Ludwig van Beethoven's "Eroica" Symphony (1805) and string quartets. More broadly conceived, the breakup of musical life took place within a context of deep instability in European politics and society between 1789 and 1848. The sovereignty of the state having been more or less achieved by around 1750, a fundamental rethinking of the nature of government developed among the educated upper and middle classes. Internal upheavals occurred widely throughout Europe. The French Revolution and Napoleon's reorganization of Europe opened up new possibilities that destabilized politics almost everywhere.[2] Along with political upheaval came an efflorescence of utopian thinking about ideal communities or the reform of professional or cultural worlds. Such movements developed separately from one other and could conflict intellectually or politically, but their influence proved mutually

---

[1] I discussed this topic in "Wagner, Wagnerism, and Musical Idealism," *Wagnerism in European Culture and Politics* (Ithaca, NY: Cornell University Press, 1984), pp. 28–71.

[2] Robert Palmer, *The Age of the Democratic Revolution: A Political History of Europe and America, 1760–1800*, 2 vols. (Princeton, N.J.: Princeton University Press, 1959–64); Jost Hermand and Michael Niedermeier, *Revolutio Germanica: Die Sehnsucht nach der "alten Freiheit" der Germanen, 1750–1820* (Frankfurt: Peter Lang, 2003); Esteban Buch, *Beethoven's Ninth: A Political History*, Richard Miller (trans.) (Chicago: University of Chicago Press, 1999).

reinforcing. Thus the idealistic movement in musical life formed part of a broader rethinking of culture and politics within Europe as a whole.

The year 1848 marked a watershed in musical life just as much as in political history. The revolutions forced members of the musical community to come to grips with its fragmented structure, and a new order came into being. Classical music achieved a hegemonic status within musical thinking, pedagogy, and public ceremony. "What was fundamentally new about nineteenth-century music culture was the overpowering presence of earlier music, a presence that has apparently become irrevocable in our century," Carl Dahlhaus noted.[3] At the same time, new types of concerts were organized for the general public – ballad concerts, music halls, *cafés-concerts*, and programs of opera excerpts and songs – that formed worlds of their own with limited relationships to classical music life. Moreover, an intense battle broke out over claims that contemporary music was now neglected in the classical music concerts. Ideological warfare broke out between those for and those against forward-looking musical styles.

Thus did a "great transformation" occur within musical culture. I use the word *great* for the title of this book because of the contrasting meanings it implies.[4] First, the word indicates the massive scale of changes that occurred in musical life. Second, it defines the cultural authority newly invested in canonic repertories, an institutionalized belief in greatness. But, third, a "great" transformation could happen only under the pressure of social and political movements. The process by which concert programs changed from replacing old works with new ones to the revering of classics was by definition political in nature. Cultural historians often take for granted that the musical classics were foreordained and use the words *canon, classic,* or *masterpiece* in ahistorical terms. It is easy to glide through the first half of the nineteenth century without recognizing how massive a set of changes was occurring in the most fundamental aspects of repertory, taste, and musical values. By contrast, the worlds of painting and sculpture came out of the Romantic period having experienced a less drastic shift from contemporary to classical standards in the definition of taste. A "high" art had long existed in those worlds but was late arriving in music, save for pedagogy and philosophical thinking. The field of painting did not undergo as major an ideological alienation from commercial culture; indeed, private

3 Carl Dahlhaus, *Nineteenth-Century Music*, J. Bradford Robinson (trans.) (Berkeley: University of California Press, 1989), p. 22.
4 Karl Polanyi used the term in his essays on the reshaping of European economy and politics, *Origins of our Time: The Great Transformation* (London: Victor Gollancz, 1945).

dealers took over from public salons in the last decades of the century. Thus, to understand how and why musical culture changed as it did, we must first define the nature of its old order before tracing the rise of the new one. We cannot understand the transformation of institutions and tastes after 1800 without laying a firm historical groundwork.

Two contrasting perspectives tend to recur in scholarly discussion of musical taste during the eighteenth and nineteenth centuries. On the one hand, those we might dub the "classicists" have as a principal concern the process by which high standards of taste and social behavior became established, and indeed can be protected, in musical life. James H. Johnson traced a movement for disciplined listening in the late eighteenth and early nineteenth centuries; Julian Johnson deplored the slippage from such standards in the late twentieth century.[5] On the other hand, scholars we might call "populists" mourn the isolation of classical music from larger musical life, indeed from society as a whole. Lawrence Levine argued that a "shared culture" whereby works by William Shakespeare and Mozart were performed without canonic definition ended with the "sacralization" of a new high culture during the late nineteenth century.[6] Still another perspective has raised questions about the declining interest in contemporary works that came with the hegemony of classical repertories in serious concerts.[7] When did the hegemony of classics create the necessity for New Music concerts?

Each of these points of view will come into our purview. While I have criticized the "classicist" viewpoint for making an overly negative assessment of eighteenth-century listening, I find its argument about the nineteenth century compelling in scope and implication.[8] This book attempts to show specifically when, and in what kinds of concerts, a macroscopic division between supposedly "light" and "serious" music arose, related to the notions of "popular songs" and "classics." Though opera overtures and selections kept alive a "common culture" among many kinds of concerts, recurrent dispute over how the music should be interpreted makes the word *shared*

[5] James H. Johnson, *Listening in Paris: A Cultural History* (Berkeley: University of California Press, 1995); Julian Johnson, *Who Needs Classical Music? Cultural Choice and Musical Value* (Oxford: Oxford University Press, 2002).

[6] Lawrence Levine, *Highbrow/Lowbrow: The Emergence of Cultural Hierarchy in America* (Cambridge, Mass.: Harvard University Press, 1988).

[7] Nicholas Slonimsky, *A Lexicon of Musical Invective: Critical Assaults on Composers since Beethoven's Time* (New York: Scribner's, 1953); Martin Thrun, *Neue Musik im deutschen Musikleben bis 1933* (Bonn: Orpheus-Verlag, 1995); Michel Duchesneau, *L'Avant-garde musicale à Paris de 1871 à 1939* (Liège: Mardaga, 1997).

[8] "Did People Listen in the Eighteenth Century?" *Early Music* 25 (1997), 678–91.

inappropriate. We will not, however, attempt to discuss philosophical aspects of taste in depth. Our perspective will instead be aimed at the conventional language whereby musicians, concert managers, and concert-goers talked about issues in the musical community. The book examines the period between 1750, when a significant number of programs can be found, and 1875, the point at which a new order in musical culture was established. The Epilogue assesses the state of the musical community in 1914 in reference to these issues.

THE TRANSFORMATION IN BRIEF

A major goal of this book is to survey the typical kinds of concert programs performed between about 1750 and 1875. In the course of several decades I have read thousands of programs, gaining an acquaintance with programming in a wide variety of places. My focus has been on Europe's four main musical cities – London, Paris, Leipzig, and Vienna – but I have also studied programs performed in such cities as Oxford, Birmingham, Edinburgh, Bordeaux, Berlin, and Boston. We will see that provincial cities were often in advance of the capitals, and that American concert life was intimately bound with what was happening in Europe, in Britain most of all – indeed, the popular song emerged earliest in Anglo-American culture. We will not examine all types of concerts. Our main concern will be in the strictly defined chamber music concert; the benefit or virtuoso concert and its successor, the recital; the orchestral series and its rival, the promenade concert; and events focused on vocal music, particularly the ballad concert, the *café-concert*, and the early form of the *opera gala*.

For an overview, let us take a brief look at the transformation of concert programming through photographed programs in the center of the book. We begin with the virtuoso or "benefit" concert, because it drew noticeable public attention during the first half of the nineteenth century. Organized by one or two musicians, it included a variety of soloists or ensembles accompanied by an orchestra. The organizer performed as soloist in a few numbers; his or her main intention was to impress the audience with a richness of musical talent mingling vocal and instrumental virtuosity equally. In 1785 a rising young violinist named Bartolomeo Campagnoli, later concert master of the Gewandhaus orchestra, gave a program that was typical for the time in its alternation between operatic excerpts and concertos (Ill. 1). The week before, a female singer from Italy gave a program with an identical pattern of genres. Concerts given in London, however, tended to be unusually long and diverse in historical periods represented. In 1801 the bass player Domenico Dragonetti offered a program of thirteen pieces, all but three vocal numbers, and he performed only in the concerto (Ill. 2). A canonic sense of Mozart's music was beginning to emerge when Dragonetti offered five of his pieces, but because none of the operas had arrived in London, selections from them counted as novelty.[9] The duet by Benedetto Marcello (1686–1739) had a firm canonic status, and his music was rarely performed anywhere else in Europe.

Benefit concerts changed a great deal from the 1820s onward, as virtuosos made them commercial undertakings, moving rapidly between cities and filling opera houses several nights in a row. Nicolò Paganini, who lent this practice prestige, gave a program in Vienna's main opera hall in 1828 (Ill. 3) that alternated between vocal and instrumental pieces but, in comparison with Campagnoli's program, was imbued more completely with operatic music – overtures, vocal selections, and fantasies on well-known themes. The aria by Mozart and the variations on a theme by Haydn carried strong canonic implications by that time. In the next fifteen years virtuoso concerts became even longer and centered on vocal pieces, the start of a major change in programming. In 1841 pianist Louise Dulcken presented what a critic called "London's present glittering galaxy" performing twenty-three numbers, sixteen from opera, aided by Franz Liszt and her brother the violinist Ferdinand David (Ill. 4). The audience paid attention to the music, for a critic admitted that the audience "of beauty and fashion . . . sat it out with exemplary patience and evident gratification."[10]

Revolutionary changes came about during the first half of the nineteenth century with the abandonment of vocal music in some programs and the focusing of a repertory on classics in others. A few pianists made a drastic break from the collegial tradition of the benefit concert by performing entirely alone at some concerts. Having originally offered conventional programs (Ill. 5), Liszt took this new path flamboyantly, pointing out what he was doing in bold type in Vienna in 1846 (Ill. 6). In the 1850s Clara Schumann and Charles Hallé took a different path, adopting a repertory focused on classical works and identifying themselves as interpreters and only occasionally as composers, shaping a new form of virtuosity. They usually included a few vocal pieces and perhaps a chamber work on their programs.

[9] Rachel Cowgill, "'Wise Men from the East': Mozart's Operas and their Advocates in Early Nineteenth-Century London," in *Music and British Culture, 1785–1914: Essays in Honour of Cyril Ehrlich*, Leanne Langley and Christina Bashford (eds.) (Oxford: Oxford University Press, 2000), pp. 39–64.
[10] "Musical Intelligence," *MW*, 3 June 1841, p. 363.

Schumann offered a concert in 1862 that was rigorous in its choice of serious works, abandoning the opera *fantaisie* and carefully selecting recent pieces, in this case by her deceased husband (Ill. 7). Julius Stockhausen likewise led in the creation of a canon for song, often aided by Johannes Brahms, as seen in a concert they gave together in 1869 (Ill. 8).

Concerts given by string quartets abandoned tradition most abruptly of all by excluding vocal music altogether and defining their public as a cultural elite separate from the general public. In 1804 the Viennese violinist Ignaz Schuppanzigh put on the first known public concert devoted entirely to string quartets and related genres, and in 1814 Pierre Baillot presented similar events in Paris. Everywhere the repertory was focused on pieces by Haydn, Mozart, and Beethoven, as we see in a program of the Beethoven Quartet Society in London in 1846 (Ill. 9). Nevertheless, in Vienna for a while, and in Britain and North America generally, chamber music concerts usually included several vocal or solo instrumental pieces deemed worthy of performance with the great quartets. In Boston in 1855 William Mason offered a program with the Mendelssohn Quintette Club that included pieces for piano by Frédéric Chopin, Stephen Heller, and Mason himself, along with chamber pieces by Beethoven, Mozart, and Brahms (Ill. 10).

Orchestral concerts moved more gradually toward programs devoted to instrumental classics. A subscription concert at the Gewandhaus in 1787 (Ill. 11) typified the carefully patterned format, featuring opera selections, that was conventional throughout Europe from the mid-eighteenth century through at least the 1830s. The programs of the Philharmonic Society of London retained such a format through the 1880s, always including at least one opera overture and vocal selection, as we see in a program from 1826 (Ill. 12). Nevertheless, Beethoven's symphonies were institutionalized systematically in almost all orchestral concert series by the 1830s. The Gewandhaus subscription concerts first gave a symphony (Beethoven's "Eroica") the privilege of being the only piece after intermission in 1807, and the Philharmonic Society did the same with the Ninth Symphony in 1825.

Concerts became either much longer or shorter during the 1830s and 1840s. On the one hand, a "Grand Miscellaneous Concert" given by the Oxford Musical Society on 16 June 1832 offered thirteen pieces by dead composers and thirteen by living ones – a mixture of oratorio and opera excerpts, parlor songs, glees, and instrumental solos (Ill. 13). On the other hand, the Viennese series called Concert Spirituel set a new benchmark Europe-wide in self-consciously serious programming. A concert in 1833, for example, offered an overture, a symphony, and a movement from each of two sacred works (Ill. 14). In the mid-1840s the Vienna Philharmonic went so far as to offer as few as three works, in one case works entirely for orchestra. But most orchestral series – even the Gewandhaus – continued to include solos for voice or instrument throughout most of the nineteenth century. The primacy of classical works in orchestral concerts led, in turn, to other events devoted to new music, as at the annual meeting of the Allgemeine Deutsche Musikverein in Hannover in 1877 (Ill. 15). We will see the origins of such concerts in the practice whereby a composer devoted a program almost entirely to his or her own music, seen in concerts given by Mozart, Beethoven, Johann Nepomuk Hummel, Hector Berlioz, and Louise Farrenc.

The origins of what North Americans now call the "pops" concert can be found at virtually the same time as that of classical music concerts. "Promenade" concerts begun in the 1830s offered just orchestral music with only occasional exceptions, chiefly waltzes, quadrilles, opera overtures, and potpourris on opera tunes or topical themes. An early such concert at London's Royal Lyceum Theatre in 1838 alternated between dance pieces and opera overtures (Ill. 16), while a program given by Johann Strauss, the Younger, while on tour in Leipzig in 1852, focused on potpourris, many of them based on music from an opera (Ill. 17). The pieces by Mozart, Weber, or Beethoven given at such events were associated in listeners' minds with the theatre rather than classical music concerts. In 1849 a group of Berlin expatriates who toured American cities as the Germania Musical Society gave a concert with a similar mixture of genres (Ill. 18).

An equally fundamental innovation arose in concerts focused on music written for the theatre and the parlor, associated with the word *popular* by the last decades of the century. Songs and opera selections were the unifying point of taste for a general public different from that for the more specialized classical music world. As early as 1787 we find a "breakfast concert" at a public house in aristocratic Bath offering a program made up almost entirely of English songs and glees (Ill. 19). In 1822 one of Boston's leading singers advertised a program focused on pieces from well-known recent Italian and British operas, only one piece more than ten years old (Ill. 20). In 1834 a singer advertised a "Miscellaneous Entertainment" in Hull as full of "popular songs" and comic acts that looked ahead to the music hall (Ill. 21). Concerts with similar ambience occurred in Germany: a show entitled "Singspiel-Halle (Salon Variété)" in Leipzig in 1866 included waltzes, comic acts, piano solos, and excerpts from German comic opera (Ill. 22). The *café-concert* and the music hall developed an unprecedented mass audience for concerts of this sort in the 1850s. A program at the Grand

Casino de Paris in 1868 opened with *vaudeville*-like acts and concluded with eighteen well-known opera duos (Ill. 23).

At the same time the opera "gala" arose, a concert of opera selections and songs. Jacques Blumenthal drew an elite audience to one he directed in London in 1857, the opera numbers punctuated by him singing and playing his own music (Ill. 24). We see how large a repertory of canonic opera selections developed in these concerts in a program performed in Paris in 1869 (Ill. 25). Finally, an edition of *potpourris favoris* published in the 1860s illustrates a canon of composers represented at that kind of concert, seen from a German perspective (Ill. 26).

Thus did canonic repertories emerge in quite different forms at concerts presented by quartets, orchestras, and singers after the middle of the nineteenth century. We will follow the transformation of musical taste through the evolution of specific practices: miscellany giving way to homogeneity of genres, vocal and instrumental pieces no longer alternating, and contemporary repertories being replaced by ones called "classical" music. Richard Taruskin has traced the history of canons and standard repertory in broad and discerning terms. Impressed by the rise of such practices during the eighteenth century, Taruskin identified aspects of the music of Handel, J. S. Bach, and Domenico Scarlatti – the "Class of 1685" – that made certain works the *foundation stone* of classical music, even though some were not widely known in the composers' lifetimes. He then raised the issue of whether the German canons, works of Beethoven most of all, can be considered authoritative as a musical *universalism* by the middle of the nineteenth century.[11] We will explore similar issues here. Chapter 1 outlines the principal concepts and contexts of the subject and then traces the evolution of musical taste within specific concert programs.[12]

---

[11] Richard Taruskin, *The Oxford History of Western Music*, 6 vols. (Oxford: Oxford University Press, 2005), vol. 2, pp. 233–5, 735–9; see also vol. 2, pp. 637–51, 691–4, and vol. 3, pp. 664–6, 676–87.

[12] See also *Concert Programmes, 1790–1914: Case Studies by William Weber*, found at http://www.cph.rcm.ac.uk/Programmes1/Pages/Index.htm.

PART I

Miscellany and collegiality, 1750–1800

CHAPTER I

Concepts and contexts

The aesthetic principles established in classical music life around 1850 still shape our assumptions today, making it difficult to look at eighteenth-century concert programs in their own terms. Even though in our time a song recital or school concert may offer eight to a dozen pieces, we think of an iconic symphony concert when we wonder about a "miscellaneous" program of varied short numbers. What did the many opera selections and virtuoso solos mean to listeners? What kinds of patterns ordered the pieces? Was greatness attributed to old or new works? To understand these problems it is necessary to choose terms that do not take for granted post-Romantic aesthetic assumptions. This chapter presents the main concepts used to discuss these issues and explores the social contexts in which concerts took place. We first inquire into *miscellany* and *collegiality* as principles within literary and musical culture. The second section explores the part played by old musical works in concert life, weighing the relative merits of speaking about their *survival* or their *canonization*. The third section outlines concepts for defining the new order of musical culture after the middle of the nineteenth century: the *homogeneity* of repertory, the *hegemony* of classics, and the role of *popular music* and *general taste* independent of such canonic authority.

MISCELLANY AS A CULTURAL PRINCIPLE

The word *miscellany* first appeared in medieval copies of prayers and meditations. When printing began it became a common title for collections of poetry, most notably in John Dryden's *Miscellany Poems* of 1684.[1] The term was intended to tell the reader that the book offered a variety of genres and

---

[1] John Dryden, *Miscellany Poem: . . . Original Poems by the Most Eminent Hands* (London: Jacob Tonson, 1684). See also *A Gorgeous Gallery of Gallant Inventions* (1578), compiled by Thomas Proctor and Owen Roydon (Menston: Scolar Press, 1972). I am indebted to Anne Cotterill on this matter.

that it was not designed for specialists.[2] Although we today react negatively to the word *miscellaneous*, in the eighteenth century it carried a welcoming connotation, telling the reader that the work would please the tastes of different people or the varied needs of any one person. The words *general* and *universal* also appeared in the titles of books and magazines for that purpose, *mélange* in French, and *allgemein* ("general") in German. Moreover, *miscellany* became a literary genre after the turn of the eighteenth century, providing a way to survey a variety of topics or ideas. Controversy over the genre demonstrated the importance of the genre to men of letters. In *Characteristics of Men, Manners and Opinions* (1711), Anthony Ashley Cooper, Lord Shaftesbury, devoted "Miscellaneous Reflections upon the Preceding Treatises" to ridicule miscellany as a "patchwork" being substituted for originality, leading to "cuttings and shreds of learning, with various fragments and points of wit, . . . drawn together and tacked in any fantastic form."[3] Yet almost all authors ended up using the miscellany, recognizing its validity when handled with discipline and intelligence.

The term likewise became common in musical life as publications and concerts proliferated in the eighteenth century. Scrapbooks of musical manuscripts served as miscellanies, the place where a person or a musical society kept pieces for later use. In 1727 the *Mercure de France* described a program of the Concert Spirituel as "the *mélange* to be given next week" (as in Ex. 2.3).[4] In 1786 an Edinburgh publisher produced a collection of songs entitled *Musical Miscellany: A Select Collection of Scots, English, and Irish Songs, Set to Music* (1786). The word became common in the titles of concerts throughout Britain in the same period, designating a program that included a variety of pieces rather than a single oratorio or ode. In 1788, for example, the Oxford Musical Society offered a "Grand Miscellaneous Concert" that combined pieces from operas, oratorios, and an ode with concertos and symphonies, representing composers from five major regions of Europe (Ex. 2.12).[5] The principle of miscellany thereby aided musicians in defining what a concert presented. "The standard design of a program was a convenient way of imposing some kind of order on an essentially disparate medley of items," Simon McVeigh suggested.[6] The

---

[2] See Elizabeth Pomeroy, *Elizabethan Miscellanies: Their Development and Conventions* (Berkeley: University of California Press, 1973).

[3] Anthony Ashley Cooper, Earl of Shaftesbury, *Characteristics of Men, Manners, Opinions, Times,* 2 vols. (Gloucester, Mass: Peter Smith, 1963), vol. 2, p. 159 (at the start of Chapter 1 of "Miscellany I"). See also Jonathan Swift, *A Tale of a Tub and Other Satires* (London: J. M. Dent, 1939), p. 93.

[4] *Mercure de France*, December 1727, p. 2941.

[5] Holywell Music Room, Concert Programs, BLO.

[6] Simon McVeigh, *Concert Life in London from Mozart to Haydn* (Cambridge: Cambridge University Press, 1993), p. 101.

term *selections* was employed for the same purpose, most commonly at
the Lenten concerts in London's theatres, when many pieces or sections
of George Frideric Handel's oratorios were performed in succession. The
principle of *collegiality* was essential to *miscellany* in concert life. By definition, a concert brought together a variety of musicians; it was out of the
question for one musician to perform alone.

Public concerts came under criticism like that from Shaftesbury at their
very start. Roger North, the Norfolk gentleman who wrote extensively on
music, recalled that the early concerts of John Banister in London "consisted
of broken incoherent parts; now a consort, then a lutenist, then a violin solo,
then flutes, then a song, and so piece after piece, the time slipping away,
while the masters blundered and swore in shifting places." North reported,
however, that the musician in charge could solve the problem if he were
"an absolute Dictator, who may coerce and punish the republican mob of
music masters." The pieces on a program could be made "to proceed . . . by
judicious steps, one setting off another, and the whole in a series connected
and concluding in a perfect acme, and then ceasing all at once."[7] Thus did
political vocabulary help people to understand how programs were made
coherent entities.

The miscellaneous program resembled the "pasticcio" opera on a certain
plane. An opera received that designation if pieces by different composers
were included, usually because singers wished to perform numbers for
which their voices were best suited. Something of the same process occurred
when movements of a symphony or an oratorio were offered in different
places on a program, as Mozart himself often did.[8] Modern reservations
notwithstanding, a pasticcio could be designed coherently, with diverse
pieces chosen by principles of mood, action, and pacing. Indeed, many of
Handel's operas were of this nature.[9] Listeners differentiated between good
and bad pasticcios. Lady Mary Coke, daughter of the 2nd Duke of Argyll,
who shared a box in the King's Theatre with Horace Walpole, said in a
letter in 1785 that she expected that night to hear "something patch'd up,
which probably will not be very good."[10]

As the main principle governing taste within the musical community,
miscellany served as the predecessor to the concept of the artwork as an

[7] *Roger North on Music, Being a Selection from His Essays Written during the Years c. 1698–1728*, John Wilson (ed.) (London: Novello, 1959), pp. 302, 305.
[8] Neal Zaslaw, *Mozart's Symphonies: Context, Performance, Practice, Reception* (Oxford: Clarendon Press, 1989), pp. 158–60, 423.
[9] Reinhard Strohm, "Händels Pasticci," *Analecta Musicologica* 14 (1974), 206–87.
[10] Lady Mary Coke to her sister, December 1785, unpublished letters, *COKE*. See also William Weber, "Did People Listen in the Eighteenth Century?" *Early Music* 25 (1997), 678–91.

indivisible whole, or the *work concept*, as Lydia Goehr termed it in *The Imaginary Museum of Musical Works*. To interpret the authority of the work concept, Goehr borrowed from Kant the notion of the "regulative" concept: the artwork could "determine, stabilize, and order the structure of practices" within musical culture.[11] From such authority came the "rules of the game" governing composition, performance, and discussion of music. Miscellany served likewise as a regulative concept during the eighteenth and early nineteenth centuries. Miscellany was inclusive, and the work concept was exclusive, indeed hierarchical, in ordering genres and tastes. The work-concept invested an aesthetic authority in the gaining of systematic musical knowledge, which was less the case in the eighteenth century. In the course of this book we shall see how, in effect, one regulative concept succeeded the other.

The principle of miscellany dictated that members of the musical community had to accommodate one another's tastes and social etiquette. All who entered a concert knew that they were expected to defer to the wishes of others to some extent. That meant being willing to hear music of varied genres, periods, tastes, and regional origins, from the cosmopolitanism of Italian opera to distinctive idioms such as a glee in London or a *Singspiel* piece in Leipzig. Quite different kinds of music – or "musics," as ethnomusicologists say – might coexist on the same program. This mixture reflected the presumption that different tastes, expectations, and social behaviors would make common company within inclusive programs. Thus in 1781 the *Journal de Paris* instructed the directors of the Concert Spirituel that, as always, they needed to apply "the intelligence needed to endow this kind of amusement with flair in choosing pieces and virtuosos to play them." That is why, the reporter wrote, "knowing that new pieces are necessary to please the audience, its directors will occupy themselves with finding novelties and varying the numbers in the different genres."[12]

An evening on the town might itself constitute a miscellany. Because only a few plays or operas were usually performed during a season, listeners got to know the music very well and therefore went to hear different parts according to their taste. The most cultured person found it conventional to visit parts of several entertainments in one day. Sir Dudley Ryder, a serious man of the theatre and later a judge, wrote in his journal in 1715

---

[11] Lydia Goehr, *The Imaginary Museum of Musical Works: An Essay in the Philosophy of Music* (Oxford: Clarendon Press, 1992), p. 121.
[12] *Journal de Paris*, 5 April 1781, p. 385.

that he "Went to the play into the side-box. Stayed the first Act. Then went to the new Playhouse, into the side-box, where stayed the first Act." After that he "Supped at the Gill House . . . [went home and] read part of [J.-B.] Molière's comedy *Ecole des Femmes*. To bed at 10, being sleepy."[13] Ryder likewise saw no need to mention the title of the play he attended in a letter or his diary, just as programs often cited only a singer but not the piece sung. People took a great deal for granted about cultural activities, because they existed in a small world where spoken communication still predominated over the written.

There is no doubt that a wider range of social etiquette was tolerated in concerts and at the opera than is true in classical music concerts today. We are amazed to hear that many people talked and moved around at concerts or the opera, and that can lead us to question the integrity of musical culture at that time. But the variety in behavior does not mean that people did not, indeed *could not*, listen, and a stricter etiquette must have been the rule in concerts compared with opera halls. Travel letters passed on the trope about social confusion in opera halls; such statements formed part of the negotiation that went on among different parts of the public. It was presumed that people with disparate tastes could coexist successfully in concert halls and at the opera, even though some complained they could not hear as well as they wished.[14] A substantial part of the talk concerned what was being performed, as is still the case in jazz clubs today. Indeed, men in the pits of eighteenth-century French theatres made spontaneous interventions concerning what was happening on stage, usually related to topics in public life.[15]

Serious listening flourished within the informal sociability that surrounded the miscellaneous concert. The motto on the ceiling of the concert hall in Leipzig's Gewandhaus – *Res severa verum gaudium*, or "A demanding matter is a source of true joy" – suggested a traditional sense of musical seriousness found before the rise of classical music and the idealistic values that buttressed it. An essay published about the musical society in Amiens, *Sentiment d'un harmoniphile sur différents ouvrages de musique* (1756), stated that its members wished both to enjoy and to learn: "Concerts aren't simply a means to combat boredom, for most people they serve as a way to learn

[13] *The Diary of Dudley Ryder, 1715–1716*, William Matthews (trans.) (London, 1939), pp. 128, 195. Quoted in Henrik Knif, *Gentlemen and Spectators: Studies in Journals, Opera and the Social Scene in Late Georgian London* (Helsinki: Finnish Historical Society, 1995), pp. 70–3.

[14] Weber, "Did People Listen in the Eighteenth Century?"; Johnson, *Listening in Paris*.

[15] Jeffrey Ravel, *The Contested Parterre: Public Theater and French Political Culture, 1680–1791* (Ithaca: Cornell University Press, 1999), pp. 58–63 and *passim*.

how music is done best in all the idioms brought together on a program."
Arguing that "variety is the soul of a concert," the essayist stated that the
concerts brought together rival factions for French and Italian music.[16]
Greatness was certainly recognized in eighteenth-century musical culture.
In *Le Parnasse français* (1723, *The French Parnassus*), Évrard Titon du Tillet
declared that "the famous [Jean-Baptiste] Lully has surpassed all musicians
who preceded him, and is regarded as the father and model of all those
who have come after him."[17] The pamphlet *Tablettes de renommée des musiciens* (1785, *Notes on Renowned Musicians*) declared concerning Haydn's
approach to the symphony: "one of the most celebrated and appealing
composers heard at the Concert Spirituel, he continues to greet the ear in
gracious and infectious ways, employing an inexhaustible genius to draw
a distinctive quality from the orchestra that has yet to be matched."[18] The
valuing of Lully, Handel, and Haydn as master composers in that time
contributed greatly to the development of canonic repertory and historical
writing during the early nineteenth century.

CAPITAL-CITY SOCIETY AND MUSICAL LIFE

The principle of miscellany was rooted in the new form of public life that
emerged in the early eighteenth century. Authority over opera, concerts, and
musical activity in general began shifting from monarchical or aristocratic
patronage to public worlds based in cities and towns. London and Paris
were the most important such centers, for in both places the monarch
withdrew from authority over musical life toward the end of the seventeenth
century. A vacuum of formal authority resulted that was filled by a fictive
principle of a unitary Public, under whose rhetorical auspices rivalries were
conducted among factions and individuals contending for influence in
cultural worlds.[19]

It is best to distinguish between the concepts of "public life" and the
"public sphere," even though the two were closely interrelated. Strictly
speaking, Jürgen Habermas's concept of the "public sphere" applies to

---

[16] *Sentiment d'un harmoniphile sur différents ouvrages de musique*, A. J. Labbet, abbé de Morambert,
and A. Léris (eds.) (Paris, 1756; Geneva: Minkoff, 1972), pp. 78–80.
[17] "Description du Parnasse français," *Le Parnasse français*, 2 vols. (Paris, 1743–1760), Supplement 3,
p. 1.
[18] *Tablettes de renommée des musiciens, auteurs, compositeurs, virtuoses, amateurs et maîtres de musique
vocale et instrumentale* (Paris, 1785; Geneva: Minkoff, 1971), pp. 18–19.
[19] See John Brewer, *Pleasures of the Imagination: English Culture in the Eighteenth Century* (New York:
Farrar Straus Giroux, 1997), pp. 3–55.

exchange of opinion concerning the state and contention surrounding it.[20] By contrast, "public life" amounted to a set of professional, social, or cultural communities, within each of which a political process took place parallel to that in the public sphere. Issues and ideas flowed back and forth between communities surrounding music or the theatre and the central sphere of public discourse, the polemical essay serving as the main vehicle of dispute. Members of the upper classes who did not play active roles in affairs of state often became deeply engaged in musical, theatrical, or literary politics, tossing off combative essays that mingled a great many levels of partisan meaning. One might even say that most people learned what politics was all about through such cultural combat. To pose an argument about a musical issue was to confront issues of concern to the community as a whole.

An investing of the public with cultural or political authority emerged in both France and Britain, despite the contrasting solutions they made to their seventeenth-century civil wars. In the two countries monarchs began to defer to metropolitan cultural leadership significantly by 1700. The departure of royal leadership left a vacuum in the world of opera that was filled, willy-nilly, by musicians, theatrical entrepreneurs, energetic amateurs, publicists, and members of the general public. The rhetorical principle was established that the public's tastes would rule over cultural institutions. An early example of that notion appeared when the Parisian man of letters Charles Dufresny declared in 1698 that "The public is a sovereign, to which all must account who strive toward high reputation, or indeed for financial gain."[21] Likewise in 1791 the London *Theatrical Guardian* stated that "The Public is the only Jury before whom the merits of an actor or actress are to be tried."[22]

Musical commentators often referred to their community as the Republic of Music, a parallel to literary commentary on the Republic of Letters. In England musical life took on an especially clear sense of political community because the King's Theatre was for all intents and purposes the center of all musical activity.[23] In 1720 a satirical article in *The Anti-Theatre* reported that the failure of a diva to arrive in England had caused great crisis: "It gives me some concern, when I reflect how prodigious the

---

[20] *Habermas and the Public Sphere*, Craig Calhoun (ed.) (Cambridge, Mass.: MIT Press, 1992); and T. C. W. Blanning, *The Culture of Power and the Power of Culture: Old Regime Europe, 1660–1789* (Oxford: Oxford University Press, 2002), pp. 1–25.

[21] Charles Dufresny, *Amusements sérieux et comiques* (Paris, 1699; Bossard, 1921), p. 126.

[22] *Theatrical Guardian*, 5 March 1791, p. 6.

[23] William Weber, "L'Institution et son public: l'opéra à Paris et à Londres au XVIIIe siècle," *Annales E.S.C.* 48 (1993), 1519–40.

demise of this unfortunate Lady must disconcert the measures of the *Musical Republick*! What councils, and what matter for debate, it must occasion to provide against a disappointment of such importance to their schemes."[24] At the turn of the nineteenth century commentators began to interpret the governance of orchestral ensembles as a form of civil polity. Gottfried Weber declared in 1807 that the director of a concert series "can be seen, like a regent of state, as the representative of the general will."[25]

Disputes over music were among the most significant episodes of cultural politics in the eighteenth century. Prior to 1700 writing on music had tended to be either pedagogical or theoretical; relatively little had been published about actual pieces of music or musical tastes. The ensuing disputes opened up musical culture to literary interest, bringing in men of letters and *salonnières*, women who guided elite social life. The first notable musical disputes occurred just after 1700, in the abbé François Raguenet's polemical defense of Italian music and John Dennis's attack on it in London. An extensive literature emerged in England over the next three decades, and a series of musicoliterary *querelles* occurred in Paris around 1737 over the challenge made to Lully by Jean-Philippe Rameau, in 1752–1754 about the Italian company called the *bouffons*, and in 1777–1778 between proponents of C. W. Gluck and Niccolò Piccinni. This literature provided the literary context in which the rethinking of musical culture began to evolve in the late eighteenth century.

By 1750 London and Paris had acquired an authority over European society and culture far more imposing than capital cities had exerted prior to that time.[26] By the end of the century these cities had become the key arbiters of cultural taste. Elite groups stayed in the capitals for more of the year than had previously been the case, creating a concentrated elite society all their own, which did not have to relate to lesser groups as much as provincial notables were accustomed to doing. A culture of consumption emerged within the two cities that stimulated specialized service industries and cultural worlds. A redistribution of wealth occurred, from the countryside to the capital cities, facilitated by the state.[27] London and Paris wielded an authority within the new culture of consumerism as

---

[24] Sir John Falstaffe, *The Anti-Theatre*, 29 March 1720, p. 1.
[25] John Spitzer and Neal Zaslaw, *The Birth of the Orchestra: History of an Institution, 1650–1815* (Oxford: Oxford University Press, 2004), p. 514.
[26] *Capital Cities and Their Hinterlands in Early Modern Europe*, Bernard Lepetit and Peter Clark (eds.) (Aldershot: Ashgate, 1996).
[27] David Ringrose, "Capital Cities and Urban Networks in the Early Modern Period," in ibid., pp. 217–40.

the arbiters of cosmopolitan taste. Culturally ambitious members of the upper classes distinguished themselves with a cosmopolitan rather than a local identity in some – though not all – of their cultural activities. Italian opera played a central role in shaping cosmopolitan identity for the nobility and upper-middle class, a subject we confront in detail in the next chapter. "The era was little swayed by nationalism," Daniel Heartz recently declared, because "it was above all cosmopolitan."[28]

Such trends dominated the fashionable press in the eighteenth century. Germans understood that to a particular extent, knowing how poorly Berlin compared with London or Paris. A new type of periodical – the *Journal des Luxus und der Moden* (Weimar, 1787–1810) and *London und Paris* (Leipzig, 1798–1826), for example – informed readers about dress, promenading, horse equipage, prostitutes, politics, theatre, and opera in the two capitals. A critique of fashion emerged within the very periodicals that promoted such taste; pressure for and against fashion interacted at close quarters. The first volume of the *Journal des Luxus und der Moden* included a poem called "Modish Novelties" that cast into question the very fashions the magazine was promoting:

> In the world of mother folly
> Does novelty unexpectedly appear.
> Suddenly comes the mob to impose
> The ways of this world upon us all,
> Waving its beautiful, streaming hair,
> Forcing people to wonder, and to adore her.[29]

Between 1750 and 1850, the cosmopolitan members of the nobility and the middle classes formed a group called the *beau monde* or "the World" in the main capital cities. The milieu was diverse in composition: international merchants and bankers; high-level doctors, lawyers, and clergymen; prestigious artists and musicians; salon hostesses of various backgrounds; and courtesans of the *demimonde*.[30] The nobility participated in the discourse of the emerging public sphere with the upper-middle class, but the *beau monde* was by no means coextensive with that class. The *beau monde* constituted a milieu larger and less intimate than that of a court but at the same time one much smaller, less diversified, and more tightly drawn

[28] Daniel Heartz, *Music in European Capitals: The Galant Style, 1720–1780* (New York: W. W. Norton, 2000), p. xx and pp. 999–1001; Blanning, *Culture of Power*, pp. 232–65.
[29] *JLM* 2 (1787), 2–3.
[30] Hannah Greig, "Leading the Fashion: The Material Culture of London's *Beau Monde*," in *Gender, Taste, and Material Culture in Britain and North America, 1700–1830*, John Styles and Amanda Vickery (eds.) (New Haven, Conn.: Yale Center for British Art, 2006), pp. 267–92.

than the upper classes found in the major metropolises by 1870. The *beau monde* was a public whose members at least knew *of* each other, mingling in a closely linked set of social, cultural, and political contexts.

The opera halls in London and Paris avoided overtly castelike conventions. There was no formal separation between nobles and commoners in the seating at the King's Theatre or at the Paris Opéra, as was the case in the equivalent halls in Vienna and Berlin. In Paris and London nobles and bourgeois sat together in the first three levels of boxes, the only major difference being that the French nobility included bourgeois tax farmers, for which there was no parallel in Britain.[31] The mingling of contrasting elites influenced the rise of "bourgeois tragedy" in the theatre, as Stefano Castelvecchi has argued: "[E]lements of contiguity between nobility and bourgeoisie, by eroding the perception that there should be an absolute, almost ontological distance between the two groups, invited novel approaches to class-based social description."[32] The *beau monde* was still small enough to function as a community. In England it was common to cite "the World" in reified form in regard to an exercise of authority. Lady Mary Coke, a long-time boxholder at the King's Theatre, often cited "the World" as the authority through which she interpreted social behavior. When gossiping about who sat with whom at the opera in 1768, she stated that "Mr Fawkener & Sir Harry Featherstone at first sat in the Pitt over against the Box & then went into it [;] each has his particular reasons, as the World says."[33] Such use of social authority generated much resentment. In a satirical work of 1785, the *fermier général* and *littérateur* Gaspard Grimod de la Reynière condemned *le monde* for telling people what to think at the theatre:

The people of the World of whom I speak exert a wide range of influence within their society and enjoy the pleasures of their status very much. They tell public opinion what to say and how to get back at it when necessary. The rest of us endure their scorn, pay for their foolishness, but . . . when such farce is badly played, we can pay to boo their acting.[34]

In a cosmopolitan milieu such as this one, women not only could exert authority over informal socializing but also mingle in public places to a certain extent. Such a public presence was just beginning in a less centrally

---

[31] Weber, "L'institution et son public."

[32] Stefano Castelvecchi, *Sentimental Opera* (Cambridge: Cambridge University Press, forthcoming).

[33] Lady Mary Coke to sister, 2 January 1779, *COKE.*

[34] [Grimod de la Reynière], *Lorgnette philosophique, trouvée par un R. Capucin sous les Arcades du Palais-Royal, & presentée au Public par un Célibataire,* 2 vols. (London: chez l'auteur, 1785), vol. 2, p. 13.

placed city such as Hamburg in the late eighteenth century, provoked criticism from people with traditional values.[35] Salons and informal socializing linked to eighteenth-century musical life gave women influence over performers, composers, and taste. Elizabeth Harris (1722–1781), wife of James Harris, Member of Parliament for Salisbury, arranged for concerts in their country house and worked with her husband to run those in the local Assembly Room; her letters show how central she was within the nationally prominent musical community. In 1776 she reported that her daughter Louisa and the musician Antonio Sacchini "are now in the deepest study of music," performing duets by Francesco Durante she thought suitable "only for the *elect*."[36] Yet the growing formality and organization of musical life after 1800 gradually limited the roles that women could play in that world. Women were barred from membership in the great majority of amateur music societies in the eighteenth century, and then from the leadership of professional concert organizations in major cities during the following century. In both the eighteenth and nineteenth centuries musical commentators applied tropes blaming women for lowering taste in musical life through an obsession with fashion. By the same token, it was assumed that women could compose only in the "lesser" genres, as Marcia Citron has shown in her pioneering volume.[37]

Although Leipzig was far smaller than London or Paris, it exerted major cultural leadership and possessed an influential cadre of citizens that was sometimes compared to the *beau monde* of the capital cities. Considerable tension existed among the different levels of Leipzig's *Bürgertum*. The most prominent families were often called patricians or aristocrats, and noble families owned town houses on the main square and came regularly to the city for business and pleasure. Not only did the city possess the most important intelligentsia in the German states, it was also a major legal center and possessed thriving businesses in textile manufacture and international trade. In 1781 a concert hall was built in the Gewandhaus, the center of the textile business, and the city's elites soon treated it as the focal point of their public social life, like the King's Theatre in London. The rule of

---

[35] Katherine B. Aslestad, "Material Identities: Tradition, Gender, and Consumption in Early Nineteenth-Century Hamburg," *Consortium on Revolutionary Europe* 27 (1998), 599–607.

[36] *Music and Theatre in Handel's World: The Family Papers of James Harris, 1732–1780*, Donald Burrows and Rosemary Dunhill (eds.) (Oxford: Oxford University Press, 2002), pp. 503–31, 892.

[37] Marcia J. Citron, *Gender and Musical Canon* (Cambridge: Cambridge University Press, 2003); Weber, *Music and the Middle Class: Social Structure of Concert Life in London, Paris and Vienna, 1830–1848*, 2nd ed. (Aldershot: Ashgate, 2003), pp. 41–2, 63–4, 69, 144.

the high bourgeoisie became institutionalized in the subscription concerts (Abonnenten-Concerte), where few outside that elite could go.[38]

Vienna took on the social characteristics of the capital of a major state more slowly than London or Paris did. Members of the major noble families resided in Vienna only to a limited extent, for seigneurial authority remained firmly in their hands, and absolutism was weakly established before the reign of Empress Maria Theresa.[39] In the Burgtheater the seating of nobles and bourgeois remained separate throughout the eighteenth century; in 1788–1789, only four boxes were subscribed by persons of rank lower than count, none of them seemingly of the business community.[40] Any order to limit ballet at the opera, as Joseph II dictated in the 1780s, would have caused major disturbances at London's King's Theatre or the Paris Opéra. By the same token, as late as the 1780s the King of Prussia told people where they would sit in the Royal Opera House in Berlin.[41] Nonetheless, French became a language of conversation in Vienna, and a salon world sympathetic to new ideas and forms of sociability emerged there during the 1770s that stimulated musical patronage in creative new ways.[42] Members of the service nobility exercised the main such leadership, thanks to their moderate wealth and extensive musical education, and they took roles as performers and composers far more extensively than in any other country as late as the 1850s.

Entrepreneurial musicians exported cosmopolitan music-making to North America as well as eastern Europe and Russia in the late eighteenth century, as Spaniards had already done in Mexico. That is why, as Michael Broyles has shown, America's musical life remained closely linked with

[38] Arnold Schering and Rudolf Wustmann, *Musikgeschichte Leipzigs*, 3 vols. (Leipzig: F. Kistner, 1926–1941), vol. 3, pp. 557–83; Hans-Joachim Nösselt, *Das Gewandhausorchester: Entstehung und Entwicklung eines Orchesters* (Leipzig: Köhler & Amelang, 1943); Gustav Wustmann, "Die Gewandhausconcerte," *Aus Leipzigs Vergangenheit: Gesammelte Schriften*, 3 vols. (Leipzig: F. W. Grunow, 1885–1909), vol. 2, pp. 458–88.

[39] James Van Horn Melton, "The Nobility in the Bohemian and Austrian Lands, 1620–1780," *European Nobilities in the Seventeenth and Eighteenth Centuries*: vol. 2: *Northern, Central and Eastern Europe*, H. M. Scott (ed.) (Harlow, Essex, UK: Longman, 1995), pp. 110–43.

[40] Dexter Edge, "Mozart's Reception in Vienna, 1787–91," in *Wolfgang Amadè Mozart: Essays on His Life and His Music*, Stanley Sadie (ed.) (Oxford: Clarendon Press, 1996), p. 75. Bruce Brown, *Gluck and the French Theatre in Vienna* (Oxford: Clarendon Press, 1991), pp. 106–7.

[41] John Mangum, "Apollo and the German Muses: Opera and the Articulation of Class, Politics and Society in Prussia, 1740–1806," unpublished Ph.D. dissertation, University of California, Los Angeles (2002), Ch. 5.

[42] James Van Horn Melton, "School, Stage, Salon: Musical Cultures in Haydn's Vienna," *Journal of Modern History* 76 (2004), 251–79. See also Brown, *Gluck and the French Theatre*, 25–63; Caryl Clark, "Reading and Listening: Viennese *Frauenzimmer* Journals and the Sociocultural Context of Mozartean Opera Buffa," *Musical Quarterly* 87 (2004), 140–75; and Blanning, *Culture of Power*, pp. 235–46.

Europe's even though it took time for the infrastructure of opera companies and a musical profession to be established. Concerts were regularly held in many towns and cities, usually similar to programs in Birmingham or Edinburgh. Boston differed from those cities insofar as its cosmopolitan upper class did not make music central to its cultural life until the 1830s.[43] The people who joined the Handel and Haydn Society at its inception in the 1810s were not major landowners or international merchants but rather teachers, mechanics, shopkeepers, clerks, and attorneys, including women as participants but not members.[44] Nevertheless, the fact that few concerts of note took place in the bourgeois City of London, or east of it, makes the numerous Boston events impressive. A loosely organized musical society came into existence by the 1760s, chiefly to aid musicians who were teaching in homes and performing in the theatre to gain a public. The main conclusion we will make is that Britain and North America worked in tandem in the evolution of ballads, songs, and theatre music toward what was called "popular songs" and then "popular music."

How did European courts figure in the rise of public concerts? Although courts staged few public events, the court concert was the chief starting point for public concerts. Court events combined cultured formality with a flexible social etiquette, a model of music-making that could be adapted to a variety of musical needs. The sound of skilled violin ensembles was by nature courtly. The twenty-four string players employed by Charles II led London's earliest concerts, court musicians designed the Parisian Concert Spirituel and the Viennese Society of Musicians (Tonkünster-Societät), and the Dresden court theatre shaped a great deal of what went on in the Leipzig Gewandhaus. Courts also gave musical access to major facilities such as the Redoutensaal in Vienna and the Palais des Tuileries in Paris. By contrast, amateur organizations – the English musical society or the central European collegium musicum – could claim little official sanction and were much less prominent in capitals than in provincial cities. A courtly manner thus left its mark upon concert life that was to persist throughout the nineteenth century.[45] Arguably, classical music taste proudly retained a courtly quality when challenged by the brazen commercialism of the music hall and the *café-concert*.

43 Michael Broyles, *"Music of the Highest Class": Elitism and Populism in Antebellum Boston* (New Haven, Conn.: Yale University Press, 1992), pp. 98–200.

44 Ibid., pp. 138–48; O. G. Sonneck, *Early Concert-Life in America, 1731–1800* (New York: Da Capo, 1978), pp. 98, 140–1, 172.

45 Rebecca Grotjahn, *Die Sinfonie im deutschen Kulturgebiet, 1850 bis 1875* (Sinzig: Studio, 1997), pp. 73–77.

HIERARCHIES OF TASTE

The authority of specialized learning is often a problematic factor in the social structure of taste. Those knowledgeable may attempt to control taste, whereas those who are not may either accept such control or ignore it. Societies approach this issue in very different ways. Present-day classical music concerts form a specialized world whose members more or less defer to an intelligentsia of critics, master teachers, scholars, concert managers, and radio announcers on classical music stations. In eighteenth-century Europe, however, the connoisseur was a gentleman rather than a professional and therefore did not distinguish himself from the music public as clearly as cultural authorities do today. Such figures brought a new discipline to their work compared with the uncritical wonder of the seventeenth-century collector or *virtuoso* toward exotic objects. The connoisseur wished to "develop subtle distinctions in order to develop a science of taste," as John Brewer put it. In so doing, the connoisseur had no need to claim special empowerment; he did not presume to dictate the public's taste.[46] The whole notion of the Public discouraged major distinctions being drawn between levels of knowledge or learning. Because the authority of public opinion was of such recent origin, endowing an intelligentsia with formal authority – as regular reviews of concerts did by 1850 – threatened to weaken the status of the Public itself. Moreover, the short historical range of most opera or concert repertories limited the need for knowledge about older styles. Simply being at opera and concert performances regularly was thought to bring a level of general knowledge deemed sufficient.

In the musical world the term *connoisseur* meant a knowledgeable person called on to evaluate musicians by the director of an opera company, a concert, or a cathedral choir. Gentlemen of standing frequently served as talent scouts for opera impresarios when they toured Italy; Horace Walpole, for example, served in that capacity for the King's Theatre. Women influenced judgment about musicians significantly as salon hostesses, but it is unlikely that many served as scouts or were called connoisseurs. If anything, the press tended to belittle the connoisseurs' influence, and indeed few such figures seem to have written on music. It was conventional for a periodical to report opinions expressed variously by connoisseurs and the general public, but the public was treated as the ultimate authority. Thus the *Mercure de France* reported in 1751 that "this aria was greatly appreciated by connoisseurs, and seemed to make a very agreeable impression upon

---

[46] Brewer, *Pleasures of the Imagination*, p. 256.

the public." A report on a new production of Lully's *Bellérophon* in 1728 asserted that "some connoisseurs believed that Neptune, while being interrogated by Jobate would have best been given a sailor's dance ... but we will leave to readers the liberty of judging whether or not that would have been better."[47]

At the middle of the eighteenth century German aestheticians began distinguishing between the *Kenner* (learned listener) and the *Liebhaber* (music-lover). Johann Georg Sulzer provided a balanced assessment of the two forms of musical attention. The *Liebhaber* possessed a "natural" listening, "a compulsive, unthinking attention mixed with astonishment." By contrast, Sulzer saw the *Kenner*'s listening "accompanied by reflection" and therefore becoming "arbitrary," tending toward the egotistical because it "draws all our attention to itself."[48] Thus was the musical community suspicious of claims to special learning; ultimately taste was thought to be rooted in the general public. The accommodation of different tastes and levels of musical learning, one to another, stands out vividly in well-known comments by Mozart and his father, Leopold. In 1780 the father wrote to the son, "I recommend you to think when at work not only of the musical but also of the unmusical public. You know that for ten true connoisseurs there are a hundred ignoramuses! Do not neglect the so-called popular, which tickles long ears."[49] Such was the conventional wisdom among musicians: it was necessary to defer to the general public as well as to learned amateurs, those who understood one's music better. Two years earlier Leopold defined the "popular" specifically as pieces simple enough for amateurs to perform. "Let your name known!" he urged, "Let it be something short, easy and popular."[50]

Aesthetic hierarchies among genres were also limited in the eighteenth century. Genres were graded in ambiguous terms, which did not make distinctions as categorical as the words *light* and *serious* were to do by the 1870s. For example, Charles Perrault's 1696 book on illustrious men of his time declared that Lully was unusual for being "solemnized" as much for

---

[47] *Mercure de France*, April 1728, p. 809. See also ibid., June 1739, p. 1389; Michel Noiray, "Connoisseur," *Vocabulaire de la musique de l'époque classique* (Paris: Minerve, 2005), pp. 21–3.
[48] Quoted in Matthew Riley, *Musical Listening in the German Enlightenment: Attention, Wonder and Astonishment* (Aldershot: Ashgate, 2004), p. 29.
[49] Leopold Mozart to his son, 11 December 1780, *Letters of Wolfgang Amadeus Mozart*, M. M. Bozman (trans.) and Hans Mersmann (ed.) (New York: Dover, 1972), p. 149. See Josef Mančal, "Zum Reise- und Konzertmanagement Leopold Mozarts für Wolfgang Mozart," *Le musicien et ses voyages: Pratiques, réseaux et représentations*, Christian Meyer (ed.) (Berlin: Berliner Wissenschafts-Verlag, 2003), pp. 43–74.
[50] Leopold Mozart to his son, 13 August 1778, *Letters of Wolfgang Amadeus Mozart*, p. 120.

his "*Light*-Music" – that is, his operas – as was for his "*Church*-Music."[51]
Opera buffa and *opéra-comique* shared common publics with *opera seria* and
tragédie lyrique to a considerable extent, as Stefano Castelvecchi suggested.
The former were seen as regional, and the latter as cosmopolitan in origin.
The contrasting genres were not thought to represent low and high culture,
and their relationships to noble and bourgeois culture are problematic.[52] A
concert-goer of 1770 would not draw nearly as strong distinctions among
a theatre song by Thomas Arne, an oratorio number by Handel, and an
opera aria by Johann Christian Bach as people do today among pieces by
Madonna, Beethoven, and Pierre Boulez. The muted hierarchical differentiation of musical genres stands out in Charles Avison's comments on ballads
in his *Essay on Musical Expression* (1753). Avison had no hesitation in putting
John Gay's *Black-ey'd Susan* among "the many excellent Ballads which our
Language affords," finding it "extremely elegant" and among the "agreeable
and familiar airs, which might properly be calculated for those Entertainments, where the public Ear should be always consulted."[53] Still, he had
no reservations about attacking the taste he saw in secular cantatas written
for family feasts. He despised them as "trifling Essays in Poetry . . . those
shallow and unconnected Compositions" that figured among "that Flood
of Nonsense in . . . our Summer Entertainments."[54]

Yet not every kind of music was offered in public concerts, because inclusiveness had limits in the eighteenth century. Some genres were excluded
from concert programs for reasons of institutional privilege, a central aspect
of authority under the Old Regime. France possessed by far the strictest lim-
itation on what could be performed in any context. The Académie Royale
de Musique, which provided a privilege to the Concert Spirituel to perform
on holy days, forbade it from offering opera numbers with French texts to
limit competition from the series. Moreover, in most parts of Europe lines
were drawn between pieces written, on the one hand, for the tavern or
the club and, on the other, those designed for opera or concerts. Women
could always attend public concerts because of the courtly manners at such
events, which differed from the distinctively male conviviality at taverns
and clubs. The latter two contexts retained something of the sexual license

[51] *Characters Historical and Panegyrical of the Greatest Men That Have Appeared in France, During the
Last Century*, 2 vols., J. Ozell (trans.) (London: Bernard Lintott, 1703–1704), vol. 1, p. 194 (emphasis
original).
[52] Robert Isherwood, *Farce and Fantasy: Popular Entertainment in Eighteenth-Century Paris* (Oxford:
Oxford University Press, 1986); Castelvecchi, *Sentimental Opera*.
[53] Charles Avison, *Essay on Musical Expression* (London: C. Davis, 1753; New York: Broude, 1967), pp.
58–86.
[54] Ibid., p. 82.

associated with traditional festivals, which were abolished or reshaped in most parts of Europe by the middle of the eighteenth century. The writing and singing of songs – the *chanson* in France, the catch and the glee in England, and the Lied in Germany – were reestablished on respectable new social bases but kept at a distance from the formal concert. A special form of learning evolved in music clubs around the writing of texts by men of letters, done in France by Charles Collé and a distinguished club called Le Caveau.[55] But the growing publication of songs as broadsheets began to bring songs into public concerts toward the end of the eighteenth century, most prominently in Britain and North America. Songs sold as sheet music were performed at the London pleasure gardens and at the main concert series in Edinburgh and Birmingham. The *romance* and the *ariette*, though often deemed serious, likewise began to appear in Parisian concerts around 1800. Then after 1850 the music hall and the *café-concert* went much further in breaking musical culture up into separate spheres.

Early tendencies toward distinguishing between light and serious music also began appearing at the end of the eighteenth century. The music historian John Hawkins used a Victorian-sounding vocabulary in calling for concerts to be given as a "sober recreation" for people drawn "not by an affectation of admiring what they could not taste [i.e., know], but by a genuine pleasure which they took in the entertainment." He nevertheless adhered to the tradition of miscellany by criticizing overly homogeneous programs given by the musicians (the "waits") employed by the City of London.[56] J. B. A. Suard looked ahead similarly in his *Mélanges de littérature* (1785), criticizing the Concert Spirituel for performing "light or inconsequential music" (probably a set of variations) and deploring a "scandalous" *opera buffa* aria placed on the same program with a "sublime" setting of the Stabat Mater.[57]

SURVIVAL VERSUS CANON

A major goal of this book is to trace the evolution of repertories of old pieces, first called "ancient music" (or *la musique ancienne*) and then "classical music." Although I have used the terms *canon* and *canonization* for

55 Charles Collé, *Chansons choisies de Piron, Collé, Gallet, Favart* (Paris: Chez tous les marchands de nouveautés, 1868), p. 171; Robert Darnton, "An Early Information Society: News and the Media in Eighteenth-Century Paris," *American Historical Review* 105 (2000), pp. 1–35.
56 John Hawkins, *A General History of the Science and Practice of Music*, 2 vols. (London: Novello, 1875; New York: Dover, 1963), vol. 1, p. xxiii; vol. 2, p. 762.
57 J. B. A. Suard, *Mélanges de littérature* (Paris: Dentu, an XII, 1803), pp. 339–40.

such a purpose, I have become concerned that they can be too categorical in portraying how a piece was perceived. Speaking of "The Canon" suggests that it is obvious what pieces held that status in global terms, and to say that a composer was "canonized" sounds as if a liturgical rite had been performed over him or her. The boundary between music that was or was not canonized can be hard to find. Some pieces – opera overtures and opera selections most of all – acquired quite different kinds of canonic identity in different performing contexts. Francis Haskell and Nicholas Penny cautioned their readers in *Taste and the Antique* that they should not assume that all pieces of classical sculpture were revered as a common corpus: "Sometimes the statues we discuss became famous quickly, at others only after many decades; sometimes fame lasted for centuries, at others for only a few years; sometimes it was universal, at others confined to specific countries; sometimes present-day taste would . . . acknowledge the justice of such fame, [but] at others it would be startled by it."[58] Wariness about these terms has led me to look more widely for concepts that adapt the concept of canon productively to historical needs.

A close-to-the ground approach to understanding the status of classics is found in the concept of *Nachleben* (survival) coined by art historian Aby Warburg early in the twentieth century. Warburg arrived at the idea out of disillusionment with rigid and teleological approaches of art historians studying the Renaissance. A methodology evolved first in writings by Edgar Wind and Gertrude Bing, and more recently those of Georges Didi-Huberman, for analyzing how artworks and traditions formed around them managed to survive.[59] Instead of seeing a style being born, rising to greatness, declining, and dying, these authors propose a multilayered survival of elements derived from different periods and continuing in "latent" form as the "residue" of the past, potentially to be revived in new ways. Didi-Huberman argues that a work's "survival entails a complex set of operations in which forgetting, the transformation of sense, involuntary memory, and unexpected rediscovery work in unison."[60] By this reckoning, artistic time is by nature impure. Residues survive from different epochs which, though anachronistic, nonetheless participate in the present as memory, as "specters" influencing the perception of old objects.

[58] Francis Haskell and Nicholas Penny, *Taste and the Antique: The Lure of Classical Sculpture, 1500–1900* (New Haven, Conn.: Yale University Press, 1981), p. xiv.
[59] Georges Didi-Huberman, "Artistic Survival: Panofsky vs. Warburg and the Exorcism of Impure Time," *Common Knowledge* 9 (2003) 273–85. See William Weber, "Survival versus Canon in the History of Ancient Music," *Age of Projects*, Maximillian Novak (ed.) (Toronto: Toronto University Press, 2008).
[60] Didi-Huberman, "Artistic Survival," p. 275.

The Warburgian approach is useful for analyzing how music persisted variously in repertory and in memory. The neutral quality of the terms *survival* and *latency* has distinct advantages compared with the grandiose implications that "canonization" can easily suggest. Through these means one can identify traditions and practices and changes within repertories and ways of perceiving old music. Although music historians are well aware that certain pieces survived, not much has been written about the subject in depth.[61] Music has long possessed a *philosophical* canon – treatises on music of the spheres – and a *pedagogical* canon – books on rules of composition. But music has lacked a *performing* canon because few ancient works had persisted and because ecclesiastical and familial festivals placed high value on new works composed for the events. For that matter, literary commentary on music rarely discussed actual pieces of music, as it often did philosophical issues relating to music, and the aesthetic principle of universalism discouraged comment on specific musical examples. By contrast, humanistic treatises had delved into paintings since the sixteenth century, endowing them with a "superintendancy" over representation in all the fine arts.[62] For example, in 1604 Carl van Mander articulated a canon of Dutch and Flemish paintings in reference to principles expressed by Virgil.[63]

A moderate amount of sacred music did by tradition survive in libraries and repertories. Because such survivals remained local in nature, little being written about them, the practice is best considered a *mentalité*. Some songs of the troubadours and *trouvères* survived in changing forms from the fourteenth century, as John Haines has shown.[64] Masses and motets became institutionalized in churches – the Venetian composer Francesco Cavalli left an endowment at his death in 1676 for his requiem masses to be sung twice annually.[65] A quite different mode of survival can be found in the academic practice called the *stile antico*: a composing style that blended techniques of Renaissance polyphony with more recent styles with little

[61] See bibliography in William Weber, "History of Musical Canons," *Rethinking Music*, Mark Everist and Nicholas Cook (eds.) (New York: Oxford University Press, 1999), pp. 340–59; and the pathbreaking studies by Jeffrey Dean, "The Evolution of a Canon at the Papal Chapel: The Importance of Old Music in the Fifteenth and Sixteenth Centuries," in *Papal Music and Musicians in late Medieval and Renaissance Rome* (Oxford, UK: Clarendon Press, 1998), pp. 138–66; and John Haines, *Eight Centuries of Troubadours and Trouvères: The Changing Identity of Medieval Music* (Cambridge: Cambridge University Press, 2004).

[62] Robert Williams, *Art, Theory and Culture in Sixteenth-Century Italy: From Techne to Metatechne* (Cambridge: Cambridge University Press, 1997), p. 6.

[63] Carel van Mander, *Dutch and Flemish Painters: Translation from the "Schilderboeck,"* Constant van der Wall (trans.) (New York: McFarlane, 1936), p. lxvii.

[64] Haines, *Eight Centuries of Troubadours*.

[65] "Cavalli," *NGD*, vol. 4, pp. 24–34; Lorenzo Bianconi, *Music in the Seventeenth Century*, David Bryant (trans.) (Cambridge: Cambridge University Press, 1987), pp. 4–6.

basis in study or performance of older music.[66] The prestigious Accademia Filarmonica of Bologna required musicians seeking admission as members – Mozart, for example – to write a piece successfully in the *stile antico*.

Music survived in new ways from the middle of the seventeenth century, often in connection with political crisis or social change. In 1641, when England was on the brink of civil war, a minor canon at St. Paul's Cathedral named John Barnard published the *First Book of Selected Church Music* to protect old pieces composed at the Chapel Royal from "perishing or corrupting in erroneous and manuscript obscurity."[67] The revival of sung services in 1660 led to growing reliance on old works that had persisted in repertory, and the term *ancient music* soon arose to denote pieces written before about 1625. The Academy of Ancient Music, a club for high-level singers and their patrons begun in 1726, performed a unique repertory of music since the Elizabethan era at its meetings (Ex. 2.11).[68] But the first major repertory of old secular music performed in public appeared at the Paris Opéra (the Académie Royale de Musique), where pieces by Lully and other composers for Louis XIV were revived until the late 1770s.[69] A similar long lifetime occurred with the operas of Carl Heinrich Graun and Johann Adolf Hasse that survived in Berlin through the 1780s.[70] All this music took on canonic roles within musical life, even though little was usually written to that effect.

For all that, however, most such pieces survived with little relationship to one another, and the process of replacing old works with new ones continued in normal fashion. The superiority of new music over the old remained a basic principle of musical life, meaning that a piece usually became anachronistic within thirty or forty years. French writers spoke often of "les progrès de la musique," that is, the process by which music became antiquated, was modified, and replaced, a "progress" in both time and musical quality. The notion of *les progrès* was of such long standing that it had nothing to do with

[66] See James Garratt, *Palestrina and the German Romantic Imagination: Interpreting Historicism in Nineteenth-Century Music* (Cambridge: Cambridge University Press, 2002), pp. 3, 40, 43, 133–4, 142–3; Christoph Wolff, "Der Stile Antico in der Musik J. S. Bachs," *Studien zu Studien zu Bachs Spätwerk* (Wiesbaden: Steiner, 1968).
[67] John Barnard, *First Book of Selected Church Musick* (London: Griffin, 1641), p. 27.
[68] William Weber, *Rise of Musical Classics in Eighteenth-Century England* (Oxford: Clarendon Press, 1992), p. 68.
[69] William Weber, "*La musique ancienne* in the Waning of the Ancien Régime," *Journal of Modern History* 56 (1984), 58–88; "Lully and the Performance of Old Music in the Eighteenth Century," *Congress for the Tricentennial of the Death of J. B. Lully*, Jérôme La Gorce and Herbert Schneider (eds.) (Laaber: Laaber Verlag, 1991), pp. 581–90; and "Mentalité, tradition, et origines du canon musical en France et en Angleterre au XVIIIe siècle," *Annales E.S.C.* 42 (1989), 849–75.
[70] Mangum, "Apollo and the German Muses."

enlightened belief in human progress. In 1764 a journalist mentioned that major changes had been made to an act of *Les Élémens* (1721), the often revived *opéra-ballets* of Michel de Lalande and his understudy André Cardinal Destouches: "One finds here [changes] necessary to the perfection of this Act... since they were composed in a time when the progress of music in France had not yet arrived at the place where it stands today."[71] Yet that very work nonetheless survived and quietly was respected.

Historical thinking began to appear in writings on music by the middle of the eighteenth century, bringing a more nuanced historical understanding than before. Charles Avison did a careful balancing act between praising ancients such as Giovanni Palestrina and acknowledging the special brilliance of composers of his time. John Hawkins and Charles Burney both published histories of music in 1776, the same year when the Concert of Antient Music arose, the first series of public performances devoted systematically to old works. Repertories and histories nonetheless went their separate ways. Carl Dahlhaus has argued that musical canon is essentially normative, not historical, and that the writing of music history, far from establishing canon, served to legitimate canonic authority.[72] We need to recall, however, that music histories were written in Germany and Italy well before canonic repertories developed in the German states: for example, Johann Forkel's biography of Johann Sebastian Bach (1802) and Esteban de Arteaga's history of opera (1783–1788).[73]

A productive accommodation can thus be reached between the concepts of survival and canon, each side conceding something to the other. On the one hand, pieces could survive in coherent fashion, not just as "residue" from the past. Listeners might understand how a tradition kept a piece in performance, even if the music did not join a canon formally. On the other hand, we need to speak less about *the canon* and a lot more about *multiple canons* and indeed about *canonic practices* and *canonic implications*. Speaking in the plural and using adjectival constructions can keep us from thinking in teleological terms. By that means we can better interpret the scraps of information that remain about old pieces – how they might persist, how people treated them, and what kinds of authority they assumed.

It is vital to use these words carefully. The term *canon* is best restricted to a genre where a fairly specific body of works can be identified. The term

---

[71] *Mercure de France*, January 1764, p. 172.

[72] Carl Dahlhaus, *Foundations of Music History*, J. B. Robinson (trans.) (Cambridge, 1983), pp. 95–100.

[73] Johann Nicholas Forkel, *Allgemeine Geschichte der Musik*, 2 vols. (Leipzig, Im Schwickertschen Verlag, 1788–1801); Esteban Arteaga, *Le rivoluzioni del teatro musicale italiano dalla sua origine fino al presente*, 3 vols. (Venice: C. Palese, 1783–1788).

classic should not be used generically (for popular songs, for example), because it was closely associated with a particular brand of aesthetic thinking. Nineteenth-century writers applied the term chiefly to symphonies, sacred works, and string quartets, but not to opera or virtuoso music. By contrast, the adjectival construction *classical music* took on a much broader meaning by the 1840s, denoting a serious repertory of old and new works. Other terms can help define the kind of canonic status held by a piece within a repertory. *Institutionalization* fits best for the survival of operas in a particular institution, as happened to *Guillaume Tell* at the Paris Opéra, or for Beethoven's symphonies at specific orchestral concerts. Although opera excerpts and instrumental solos were not called classics, they were performed *canonically* on a long-term basis. The *coalescence* of numerous works defines an informal relationship that a variety of pieces, or even genres (old opera selections notably), might assume in a repertory. The concept of *museum culture* has proven useful to define canonic repertories succinctly but needs reexamination as to the major differences between such matters in art and music, specifically in museums and concerts.[74] Another question suggests itself: in what terms can a composer be seen to have acquired canonic status before the time of death? By tradition music of a master composer might be performed for a number of years after he died, such as was done with Arcangelo Corelli.[75] Mary Sue Morrow suggested the useful term *iconic* for identifying the honor accorded a composer during his lifetime, even though that status usually disappeared shortly after he died.[76]

The key point here is that simply the survival of a piece in repertory carried canonic implications. One thus modifies Joseph Kerman's useful distinction between canon and repertory by accepting long-term performance itself as a form of canonic recognition.[77] If aesthetic thinkers attributed canonic status to symphonies, musicians endowed opera selections and popular songs with canonic identity as they kept them in repertory. A piece of music earned special status by surviving the seemingly inevitable recycling of old works for new. We shall see this process occurring in music halls, *cafés-concerts*, and opera "galas" just as much as in "symphony" concerts. A second major point is that canon-building in nineteenth-century concerts

---

[74] James Sheehan, *Museums in the German Art World: From the End of the Old Regime to the Rise of Modernism* (Oxford: Oxford University Press, 2000).

[75] John Hawkins, *A General History of the Science and Practice of Music*, 2 vols. (London: Novello, 1875; New York: Dover, 1963), vol. 2, p. 676.

[76] Mary Sue Morrow, *German Music Criticism in the Late Eighteenth Century: Aesthetic Issues in Instrumental Music* (Cambridge: Cambridge University Press, 1997), pp. 60–1, 113.

[77] Joseph Kerman, "A Few Canonic Variations," in *Canons*, Robert von Hallberg (ed.) (Chicago: University of Chicago Press, 1984), pp. 177–96.

grew to a considerable extent out of the old practices that enabled pieces to survive. The traditional practice of quietly retaining a mass by Byrd or a well-known *air* by Lully was then transformed into a much larger and aesthetically more defined process. Pieces by Mozart, Beethoven, Gioachino Rossini, and Hector Berlioz thus became established in concert life in close association with surviving repertories of music by Giovanni Pergolesi, Niccolò Jommelli, Handel, and Graun.

TOWARD THE NINETEENTH CENTURY

Several concepts will guide how we define the transformation of concert life in the first half of the nineteenth century. As the musical community broke apart into separate areas, concert programs became more *homogeneous* than *miscellaneous*, classical music achieved an imposing, if limited, *hegemony*, and new kinds of concerts emerged that were oriented toward the *general public* by offering repertories of *popular songs* that prefigured what we call *popular music*.

   The principle of *homogeneity* arose as the largest principle of concert programming as areas of concert life moved farther apart from one another. Although *homogeneity* did not enter the musical vocabulary as *miscellany* had done, the term defines how a program was now expected to include genres sharing similar performing forces and a common level of taste, defined hierarchically. If miscellany had been inclusive, homogeneity was now exclusive. The former bound disparate musics together, but the latter distinguished major types from one another. Ballads such as Henry Bishop's *Home! Sweet Home!* were now excluded from some classical music concerts because they were popular songs, as had not been the case in the eighteenth century. Homogeneity was not applied rigidly; each concert institution defined it in a particular way according to its musical and social identity. Programs became homogeneous partly because music from so many historical periods began entering concert programs. The music Clara Schumann performed in 1862 (Ill. 7) spanned 150 years, five times more than the pieces Bartolomeo Campagnoli offered in 1785 (Ill. 1). Because listeners can absorb only so much variety overall, the increasing historical diversity required greater homogeneity in other respects. During the 1880s some singers and pianists began designing recitals chronologically, clarifying what could be a confusing array of periods, and early music specialists began putting the birth and death dates of composers on their programs. A pedagogical dimension began entering programs that had been entirely foreign to concert life before that time.

The term *popular music* has been used with substantially different meanings both in the nineteenth century and in recent scholarly literature. The two main options are to see it in social terms or aesthetic terms, that is, either as music of the lower classes or as music designed to entertain, no matter which social classes are involved. Richard Middleton focused on the second meaning productively when he defined "popular music" as "types of music that are considered to be of lower value and complexity than art music, and to be readily accessible to large numbers of musically uneducated listeners rather than to an elite."[78] In this context "elite" relates to aesthetic hierarchy more than social class. Still, the term *uneducated listener* does imply social class, suggesting that the two definitions were always bound in with one another to some extent. Although some observers might object to the term *lower value* in Middleton's definition, it is justified if one can show that hegemonic authorities judged popular songs in such terms, even though by no means everyone agreed with them. Derek Scott contributed to such analysis by suggesting that we think of "contested taste" occurring between taste groups in musical commentary. Such dispute occurred primarily over the commercialism determining how popular songs were designed and marketed. The ideology of classical music rejected commercialism even though most of its music was sold by the same publishers who peddled ballads. Scott has also stressed a complicated interaction among social classes in the early stages of the "revolution of popular music" he portrays. He argued that we should not see the music hall or the *café-concert* essentially reflecting the working classes or any one group for that matter.[79]

Because the term *popular music* carries so complex a set of meanings, I have come to speak instead of *general taste* and the *general public* to identify music that is thought approachable for anyone within a broad area of society.[80] The word *general* was often used to mean the opposite of "specialized," for we have already seen how the word was used in magazines to differentiate themselves from learned journals. Thus the opera overture was thought *approachable* by the general public even though not every

---

[78] Richard Middleton, "Popular Music," *NGD*, vol. 20, pp. 128–30. See also Andreas Ballstaedt and Tobias Widmaier, *Salonmusik: zur Geschichte und Funktion einer Bürgerlichen Musikpraxis* (Stuttgart: Steiner Verlag, 1989).

[79] Derek Scott, *Sounds of the Metropolis: The 19th-Century Popular Music Revolution in London, New York, Paris and Vienna* (New York: Oxford University Press, 2008); and "Music and Social Class," in *Cambridge History of Nineteenth-Century Music*, Jim Samson (ed.) (Cambridge: Cambridge University Press, 1992), pp. 544–67.

[80] Otto Biba, "Beobachtungen zur Österreichischen Musikszene des 18. Jahrhunderts," *Österreichische Musik/Musik in Österreich: Theophil Antonicek zum 60. Geburtstag*, Elisabeth Hilscher (ed.) (Tutzing: Schneider, 1998), p. 224.

person would necessarily *enjoy* any example of it. No one naturally presumed that *general* had to mean wholly *universal* taste. In 1773 a French magazine used the word *general* diplomatically: "Let us hope that artists and amateurs, indeed also those who have not learned much on music, will come to agree on the general nature of the art and the knowledge needed to enjoy it."[81] Members of a particular social group might regard a genre – Italian opera selections among the English upper classes, for example – as "general" to them all, even though (perhaps *because*) people lower down the social scale found it foreign to their culture.[82] A genre occupied a place on the continuum from general to esoteric taste at any one time. Between around 1750 and 1830 the opera overture stood on one end and the fugue on the other. The most drastic change occurred with the instrumental pieces of J. S. Bach, which went from being regarded as academic in nature to being played often by pianists by 1850. Haydn's symphonies went in the opposite direction, because although around 1800 they opened many benefit concerts, by 1840 they were performed only at learned classical music concerts. Oratorios, *Messiah* most of all, continued to suit general taste to an unusual extent. Mozart's *Die Zauberflöte* and Haydn's *Die Schöpfung* were able to "transcend the distinction between popular and esoteric music," Dahlhaus observed.[83]

The concept of *hegemony* will serve here to define the authority held by Italian opera in the eighteenth century and classical music from the middle of the nineteenth century. As defined by Antonio Gramsci, the concept has proved useful for historians who want to analyze the fluid ways in which authority has been exerted in cultural spheres. In this usage, "hegemony" does not mean a wholesale or permanent vesting of power in one group or institution over another. Rather, hegemony emerges and is maintained through negotiation among groups on an ongoing basis, even though one group may end up predominating. As one historian argued, "subordinated groups accept the ideas, values and leadership of the dominant group not because they are physically or mentally induced to do so, nor because they are ideologically indoctrinated, but because they have reasons of their own."[84] Derek Scott has defined the bourgeoisie culturally as a "hegemonic

---

[81] "Prospectus," *Journal de musique*, 1773, p. 6.
[82] I first used the term in "Learned and General Musical Taste in Eighteenth-Century France," *Past and Present* 89 (1980), 58–85.
[83] Carl Dahlhaus, *Nineteenth-Century Music*, J. Bradford Robinson (trans.) (Berkeley, Calif., 1989), p. 35.
[84] See Gwynn William, "Gramsci's Concept of 'Egemonia,'" *Journal of the History of Ideas* 21 (1960), 586–99.

bloc" that "aims to win its position of ascendancy through consent rather than impose itself by force."[85]

Although the ultimate hegemony in the modern era resides in the state, particular communities within societies have also possessed a political structure with a hegemonic authority. An identifiable community – or "art world," as sociologists put it – developed in each theatre, art, and music in the early eighteenth century in which practices of rhetoric and negotiation evolved, guiding the communities. The terms *musical world* in Britain, *Musikleben* in Germany, and *monde musical* in France – all of which made their way into the titles of periodicals – expose such social structures. Italian opera exerted a broad hegemony in eighteenth-century concert life, though rivaled by regional or national idioms of comic opera. Classical music achieved an imposing hegemonic status by the 1860s but on a more limited basis. Even though classical music came to dominate music criticism, pedagogy, and civic ceremony, the breakup of concert life limited its authority significantly within concerts of popular songs designed for the general public.

In 1890 George Bernard Shaw denounced the miscellaneous concert, flaunting the hegemony of idealistic musical values over traditional ones in concert life. Unlike Roger North, Shaw rejected such a concert out of hand: "There are few things more terrible to a seasoned musician than a miscellaneous concert, . . . A ballad concert, a symphony concert, a pianoforte recital: all these are welcome when they are not too long; but the old-fashioned 'grand concert,' with an overture here, a *scena* there, and a ballad or an instrumental solo in between, is insufferable." He articulated a fear of mass culture within his musical world, saying that a miscellaneous concert was "a vast crowd of people without definite musical ideas, loosely strung good-natured creatures who are attracted solely by the names of the performers, and can distinguish between Edward Lloyd and Sims Reeves, but not between a Donizetti cavatina and a Bach fugue."[86]

CRITIQUES OF MISCELLANY IN 1726 AND 1890

The words of North and Shaw suggest the virtues and the vices of their contrasting musical cultures. Eighteenth-century musical culture had to tolerate contrasting tastes and behaviors, making it seem intellectually lazy,

[85] Derek Scott, *The Singing Bourgeois: Songs of the Victorian Drawing Room and Parlour* (Aldershot: 2nd ed., Ashgate, 2001), p. x. See also Patricia Anderson, *Printed Image and the Transformation of Popular Culture, 1790–1860* (Oxford: Clarendon Press, 1991).
[86] George Bernard Shaw, *Music in London, 1890–1894*, 3 vols. (London: Constable, 1932), 16 November 1890, vol. l, p. 80.

because the musical community was small in size and presented limited performing opportunities. By the middle of the nineteenth century many more options were available to listeners, leading some to demand a much higher order of musical taste and to be intolerant toward those who did not share that goal. Critics like Shaw defined the classical music world ideologically and in hierarchical terms foreign to musical outlooks of the eighteenth century. Idealists such as he saw no other choice because they feared that ballads and music halls were going to overwhelm the world of serious music.

CHAPTER 2

Variations on miscellany

The principles of miscellany and collegiality governed concert programming for well over a century. Organizing a concert was a collegial undertaking, a sorting out of priorities among professionals accustomed to working together. Highly patterned, often symmetrical, programs brought order to a community beset with rivalries between local and foreign composers and literary quarrels over taste for old works or new ones. Around 1780 every major concert series offered opera selections, concertos, cantatas, and symphonies, and almost every concert-goer learned the music of Haydn, Domenico Cimarosa, Giovanni Paisiello, and the long-deceased Giovanni Pergolesi. Indeed, some old works, often called "ancient" music, were performed in most places, even though that music took second place to newer products.

"Miscellany" took substantially different forms in the major cities of Europe. The most important difference among the four cities we are studying was whether a central institution held privileges to control concerts and programs, which therefore tended to follow common guidelines. In Paris and Leipzig institutional monopolies kept formats remarkably consistent; in London, and to a lesser extent Vienna, a free-market atmosphere led to considerable variety in program design. The strictest controls were found in absolutist Paris, where state monopolies governed musical life, and the weakest ones existed in London, whose municipal decentralization and liberties dating back to the Civil War allowed a diverse array of concerts and programs. This chapter will first explore basic principles of programming in the late eighteenth century and examine a prototypical concert offered in each city. The second section will raise the question of how cosmopolitan, regional, or national identities were given to music and how the identities related to one another in each city. The final section analyzes the repertories of old works that survived within programs in this period.

BASIC PATTERNS IN CONCERT PROGRAMS

An eighteenth-century listener would have thought a piano recital or a purely orchestral concert monochromatic, strange, and dull.[1] The principle of miscellany dictated that a program maintain contrast in its sequence of pieces. Most basic of all, a public concert had to include both vocal and instrumental pieces, opera selections to a particular extent. Two or more examples of the same genre could not occur back to back, and contrast was maintained among male and female singers and soloists playing on different instruments. These practices reflected a deep fascination with virtuosity in its contrasting forms. Voices and instruments had long been thought to depend on one another in what one musicologist has called the "love duet" inherent in the long tradition of *bel canto*.[2] Around 1785 listeners would flock to concerts to hear a rondo by Domenico Cimarosa followed by a violin concerto by Giovanni Viotti. Love of virtuosity made the contrasting genres succeeding one another on a program appear seamless to the attentive listener.

Programs usually followed a format that was standard in a concert series and perhaps even in a city generally. Although any one program had to display variety, program formats tended to remain constant over time. A concert always opened with an orchestral piece, often the allegro first movement of a symphony, a practice derived from the overture opening an opera. How many movements of a symphony were performed is a nagging question, because different practices seem to have prevailed. In Vienna and German cities, movements of a symphony were often performed individually, or put in different parts of a program; in London a single movement was often done at the end of a concert, called a "full piece," but a symphony opening the second half would probably be done complete (Ex. 2.4).[3] The last piece in each half of a concert – often called the Finale, again a derivative of opera – could be an operatic ensemble as large as a sextet. The main concert series did not present orchestral concerts as such, because at least half of a program usually consisted of accompanied instrumental solos or vocal

[1] Mary Sue Morrow, *Concert Life in Haydn's Vienna: Aspects of a Developing Musical and Social Institution* (Stuyvesant, N.Y.: Pendragon, 1989), p. 141.
[2] Rodolfo Celletti, *A History of Bel Canto*, Frederick Fuller (trans.) (Oxford: Clarendon Press, 1991), p. 3.
[3] Rebecca Grotjahn, *Die Sinfonie im deutschen Kulturgebeit 1850 bis 1875* (Sinzig: Studio, 1998), p. 76; Zaslaw, *Mozart's Symphonies*, pp. 158–60, 423; McVeigh, *Concert Life in London*, pp. 101, 193–204.

pieces. Thus a series served as a staging area for a variety of ensembles and soloists. The most imposing musical forces appeared in choral-orchestral sacred works for Advent, Christmas, or Lent or in a choral piece from an opera.

Instrumentalists sometimes followed different rules in the "benefit" concerts they organized. Two instrumental works might come in a row, though always in different genres; the practice of playing several pieces in the same genre together did not become common until at least the 1840s. Military bands offered concerts without any singers, a practice virtually unique to them in the eighteenth century. But the main exception to the rule occurred in elite private concerts, where an unusually high proportion of vocal or instrumental pieces might be heard. We do not discuss private concerts in depth, but it is clear that the need to accommodate the public did not apply to an aristocrat presenting music in a stately home. For example, around 1800 the Habsburg Empress Marie Therese, a singer in her own right, presented several concerts a week made up almost entirely of vocal pieces, usually focused either on *opera buffa* or *opera seria*.[4] The patrons of Beethoven's chamber music likewise held private performances dedicated strictly to quartets and related genres. The English heir apparent gave a concert in Devonshire House in 1823 made up of ensemble numbers from Rossini's *Il Turco in Italia* (1814), each half introduced by a sonata for horns.[5]

Leipzig was a key musical city in the German states during the 1780s even though it did not possess its own opera company. The Grosses Concert, a series founded in 1743, served as the center of musical life, featuring opera singers drawn from court theatres, until a new series was begun in the Gewandhaus in 1781. A series of twenty-four annual subscription concerts (Abonnenten-Concerte) and numerous Extra-Concerts by individual musicians were held in the new hall. Between 1720 and 1817 the only opera produced in Leipzig came from intermittent performances offered by a variety of companies in the Rannstädter Theater.[6] The new concert series was governed by a privately incorporated board, the *Direktorium*, that was closely linked to the city council. Members of the board – chiefly clothing

---

[4] John Rice, *Empress Marie Therese and Music at the Viennese Court, 1792–1807* (Cambridge: Cambridge University Press, 2003), pp. 90–2, 170–3.

[5] "London," *QMMR* 5 (1823), 252.

[6] [Johann Friedrich Erst von Brouve], *Raisonnirendes Theater Journal von der Leipziger Michaelmesse 1783* (Leipzig: Jacobaer, 1784), pp. 32–33; Schering and Wustmann, *Musikgeschichte Leipzigs*, vol. 3, pp. 557–83.

merchants, publishers, judges, and law professors – worked with the music director of the series to choose programs and performers and to determine which musicians could present their own concerts in the hall.[7] Although the board did not exercise a legal privilege over concerts in the city, it in effect held a monopoly over prestigious events. Concerts appeared in numerous public houses, most outside the city walls, but none came close to the Gewandhaus in size or renown.

The order of musical genres expected at concerts – in effect, the principle of miscellany – was written into the Gewandhaus's founding document.[8] The great majority of programs (Ex. 2.1) adhered to this format until the 1830s.

2.1 *Sequence of Genres, Abonnenten-Concerte, Leipzig Gewandhaus,*
   c. 1781–1820[9]

Overture or Symphony
Opera number, usually an aria
Concerto, done by the principal player, often composed by that person
Opera ensemble number, duo to sextet

—

Overture or Symphony
Opera aria or ensemble number
Operatic choral number
Symphony or other instrumental piece

The centrality of opera selections appears in a program performed in 1787 that included four different types of excerpts (Ill. 11). The works were recent: a scene by Giuseppe Sarti (*Giulio Sabino*, 1781), a terzetto by Paisiello (*Il re Teodoro*, 1783), and a chorus from Franz Seydelmann's *Il mostro ossia Da gratitudine amore* (1785). The rondo for bass by Cimarosa, "Care donne giovinette che gelosi sposi avete," may have been a free-standing song.[10]

7 Schering and Wustmann, *Musikgeschichte Leipzigs*, vol. 3, pp. 259–61, 427, 477–78; Margaret Menninger, "The Serious Matter of True Joy: Music and Cultural Philanthropy in Leipzig, 1781–1933," in *Philanthropy, Patronage and Civil Society: Lessons from Germany, the United States, Britain and Canada*, Thomas Adam (ed.) (Bloomington: Indiana University Press, 2004), pp. 120–37.
8 Schering and Wustmann, *Musikgeschichte Leipzigs*, vol. 3, pp. 271–5; Wustmann, *Aus Leipzigs Vergangenheit*, vol. 2, p. 262; Friedrich Schmidt, *Das Musikleben der bürgerlichen Gesellschaft Leipzig im Vormärz, 1815–48* (Langensalza: Beyer, 1912), pp. 42–6.
9 Abonnenten-Concerte, SGML. See "Nachricht von der künftigen Einrichtung des Leipziger Concerts," in Eberhard Creuzburg, *Die Gewandhaus-Konzerte zu Leipzig, 1781–1931* (Leipzig: Breitkopf & Härtel, 1931), opposite p. 19.
10 A manuscript copy is held in Perugia: Istituto Centrale per il Catalogo Unico, http://opac.sbn.it/cgi-bin/IccuForm.pl?form=WebFrame.

The program carefully balanced composers of different national origin: four Germans, three Italians, and one Bohemian – Antonio Rosetti, by birth Anton Rösler, whose much-admired symphonies were also performed in London and Paris. Sarti was the leading opera composer of his generation, Paisiello and Cimarosa were the rising stars in that field, and Naumann and Carl Stamitz led German-born composers of their generation. The eight composers were between thirty-seven and fifty-seven years in age; Seydelmann was a student of Naumann. Karl Gottlieb Berger, the orchestra's principal violinist, probably composed the concerto.[11]

The Concert Spirituel in Paris held an exclusive royal privilege for permission to present concerts in Paris. In 1725 the Académie Royale de Musique authorized the concert series to present events in the Salle des Tuileries on the twenty-five holy days when the opera was required to be silent.[12] Though the repertory was predominantly secular, one to three sacred pieces – oratorios, motets, or movements from masses – were presented at each concert up to the time of the Revolution. In regulating all public concerts in the capital, the series allowed far fewer musicians to give benefit concerts than was done in most European cities and did not permit outdoor concerts at all. Amateur concerts modeled on the Concert Spirituel provided the only other major type of concerts in the city.[13] Although concerts did not follow a standard sequence of genres as was done in Leipzig, programs were nonetheless patterned with great care. A program in 1782 was highly symmetrical, for it opened with a symphony, an aria, a concerto, and a sacred piece and then did the same but in reverse, with a concerto placed in between (Ex. 2.2). As in Leipzig, balance was maintained among regional origins for genres and therefore among the composers: at this concert four pieces were by Frenchmen, two by Germans, and two by Italians, though other events had more by the latter. Programs often offered more opera selections than this one did.

[11] "Karl Gottlieb Berger," *Biographisch-Bibliographisches Quellen-Lexicon der Musiker und Musikgelehrter,* 11 vols., 2nd. ed., Robert Eitner (ed.) (Leipzig, 1900–1904; Graz: Akademisches Druck- und Verlangsanstalt, 1959), vol. 1, pp. 458–9. It is very unlikely that the symphony was by Johann Stamitz, Carl's father.
[12] On concerts held in churches for a paying audience, see Thierry Favier, "Aux origines du Concert Spirituel: pratiques musicales et formes d'appropriation de la musique dans les églises parisiennes de 1680 à 1725," in *Les Formes d'organisation collective du concert en Europe 1700–1900,* Patrice Veit and Michael Werner (eds.)(Berlin: Berliner Wissenschaftsverlag, forthcoming).
[13] Michel Brenet [Marie Bobillier], *Les Concerts en France sous l'ancien régime* (Paris: Fischbacher, 1900; New York: Da Capo, 1970); Joann Élart, "Musiciens et répertoires de concert en France à la fin de l'Ancien Régime," unpublished Ph.D. dissertation, University of Rouen (2005), vol. 2, Appendix III, pp. 14–25.

2.2 *Concert Spirituel, Paris, Salles des Tuileries, 9 December 1782* [14]

Symphony	Haydn
Italian Aria	Sarti
Concerto for bassoon	P.-D. Deshayes
O Salutaris, motet *a capella*, 3 voices	F.-J. Gossec
Concerto for oboe "composed upon several known melodies" (Besozzi)	[? *Carlo Besozzi*]
Ode sacrée, words by Jean-Baptiste Rousseau	N.-J. Chartrain
Concerto for violin	*Chartrain*
Italian aria	Niccolò Piccinni
Symphony	J.-F. Sterkel

In Vienna no central concert society exerted a monopolistic authority such as did the Gewandhaus and the Académie Royale de Musique. The court and the police nonetheless controlled the city's two theatres, where concerts often replaced shows on thirty-five holy days, and the Grosser and the Kleiner Redoutensaal were sometimes used for concerts. The loosening of the rule against theatre on holy days in 1786 limited access to their calendars even more.[15] But musicians overcame this problem by making imaginative use of public houses and parks for an increasing number of entrepreneurial concert ventures. A decline in funding for music at the court helped turn the Viennese musical world into a free market similar to that in London.[16] The Society of Musicians (Tonkünstler-Societät) enjoyed special access to the Kärntnertor Theater because of its role as the corporate body raising funds for musicians' pensions. Although its concerts were not as central to musical life as the Concert Spirituel was in Paris, they did amount to about a quarter of all public concerts in Vienna in the 1770s and 1800.[17] Many of the Society's early programs combined an oratorio or a cantata, by either an Italian or Austrian composer, with a concerto or a symphony or both. Programs of a miscellaneous nature became even more common at the series, often with design as symmetrical as at the Concert Spirituel.

---

[14] Constant Pierre, *Histoire du Concert Spirituel (1725–1790)* (Paris: Société Française du Musicologie, 1975), p. 321.

[15] Otto Biba, "Grundzüge des Konzertwesens in Wien zu Mozarts Zeit," *Mozart-Jahrbuch*, 26 (1978–1979), pp. 132–43, and "Beobachtungen zur Österreichischen Musikszene des 18. Jahrhunderts," *Österreichische Musik/Musik in Österreich: Theophil Antonicek zum 60. Geburtstag*, Elisabeth Hilscher (ed.) (Tutzing: Schneider, 1998), pp. 213–30.

[16] Spitzer and Zaslaw, *Birth of the Orchestra*, pp. 421–2.

[17] Morrow, *Concert Life in Haydn's Vienna*, pp. 46–50, 68–71 and *passim*; Rice, *Empress Marie Therese*, pp. 170–72. Dexter Edge, "Concert Life in Haydn's Vienna: Aspects of a Developing Musical and Social Institution" (review), *Haydn Yearbook/Haydn-Jahrbuch* 16 (1992), 116.

A program given in 1778 presented a sequence of aria, chorus, and instrumental piece four times (Ex. 2.3). Here we find a balance tilted toward local composers: three opera pieces by Italian composers and two by Austrians, four instrumental works by Austrians, and three selections by the cosmopolitan G.-F. Handel. Concerts in the Burgtheater followed similar practices, although with more focus on Italian than German composers and less attention to Handel.[18]

2.3 *Tonkünstler-Societät, Kärtnertor Theater, 20 December 1778*[19]

Symphony	Johannes Sperger
Aria [opera or oratorio]	Carl Ditters von Dittersdorf
Chorus [oratorio]	†Handel
Concerto for Contrabass	*Sperger*
Aria [German opera]	Franz Teyber
Chorus [opera]	Antonio Sacchini
Symphony	[?Gottfried van Swieten]
Aria [opera]	[?Giuseppe] Giordani
Chorus [oratorio]	†Handel
Concerto for violin	Joseph Zistler
Trio [opera]	Sarti
Chorus [oratorio]	†Handel

London concert life was unusually free of central institutional control. Although the King's Theatre held a monopoly over the staging of opera with Italian texts, no concert series dominated the city as did the Concert Spirituel or the Gewandhaus. Moreover, many public rooms were available for concert use, most significantly the Hanover Square Rooms constructed in 1776 specifically for concerts. Government control of taverns and concert rooms was minimal, due to disputes following the Civil War and to the lack of unity among municipalities in the metropolis. The City of Westminster, where the majority of concerts took place, required licenses for daytime concerts but exercised much less control than comparable bodies in other cities. Concerts indeed had flourished to an unusual extent in London since the 1670s. The little-regulated, entrepreneurial nature of concerts

---

[18] Brown, *Gluck and the French Theatre*, pp. 14–15, 129–30.

[19] C. F. Pohl, *Denkschrift aus Anlass des hundertjährigen Bestehens der Tonkünstler-Societät* (Vienna: Tonkünstler-Societät, 1871), p. 59; Bernd Edelmann, "Händel-Aufführungen in den Akademien der Wiener Tonkünstlersozietät," *Göttinger Händel-Beiträge* 1 (1984), 172–4, 178–9; Morrow, *Concert Life in Haydn's Vienna*, p. 246.

(not found in opera) was essentially a postrevolutionary condition caused by the cycle of regime changes and the lack of a central municipal authority.

In London the closest parallel to the Concert Spirituel or the Gewandhaus series was a succession of subscription series in existence between 1764 and 1793. Concerts begun by Johann Christian Bach and Carl Friedrich Abel in 1764 became the premier locale where one could hear virtuoso pieces and Italian opera selections. In 1783 a venture led by violinist Johann Salomon began, joined two years later by a series called the Professional Concerts. These concerts attracted both the musical *cognoscenti* and the elite public in general; the players counted among the most distinguished musicians in London, enjoying the patronage of the main families involved in musical life.[20] A program presented at the Hanover Square Rooms by Salomon during Haydn's first visit to London in 1791 looked like an expanded version of the 1787 Gewandhaus concert in its alternation between Italian opera numbers and concertos (Ex. 2.4). The twelve works on this program display a distribution of genres similar to that in the other cities: an overture opening each half, four opera pieces, three concertos, and a cantata. String quartets, an example of which we see here, were more common in London than in Leipzig and Paris. What most differentiated this program from those in the other cities was the relative absence of British composers, a lack not found in most other London concerts.

2.4 *Salomon Subscription Concerts, Hanover Square Rooms, London, 27 May 1791*[21]

Symphony ["Overture"]	Rosetti
Italian opera aria (Theresa Negri)	
Concerto for violin	*Salomon*
Italian opera aria (Giacomo Davide)	
Concerto for flute and bassoon	[? *J. & F. Küchler*]
—	
Symphony ["Overture"]	Haydn
"Cantata," [? scene, *L'Anima del filosofo*, 1791]	Haydn

---

[20] Simon McVeigh, "The Professional Concert and Rival Subscription Series in London, 1783–1793," *Royal Musical Association Research Chronicle* 22 (1989), 1–135.

[21] Quoted in H. C. Robbins Landon, *Haydn in England, 1791–1795*, vol. 3, *Haydn: Chronicle and Works* (Bloomington: Indiana University Press, 1976), pp. 80–1. The Haydn "cantata" might also have been his *Arianna a Naxos* ("Teseo mio ben," 1790), Hoboken XXVIb:2, probably orchestrated; see Julian Rushton, "Viennese Amateur or London Professional? A Reconsideration of Haydn's Tragic Cantata *Arianna a Naxos*," in *Music in Eighteenth-Century Austria*, David Wyn Jones (ed.) (Cambridge: Cambridge University Press, 1996), pp. 232–45.

New string quartet	Haydn
Italian opera aria (Negri)	
Concerto for pedal harp	*Anne-Marie Krumpholtz*
Italian recitative and aria (Davide)	
Finale [Symphony movement]	Rosetti

A traveler could thus experience comparable concerts in all four cities, hearing a few pieces everywhere – most likely Haydn's best-known "London" symphonies and pieces from Cimarosa's *Matrimonio Segreto*. The careful patterning of the programming was essential to this cosmopolitan musical world. Yet we will see different formats in other kinds of concerts in each city. The free-market condition in London concerts stimulated particular variety in program formats. The Concert of Antient Music arose as the first public series devoted to canonic repertory, and specialized concerts developed featuring British music. In Vienna new formats appeared widely in benefit concerts from the late 1780s. These tendencies presage the end of miscellany as the principle governing programming in the 1830s.

COSMOPOLITAN VERSUS REGIONAL IDENTITIES

Because excerpts from Italian opera long dominated programs at leading concerts, we will inquire into the nature of cosmopolitanism found in musical life generally. As applied here, the term *cosmopolitan* indicates the authority carried by a genre that was widespread and as such hegemonic in contexts where the music was performed. No single country or region could exist on its own; involvement internationally, whether in collaborative or competitive terms, was basic to musical culture. By 1710 opera from diverse parts of the Italian peninsula had become established as the principal repertory in almost all courts and cities. Though still Italian in identity, the works exerted authority as the cosmopolitan standard in opera. The concertos and symphonies by central European composers, often identified as German, acquired a similar if less powerful such role in the late eighteenth century. Thus M.-P.-G. Chabanon spoke mostly for Italian opera when he declared that "in their free circulation, the arts lose all of their indigenous character; . . . In this regard Europe can be thought to be a mother country of which all the arts are citizens."[22] By the 1850s classical music repertories at orchestral and chamber music concerts assumed a cosmopolitan status even though the music still carried a German identity.

[22] Quoted in Noiray, *Vocabulaire*, p. 119.

At the same time, local composers were sometimes favored on programs in opposition to cosmopolitan rule. Moreover, musical theatre with vernacular texts – *opéra-comique, Singspiel,* and English ballad opera – was thought distinctive to a region and thereby attempted to rival cosmopolitan genres. The French idiom acquired a limited international status because it was also performed in Vienna and in Berlin during the second half of the eighteenth century. The word *regional* is more precise than *national* for designating the opposite of *cosmopolitan,* because musical genres or styles were neither linked to the state nor congruent with state boundaries. One can indeed speak of "indigenous" composers in some cases. The relationships between music by local and by foreign composers differed widely in the four major musical cities. In the early and mid-eighteenth-century France and England stood at opposite poles as to the primacy of Italian versus domestic opera. Although the King's Theatre offered Italian opera exclusively, the Paris Opéra allowed few such productions until the 1770s. In Vienna, Dresden, Berlin, and other cities, however, non-Italians – Graun, Hasse, Mozart, and Gluck most of all – wrote successfully in Italian opera even though their origins made them subordinate to Italian composers.

Paris and Bordeaux

The Bourbon monarchy, recovering from the civil war of the Fronde and embattled militarily for half a century, gave an extraordinary privilege to French opera at the Académie Royale de Musique in 1669. Favoring local music grew from an introverted tendency in French absolutism, puzzling visitors from elsewhere in Europe. All of the licensed theatres had virtually year-round schedules, unusually long ones in the case of the Opéra, and the cost of developing new repertory meant that old works were revived regularly. Works by Lully and Rameau dominated the repertory in the 1750s and 1760s, a piece by the former last revived in 1779 and one by the latter in 1785.[23] A complete recycling of old for new works occurred at both the Opéra and the Concert Spirituel in the 1770s, bringing the institutions back into harmony with the cosmopolitan expectations of the European upper classes. Italian repertory entered the Opéra and became more common at the Concert Spirituel, leading some to speak of an "Italianization" of the two institutions.[24] French musicians drew on the

---

[23] Pierre, *Concert Spirituel,* pp. 71–4; Daniel Heartz, "The Concert Spirituel in the Tuileries Palace," *Early Music* 21 (1993), 240–8; Patrick Taïeb, *l'Ouverture d'opéra en France de Monsigny à Méhul* (Paris: Société Française de Musicologie, 2007), pp. 299–375.

[24] Pierre, *Concert Spirituel,* p. 334. See Brenet, *Concerts sous l'ancien régime,* p. 320 and Michel Noiray, "Le répertoire d'opéra italien au Théâtre de Monsieur et au Théâtre Feydeau (janvier 1789–août 1792)," *Revue de musicologie* 81 (1995), pp. 259–275.

growing tendency toward nationalistic rhetoric in the press. The author of a *Dialogue entre Lulli, Rameau et Orphée, dans les Champs Elisées* (1774) complained in the preface: "Today we cling to a host of prejudices: the most ridiculous of them all for our Nation is to think that our Music must cede to the dominance of those of Italy or Germany." England was thus not alone in holding an inferiority complex about its music, as was still the case in the nineteenth century.[25] "I'm not about to say, as has been claimed," the essayist concluded, "that we really have no music; that sweeping reproach has no basis whatsoever in fact."[26] Concert repertories became more diverse as the Revolution broke down privileges of the old order. The monopoly of the Académie Royale de Musique over French vocal music came to an end, as did the Concert Spirituel itself, and excerpts from French opera became central to new concert programs. In 1796, for example, a concert in the prominent series held at the Théâtre Feydeau offered excerpts from Gluck's *Alceste* (1776), Mozart's *Don Giovanni*, and an ariette seemingly from Jean-Jacques Rousseau's *Le Devin du Village*.[27] Excerpts such as these (the Rousseau excepted) were to remain in repertory throughout the nineteenth century.

A forward-looking expansion of repertory developed even earlier in Bordeaux than in Paris.[28] Every two weeks from January to September between 1783 and 1793, the Musée de Bordeaux presented a lecture or a poetry reading, followed by a concert directed by Franz Beck, a violinist born in Mannheim and trained in Italy. Musicians performed for free in the orchestra because they were thereby allowed to present benefit concerts in the museum for their own profit or loss. The Bordeaux programs included a profusion of French opera numbers that could not be offered in public concerts in Paris until after 1790. A concert in 1784 offered an excerpt from an *opéra-comique* by Pierre Monsigny as well as three opera numbers by Gluck, along with a motet and a secular cantata (Ex. 2.5). The music of Piccinni normally dominated these programs, however.

[25] Katharine Ellis, *Interpreting the Musical Past: Early Music in Nineteenth-Century France* (Oxford: Clarendon Press, 2005), pp. 16–21.
[26] *Dialogue entre Lulli, Rameau et Orphée, dans les Champs Elisées* (Amsterdam: Stoupe, 1774), p. vi. He was of course referring to the denunciation of French as an operatic language made by Jean-Jacques Rousseau.
[27] Patrick Taïeb, "L'exploitation commerciale du concert public en l'an V (1797)," in *Les Formes d'organisation collective du concert en Europe 1700–1900*, Patrice Veit and Michael Werner (eds.) (Berlin: Berliner Wissenschaftsverlag, forthcoming).
[28] See William Weber, "Les programmes de concerts, de Bordeaux à Boston," *Le Musée de Bordeaux et la musique de concert, 1783–93*, Patrick Taïeb, Natalie Morel-Borotra, and Jean Gribenski (eds.) (Rouen: University of Rouen, 2005), pp. 175–93; Joann Élart, "Les origines du concert public à Rouen à la fin de l'Ancien Régime," *Revue de musicologie* 93 (2007), 53–74. On nineteenth-century provincial concerts, see Ellis, *Interpreting the Musical Past*, pp. 36–41, 62–63.

2.5 *Concert Publique, Musée de Bordeaux, 3 July 1784*[29]

Symphony	Haydn
Air, "Est-il un sort plus glorieux?"	
La Belle Arsène (1776)	Pierre Monsigny
Symphonie concertante	J.-B. Davaux
Motet, *O Salutaris hostia*	F.-J. Gossec
Overture, *Roland* (1778)	Piccinni
Duo, "Ne doutez jamais de ma flame,"	
Iphigénie en Aulide (1774)	Gluck
Concerto for violin	*Marchal, Sen.*
Duo, "Et tu preténds encore que tu	
m'aimes," *Iphigénie en Tauride* (1779)	Gluck
Airs variés for violin	*Marchal, Sen.*
"Hymne à l'amour," *Echo et Narcisse* (1779)	Gluck

The Bordeaux concerts also served the growing market for domestic music much more explicitly than did the Concert Spirituel. The *airs variés* (variations on melodies) by violinist Marchal were typical of the instrumental solos performed at Bordeaux's benefit concerts, pointing ahead to the salon music of the early nineteenth century. Indeed, the potpourri – a medley on a well-known opera or folk tune – was often performed, as did not happen at the Concert Spirituel (though the concerto "upon several known melodies" in Ex. 2.2 may have been similar). At a program in 1786 a young violinist performed a potpourri for mandolin, whereas his father played a concerto by the distinguished Viotti.[30] A culturally and politically active middle class existed in Bordeaux, for the leaders of the Musée tended to come from outside the local elite. Indeed, many were killed in the Terror.[31]

Leipzig

A working compromise existed between Italian and German genres and composers in the planning of the Gewandhaus subscription concerts. As we saw in the 1787 program, selections by Naumann and Seydelmann were performed alongside pieces by Sarti, Cimarosa, and Paisiello (Ill. 11).[32] The

---

[29] "Concerts du Musée," Archive, Musée de Bordeaux, courtesy of Patrick Taïeb. See also Patrick Taïeb, "Le Concert de Reims, 1749–1791," *Revue de musicologie* 93 (2007), 17–52.

[30] *Journal de Guyenne*, 25 June 1786, p. 704.

[31] Stephen Auerbach, "'Encourager le commerce et répandre les lumières': The Press, the Provinces, and the Origins of the Revolution in France, 1750–1789," unpublished Ph.D. dissertation, Louisiana State University (2001).

[32] A. G. Meissner, *Bruchstücke zur Biographie J. G. Naumann's*, 3 vols. (Prague: A. Doll, 1803).

Extra-Concert given in 1785 by Bartolomeo Campagnoli likewise included an aria from an *opéra-ballet* by Naumann (Ill. 1). Vocal pieces in other languages also appeared occasionally at these concerts. In 1783 a female singer named Schröter offered a piece from Monsigny's *La Belle Arsène* (1776) in French ("Non, non, j'ai trop de fierté") as well as several in English by Johann Christian Bach ("By my sighs you may discover," probably a song written in an English genre).[33]

Patriotic rhetoric supporting the region's music emerged in Germany in a fashion similar to that in France. In 1779 a Leipzig periodical deplored the cosmopolitan musical taste Germans tended to follow, for, just as the Italian-born Lully "endowed the French with their kind of music, ... so German music has been in the situation of mostly borrowing from other countries." Thus, "[w]e must differentiate ourselves by virtue of our careful craftsmanship, proper definition of pieces, and through the depth of feeling with which we endow our music."[34] Music by German composers was chiefly represented at the subscription concerts by texts on religious or civic themes, setting that region's music apart from the supposed frivolity of Italian opera. The cantata and the ode were thought to fulfill civic purposes; Johann Reichardt's *Hymne an die Musik*, for example, was performed in an amateur concert series in 1779 and four times at the subscription concerts by 1800.[35] His *65. Psalm*, set to words by Moses Mendelssohn, also appeared there often. A civic theme is particularly strong in a cantata by Johann Adam Hiller called *Auf, Volk! Auf, auf zur Freude!* (Oh, people, arise with joy!). Still, many Bohemians such as Rosetti and Johann Baptiste Vanhal wrote symphonies performed at the Gewandhaus that were usually perceived as German in style. Thus did music written for a sacred or civic purpose give the German music at the concerts a serious tone that pointed ahead toward an essential characteristic in the culture surrounding classical music.

Pieces from German operas were also occasionally performed at the subscription concerts. Thomas Bauman explains that in this period German musical theatre "grew from a fairly homogeneous conception – one of rustic comedy or farce peppered with relatively modest musical items – into a multivariate, complex activity."[36] One of the oldest German opera composers represented was Ignaz Holzbauer, an Austrian who served as

[33] Extra-Concerte, 1777–92, SGML.
[34] "Über die Tonkunst," *Olla Potrida*, April 1779, p. 240.
[35] "Musikübende Gesellschaft and Abonnenten Concerte," SGML. See the valuable discussion of Beethoven's occasional works in Esteban Buch, *Beethoven's Ninth: A Political History*, Richard Miller (trans.) (Chicago, Ill.: University of Chicago Press, 1999), pp. 66–86.
[36] Thomas Bauman, *North German Opera in the Age of Goethe* (Cambridge: Cambridge University Press, 1985), p. 3.

Kapellmeister in Mannheim. Excerpts from his *Günther von Schwarzburg* were done frequently during the mid-1790s, and Mozart had expressed his admiration for it while in Mannheim when it was first performed in 1777.[37] Numbers from stage works by Johann Peter Schulz were also performed, most important of all a setting of an adaptation of Racine's *Athalia*. Yet not all of Mozart's German operas were performed often at the Gewandhaus. Although excerpts from his Italian operas were done at least a half dozen times almost every season from 1790 onward, only twice did pieces from *Die Zauberflöte* appear on a program before 1832, three decades after the Private Concerts in Birmingham offered a duet from what it called *Il flauto magico*.[38] Pieces from *Die Entführung aus dem Serail* appeared six times between 1792 and 1810 but not again until 1835. Mozart indeed puzzled some critics. In a critical survey of productions done at the Rannstädter Theater in 1783, the author, a military officer, declared that, although fascinated with *Entführung*, he knew nothing similar and was at a loss to evaluate it.[39]

Social tension arose in Leipzig's musical life chiefly between levels of the bourgeoisie, because the subscription series drew more criticism in the press than did comparable institutions in any of the other major cities. Political dissension grew significantly in many parts of Germany during the 1780s and 1790s, and in some cases radical positions surfaced. Satirical tracts similar to those published in London and Paris appeared in Leipzig, complaining that the governing class was too rich and obsessed with fashion. A book called *Leipzig im Profil* (1799) criticized the Leipzig elite sharply and attacked the Gewandhaus for monopolistic control of musical life. The author deplored the concerts' formality and stood up for traditional events in public houses:

It's hard to tell who the entrepreneur is at the [Gewandhaus] hall; the orchestra is big and busy, though it costs a risky amount of money to keep it going. Ordinary people instead go to six- or eight-Groschen concerts in the Rannstädter Schiessgraben to satisfy their musical needs, or to [Christian Gottfried] Thomas's hall, which they like a lot. Also, Herr Richter gives weekly concerts summers in his garden on Hintergasse – there you can hear the top musicians in the city, which old folks say they remember being better than what is done now.[40]

---

37 Gloria Flaherty, *Opera in the Development of German Critical Thought* (Princeton, N.J.: Princeton University Press, 1978), p. 267; Jost Hermand, "Die erste deutsche Nationaloper," in *Revolutio germanica: die Sehnsucht nach der "alten Freiheit" der Germanen, 1750–1820*, Jost Harmand and Michael Niedermeier (eds.) (Frankfurt am Main and Leipzig: Peter Lang, 2002), pp. 158–71.

38 Birmingham Private Concerts, 30 November 1801, BCL.

39 *Raisonnirendes Theater Journal*, pp. 32–3.

40 [Moritz Cruciger], *Leipzig im Profil: Ein Taschenwörterbuch für Einheimische und Fremde* (Leipzig: Solothurn, 1799), pp. 64–5. On satirical literature (often called *Pasquillen*), see Robert Beachy, *The Soul of Commerce: Credit, Property and Politics in Leipzig, 1750–1840* (Leiden: Brill, 2005), pp. 99–136.

An entrepreneur, composer, and publisher, Thomas was one of the guiding forces in Leipzig musical life. In a polemic entitled *A Non-Partisan Critique* (1798), Thomas presented himself as representative of the larger public (the "middling" classes, historians would say) and claimed that the *Direktorium* had prevented him from producing a series of Concerts Spirituels during Lent. Still, he produced concerts in as many as ten of the public houses proliferating in this period and was later connected with the Gewandhaus.[41] In 1799 he put on an outdoor concert that involved the local elite: "A Public Assembly and Grand Academy of Music" honoring the birthday of the Saxon Erzherzog and Grand Field Marshall Carl (Ex. 2.6). Held in the evening at Reichel's Garten, a prominent public house outside the city walls, the concert involved a military band and a string ensemble. Though Thomas composed or arranged all the music, a Haydn symphony that opened the event lent the occasion a certain aesthetic legitimacy.

2.6 *"Assemblée Publique avec Grande Académie de Musique, Reichels Garten," Leipzig, 5 September 1799* [42]

Symphony, with Janissary music [?No. 94, 1794]	Haydn
Introductory Music	C. G. Thomas
Battle Song, words by Klopstock, 30 Instruments and 8 Voices, 4- and 8-voice canons and solo movements	*Thomas*
–	
Volksgesang in honor of the Name Day of the Erzherzog	*Thomas*
Volksgesang in Honor of the Birthday of the Erzherzog	*Thomas*
Poem of Praise for Erzherzog Carl, words by Pastor Veith zu Andelfinger	*Thomas*

Vienna

In Vienna throughout the eighteenth century local musicians worked very much under the shadow of Italian – essentially Neapolitan – opera. The first stop northward on the tour of a rising Italian singer or composer was usually the Habsburg court, where both royalty and aristocrats lavished more on them than perhaps anywhere else but in England. "Taste in music

---

[41] [C. G. Thomas], *Unpartheiische Kritik der vorzüglichsten zu Leipzig aufgeführten, und fernerhin aufzuführenden Concerte und Opern, wie auch anderer, die Musik betreffende Gegenstände* (Leipzig, Verlag der Verfassers, 1798); Schering and Wustmann, *Musikgeschichte Leipzigs*, vol. 3, pp. 162, 525–6, 613–14; "J.-C. Thomas," *NGD*, vol. 25, pp. 408–9; F. G. Leonhardi, *Geschichte und Beschreibung der Kreis- und Handelstadt Leipzig nebst der umliegenden Gegend* (Leipzig: J.-G. Beygang, 1799), pp. 660–1.

[42] Garten-Konzerte, 1787–1858, SGML.

here is ruled by the Italians," reported a magazine in 1803.[43] An aristocrat articulated the hegemony of cosmopolitan opera in Vienna when he recorded in his diary that the London-based oboist Christian Fischer "draws sounds that are quite sweet, quite pure, quite subterranean, quite difficult from his instrument, but the choice of music – all English and French – did not please."[44]

Viennese musicians entered into free-wheeling experimentation in their benefit concerts from around 1785. A program was given in 1788 by Stefano Mandini, the baritone who created the role of Count Almaviva in *Nozze di Figaro*, that offered pieces by eight Italians and a *canon a capella* apparently by the learned Giovanni Battista Martini (Ex. 2.7). Though one or two instrumental pieces might also have been played, the performance of four opera selections in each half of the program departed from the tradition of alternating between vocal and instrumental music. The program contained a rich variety of composers and genres; it gives the sense of a musical community going in interesting new directions.

2.7 *Singer Stefano Mandini, Burgtheater, 5 February 1788* [45]

Symphony	Mozart
Recitative/aria	Gioacchino Albertini
Scene/aria, *L'Olimpiade* (1784)	Cimarosa
Aria	Paisiello
Trio, "Che vi par Dorina," *Fra i due litiganti il terzo gode* (1782)	Sarti
Concerto for violin	
Symphony	Haydn
Canon a capella, 3 voices	[? †Giovanni Battista] Martini
Aria, *L'Impresario in angustie* (1786)	Cimarosa
Scene/Rondo	Antonio Bianchi
Exit aria, *Axur re di Ormus* (1788)	Antonio Salieri
Trio	[?Pietro Alessandro] Guglielmi
Symphony	

[43] Quoted in Morrow, *Concert Life in Haydn's Vienna*, p. 214. Hermann Abert commented on the limited national identity apparent in Mozart's letters in *W. A. Mozart*, 2 vols. (Leipzig: Breitkopf & Härtel, 1955–1956), vol. 2, pp. 10–11, and on his setting of Italian librettos, vol. 1, pp. 357–82. See also the 1829 comment on Mozart in *The Musical Reformer* cited in Ch. 5, n. 10.
[44] Quoted in Morrow, *Concert Life in Haydn's Vienna*, p. 230.
[45] Ibid., p. 270; "Mandini family," *NGD*, vol. 15, pp. 736. David Wyn Jones discusses aspects of the city's concert life in *The Symphony in Beethoven's Vienna* (Cambridge: Cambridge University Press, 2006), especially pp. 8–10, 32–3.

The learned tradition among Viennese composers nonetheless posed a significant counterpoint to cosmopolitan opera in this period. Composers such as Johann Albrechtsberger, Joseph Weigl, and Joseph Eybler were noted for their "craftsmanship, harmonic sophistication, and richness of instrumental color," music favored by Empress Marie Therese.[46] Their pieces were performed regularly at the concerts of the Society of Musicians, often in greater numbers than at the one given in 1778 (Ex. 2.3). But although they acquired significant high patronage, they were unsuccessful on the whole in achieving recognition internationally. A variety of other composers – civil servants and members of the lower nobility, most notably Ignaz von Seyfried – devoted most of their lives to musical activity. We shall see how they led the idealistic movement for reform of musical culture in the early nineteenth century.

For organizers of benefit concerts to perform almost entirely their own music was another example of how practices in programming loosened up in Vienna during this period. The benefit concert was inherently collegial, because the public expected to hear a variety of composers, performers, and genres. Oboist Fischer, for example, was typical of practice in Vienna and the other cities in devoting no more than a third of a program to his own music. Departing from this convention was most likely done by a leading musician intent on self-promotion. Thus it is striking that in 1783 and 1784 Mozart put on two concerts where, it seems, at least two-thirds of the known pieces were his own and that in 1789 he presented a concert in Leipzig where no other composer was mentioned on the printed program.[47] Because perhaps only about half of all Viennese programs produced in the period are known today, it is probable that other musicians did the same. It is nonetheless hard to find comparable examples of such a concert in the major cities, partly because a musician was normally not well known in as wide a range of genres as was Mozart. Soon after 1800 five major Viennese

---

[46] Rice, *Empress Marie Therese*, p. 2 and *passim*.

[47] Cramer's *Magazin der Musik* identified the program of 23 March 1783 as entirely by Mozart; the one on 1 April 1784 included three unidentified arias, one certainly by him; see Morrow, *Concert Life in Haydn's Vienna*, pp. 253, 256. Mozart suggested the unusual nature of the 1783 program when he gave a detailed list of pieces performed in a letter to his father, 29 March 1783; see *Mozart: Briefe und Aufzeichnungen*, Wilhelm Bauer and Otto Erich Deutch (eds.), 7 vols. (Kassel: Bärenreiter, 1962–1975), vol. 4, pp. 261–2. The program of the Leipzig concert, on 12 May 1789, stated "All of the pieces of music named here are compositions of Kapellmeister Mozart"; see Extra-Concerte, 1779–1792, SGML and letter of Mozart to his wife Constanza, 16 May 1789, *Mozart: Briefe und Aufzeichnungen*, vol. 4, p. 86. An even more exceptional concert devoted to one composer occurred in the performance of Carl Ditters von Dittersdorf's twelve symphonies on Ovid's *Metamorphoses*, called *Four Ages of the World* (1786); see Richard Will, *The Characteristic Symphony in the Age of Haydn and Beethoven* (Cambridge: Cambridge University Press, 2002), p. 29.

musicians – Ferdinando Paër, Georg Vogler, Anton Eberl, Theodor von Schacht, and Beethoven – offered programs devoted to their own music (the singer Paër and the cellist Eberl also serving as performers). It is well known that Beethoven continued to produce concerts of this nature.[48] We will follow the evolution of this type of program as it developed into what today is called the New Music concert.

Another important new type of concert came with the performance of substantial works in public parks. Events held in the Augarten seem to have been variously outdoors and in a hall within the park, and we can presume that the concerts organized by Ignaz Schuppanzigh and other entrepreneurs occurred mostly in the hall.[49] Mozart performed a concerto for two pianos at an Augarten concert in 1782, along with one of his symphonies and another by Gottfried van Swieten, all naturally separated by vocal pieces.[50] Opera selections provided most of the vocal selections, differing from the songs that dominated at Ranelagh or Vauxhall in London. Musical entrepreneurs also began inventing programs that looked ahead to promenade concerts and the music halls. In 1795 a family of musicians presented eighteen pieces that blended opera excerpts (by Sarti, Cimarosa, Pasquale Anfossi, and Pietro Alessandro Guglielmi) with popular songs probably drawn from *Singspiel* ("Addio, der Abschied," "Filomena, die Nachtigal," and "Non plus ultra"). A sonata was performed by three people bowing on one violin, and the final piece was described as "a noisy concluding chorus by the family and orchestra."[51] Although we know of only a few other such events, this one illustrates how musicians were feeling their way toward concerts devoted to what Leopold Mozart referred to as "the so-called popular [music], which tickles long ears."[52] The Emperor's wind ensemble went in the opposite direction aesthetically: instead of performing in the open air, it began presenting formal concerts in the Kärntnertor Theater.[53] A program given in 1787 included arrangements of music from comic operas – Vicente Martin y Soler's *Una*

[48] Morrow, *Concert Life in Haydn's Vienna*, pp. 253, 256, 263, 312, 319, 323, 327–8, 339. On 7 May 1824, Beethoven gave a concert including his Overture, Op. 124, "The Three Grand Hymns" (Mass in D, "Missa Solemnis"), and the Symphony no. 9; see *Thayer's Life of Beethoven*, revised and edited by Elliot Forbes (Princeton: Princeton University Press, 1967), pp. 907–8, and also pp. 254–5 (2 April 1800) and p. 446 (22 December 1808).

[49] Morrow, *Concert Life in Haydn's Vienna*, pp. 56, 59.

[50] Ibid., pp. 55, 251. A similar report involving Ignaz Schuppanzigh mentioned vocal pieces; see ibid., p. 60. See Biba, "Grundzüge des Konzertwesens in Wien zu Mozarts Zeit," pp. 132–42.

[51] Morrow, *Concert Life in Haydn's Vienna*, pp. 288–9.

[52] Leopold Mozart to his son, 11 December 1780, *Letters of Wolfgang Amadeus Mozart*, p. 149.

[53] Biba, "Beobachtungen zur Österreichischen Musikszene des 18. Jahrhunderts," pp. 213–19.

cosa rara (1786) and Dittersdorf's *Der Apotheker und der Doktor* (1786).[54] These novel programs suggest the energy with which Viennese musicians began giving unconventional concert formats and in so doing broke free of the nobility.

London

No compromise was struck between local and Italian composers at the King's Theatre in London such as was done in other cities. Nowhere else were local composers excluded as fully from writing for the main Italian opera theatre as in London. The only known performances of music by British-born composers at that theatre between 1708 and 1838 were two works by Stephen Storace, son of an Italian bass player, and a one-night production, *l'Olimpiade*, by Thomas Arne (1710–1778).[55] Most importantly, there is no evidence that Arne's widely produced *Artaxerxes* (1762) was ever performed at this privileged theatre. Innumerable works by British composers were performed at other theatres, however.

Italian opera achieved hegemony at the King's Theatre in direct relationship to the reconstitution of the nobility during the political crisis of the early eighteenth century. The "Whig ascendancy" dominating British politics between 1714 and 1760 took cultural form in the rigid monopoly given to Italians for productions in the King's Theatre.[56] By the 1720s its directors formed part of the firm-handed – in some respects authoritarian – politics by which Robert Walpole brought England stability for the first time since the Civil War of 1642. Taste for Italian music was seen as "general" among the upper classes, but that music held a more particular class basis than was found in the other cities, separate from taste for British music. Associating the nobility with the authority of cosmopolitan culture reinforced the preeminence of that social class in the uncertain search for political stability in the period. As the London *Weekly Journal* put it in 1725, Italian opera was "so generally approv'd of in *England,* that it is look'd upon as a want of Breeding not to be affected by it."[57] Yet this happened just as England was acquiring a bourgeoisie wealthier than that of any other

---

[54] Edge, "Concert Life in Haydn's Vienna," pp. 152–3; Morrow, *Concert Life in Haydn's Vienna*, p. 264.

[55] "Stephen Storace" *NGD*, vol. 24, pp. 442–4; "Arne," *NGD*., vol. 2, pp. 41–5. Storace's pieces were done in 1788 and 1792 and Arne's in 1765. Michael Balfe's *Falstaff* had its première at the Queen's Theatre in 1838.

[56] *Whig Ascendancy: Colloquies on Hanoverian England,* John Cannon (ed.) (London: Edward Arnold, 1981), *passim*; Weber, "L'Institution et son public"; Paul Monod, "Politics of Handel's Early London Operas, 1711–1719," *Journal of Interdisciplinary History* 26 (2006), 445–72.

[57] *Weekly Journal; or, Saturday's Post,* 18 December 1725, quoted in Elizabeth Gibson, *Royal Academy of Music, 1719–1728: The Institution and Its Directors* (New York: Garland, 1989), p. 388.

European country. In 1868, as the English middle classes were enjoying newly won parliamentary representation, the nationalist George Macfarren looked back to the Hanoverian Succession to condemn the aristocracy for "ignoring everything Anglican in connection with music."[58]

The subscription series at the Hanover Square Rooms extended the hegemony of cosmopolitan opera into the concert hall. As we have seen (Ex. 2.4), programs performed at such concerts included relatively little music by British composers or, for that matter, "domesticated" music by Handel. But the subscription concerts were atypical of London's concert life as a whole. Anyone who did a tour of concerts and musical societies across Britain during the 1780s would have heard works by British composers frequently. Opportunities for performance of their music opened up for them within provincial musical societies, prestigious gentleman's clubs, and a growing number of prominent London concerts. Composers such as Arne, Charles Dibdin, William Shield, Samuel Webbe, and John Wall Callcott flourished in these contexts, and some of their vocal music was performed right up to the First World War.

Two uniquely English genres proved especially popular between 1760 and 1830: the glee and the catch. The term *glee* first appeared in the middle of the seventeenth century as a song written for three to six unaccompanied solo male voices, eventually with contrasting choral sections. Following in the tradition of Italian canzonets and the simpler English madrigals, the glee did not usually have much contrapuntal activity among its parts.[59] The genre became prominent chiefly with the founding of the Noblemen's and Gentlemen's Catch Club in 1761, at whose meetings (for men only) leading singers and composers found patrons among gentlemen and nobles. Glees also became a major component of English opera, the best known by Arne and Shield, but were also sung widely by amateurs. Catches, by comparison, involved imitative counterpoint that was variously simple or complex, set to texts of love and conviviality similar to those of the glee. Catch clubs sprang up all over the British Isles in imitation of the original organization. In the south coastal city of Chichester, for example, there existed both a catch club and a musical society; the latter closed its meetings by singing catches.[60] The best known catches and glees were

---

[58] George Macfarren, "'The English Are Not a Musical People,'" *Cornhill Magazine* 18 (1868), 356.

[59] Brian Robins, *Catch and Glee Culture in Eighteenth-Century England* (Woodbridge, UK: Boydell, 2006); McVeigh, *Concert Life in London*, pp. 94, 100, 109–11, 152, 196, 243–9.

[60] *John Marsh Journals: The Life and Times of a Gentleman Composer (1752–1828)*, Brian Robins (ed.) (Stuyvesant, N.Y.: Pendragon, 1998), pp. 399–758.

performed in public concerts after 1790, most prominently at the Academy of Ancient Music and the Anacreontic Society.

British music took special prominence at the eighteenth-century pleasure gardens Vauxhall and Ranelagh. Even though aficionados of opera and virtuosity took the Professional Concerts more seriously than those at Vauxhall, they did not draw a sharp distinction between what they heard in the gardens and in formal concerts.[61] Lady Mary Coke went regularly to concerts at both pleasure gardens, indicating how prestigious a public was present there: in 1781 she wrote her sister that "many of the Young Ladies having made their parties went to Ranelagh."[62] The orchestra was a good one, drawn from players at the main theatres. The Vauxhall music director James Hook (1745–1827), winner of a song prize from the Catch Club, wrote many songs and organ concertos for the pleasure gardens. His songs resembled those written for English opera and for domestic use. The first half of a program at Ranelagh or Vauxhall usually alternated between theatre songs and overtures, symphonic movements, or concertos by well-known Continental composers; the second half often was the act of an English opera. Works by Handel and Haydn gave the programs a canonic basis, contrasting with the presence of recent English ballads.[63] A concert would often open or close with a piece by Arne, who was recognized in canonic terms after his death in 1778.

Programs at the Pantheon, a large hall on Oxford Street that opened in 1772, also indicate how strong a public British music enjoyed. Offering both seats and a promenade area, the Pantheon became known for the high level of its performers and the prestige of its audiences. In 1783 Lady Mary Coke wrote her sister that Lady Ailesbury had insisted they go to the "great concert" at the Pantheon organized to raise money for singers and dancers "defrauded" by the manager of the King's Theatre.[64] A program from 1786 (Ex. 2.8) blended British and cosmopolitan repertory: concerto grossos by Giuseppe Sammartini and the celebrated Corelli followed by pieces by four Englishmen, three Italians, one Austrian, and the London-based F. J. Barthélemon. Nowhere else in Europe would one hear in public a piece as old as the glee "Turn, Amarillis," by the seventeenth-century Thomas Brewer, along with a new song modeled on it.

---

[61] Charles Cudworth, "The Vauxhall 'Lists,'" *Galpin Society Journal* 20 (1967), 26.
[62] Lady Mary Coke to sister, 21 December 1781, *COKE*.
[63] Cudworth, "Vauxhall 'Lists,'" p. 40; Simon McVeigh, Database of London Concert Programs, 1750–1800.
[64] Lady Mary Coke to sister, 28 May 1783, *COKE*.

2.8 *Pantheon, 26 December 1786* [65]

Overture [probably symphony]	†G.-B. Sammartini
Song (Mr. Arrowsmith)	
Song	F.-J. Barthélemon
Concerto grosso	†Corelli
Duet, "Time has not Thinned my Flowing Hair"	William Jackson
Glee, "Turn, Amaryllis, thy Swain"	†Thomas Brewer
Catch, "Which is the Properest Day to Drink"	†Arne
—	
Overture	Haydn
Aria, "Care luci, nel mirarvi"	†Sacchini
Concerto for violin	Barthélemon
Glee, "The Answer to Turn Amaryllis"	Stephen Paxton

Thus did songs in the vernacular assume great prominence in public concerts in London. The glee became so popular in the early 1790s that it was sometimes done on programs that formerly had offered little British music of any kind. On 5 January 1791, for example, the Neapolitan violinist Ignazio Raimondi put on a benefit concert that mingled glees by Samuel Webbe and Garrett Wellesley, Lord Mornington, with Italian opera numbers sung by the star singers Gertrude Mara and Gasparo Pacchierotti, along with the sponsor's "Battle" Symphony. On 18 May 1793, the Professional Concert followed suit by presenting a glee by Webbe.[66]

An ideology of musical nationalism grew up around concerts of this sort. The very hegemony of cosmopolitan taste at the King's Theatre and the Hanover Square Rooms stimulated British musicians to promote their music elsewhere. In existence 1792–1795 and then periodically for some time after 1801, the Vocal Concert was arguably the first musical institution devoted explicitly to music by indigenous composers in the four cities we are studying. A memoir of concert life published in 1818 indeed stated that events were "almost exclusively dedicated to the performance of English music."[67] A program given in 1793, for example, included eleven pieces by British composers out of sixteen in all, only one by an Italian, with instrumental pieces only at the start of each half.[68] While challenging the primacy

---

[65] McVeigh, Database of London Concert Programs, 1750–1800; and the detailed discussion in Robins, *Catch and Glee Culture*.
[66] McVeigh, Database of London Concert Programs.
[67] "Memoirs of the Metropolitan Concerts III," *QMMR* 1 (1818), 186.
[68] *Harrison and Knyvett's Vocal Concert*, BL.

of cosmopolitan repertory, the musicians began going so far as to design programs made up almost entirely of vocal selections.

American and British provincial cities

As in concerts at the Musée de Bordeaux, programs tended to be particularly inclusive in Britain's provincial cities and in North America. Songs originating in ballad operas took root at an early date in provincial concert life, serving broader publics than those who went to specialized London venues. In her study of local musical societies, Jenny Burchell showed that musical societies offered two kinds of events: "polite" performances among the members and "commercial" concerts for the general public.[69] The members – usually just men – would meet every week or two, without an audience, and perform chiefly instrumental pieces. But periodically they put on public concerts designed to give their club prominence and financial support, with women appearing as singers and as a major portion of the audience. Programs at such events were usually centered on vocal pieces, chiefly opera selections and cantatas or odes, and subsequently ballads and glees.

Tension over goals was built into the life of musical societies. Some members preferred that the club dedicate itself to amateur instrumentalists performing for one another rather than for a less musically educated public. Here we find an early example of conflict between learned and general taste: those with more training in music wished to remain apart from those with less. By the same token, Johann Forkel, music director at the University of Göttingen, vented his frustration in 1779 that a program focused on instrumental pieces would turn away those lacking "sufficient knowledge of art and practice" needed to understand such music.[70] Still, meetings of private music societies were by no means learned seminars. The players usually ate, drank, and smoked, and the evening would end up with everyone singing songs or catches. Issues of gender figured deeply in the dichotomy between public and private meetings. Women were seen as the defining force for fashion, thereby investing public musical life with tastes thought contrary to the learning of private musical meetings, even though their presence was vitally needed by such an organization. The minutes of the Edinburgh Musical Society, for example, urged in 1789 that the officers "endeavor to prevail on ladies of fashion to honor the Concert as a place

---

[69] Jenny Burchell, *Polite or Commercial Concerts? Concert Management and Orchestral Repertoire in Edinburgh, Bath, Oxford, Manchester, and Newcastle, 1730–1799* (New York: Garland, 1996), pp. 3–29.
[70] Quoted in Matthew Riley, *Musical Listening in the German Enlightenment: Attention, Wonder and Astonishment* (Aldershot, UK: Ashgate, 2004), p. 97.

of fashionable amusement."[71] One senses male jealousy toward confident leadership exerted by women in upper-class gatherings.

A particularly detailed record of learned local musicians appears in the autobiography of John Marsh, a lawyer of moderate wealth who served as head of the musical societies in Salisbury, Canterbury, and Chichester between the 1780s and 1810s. While in Chichester, he reported that obtaining better singers and the Sussex military band allowed the concerts to move to a large hall and draw bigger audiences than before. In 1788 he remarked that he was trying to make the second half of the program a particularly attractive "miscellaneous act." He worried chiefly about finding good singers and answering complaints that he had abandoned the intimate old instrumental concerts.[72]

A program presented by the Edinburgh society in 1752 illustrates a particularly active effort to please the general public. Including eight vocal and seven instrumental numbers, the program relied on genres thought widely popular. Three visiting Italian musicians performed melodies on Polish, Scottish, and "Hossack" airs, though we can be sure that the music was cosmopolitan in style.[73] Three selections from Handel's widely performed *Acis and Galatea* (1718/1732) were offered along with several instrumental solos. Still, musical societies sometimes did offer programs of a more learned nature. A concert at the Oxford Musical Society in 1765 included only two vocal pieces out of ten, focusing instead on concerto grossos by Corelli, Francesco Geminiani, and Charles Avison that the amateur players knew almost by heart.[74] Indeed, these works survived in large part because amateurs could play them. The music did not survive in performance in Italy, where amateur music societies were less common and the whole framework of musical culture discouraged the survival of repertory.

A concert held in Bath in 1787 went unusually far toward focusing a program on popular songs. The Villa Gardens, a public house in the prestigious spa town, offered the "Annual Breakfast Concert" performed by an

---

71 Burchell, *Polite or Commercial Concerts*, pp. 48–9. See Georges Escoffier, "De la tentation à la civilisation: La place des femmes au concert en France au XVIIIe siècle," *Sociétés de concert en Europe, 1700–1920: Structures, pratiques musicales et sociabilités*, Hans-Erich Bödeker and Patrice Veit (eds.) (Berlin: Berliner Wissenschaftsverlag, 2007), pp. 101–27.

72 *John Marsh Journals*, pp. 415–16, 434, 443–44, 462, 467; Brewer, *Pleasures of the Imagination*, pp. 531–72.

73 Burchell, *Polite or Commercial Concerts*, p. 84. Since Madonis had just been in St. Petersburg, "Hossack" might have meant "Cossack," though the former word was also a common Scottish name. On Scottish musical life, see Claire Nelson, "The Influence of Scotland in London's Musical Life during the Eighteenth Century: With Specific Reference to Violin Repertoire," unpublished Ph.D. thesis, Royal College of Music (2002); and Matthew Gelbart, *The Invention of "Folk Music" and "Art Music": Emerging Categories from Ossian to Wagner* (Cambridge: Cambridge University Press, 2007).

74 Oxford Musical Society, BLO.

ensemble of twelve winds and strings that included such notable Londoners as oboist John Ashley and singer Charles Incledon (Ill. 19).[75] Aside from the overture or concerto that opened and closed each half, the music consisted entirely of British songs, the best known being "The soldier tired" from Arne's *Artaxerxes.* Some of the songs were probably unaccompanied, such as "Joan said to John," a catch by Osmond Saffery, and the glee, "Come live with me and be my love," by Samuel Webbe, Senior. Other songs – "Zooks that an old man can't keep a chicken," for example – probably originated as broadsides, written for taverns. Thus members of the aristocracy heard a lot of British music when on holiday. Pieces from English opera such as Arne's, which we have seen at the Pantheon and Vauxhall, became increasingly linked with songs from private contexts, a repertory that became central to programs external to classical music during the nineteenth century. That tendency is apparent at the turn of the century; the Private Concerts in Birmingham, for example, included a ballad at most of its events after their initiation in 1800.[76] The French *romance* was likewise included in many programs of the prominent concerts given in Paris on the rue de Grenelle from 1802.[77]

Concerts presented in Boston in the 1790s were not far different from those in Edinburgh or Bordeaux in the variety of their offerings. One given in 1799 included many of the same genres as in British cities but involved familiar names of composers from a particular number of regions – Austria, Germany, Bohemia, France, England, Ireland, and North America (Ex. 2.9).

2.9 *Catherine Graupner and Peter Van Hagen, Concert Hall, Boston, 25 June 1799* [78]

Overture	Ignace Pleyel
Song	Samuel Arnold
Sonata for pianoforte, 4 hands	Johann Kozeluch
"By my Tender Passion," *Haunted Tower* (1789)	†Storace
Solo for clarinet	†Johann Christoph Vogel
Glee, "Lullaby"	Samuel Harrison
Concerto for violin (Van Hagen)	Giovanni Giornovichi
–	

[75] *Bath Chronicle,* 6 April 1787, p. 3.
[76] Birmingham Private Concerts, BCL, Programs, 1801–45, vol. 1.
[77] See, for example, *CORR,* vol. 2, no. 1, 1 January 1804, p. 2.
[78] Sonneck, *Concert-Life in America,* pp. 315–16. Catherine Graupner was an English actress and singer married to the German violinist Gottlieb Graupner; the two become key figures in Boston musical life.

Concerto, performed on the piano	Haydn
Song, "Columbia's Bold Eagle"	A Gentleman of Salem
Concerto for oboe	Jean Le Brun
Glee, "Play'd in Air," *Castle Spectre* (1798)	Michael Kelly
Vocal quartet	
Song, "To Arts, to Arms," words by Tom Paine	*P. A. Van Hagen*

Some concerts given in New England seem to have been more homogeneous in their focus on songs written for the home or the theatre than was the case in Britain. A touring musician might give a concert almost entirely on his or her own, limiting the collegial format of the benefit concert and performing primarily theatre or parlor songs in English. The listing of a concert by Mrs. Tubbs, "late Mrs. Arnold," of Covent Garden, in 1796, at the assembly room in Portsmouth, New Hampshire, only mentioned "a voluntary piece" for organ in addition to the many songs that she would sing to piano accompaniment. The titles had Scottish and English themes, for example, "The market lass," "The bonny bold soldier," "Mary's dream, or Sandy's ghost," and "Ellen, or the Richmond primrose girl."[79] A melody originally set to a bawdy text, "By moonlight on the green," had been published in Thomas D'Urfey's *Pills to Purge Melancholy* (1719) and James Oswald's *Caledonian Pocket Companion* (175?). Interestingly enough, the only concert by a single musician thus far discovered for London in the second half the eighteenth century occurred when a French woman sang and played the piano in a local tavern in 1786.[80]

REPERTORIES OF ANCIENT MUSIC

The principle of miscellany encouraged the survival of old works in repertories but limited their number and the authority given such music. Although a revolving door took works in and out of performance, some pieces managed to find institutional niches where they would stay for substantial periods of time. Few pieces were revived after several decades of disuse, save when occasionally a connoisseur brought back a piece by a major figure such as Handel. Works survived attached to a feast day and the tradition of an institution, in so doing earning canonic status. "Ancient music," as it was called in Britain and France, came to predominate in a few repertories, establishing old music more firmly than seems ever to have been the case save at a few institutions such as the Sistine Chapel. But this music did not define musical taste as a whole or develop as extensive an aesthetic

---

[79] Ibid., p. 319.   [80] McVeigh, *Concert Life in London*, p. 101.

definition as the repertory of classical music was to do. In this section we compare what kinds of music survived in concerts in our four cities before 1800.

Need for repertory contributed to the survival of old works. Before 1700 a stable balance existed between supply and demand for composers and new works. A complex of institutions – courts, churches, and municipalities – limited the number of people who could emerge as aspirants to prestigious musical careers. But by 1750 opera seasons had become significantly longer than before, and the number of public concerts had grown drastically, creating a significant need for more repertory. Because commissioning new works was expensive and time-consuming, well-regarded pieces tended to remain in use, building up reputations of a canonic nature. We have already mentioned the virtually year-round schedule of the Paris Opéra, where in 1714 the court ordered an opera by Lully to be ready in the event that a new production failed. The operas of Graun and Hasse remained on stage in Berlin and at the Gewandhaus concerts, earning a deep respect among critics and the public.[81] By the same token, Henry Purcell's *Te Deum* and Handel's oratorios, odes, and masques provided ready repertory for a variety of concerts all over Britain. The annual musical festivals in cathedral cities grew to four days of productions by the 1750s, thanks to the readiness of established works of ancient music.

Interestingly enough, repertories of old works coalesced during the 1720s and 1730s in both England and France. Performance of the music was nurtured by court musicians in both places, implicitly under the aegis of the state. Revivals of operas by Lully and later composers such as André Campra occurred regularly at the Académie Royale de Musique, called *la musique ancienne* by around 1740. After the Academy of Vocal Music was founded in London in 1726, the word *ancient* was substituted for *vocal* in 1731. By contrast, little old music survived in public concerts in the German states or the decentralized Habsburg Empire until around 1770, and no term for such pieces emerged before the term *classische Musik* began appearing in the 1810s.

It is not surprising that most of the pieces that survived in concerts in all four cities were by Italian composers or written in Italian idioms. Music by "the immortal Pergolesi," as he was called idiosyncratically, was performed the most widely of all, his *Stabat Mater* (1736) more often than excerpts from *La Serva Padrona* (1733). The Concert of Antient Music in London offered pieces from his works in *opera seria* (chiefly *l'Olimpiade*,

[81] Mangum, "Apollo and the German Muses."

1735) but none in *opera buffa*, and few excerpts from his famous *opera buffa* seem to have been performed in Viennese concerts. Moreover, a few pieces in *opera seria* by Hasse, Jommelli, Tommaso Traetta, and Gian Francesco Maio were heard in London, Paris, and Leipzig after their deaths, all but Hasse having died fairly young. Excerpts from Hasse's operas and sacred works were often performed not only at the Gewandhaus but also fifteen times at the Concert Spirituel. Music by other composers had more limited circulation. Corelli's music was represented six times in Paris during the century, but none was offered at the Gewandhaus until 1875. Overtures by Rameau were performed several times at the Concert of Antient Music in the 1790s but seemingly not in concerts in Leipzig or Vienna. Aside from the special prominence of Pergolesi, pieces survived on a local basis, not perceived as a common repertory. Only a knowledgeable, well-traveled concert-goer would have known what different old works were still being performed across Europe. If anything, people tended to be puzzled by repertories of old pieces, most of all the antiquated music heard at the Paris Opéra. Friedrich Grimm, discussing the death of Jean-Joseph Mondonville in 1772, stated that "[t]hose who are knowledgeable about music . . . will judge in what state this art is now in France, [that] none of these great masters of music would ever have succeeded in gaining a hundred *écus* in any other country."[82]

Handel's oratorios, odes, and masques were the starting point of an international repertory of canonic works. Before 1770 his music enjoyed little circulation outside Britain; his pieces appeared five times at the Concert Spirituel (an Italian and an English aria and three concerto grossos), but none was heard at the Gewandhaus subscription concerts until 1803.[83] Handel's music began sweeping across Europe in the late 1770s, first in Berlin and Vienna and then in other German cities and reached Paris around 1800.[84] The 1784 Handel festival in Westminster Abbey stimulated an awareness of his music on an extraordinary international scale. For example, in 1788 a writer in Breslau, the capital of Prussian Silesia, reported with great interest that *Messiah* had recently been performed in London,

[82] Friedrich Melchior, Freiherr von Grimm, *Correspondance littéraire, philosophique et critique*, 16 vols. (Paris: Longchamps, 1829–43), vol. 8, pp. 80–1. See also *Correspondance secrète entre Marie-Thérèse et le comte de Mercy-Argenteau*, 3 vols., 2nd ed., M. A. Geffroy (Paris: Firmin-Didot, 1875), vol. 2, p. 285.

[83] Alfred Dörffel, "Statistik der Concerte im Saale des Gewandhauses zu Leipzig," in *Geschichte der Gewandhausconcerte zu Leipzig vom 25. November 1781 bis 25, November 1881*, 2 vols. (Leipzig: Breitkopf & Härtel, 1881–1884), vol 1, pp. 23–5. Citations of performances from the subscription concerts below derive chiefly from this index.

[84] "G. F. Handel," *CORR*, 6 June 1802, p. 367, and numerous programs cited.

Berlin, and Leipzig, motivating local musicians to bring Johann Hiller to perform programs similar to those done at the Abbey.[85]

Britain

The principle of miscellany proved especially sympathetic to older music in eighteenth-century Britain. Because British concert programs were unusually long and variable in format, a variety of old works found niches there – anthems, services, madrigals, concerto grossos, oratorios, odes, and theatre songs.[86] One or two pieces by dead composers were usually present in most concerts in London and in the provinces by 1760. We will examine programs designed for contrasting publics at the Academy of Ancient Music (1726–1802?), the Concert of Antient Music (1776–1848), and the Oxford Musical Society (c. 1748–1840).

A concert at the Oxford Musical Society in 1765 was typical of the period in offering one work by a dead composer in each half of a program of ten pieces. The overture to Handel's *Pastor Fido* (1712) and a concerto grosso by Corelli (published in 1714) were accompanied by concertos by Avison and John Stanley, music more accessible to amateur performers than the demanding virtuosic concertos of Geminiani or Giuseppe Tartini.[87] By this time, however, Handel's style must have seemed like a "spectre," as Aby Warburg would put it, because such a major musical transformation had occurred since the 1720s.

2.10 *"Motets, Madrigals, and other Pieces Performed at the Academy of Ancient Music," Crown and Anchor, 24 April 1746*[88]

Motet, 5 voices, "Angelus Domini" (1575)	†Palestrina
Canzonet, 3v, "Old I Am, Yet Can, I Think" (1746)	John Travers
Song, *Indian Queen*, "While thus We Bow before your Shrine" (1695)	†Henry Purcell
Kyrie eleison, 4v [1621]	"Edv. Lupi" [†Duarte Lobo]

[85] "Nachrichten," *Neue Bunzlauische Monatschrift zum Nutzen und Vergnügen* 5 (1788), 125–6.

[86] Weber, *Rise of Musical Classics*, Ch. 6, "Repertory of the Concert of Antient Music," pp. 168–97.

[87] 7 January 1765, Oxford Musical Society Programs, BLO; Susan Wollenberg, *Music at Oxford in the Eighteenth and Nineteenth Centuries* (Oxford: Oxford University Press, 2001).

[88] Programs of the Academy of Ancient Music, Leeds Public Library. The setting of "Non nobis domine," almost always sung at the end, was incorrectly attributed to Byrd. I appreciate the advice of Bonnie Blackburn in identifying Edv. Lupi as Duarte Lobo; see Owen Rees, "Adventures of Portuguese 'Ancient Music' in Oxford, London, and Paris: Duarte Lobo's 'Liber Missarum' and Musical Antiquarianism, 1650–1850," *Music & Letters* 86 (2005), 42–73.

Madrigal, 4v, "Say, Gentle Nymphs" (1594)	†Thomas Morley
Magnificat [before 1721]	Johann Pepusch
Motet, 4v, "Quam pulchri" (1572)	†Tomás Luis de Victoria
Madrigal, 3v, "The Eagle's Force Subdues each Bird that Flies" (1611)	†William Byrd
Te Deum	Handel
Non nobis Domine	"W. Byrd" [Anon.]

By comparison, a program given at the Academy of Ancient Music demonstrates a specialized, wide-ranging repertory such as could be heard nowhere else in Europe until the early nineteenth century (Ex. 2.10). A club that met at the Crown & Anchor on the Strand, the Academy drew members from the choirs of the Chapel Royal, Westminster Abbey, and St. Paul's Cathedral, as well as a few amateurs, William Hogarth most notably.[89] Among the ten pieces on the program, six dated from the late sixteenth or early seventeenth century, and the four written between 1695 and 1746 followed conservative styles. Most of the Academy's programs included a piece by Palestrina, whose works had been performed regularly in the Sistine Chapel's unique canonic repertory.[90] Although it is difficult to trace the routes by which madrigals survived, we can presume that those by Morley and Byrd had been performed at least occasionally, probably with drinks after dinner, among men and perhaps women unusually knowledgeable of the "ancient" style. Records of the Madrigal Society (1740) and the Catch Club (1761) indicate that secular works of that vintage had persisted.[91] The canzonet for three voices by John Travers (c. 1703–1758) formed part of that tradition; his pieces cropped up in many places through the middle of the nineteenth century. No concert repertory included so many pieces of such antiquity until the private concerts of Raphael Kiesewetter in Vienna and the Concerts Historiques of François Fétis in the 1830s.

Still, the Academy's repertory remained a curiosity in its day, for it was much too antiquated and specialized for the general public. A pamphlet published in 1733 ridiculed the academy as "Gropers into Antique Musick, and Hummers of Madrigals," and described the works of its "venerable President" [Johann Pepusch] as "dress'd up in Cobwebs, and powdered with

[89] See Index, Weber, *Rise of Musical Classics.*

[90] Jeffrey Dean, "The Evolution of a Canon at the Papal Chapel," pp. 138–66. Scholars have found Palestrina performed in Vienna (see n. 122) but nowhere else in Italy to a significant extent.

[91] Minutes of the Madrigal Society and Catch Club, BL; Robins, *Catch and Glee Culture,* pp. 23–5, 32–81, 106–7.

Dust."[92] By the 1740s few people probably knew about its meetings. Indeed, Jeffrey Dean has raised the important question of how much Renaissance polyphony was valued in its own time outside the small world of learned cathedral musicians.[93]

A separate institution arose with a quite different repertory in the Concert of Antient Music in 1776. Programs confirm the claim that no piece less than twenty years old could be performed there, but, despite the antiquated spelling of "antient," the series only occasionally offered pieces prior to Henry Purcell. The Antient Concerts, as they were called, constituted a subscription series rather than a professional club, for they drew people of high landed or aristocratic lineage similar to those who attended the concerts begun by Bach and Abel. The presence of King George III as patron from 1785 drew people just to see the Royal Family. The series was the most direct predecessor to classical music concerts of the nineteenth century in associating a canonic repertory with an elite clientele. The Academy of Ancient Music, for its part, was remodeled along similar lines in the late 1770s, now including recent glees, symphonies, and opera excerpts as the new series did not.[94]

The Antient Concerts followed the principle of miscellany loosely, offering programs of nine to fifteen pieces, several concertos or concerto grossos standing between opera and oratorio excerpts, movements from sacred works, and a few madrigals (Ex. 2.11).

2.11 *Concert of Antient Music, Tottenham Street Rooms, 14 February 1780* [95]

Concerto for oboe	†Handel
Madrigal, "Fair, sweet, cruel"	†Thomas Ford
Aria, "Rendi il sereno al ciglio," *Sosarme* (1732)	†Handel
Duet and chorus, "Sion Now her Head shall Raise,"	
Esther (1718)	†Handel
Concerto, Op. 3, no. 2	†Geminiani
Air, "La dove gli occhi io giro," *Admeto* (1727)	†Handel
Aria, "Jehovah Crowned with Glory Bright," *Esther*	†Handel
—	
Overture, *Radamisto* (1712)	†Handel
Kyrie eleison	†Francesco Feo

[92] *Harmony in an Uproar*, incorrectly attributed to John Arbuthnot, in *Miscellaneous Works of John Arbuthnot*, 2 vols. (Glasgow: Carlile, 1751), vol. 2, p. 34.
[93] Jeffrey Dean, "Listening to Sacred Polyphony c. 1500," *Early Music* 25 (1997), 611–36.
[94] Weber, *Rise of Musical Classics*, Chs. 5–6, pp. 143–97.
[95] Programs of the Concert of Antient Music, BL and Yale University Library.

Such a program was much less esoteric than those the Academy of Ancient Music had offered. In this instance the only Elizabethan piece was a well-known madrigal by Thomas Ford published in 1607. After 1785 as much as two-thirds of a program was often by Handel, and some programs had nothing written before 1710. Still, the musically more learned directors chose pieces or composers not well known among the general public. The piece of greatest interest to connoisseurs on this program was a movement from a mass by Francesco Feo (1691–1761), a prominent music teacher in Naples much admired by Charles Burney.

Handel's music was the binding agent within the repertory of "ancient" music, just as Palestrina had been in the concerts of the Academy of Ancient Music or as Beethoven would be in classical music concerts in the early nineteenth century. When a canonic repertory was one or two generations old, a single great composer would almost always take a privileged role, providing strength and focus to a novel direction in musical taste. Handel's music was omnipresent in provincial concerts, becoming central to the taste of the general public. A diverse mixture of historical epochs appeared on provincial programs by the end of the eighteenth century, such as was found nowhere else in Europe. The "Grand Miscellaneous Concert" given by the Oxford Musical Society in 1788 typified how a six-decade-old Italian opera number by Handel could coexist with a recent symphony by J.-B. Davaux and an aria by Cimarosa (Ex. 2.12).

2.12 *"Grand Miscellaneous Concert," Oxford Musical Society, Holywell Music Room, 11 November 1788*[96]

Overture	Dittersdorf
Song, "What Passion cannot Music Raise and Quell,"	
Ode to St. Cecilia's Day, cello obligato	†Handel
Concerto for oboes	†Handel
Sinfonia	Gossec
Aria, "Torna al primiero affetto"	Cimarosa
Concerto for organ	Philip Hayes
—Between the Acts: "The Soldier Tir'd," *Artaxerxes*	†Arne
Overture to *Deidamia* (1741)	†Handel
Song, "Let the bright Seraphim," *Samson* (1743)	†Handel
Symphonia Concertante	Davaux
Sinfonia	Haydn
Aria, "Dove sei amato bene," *Rodelinda* (1725)	†Handel
Sinfonia, with drums	Vanhal

[96] Holywell Rooms, Programs, BLO.

Because ancient music was so drastic an innovation, it remained on weak ground intellectually and became subject to harsh criticism. Only a limited aesthetic definition emerged around the music, for the most part more historical than philosophical. Dispute between factions of "ancients" and "moderns" continued until the principle of "classical" music superseded the "ancient" in the 1820s.[97] A history of Edinburgh published in 1788 warned that the city's musical society needed to ensure that proponents of the "prevailing taste" for recent music not "debar the amusement of those, who find more pleasure in the old compositions."[98]

Ideological promoters of British music attacked the Antient Concerts, and thereby the King, in brazenly partisan terms. Whig opponents of the government had for some time been making a far-reaching critique of the monarchy, demanding that strong new powers be given to Parliament. The composer and author Charles Dibdin drew on such opinion in a periodical called *The Bystander* in 1790, condemning the monarch for focusing patronage on Handel rather than on living composers. He called his authors an "association," a political faction, and made clear their allegiance to the Prince of Wales, admitting "it were treason" to suppose that the King had maintained "distance between the sovereign and his children." He also objected to the "cognoscenti" surrounding the monarch who elevated Handel as "the sole possessor of all musical genius," but not Thomas Arne.[99] Thus did a nationalistic ideology for British music arise linked closely to state politics. Dibdin's argument grew out of the exclusion of British composers from the King's Theatre and looked ahead to the nationalism active in the composing profession during the 1830s.

France

It is extraordinary how long and how often pieces by Lully and his successors were performed in France during the early and middle decades of the eighteenth century. At points in the 1760s pieces by dead performers dominated the Opéra; the last Parisian *reprise* of *Thésée* (1685) occurred in 1779. Although some aspects of old works were redrafted, and new ballets

---

[97] Howard Irving, *Ancients and Moderns: William Crotch and the Development of Classical Music* (Aldershot, UK: Ashgate, 1999).

[98] Hugo Arnot, *The History of Edinburgh from the Earliest Accounts to the Present Time* (Edinburgh: William Creech, 1788), p. 380.

[99] *Bystander, or, Universal Weekly Expositor, by a Literary Association* (London, 1790), pp. 45, 399. By Marilyn Morris, see "Impact of the French Revolution on Debate about the British Monarchy," *Consortium on Revolutionary Europe* 23 (1994), 526–37; and *The British Monarchy and the French Revolution* (New Haven: Yale University Press, 1998), pp. 160–87.

inserted, no operas lasted near that long anywhere else in Europe.[100] In this regard *la musique ancienne* well outdid the survival of ancient music in Britain. The operas of Purcell and Matthew Locke did not loom as large in eighteenth-century London as Lully's did in Paris, and he was born a generation before Purcell. The canonic status held by music from the reign of Louis XIV became evident during the legendary *querelle des bouffons* between 1752 and 1754, when the arrival of a troupe offering Italian *opera buffa* stimulated a wild array of publications for and against that kind of musical theatre. Politics of state were directly involved in the dispute, for supporters of the *Encyclopédie* – termed *les lumières* – took up the cudgels for Italian opera against *la musique ancienne* to combat the monarchy in the constitutional crisis over the right of the Parlement of Paris to refuse to register a royal edict.[101] Thus was support for musical tradition – the recycling of old music – brought against the first challenge to the absolutist régime of 1661. Though the monarchy lost the legal battle, its repertory became even more predominant at the Opéra for fifteen years.

Quite different genres and composers survived in the Concert Spirituel and at the Opéra. Although only a few transcriptions of music by Lully were done at the concerts, almost every program included one or two motets written for Louis XIV. Commentators saw the grand literary notion of the Sublime realized in imposing *petits et grands motets*, pieces that involved one or two choruses, instrumental ritornellos with trumpets and timpani, and solos for voices, oboe, or flute.[102] Not until the symphony took on heightened importance in the 1770s did orchestral pieces become as important in the concerts. Older works tended to be attached to feast days: Lalande's motet *De profundis* was always performed on All Saint's Day, Pergolesi's *Stabat Mater* held pride of place in Lent, and collections of carols (one by Corelli) were offered at Christmas. Secular feasts were also honored; Jean-Baptiste Morin's *Chasse du cerf* appeared in hunting season.

By far the most often performed composer of *la musique ancienne* was Lalande (1657–1726), who entered the court just as the King was turning from a public to a private life in the early 1680s, declaring himself the champion of universal Catholicism. Court factions identified Lalande's music as a bastion of French tradition against the forward-looking Italian

---

[100] Lois Rosow, "From Destouches to Berton: Editorial Responsibility at the Paris Opéra," *JAMS* 40 (1987), 285–309.

[101] William Weber, "*La musique ancienne* in the Waning of the Ancien Régime," *Journal of Modern History* 56 (1984), 71–4.

[102] Thierry Favier, "Lalande et le sublime," in *Lalande et ses contemporains*, Lionel Sawkins (ed.) (Paris: Éditions des Abesses, 2005).

style.[103] His works obtained a far wider public at the Concert Spirituel than at court; by the 1730s it was customary for a singer to make his or her debut in Paris by singing a solo in a piece by de Lalande.[104] A typical program in the 1750s included ten pieces, one, two, or three of them sacred works by deceased composers, a particularly familiar one coming at the end. The concert on 8 September 1752, for example, presented a Te Deum by Lalande and a motet, *Diligam te*, by the abbé Henri Madin, along with two Italian opera selections and a cantata on the convalescence of the Dauphine.[105] Still, *la musique ancienne* did not dominate the Concert Spirituel as much as it did at the Opéra. During the 1760s the proportion of pieces by dead composers at the former was between 14 and 24 percent between 1750 and 1767, whereas at the Opéra the figure was at least 50 percent in a season, and at a few points as high as 90 percent.[106]

The concert repertory of *la musique ancienne* did not draw criticism as harsh as that directed against the Opéra. Indeed, we can see a certain authority invested in the *grands motets*, with commentators from opposite ends of the political spectrum speaking kindly of them. In 1746 the royalist Louis Bollioud de Mermet declared that they were "true good taste" and that "it is the duty of true connoisseurs to raise their voices against abusive new customs." In 1765 Rousseau stated in the article "Motet" in the *Encyclopédie* that "Frenchmen have been successful in this idiom, their motets being attractive and well crafted, those of Lalande being the *chefs-d'oeuvres* in the genre."[107] But tradition reasserted itself in the late 1760s as musicians dropped *la musique ancienne* from repertory. A scathing report on the Concert Spirituel in 1773 announced that the motet had fallen into complete discredit, because the directors of the Concert Spirituel foolishly kept offering pieces composed by Michel Mouret in the 1720s, a time from which taste had since progressed.[108] Another commentator asked why people had to hear music "of a taste entirely contrary to that of our day."[109] In the mid-1760s the renewal of repertory began with a prize for new motets

---

[103] *Journal de Trévoux*, December 1746, p. 2633. See the recent biography by Catherine Massip, *Michel-Richard Delalande ou le Lully latin* (Geneva: Papillon, 2005).

[104] Brenet, *Les Concerts en France*, p. 122; Castil-Blaze, *Académie Impériale de Musique de 1665 à 1855*, 2 vols. (Paris: Castil-Blaze, 1855), vol. 1, p. 157.

[105] Pierre, *Concert Spirituel*, p. 263.

[106] Weber, "*La musique ancienne* in the Waning of the Ancien Régime."

[107] Bollioud de Mermet, *De la corruption du goust*, pp. 41, 46; "Motet," *Encyclopédie, ou, Dictionnaire raisonné des sciences, des arts et des métiers*, 14 vols. (Paris: Briasson, 1751–1780), vol. 10, p. 765.

[108] "Concert Spirituel," *Journal de musique*, March 1773, pp. 206–7, 212.

[109] *Mercure de France*, 2 October 1777, p. 173.

sponsored by the Chapelle Royale and the Concert Spirituel.[110] By 1768
pieces by dead composers performed at the Concert Spirituel had fallen to
11 percent and by 1772 to 2 percent; at the Opéra the number was down
to 23 percent in 1775–1776 and 2 percent in 1783–1784.[111] Pergolesi's *Stabat
Mater* escaped the purging of repertory, as did Rousseau's *Le Devin du Village* (1752), which remained on stage until 1829. Still, a few pieces written
between the late 1740s and the 1760s remained in use, excerpts not only by
well-known composers such as Jommelli, Traetta, and Hasse but also by
the highly respected Gian Maio and Josef Mysliveček.

Even though *la musique ancienne* disappeared from repertory, a historical
understanding had become integral to French musical thinking. In the
spring of 1778 the Opéra staged a production called *Les Trois Âges de l'Opéra*
(The Three Epochs of the Opéra), a medley of pieces from works by Lully,
Rameau, and Gluck arranged by Grétry. Its allegorical text portrayed the
three composers as gods achieving immortality upon the abandonment of
their works on earth.[112] The production helped forge a compromise between
French tradition and the arrival of foreign works at the Opéra; Gluck
and Lully were absorbed into a national conception of the institution's
history, the latter having arrived in France at age twelve. The preface to
the libretto posed the problem in political terms, concisely stating the
tension between cosmopolitan and national interests: "One must admire
all eminent musicians, whether National or Foreign, who devote their labors
to the progress of the art, and one must support the Spectacle that has been
tasted by the Public for a hundred and twenty years." Yet it concluded that
"one only wishes that those same people will never forget that our own
Operas cannot reach perfection save by reuniting different Parties, the least
of which are essential to them all."[113]

Leipzig and Berlin

In Leipzig one could not hear music as old as the madrigals sung at the
Antient Concerts or the motets at the Concert Spirituel, but quite a few

[110] Brenet, *Les Concerts en France*, pp. 284–6.

[111] Weber, "*La musique ancienne* in the Waning of the Ancien Régime," pp. 71–4.

[112] *Les Trois Âges de l'Opéra*, BNF; *Mercure de France*, April 1778, p. 160; May 1778, p. 152; *Almanach
des spectacles de Paris* (Paris, 1779), p. 220; "Lully and the Performance of Old Music in the 18th
Century," pp. 581–90; M. Elizabeth C. Bartlet, "Jean-Baptiste Lully and the Music of the French
Baroque," in *Essays in Honor of James R. Anthony*, John Hajdu Heyer (ed.) (Cambridge: Cambridge
University Press, 1989), pp. 291–318. See also *Dialogue entre Lulli, Rameau et Orphée*. A few pieces
by early eighteenth-century composers did survive in provincial churches; see Ellis, *Interpreting the
Musical Past*, p. 74.

[113] *Les Trois Âges de l'Opéra*, p. 4.

works dating from the 1740s did survive at the subscription concerts. During the 1780s, between 8 and 14 percent of all pieces performed were by dead composers, substantially more than in Paris at the time. Selections from operas by Hasse and Graun written in the 1740s and early 1750s survived in Berlin and also in Leipzig, thanks to the close musical links between the two cities. Once again we find an old repertory surviving in relationship to a strong developing state, for Prussia stood in the forefront of military and bureaucratic organization. Although this repertory earned no conceptual denomination like that of "ancient" music, a learned interest in the two musicians continued into the nineteenth century along with the canonic survival of music by a whole host of opera composers, Cimarosa and Mozart most notably.

By the time Frederick II founded a court opera in 1740, relatively few monarchs exercised much leadership over court opera in Europe generally. He nonetheless involved himself deeply in the Berlin company, particularly in the works of Graun and Hasse, even though some of the works performed there had been first mounted in Dresden or Rome.[114] After the Seven Years War ended in 1763, Frederick had neither the money nor the will to mount major new productions, further encouraging him to keep the old works on stage. Although a variety of troupes came and went from Berlin, offering *opéra comique, opera buffa,* and *Singspiel,* from 1773 the old works returned for about half of the performances. *Cajo Fabricio,* for example, first performed in Rome in 1732, was revived as late as 1785. It was with good reason that Charles Burney shook his head in 1772 about the predominance of old works in Berlin, saying that although some saw it as an "Augustan age," he thought that "music is truly stationary in the country."[115] Frederick died on 17 August 1786, and the old repertory came to an end with Hasse's *Piramo e Tisbe* on 13 December 1787.

Selections from operas by both Graun and Hasse remained just as prominent at the Gewandhaus. Not only did the subscription concerts regularly offer excerpts by both composers, but also the city's Amateur Musical Society (Musikübende Gesellschaft) performed one at every other concert in the year 1779.[116] Although Hasse kept composing right into the early 1780s, it is remarkable that pieces by Graun continued to be performed so long after his death in 1759. We can take this problem further by quantifying the

[114] Mangum, "Apollo and the German Muses." See also Heartz, *Music in European Capitals,* pp. 204–44 and 38–71.
[115] Quoted in Heartz, *Music in European Capitals,* pp. 385–6.
[116] Musikübende Gesellschaft, SGML; Schering and Wustmann, *Musikgeschichte Leipzigs,* vol 3, pp. 465–80.

repertory of the Gewandhaus in one season to determine the relative age of pieces in the different genres. In the season 1782–1783, 12 percent of the pieces performed (20 of 174) were by dead composers, significantly more than that at the Concert Spirituel at the time. The average year in which composers of all pieces were born – in reference to all performances of each piece – was 1730. By comparison, concertos were the youngest (1753), opera selections were the oldest (1720), and sacred works and symphonies stood in the middle (1728 and 1730, respectively). The oldest composers were Hasse (1699–1783), Graun (1703–1759), Pergolesi (1710–1736), and Davide Perez (1711–1778), and the youngest was Anton Zimmerman (1741–1781), whose symphonies were widely performed for a while after his death. Thus we find that opera selections in the concert hall tended to be a good deal older than productions on stage.

An interesting Anglo-German parallel can be seen in the canonic role played by Graun's passion oratorio *Der Tod Jesu* (1755) and Purcell's setting of the Te Deum (1694). Graun's work was performed regularly, in some cases on an annual basis, in Berlin and other parts of Germany, and a French magazine recounted the composer's life in 1773.[117] Both works served as the starting point for larger repertories of choral-orchestral music: Purcell's setting led to the institutionalization of Handel's settings of the Te Deum as well as his oratorios, odes, and masques; and Graun's oratorio was succeeded by Haydn's *Die Schöpfung* and *Die Jahreszeiten*, Mozart's *Requiem*, and Handel's choral-orchestral works. Still, *Der Tod Jesu* was performed at the Leipzig concerts only in 1789 and a few times after 1819, possibly because it was associated too closely with the Prussian monarchy in that time of great diplomatic strife. Other sacred works by Hasse and Graun were nonetheless performed at the Gewandhaus for over a hundred years. Hasse's Te Deum seemed to add the weight of authority to programs given on important occasions. In 1787 the city's Amateur Musical Society performed it with his setting of the text "Puer natus est"; on New Year's Day 1807 the subscription concerts presented it along with August Eberhard Müller's cantata *Gerechte, frohlocket!* (Rise up, rejoice!).

The honoring of Graun and Hasse was arguably the main German precedent to the canonic repertories formed in the early nineteenth century. At the court in Dresden, where Hasse had been based, several of his sacred

---

[117] Christoph Hellmut Mahling, "Zum 'Musikbetrieb' Berlins und seinen Institutionen in der ersten Hälfte des 19. Jahrhundert," *Studien zur Musikgeschichte Berlins im frühen 19. Jahrhundert,* Carl Dahlhaus (ed.) (Regensburg: Bosse, 1980), pp. 27–285; "Vie de Charles-Henri Graun," *Journal de musique,* 1773, no. 4.

works continued to be sung in the chapel on feast days, a tradition that has supposedly lasted to the present day.[118] Johann Hiller went so far as to publish a set of Hasse's arias with ornamentation written out (*Sechs italiänische Arien*, 1778), as well as a keyboard reduction of a passion oratorio (*Die Pilgrimme auf Golgotha*, 1784). He and Johann Reichardt also composed pieces in a style associated with Hasse. A biographical dictionary published in 1794, edited by Friedrich Carl Hirsching, devoted more space to Hasse than to almost any other composer. The article on him discusses his travels among courts in great detail and speaks in awe of his ability to mingle with the upper classes: "Hasse took on a strong presence in his time, far more than almost any other composer. Having become highly educated, he conducted himself in a manner that impressed the aristocratic temperament and left all convinced by his sincerity."[119]

The practice of performing sacred and fugal works of Johann Sebastian Bach was quietly developing at the same time. Bach's keyboard music and fugal exercises became increasingly well known among learned musicians, and some of his chorales, organ pieces, and motets were performed in church by his sons and students.[120] The *Allgemeine musikalische Zeitung* displayed a portrait of Bach on the frontispiece of its first issue in 1798, and Johann Nicolai Forkel published the first biography of him in 1802. Indeed, in 1805 the Kyrie and Gloria from a mass for two choirs were performed at the Gewandhaus subscription concerts. A movement was well underway that would culminate in the first concert performance of the St. Matthew Passion in Berlin in 1829.[121]

Vienna

Viennese concert-goers began discovering the choral-orchestral music of Handel in the late 1770s, but little other music more than twenty years old was performed there in public. We do know that the court chapel choir sang hymns by Palestrina and a few other composers of his time as late as the

---

[118] Heartz, *Music in European Capitals*, p. 337.
[119] *Historisch-literarisches Handbuch berühmter und denkwürdiger Personen*, Friedrich Hirsching (ed.) (Leipzig: Schwickert, 1795), p. 8; Johann Friedrich Reichardt, *Briefe eines aufmerksamen Reisenden die Musik betreffen*, 2 vols. (Frankfurt, 1774–1776; Hildesheim: G. Olms, 1977), vol. 1, p. 6. On nineteenth-century study of Hasse, see Otto Jahn, "Beethoven und die Ausgaben seiner Werke: Beethovens Werke, in der Ausgabe von Breitkopf und Härtel," *Die Grenzboten* 23 (1864), 265.
[120] *Bach und die Nachwelt*, vol. 1, *1750–1850*, Michael Heinemann and Hans-Joachim Hinrichsen (eds.) (Laaber: Laaber Verlag, 1997); Dörffel, *Geschichte der Gewandhausconcerte*, vol. 1, p. 3.
[121] Celia Applegate, *Bach in Berlin: A Cultural History of Mendelssohn's Revival of the St. Matthew Passion* (Ithaca, N.Y.: Cornell University Press, 2005).

1730s.[122] But the close links between the Viennese court and Italian musical culture probably discouraged musicians from keeping secular works long in use. Likewise, musical pedagogy there was rooted in the *stile antico* as adapted by J. J. Fux, a tradition that tended to resist study or performance of old works. Thus we see that canonic performing repertories grew up instead in France and England, where few musicians practiced the *stile antico* extensively.

A coterie of learned musicians and amateurs formed in the early 1780s whose successors were to lead the movement toward idealistic values and repertories of classical music. The group was led by Gottfried, Baron van Swieten, son of a Dutch physician who served as Habsburg ambassador to Prussia and then became Imperial Councillor and Senior Librarian in Vienna. The 1796 *Jahrbuch der Tonkunst* spoke of him as "the patriarch of music" whose opinions "half-connoisseurs" would repeat to impress other people.[123] In 1782–1783 Swieten held meetings at his home with Mozart, Weigl, Antonio Salieri, and Joseph Starzer, leader of the Society of Musicians, to perform and discuss older music, primarily by Hasse, Graun, Handel, and Bach.[124] Their interests included composers whose music had survived in widely separated contexts in Britain, Austria, and Germany, the main stimulus deriving from Swieten's activities in Berlin. A report on the meetings employed the phrase "pieces by older masters" ("Stücke von alten Meistern"), thus turning the traditional term "der Meister" – a leading contemporary musician – to a larger and quite different purpose.

Performance of Handel's choral-orchestral works emerged in repertories of oratorios set by Italian and Austrian composers to texts by Pietro Metastasio. Impressively enough, five oratorios and two odes by Handel are known to have been performed prior to 1800, though chiefly in private settings. Save for the public performance of *Judas Maccabaeus* at the Society of Musicians in 1779, public concerts offered primarily excerpts from these works (Ex. 2.3). Selections were common at benefit concerts; Mozart, for example, drew pieces from *Acis and Galatea* for such an event in 1788. A group of noblemen called the Society of Cavaliers presented a variety

[122] Friedrich W. Riedel, *Kirchenmusik am Hofe Karls VI. (1711–1740)* (Munich: Katzbichler, 1977), pp. 76, 78, 86.

[123] Johann Ferdinand Ritter von Schönfeld, *Jahrbuch der Tonkunst Wien und Prag*, Otto Biba (ed.) (Vienna, 1796; Munich: Katzbichler, 1976), p. 72; translated by Katherine Talbot in *Haydn and his World*, Elaine Sisman (ed.) (Princeton: Princeton University Press, 1997), p. 319.

[124] Edelmann, "Händel-Aufführungen in den Akademien der Wiener Tonkünstlersozietät," pp. 172–74 and *passim*; Teresa M. Neff, "Baron van Sweiten and Late Eighteenth-Century Viennese Musical Culture," unpublished Ph.D. dissertation, Boston University (1998).

of works in their homes – *Judas Maccabaeus* in 1786, *Messiah* in 1789 and 1790, and *Alexander's Feast* and the *Ode for St. Cecilia's Day* the year after. Another group of nobles offered *Athalia* in 1794 and *Acis and Galatea* in the Schwarzenburg palace in 1797.[125] Full-length performances of these works did not become common in the Austrian capital until the mid-1820s. By contrast, Haydn's two major oratorios, first performed in 1799 and 1801, became standard repertory more or less complete from the start.[126]

Swieten's learned cabal aside, repertories tended to cast off ageing works particularly quickly in the Habsburg capital. The main exceptions included a concert version of Traetta's *Iphigenia in Tauride* (1763), five years after his death in 1779, and choruses by Florian Gassmann, a founder of the Society of Musicians after his death in 1774. Excerpts from Hasse's opera *Alcide al bivio* (1760) were done at a concert in 1781, and his oratorio *Isacco figura del Redentore* (1746) appeared the year after. But much less music by Graun and Hasse was presented in Vienna than in Leipzig. Although a piece called *Der Tod Jesu*, possibly by Graun, was performed in 1786, the wave of performances of that work in many parts of Germany did not seem to reach Vienna. It is notable that we find little mention of Pergolesi or Jommelli in public concerts, music that was so common in London and Paris at the time.

CHANGE AND CONTINUITY, 1750–1800

Although early tendencies toward the transformation of musical culture were evident around Europe by 1800, the principle of miscellany was still in place in concert life. On the one hand, musicians began designing many new kinds of concerts, changing formats in provocative ways. Tension between taste for cosmopolitan and local music increased as musicians drew on nationalistic rhetoric to defend their interests. Repertories of old music began to extend the historical range of programming significantly. The intellectual challenge often imbedded in the mature Classic style was closely involved with these innovations. Yet, on the other hand, long-standing principles and practices remained much in force. Alternation between vocal and instrumental music and subordination of old music to new was still expected by musicians and the public. Performing Pergolesi's *Stabat Mater* or excerpts from Handel's *Messiah* did not fundamentally alter the nature

---

[125] Morrow, *Concert Life in Haydn's Vienna*, pp. 176–8.
[126] Pohl, *Denkschrift... Tonkünstler-Societät*, pp. 62–79.

of concert programs. The forces changing concert life as well as European politics would have much deeper effect in the ensuing decades, breaking down the principle of miscellany and the unity of musical life as a whole. Ignaz Schuppanzigh took the first major step in that direction when in 1804 he excluded vocal music in designing public concerts for his string quartet.

PART II

Crisis and experiment, 1800–1848

CHAPTER 3

Musical idealism and the crisis of the old order

Between 1800 and 1850 European musical life underwent a fundamental transformation in values, practices, repertories, and institutions. The expansion of musical life in that period brought about more new kinds of music and taste than could coexist within the "miscellaneous" program or within the musical community as it had been traditionally defined. "An expanding horizon of musical meaning, like expanding rings on the water's surface, still contained what earlier boundaries enclosed," James H. Johnson has suggested.[1] For several decades many concert programs became longer and more diverse than ever before, putting together symphonies or chamber works, opera excerpts, fantasies on opera tunes, harmonized folk songs, sentimental ballads, and the latest quadrilles. The locus and nature of authority over musical taste and institutions came into question, as traditional privileges disappeared, new kinds of halls and concerts grew up, and an aesthetic authority was vested in classical music. The old order of musical life accordingly went into crisis, and the nature of the musical community had to be reconceived. By the mid-1840s major arenas of musical activity began to separate, and after the upheaval of 1848–1849 a new musical order came into place based on the relative independence of different kinds of music.[2]

Léon Escudier, editor of the magazine *France musicale*, depicted the contemporary crisis within the musical world in the prospectus to its first issue in 1837:

What a strange set of anomalies! Music is proliferating with astonishing speed today. The art has passed from the theatre into the salons, from salons into the shops, from there onto the street, seeking to become a force among the masses; the number of those who understand music, whether more or less, has become immense; new

---

[1] Johnson, *Listening in Paris*, p. 281.
[2] See William Weber, "Redefining the Status of Opera: London and Leipzig, 1800–1848," *Journal of Interdisciplinary History* 46 (2006), 507–532.

kinds of music giddily appear; top artists become ever more numerous; music schools proliferate; and yet music criticism is still in its infancy.... While a new language of musical practice is in place, found from one end of Europe to another, it awaits discovery of its grammar.[3]

Escudier was both excited and alarmed at how fundamentally the Parisian musical world was changing and how unstable it had become. The most telling word he used to make this point was *grammar*, meaning a new authority that could bring order to the "strange set of anomalies" in musical culture. Music criticism, he thought, might provide standards to give musical taste firmer intellectual roots. Another key point was his worried distinction between those who "understand music, whether more or less," primarily those who thought they knew a lot but didn't. Far more people now learned to sing or play the piano, went to concerts or the opera, or simply heard opera numbers at home than had been the case fifty years before. The newer musical publics transformed – some thought corrupted – the relationship between amateurs and learned musicians. Against this backdrop expectations about musical learning became an ideological issue as they had not been previously. Escudier worried that serious music might be engulfed by musicians "seeking to become a force among the masses" ("pénétrer dans les masses populaires"). Indeed, his family's publishing firm was contributing to that very process. Sweeping changes in the commercialization of sheet music had intensified the differences between music written for the more and the less well educated. Technical advances in building pianos and printing sheet music led to expanded marketing strategies, changing from the prepaid subscription to speculative sale of spin-offs from popular operas.[4]

This chapter concerns the movement that arose among self-consciously serious musicians, amateurs, and commentators all over Europe who attempted to reform and reshape musical culture fundamentally. Best called "musical idealism," this movement laid the groundwork for the world of classical music.[5] We will explore writings of that kind published during the

---

[3] "Prospectus," *FM*, 31 December 1838, p. 1.

[4] Scott, *Sounds of the Metropolis*, Ch. 1; Arthur Loesser, *Men, Women and Pianos: A Social History* (New York: Simon & Schuster, 1951); Andreas Ballstaedt and Tobias Widmaier, *Salonmusik: zur Geschichte und Funktion einer Bürgerlichen Musikpraxis* (Stuttgart: Steiner Verlag, 1989).

[5] I originally used the term *musical idealism* in "Wagner, Wagnerism & Musical Idealism," in *Wagnerism in European Culture and Politics*, David C. Large and William Weber (eds.) (Ithaca, N.Y.: Cornell University Press, 1984), pp. 28–71; as did Michael Broyles in *"Music of the Highest Class": Elitism and Populism in Antebellum Boston* (New Haven, Conn.: Yale University Press, 1992), pp. 1–14; and Raymond Knapp in *The American Musical and the Performance of Personal Identity* (Princeton, N.J.: Princeton University Press, 2006), *passim*.

first half of the nineteenth century. Idealistic musical values were more journalistic than philosophical in nature, even though links evolved between
musical commentary and formal aesthetic thought. The people who took
up idealistic musical values were relatively small in number but knew how
to make their opinions known. They rejected the assumption that members of the musical community had to accommodate themselves to lesser
kinds of music, and instead called for musical culture to be based on a
learned high culture. To a certain extent, the movement arose as a reaction against the growing commercialization of opera and concert life. But,
more fundamentally, musical idealism was born from a utopian vision of
music-making rooted in Romantic thinking that made claim to a kind of
artistic truth. This chapter will examine the larger political context of the
transformation of taste, discuss different approaches for analyzing it, and
finally compare tendencies in the four cities we are studying.

Musical idealism sprang up in almost every major region of western and
central Europe – save Italy for the most part – during the first half of
the nineteenth century. We will see how different regions contributed to
musical idealism in complementary ways. Although German and Austrian
periodicals figured centrally in the early history of the movement, leadership arose at much the same time in England and France. After all, canonic
repertories had appeared in those two countries during the eighteenth century, helping guide such developments Europe-wide after that time. The
vision of a higher order of musical taste radiated from the major musical
cities, reshaping musical life in eastern Europe and North America, in small
towns as much as in big ones. Cities such as Manchester, Boston, Brussels,
and Frankfurt ended up influencing major musical cities significantly.

The movement arose within the context of the breakdown of the old
political order brought about by the French Revolution and the Napoleonic
Wars. In Vienna in 1804 and in Paris in 1814, public concerts were begun
that were devoted entirely to string quartets and related genres, a revolutionary change. In 1807 the subscription concerts at the Leipzig Gewandhaus
broke from concert tradition by performing Beethoven's "Eroica" Symphony as the only work after intermission. The Philharmonic Society of
London (1813) and the Society of the Friends of Music in Vienna (1814)
set up a new set of principles for musical organizations. By the late 1820s a
Viennese series called the Concert Spirituel (on the Parisian model) established the first orchestral repertory to be focused on classical works and
identified with a "high" aesthetic. The Parisian Society of Concerts of the
Conservatoire (1828) and the Vienna Philharmonic Orchestra (1842) developed broad classical repertories systematically from the start. In the midst

of all this, a militant faction set forth an ideological agenda for reforming musical life, publicizing it in the fast-growing musical press. In all four cities at least one substantial music magazine expressed this point of view, though not consistently. Music-lovers read these periodicals voraciously, spending far more time doing so than is the case today.

Yet idealistic musical issues remained secondary in importance for most of the music public. Grand opera and virtuoso concerts must be seen as "the most representative sites of music-making" at that time.[6] New operas by Donizetti, Bellini, Meyerbeer, also by Giovanni Pacini and Saverio Mercadante, captured public attention, as did *fantaisies* on that music by such virtuosos as pianist Sigismond Thalberg and cellist Adrien Servais. Indeed, the orchestras that performed Beethoven's symphonies depended on opera as their main employment and on virtuosos for attracting a public larger than the dedicated few. A Viennese journalist exemplified the hostility of the mainstream press to idealistic values in 1846 when he derided the "missionaries of the classics" who were trying to take over musical life against the public's wishes.[7]

THE POLITICAL CONTEXT

The breakdown of the old musical order and the building of a new one developed in close relationship to political crises dating from the French Revolution of 1789 and the Napoleonic Wars. During the late eighteenth century the locus of political authority came into question in most parts of Europe and North America. Notions of representative government were voiced variously by aristocrats wishing to revive older assemblies and by "enlightened" thinkers intent on reform either through monarchical or legislative leadership. The French Revolution came about less from those ideas than from the breakdown of absolutism, specifically the failure of elite factions to reach compromise regarding taxation and privileges. The Napoleonic invasion of central Europe, and political reconstitution of that region, brought political turmoil and in addition raised issues of governance in places not controlled by the Napoleonic Empire. The question "Who is to govern?" became an issue not only in state and local politics but also in professional and cultural communities as a whole and indeed in musical life itself.[8]

---

[6] Jim Samson, "The Great Composer," *Cambridge History of Nineteenth-Century Music*, Jim Samson (ed.) (Cambridge: Cambridge University Press, 1992), p. 264.

[7] *Der Wanderer*, 21 March 1846, p. 275.

[8] James Sheehan, "The Problem of Sovereignty in European History," *American Historical Review* 111 (2006), 1–15; Buch, *Beethoven's Ninth*; Stephen Rumph, *Beethoven after Napoleon: Political Romanticism in the Late Works* (Berkeley: University of California Press, 2004).

Historians now apply the word *revolution* broadly, finding that before the twentieth century such events took forms big and small, involving areas of society in multiple ways. Charles Tilly has argued that the progress of a revolution can be compared to that of a traffic jam. A breakdown in state authority, he contended, grows out of loose, changing coalitions among groups whose political activity tends to "merge imperceptibly into routine vehicular flows." Almost everyone ends up affected as a result: "In the course of a revolution non-contenders often mobilize and become contenders . . . [because] every interest that depends on state action is at risk."[9] For that reason, a fundamental instability, a kind of proto-revolutionary condition, may exist in a state where revolutionary breakdown does not eventually occur.

What historians call the Restoration, occurring between 1814–1815 and 1830, was in reality a deeply unstable status quo where revolution often seemed imminent. As Eric Hobsbawm once wrote, "never in European history and rarely anywhere else, has revolutionism been so endemic, so general, so likely to spread by spontaneous contagion as well as by deliberate propaganda."[10] Many among the upper orders of society harbored serious doubts about the reconfiguration of the old order and were ready to entertain alternatives when the opportunity arose. Utopian thinkers proposing ideal communities abounded, showing how open-ended political allegiances had became among many people. Just as utopians saw representative government as a chimera, so musical idealists called for the stern rule of learned taste over concerts and opera. We shall find some tough-minded musical idealism published in Boston's Fourierist magazine *The Harbinger, devoted to Social and Political Progress.*

European revolutions and riots between 1830 and 1835, together with their forceful repression, stirred the political pot once again, heightening tension all the more because the press was reaching an increasingly large public. Diverse movements among workers or intellectuals – Chartism in England, the *Vormärz* in Germany, and widespread discontent in France – unsteadied government and society. That is why most historians no longer speak of the revolutions in 1848–1849 as having truly failed. The crowd actions that forced the breakdown of the State in so many places, even if for just a few months, had no parallel in Western history. The revolutions brought long-term consequences, opening up politics to a much wider population.[11]

9 Charles Tilly, *European Revolutions, 1492–1992* (Oxford: Blackwell, 1993), pp. 7, 9.
10 Eric Hobsbawm, *Age of Revolution, 1789–1848* (London: Weidenfeld & Nicolson, 1962), p. 109.
11 Jonathan Sperber, "The Mid-Century Revolutions in European History," in *The European Revolutions, 1848–1851* (Cambridge: Cambridge University Press, 1994), Ch. 6, pp. 239–58; *1848: A European*

The ongoing crisis of political legitimacy in European states from the 1780s spurred members of political, professional, and cultural communities to rethink the nature and locus of authority and to try to bring change aggressively. Such efforts were often opportunistic. People not necessarily involved in national politics attempted to take advantage of the unstable condition of society to alter how a community was governed and by whom. It has been argued that the field of psychiatry underwent a fundamental transformation in close relationship to the larger political crisis, for example.[12] Within both Catholic and Protestant churches a fundamental rethinking of purpose went on in this period, stimulating reform movements that set up new high ideals in ways not dissimilar to what went on in musical life.[13] Comparable reform movements sprang up in a variety of communities largely independent of one other as to ideology or party identity; indeed, they sometimes conflicted with one another. Musical and political leadership became the most closely linked in Vienna, where several major figures participated in the Revolution of 1848, one of them having been in charge of police control of foreigners. The group surrounding Robert Schumann, called the *Davidsbündler*, was linked with the Young Germany movement even though its writings avoided political commentary. English musical idealists borrowed from the political vocabulary of Reform but attacked the bourgeois leaders of the Philharmonic Society just as much as they did nobles running the King's Theatre.

Did musical idealism come from a rising middle class? It is necessary to think about this question in multidimensional terms. From one perspective, middle-class leadership unquestionably was central to the concerts and periodicals that generated the movement of musical idealism, and the critique of traditional opera life often was portrayed as the middle-class challenging the nobility.[14] From another angle, however, we can see major divisions among the middle classes. Families in business and the professions tended to have quite different economic situations and social values, which we shall see contributing to major divisions in musical taste. Moreover, the upper-middle class was severing itself from the "middling classes" in this period as a social elite. The premier orchestral concerts thus

Revolution? Alex Körner (ed.) (Basingstoke, Hants, UK: Macmillan, 2000); Peter Uwe Hohendahl, *Building a National Literature: The Case of Germany, 1830–1870*, Renate Franciscono (trans.) (Ithaca, N.Y.: Cornell University Press, 1989).

[12] Jan Goldstein, *Post-Revolutionary Self: Politics and the Psyche in France, 1750–1850* (Cambridge, Mass.: Harvard University Press, 2005).

[13] R. W. Franklin, *Nineteenth-Century Churches: The History of a New Catholicism in Württemberg, England, and France* (New York: Garland, 1987).

[14] Johnson, *Listening in Paris*.

became isolated institutions that did not offer cheap seats in a gallery, as did most opera halls. We have already seen pamphleteers accusing the subscribers to the Gewandhaus concerts of excluding the general public from its concerts.

Yet from a third perspective we see a coming together of the bourgeois and the aristocrat within movements of taste that cut across class boundaries. We will borrow from Pierre Bourdieu the term *class fractions* to define how a social class can become "fractionalized" among groups adhering to conflicting values and tastes.[15] The new dichotomy of taste between light and serious music brought together people from parts of the middle classes and the nobility under common cultural identities. Thus the quartet series and the fashionable virtuoso concert each brought together people from diverse social levels under the aegis of a unifying musical outlook. During the 1830s and 1840s concerts and salons provided the upper-middle class and the nobility opportunities to engage socially.[16] The fractionalization of social classes contributed to the gradual integration of upper-middle-class and aristocratic people into a common "upper class," such as would develop variously in different countries. Still, we must also consider the possibility that any one listener might well pursue diverse tastes, being "fractionalized" internally. For example, Louis-Philippe Girod de Vienney, baron de Trémont, was a patron of Auber as well as Baillot and wrote on opera singers as well as on Beethoven.[17]

National politics and musical culture thus shared a common instability during the early nineteenth century. Something of the same interaction between music and politics had taken place in the rise of "ancient music" in England during the crisis following the constitutional settlement of 1689. That first term for defining canonic repertory was invented by High Tories and singing men from the cathedrals who gathered in the rooms of the Rector of Christ Church College, Oxford, singing Elizabethan anthems and madrigals and talking politics.[18] Conflict over political authority at both

---

[15] Pierre Bourdieu, *Distinction: A Social Critique of the Judgment of Taste*, Richard Nice (trans.) (Cambridge, Mass.: Harvard University Press, 1984), pp. 260–7; and Scott, "Music and Social Class," *Cambridge History of the Nineteenth Century*, Jim Samson (ed.) (Cambridge: Cambridge University Press), p. 545.

[16] For bibliography, see Preface, *MMC*, pp. xi–xxiv; Dror Wahrman, *Imagining the Middle Class: The Political Representation of Class in Britain, c. 1780–1840* (Cambridge: Cambridge University Press, 1995); Jürgen Kocka, "The Middle Classes in Europe," *Journal of Modern History* 67 (1995), 783–806; *Adel und Bürgertum in Deutschland, 1770–1848*, Elisabeth Fehrenbach (ed.) (Munich: Oldenbourg, 1994).

[17] "Baron de Trémont," *Le Ménestrel* 38 (1927), 339–41, 401–5.

[18] See Introduction, Weber, *Rise of Musical Classics*.

times – in 1700 and 1840 – encouraged new forms of intellectual authority in the musical world.

PHILOSOPHICAL VERSUS MUSICAL IDEALISM

Because Romanticism has proved problematic in the study of music history, scholars have sought other ways to delineate the transformation of music and musical culture either in philosophical or social terms. A variety of philosophical or social approaches have arisen, concentrating either on formal thought or journalistic commentary. Whereas the philosophical approach has focused on German Idealism from Kant to post-Hegelian thinkers, social analysis of musical life has emphasized ideological agendas in the public press. Even though philosophical idealism influenced musical thinking significantly, journalists developed their own vocabulary for "higher" musical values, linked to taste for classical music. We will explore the approaches of such scholars as Mark Evan Bonds, David Gramit, and Lydia Goehr in defining musical idealism and the authority of the classics.

Bonds has, in effect, rethought the nature of musical romanticism in his study of the impact of idealism on musical aesthetics in early nineteenth-century Germany. Kant, Schiller, Herder, and Schelling, he suggested, broke with the eighteenth-century principle of mimesis – art as imitation of nature – as they sought to lift musical thought above the nominalism inherent in that principle. They posited instead "that the aesthetic effect of an artwork resides in its ability to reflect a higher ideal." In the 1810s E. T. A. Hoffmann formulated that ideal as the "wondrous realm of the infinite," sought in what Bonds characterizes as a "refuge from the failed world of social and political life." W. H. Wackenroder thought that music helped the mind forget "all earthly trivialities that are truly dust on the radiance of the soul."[19] The notion of a lofty order of musical experience led to a new hierarchy in levels of genres and taste, a scheme that was invested with the status of Truth. Still, Hoffmann aside, the idealist philosophers did not derive their notions about music and the higher sphere from actually hearing or studying music, and they had little concern with reforming musical life as such. But in the 1810s the more learned members of the music public – some of whom read philosophy, and some did not – began to hear symphonies, indeed instrumental music in general, in a fundamentally new manner, because they "no longer approached these works as a source

---

[19] Mark Evan Bonds, "Idealism and the Aesthetics of Instrumental Music at the Turn of the Nineteenth Century," *JAMS* 50 (1997), 392, 397. Sanna Pederson has explored nations of "autonomous" music in relationship to "social projects" during this period, in "A. B. Marx, Berlin Concert Life, and German National Identity," *NCM* 18 (1994), 87–107.

of entertainment, but increasingly as a source of truth." The symphony became a vehicle for knowing music systematically and thereby became associated with the "quest for truth" and the "infinite sublime."[20] Poetic language helped bestow such an authority on music more than did a belief in "absolute" music, because poetic and visual imagery continued to be central to musical commentary. In Bonds's view, the principle of "absolute" music did not arise until after 1850, led chiefly by Eduard Hanslick.[21]

As posited around 1815, the notion of higher musical experience was essentially introverted in nature, rooted in individual contemplation. After about 1830 the new musical ideals displayed an increasingly extroverted sensibility as they were turned into ideological vehicles for reform of taste. Bonds finds a potential for such change in philosophical idealism, in the presumption that listening to music sprang from the actions of "a free and absolute self" that was empowered to interpret an art-work in its own terms or indeed to "reconstruct" it mentally.[22] Thus did the notion of an egotistical individual become central to assumptions about a "higher" musical sphere, assumptions that guided the leadership of the evolving classical music world. A sociable definition of musical truth grew up in commentary in the word *genial*, identifying a union between introversion and extroversion both in the music and in the listener's experience. Commentators spoke often about the mingling of reflection and sociability that they heard in music by Franz Schubert, Louis Spohr, Robert Schumann, and Felix Mendelssohn.

The self-willed individual was often deeply involved in musical politics and, by extension, national politics. Something of this process came about in the popularization of Kant's philosophical and political imperative among lower nobles and upper bourgeois in the Rhineland around 1810. Reading groups in that region were attracted, Timothy Blanning tells us, by "notions of personal autonomy and self-determination, as tempered by the categorical imperative, which in turn gave an ethical content to every individual act." They came to see "liberty as a duty rather than a right," just as musical idealists interpreted their responsibility to raise musical culture to a new level.[23] We shall see a similar lofty mentality developing within cultlike chamber music concerts.

---

[20] Mark Evan Bonds, *Music as Thought: Listening to the Symphony in the Age of Beethoven* (Princeton, N.J.: Princeton University Press, 2006), pp. xv, 45.

[21] Ibid., pp. 107–15; Robin Wallace, *Beethoven's Critics: Aesthetic Dilemmas and Resolutions during the Composer's Lifetime* (Cambridge: Cambridge University Press, 1986).

[22] Bonds, *Music as Thought*, p. 30.

[23] Blanning, *The French Revolution in Germany: Occupation and Resistance in the Rhineland, 1792–1802* (New York: Oxford University Press, 1983), p. 263. For recent discussion of this problem, see James Brophy, *Popular Culture and the Public Sphere in the Rhineland, 1800–1850* (Cambridge: Cambridge University Press, 2007).

The very word *idealism* was widely used in England to denote a high social purpose. In 1822, in his *Essays and Letters*, Percy Bysse Shelley spoke about "the highest idealisms of passion and power." In 1867 John Ruskin declared that "[t]hree-fourths of the demands existing in the world are romantic; founded on visions, idealisms, hopes, and affections.[24] Writers employed such broad, culturally suggestive words to convey how high they were aiming in their intellectual ambitions. Samuel Taylor Coleridge, too, defined his personal ideals in political and ideological terms. In his essay "Constancy to an Ideal Object," Coleridge declared that, "in the genuine enthusiasm of morals, religion, and patriotism, this enlargement and elevation of the soul above its mere self attest to the presence, and accompany the intuition of, ultimate principles alone."[25] In his book *Table Top*, published in 1835, Coleridge analyzed the breakdown of eighteenth-century elite institutions as an important context wherein he shaped his ideas. He declared that "There have been three silent revolutions in England: first when the professions fell off from the Church; secondly, when literature fell off from the professions; and, thirdly, when the press fell off from literature."[26] This breakup of established professional authority opened the way for musical writers to claim a new authority within intellectual life in the second quarter of the nineteenth century.

Musical idealism had roots in eighteenth-century polemics on moral aspects of musical life. As concerts and opera expanded independent of monarchs after 1700, writers claimed to represent public opinion with high-minded points of view: Johann Kuhnau condemned musical charlatans in 1700, and Arthur Bedford attacked licentious theatre songs in 1711.[27] In *The Great Abuse of Musick*, Bedford declared that "in this degenerate Age" irresponsible musicians had abandoned the craft of "our ancient musicians" to write "easy tunes to pious words."[28] In the 1830s, utopian thinkers sent the polemical tradition into a new direction. In *Philosophy of Music* (1835), Giuseppe Mazzini called for his countrymen to reform opera so that it

---

[24] "Idealism," *Oxford English Dictionary Online*, http://dictionary.oed.com.

[25] Jerome J. McGann, *Romantic Ideology: A Critical Investigation* (Chicago, Ill.: University of Chicago Press, 1983), p. 4.

[26] Samuel Taylor Coleridge, *Table Talk and Omniana, with a Note on Coleridge by Coventry Patmore* (London: Oxford University Press, 1917), p. 176.

[27] François Raguenet, *Comparison between the French and Italian Operas* (London, 1709; repr. Farnborough, UK: Gregg Publishers, 1968); Johann Kuhnau, *Musical Charlatan*, John R. Russell (trans.) (Columbia, S.C.: Camden House, 1997); Henry Aldrich, *Great Abuse of Musick* (London: Wyatt, 1711).

[28] Aldrich, *Great Abuse of Musick*, pp. 232, 182.

might serve art and Christian principle rather than materialism.[29] In the *Revue et Gazette musicale* in 1844, Hector Berlioz sketched out a musical community, Euphonia, where musicians could control all aspects of festival performances.[30] Robert Schumann speculated about a better musical world in writing aphorisms for the *Neue Zeitschrift für Musik*. Richard Wagner got quite specific about what utopian musical communities should be like in his essays published during and after the Leipzig uprising in 1849. Yet one of the pithiest declarations came from a little-known British musician, Thomas Danvers Worgan, who wrote an essay, "The Musical Utopia in Dominions of Prince Posterity," in *The Musical Reformer* (1829), saying that:

amateurs, and the patrons of music, are too well instructed to countenance trash; the composer is not at the mercy of the performer, and variety of excellence in composition is too generally heard to suffer the incessant repetitions of a vocal or instrumental performer, however excellent, to be tolerated. This literary and musical union would form a potent engine for effectuating that reformation which, when completed, would realize the Utopia I am about to fabricate, as a relief from the contemplation of degeneracy, disorder, and fatuity.[31]

It should not be assumed, however, that ideas derived from German Idealism defined the values of classical music life throughout Europe. The writings of William Crotch in England illustrate how a musical thinker could start from different aesthetic bases but end up with views on musical life and classics quite similar to those found in Germany by the early 1830s. After becoming Heather Professor of Music at Oxford in 1797, Crotch gave lectures on music in many places for three decades. Those he gave at the Surrey Institution in 1818 involved neither Romantic introspection into the "infinite" nor the idea of a "refuge" from the mundane world. Yet Crotch founded music criticism on knowledge and truth, basically the same principles as the German Idealists followed. He went so far as to argue that "there is a kind of Truth even in matters of taste which will ultimately prevail" and called on critics to "discover this Truth" by proceeding from universal knowledge rather than individual prejudice.[32] Thus Crotch shifted

[29] Giuseppe Mazzini, *Philosophie de la musique: vers un opéra social*, Martin Kaltenecker (trans.) (Paris: Van Dieren, 2001).

[30] Hector Berlioz, "Village of Euphonia, the Musical City: A Tale of the Future," in *Evenings with the Orchestra*, Jacques Barzun (trans.) (Chicago, Ill.: University of Chicago Press, 1973), pp. 258–97.

[31] T. D. Worgan, *Musical Reformer* (London: S. Maunder, 1829), pp. 46–7.

[32] William Crotch, *Substance of Several Courses of Lectures on Music* (London: Longman, 1831); Howard Irving, "Crotch's 1818 Lectures," in Howard Irving, *Ancients and Moderns: William Crotch and the Development of Classical Music* (Aldershot, UK: Ashgate, 1999), p. 224.

the eighteenth-century idea of the sublime from the music public as a whole into a sphere of elevated taste. To determine the "comparative value" of any piece of music he proposed a series of questions for the reader that set up hierarchies much like those proposed in the *Allgemeine musikalische Zeitung*:

> Let [the student] consider in what manner the music affects him. Does it surprise and amuse him? Does it soothe and tranquilize him? Or does it elevate his mind and fill it with serious admiration? Whatever, in our art or indeed in any other art, produces merely surprise and entertainment, is inferior to what excites our complacency and love, and both are surpassed by that which awakens in us awe and wonder and veneration.[33]

A spiritual element figured powerfully in idealistic thinking on music, with origins both secular and sacred. Discussing Handel's *Dettingen Te Deum*, for example, Crotch noted that "these early masters are still the great and unrivalled models of all that is sublime and sacred in our art."[34] A search for musical spirituality continued to penetrate classical music discourse, for understanding Schubert's songs as much as Beethoven's *Missa Solemnis*. Just as the Society of Concerts in Paris was repeatedly described as a "sanctuary" of great music, so a report of the Philharmonic Society of New York stated that the "science of music . . . is not of human invention, but of divine appointment."[35] Yet the religious aspect was absorbed into the basically secular nature of classical music concerts so fully that the word *spiritual* better describes this musical sensibility, referring to the contemplative process essential to musical idealism. Sacred works became less central to repertories from the middle of the nineteenth century, or were performed in separate contexts, save for the Parisian concerts that remained tied to French Catholicism. As Celia Applegate has argued, the revival of Bach's *St. Matthew Passion* is best seen as a partial secularization of religious music.[36] Musical and religious considerations accommodated one another in subtle ways in the performance of this work.

Values of musical idealism also began appearing in North America, most prominently in Boston, as an infrastructure of musical institutions developed during the early nineteenth century. The city's upper class began to invest itself more fully in musical life, attracting major performers in increasing numbers, some presenting classical repertories. During the 1810s the Handel and Haydn Society began laying down a repertory of selections from oratorios, followed in the 1840s by choral and orchestral concerts of

---

[33] Irving, "Crotch's 1818 Lectures," p. 223.   [34] Ibid., p. 254.
[35] Quoted in Levine, *Highbrow/Lowbrow*, p. 132.
[36] Applegate, *Bach in Berlin*, pp. 173–233; see also Joël-Marie Fauquet and Antoine Hennion, *La Grandeur de Bach: L'amour de la musique en France au XIXe siècle* (Paris: Fayard, 2000).

the Boston Academy of Music and chamber music series offered by the Harvard Musical Association (not tied to the university). *The Harbinger*, edited by John Sullivan Dwight (1812–1893), brought the idealism of the utopian movement to its critique of the city's evolving musical life. In 1846 an article attacked the Academy's directors for "pandering to a medium and uneducated taste" after initially trying to elevate standards. "From Mozart and Haydn and Spohr they fell down to Auber, and then slipped a stage lower in wearisome solos by second-rate performers."[37] In *Dwight's Journal of Music*, founded in 1852, he took a more accommodating stance, that of *France musicale* rather than the *Musical World*, defining musical idealism with a canny diplomacy. "Miscellaneous programme-making should be more a work of art," he declared in the second year of the journal, asking why a musician offered so short a song by Spohr in the midst of less serious fare.[38] Thus did Boston join the "transatlantic musical culture," it has been argued, bringing "a hierarchical attitude toward music in which aesthetic value was subordinated to moral value."[39]

A common agenda emerged among idealistic writers by 1848 that seems familiar to followers of classical music today. Principles emerged from this discourse in the succeeding decades that can be summarized as:

- Serious demeanor during musical performance;
- Respect for the integral work of art;
- Vesting of authority over musical taste within musical classics;
- Hierarchical ordering of genres and tastes;
- The expectation that listeners learn about great works to understand them appropriately.

In the 1830s and 1840s, however, commentators had not defined their cause in such general terms. They wrote chiefly in negative terms against specific offenses to good taste:

- Performance of opera excerpts at concerts or in poorly crafted editions;
- Craven appeal to popular taste in the opera *fantaisie*;
- Mixture of genres in programs condemned as incoherent;
- Performance of dance music and lesser songs alongside works of art;
- Music teachers who pandered to fashion;
- Public disinterest in learning about music.

---

[37] "Sixth Concert of the Boston Academy," *Harbinger*, 7 March 1846, p. 204; Broyles, *"Music of the Highest Class,"* p. 28. The magazine was sponsored by the American Union of Associationists.
[38] *Dwight's Journal of Music; A Paper of Art and Literature*, 12 January 1854, p. 127.
[39] Broyles, *"Music of the Highest Class,"* p. 11; see also Ch. 6.

Writers translated these issues into code words to which readers were exquisitely sensitive – on the one hand, *fashion, mode,* or *miscellany* and, on the other, *classical, serious,* or *high-class.*

The hot-button words of musical idealism amounted to some extent to a critique of modernity, as was the case in Romanticism generally.[40] David Gramit has made a detailed analysis of German thinking in this regard, defining what was proper to music and to the concert on a high plane.[41] Central to his argument is the impact on musical life that came from the precipitous decline in privileged positions in courts and churches, a trend that made musicians fearful that public taste would lose its intellectual moorings and be manipulated by purely commercial motives. Would good music survive if piano teachers kept feeding their students' banal arrangements of "folk" melodies? Could serious musicians satisfy that musical need but not be degraded by it? The crisis of taste demanded new ideals for "proper" or "worthy" music, as opposed to pieces condemned as trivial or degenerate. Although essayists had raised the specter of moral decline in musical taste since the early eighteenth century, a new trope arose calling specifically for unworthy genres to be expelled from concerts – dance music, the variation, and the potpourri most of all. Reviewers began sketching out a hierarchy among genres, from the potpourri at one end to the symphony and the quartet at the other. Still, as Gramit points out, a systematic hierarchy never emerged because too many ambiguities and disagreements arose about pieces fitting in between the higher and lower levels for agreement to be reached.

Letters between Felix Mendelssohn and the pianist Ignaz Moscheles illustrate how central the vocabulary of musical idealism had become to musicians by the 1840s. Moscheles, disillusioned with musical taste in London, had decided to return to Leipzig, telling Mendelssohn that "If a musician wants to play for public taste here, he has to make too many concessions [;] I myself don't want either to compose for purely business purposes or to function just as a teacher who has little impact upon the art and ends up mostly serving the latest modes." They spoke of a dichotomy between "light" and "serious" music much more explicit than one can find around 1800. "Modish taste is degrading," wrote Moscheles, because it

[40] Michael Löwy and Robert Sayre, *Romanticism against the Tide of Modernity,* Catherine Porter (trans.) (Durham, N.C.: Duke University Press, 2001).
[41] David Gramit, *Cultivating Music: Aspirations, Interests, and Limits of German Musical Culture, 1770–1848* (Berkeley: University of California Press, 2002), pp. 125–60.

"makes people only want light music."[42] Mendelssohn replied that things weren't much better in Leipzig. What had occurred, Matthew Riley argues, was "a loss of faith in the fragile continuity between amateur and expert listening practices."[43]

Yet the ideological slogans of the time tended to overstate how far apart idealistic and commercial values for music tended to be. For one thing, publishers promoted editions of classical music just as vigorously as opera editions. The London firm of Novello's prospered without publishing anything related to operatic or virtuosic music, and Schlesinger's in Paris and Berlin balanced its lists carefully between the two.[44] Although "salon music," as it came to be called, developed a considerably bigger market than classics, the latter had a commercial staying power that made it attractive to publishers. Furthermore, virtuosos were beginning to play Beethoven's music, and many composers still wrote music suited for the less intellectual public. Mendelssohn and Schumann both wrote songs for amateur singers that were performed for the rest of the century in contexts far from the classical music world. In Leipzig in 1893, for example, a group of singers calling themselves the Wilfferodt'sches Quartett put on a "family night" in a venue called Wiegner's Gesellschaftshaus, offering Mendelssohn's duet "Gruss" and Schumann's part-song "Wanderlied," along with recent operetta pieces, comic skits, and a quadrille set for four voices. A small band rendered polkas and waltzes for dancing to end the evening.[45]

Where did opera and opera selections stand within the thinking of musical idealism? This question needs to be seen from different angles. First, idealistic values emerged in the opera world similar in some respects to those found in concerts. By the 1830s the growth in the size and the anonymity

[42] Quoted in Johannes Forner, "Mendelssohns Mitstreiter am Leipziger Konservatorium," *Beiträge zur Musikwissenschaft* 14 (1972), 188, 191. See also Rebecca Grotjahn, "'Musik als Wissenschaft und Kunst': Das Leipziger Konservatorium als Modell einer höheren musikalischen Bildung," in *Musik, Wissenschaft und ihre Vermittlung. Bericht von der Internationalen Tagung in Hannover 2001*, Arnfried Edler und Sabine Meine (eds.) (Mainz: Schott, 1995).

[43] Riley, *Musical Listening*, p. 109.

[44] Victoria Cooper, *House of Novello: Practice and Policy of a Victorian Music Publisher, 1829–66* (Aldershot, UK: Ashgate, 2003), pp. 121–47; Weber, "Mass Culture and the Reshaping of Musical Taste, 1770–1870," *International Review of the Aesthetics and Sociology of Music*, 8 (1977), 5–21.

[45] Concerte in verschiedene Stätten im 19. Jh., SGML. The duet is no. 3 in the *Sechs zweistimmige Lieder* (1844); "Wanderlied" is from *Zwölf Gedichte*, op. 35, no. 3 (1840). On Mendelssohn's attention to the general public, see Leon Botstein, "The Aesthetics of Assimilation and Affirmation: Reconstructing the Career of Felix Mendelssohn," *Mendelssohn and his World*, R. Larry Todd (ed.) (Princeton, N.J.: Princeton University Press, 1991), pp. 32–7.

of the opera public made audiences quieter, and socializing somewhat less important, than had been the case before. Going to the Paris Opéra made Henri Beyle, or Stendahl, wonder, "What will result from this scrupulous silence and continuous attention?"[46] The King's Theatre in London likewise acquired a more sedate decorum in the "refashioning" of the institution, as Jennifer Hall-Witt has demonstrated.[47] One could argue that a variety of elite publics – at the Gewandhaus as well as at opera halls – took on a high-minded aesthetic in response to the political and social challenges they faced in that period. But, second, no clearly demarcated body of great works, empowered through critical discourse, emerged in opera comparable to what had arrived in concerts by 1848. Although study of opera canon has only just begun, present opinion sees such a repertory arriving fairly late in the nineteenth century.[48] By 1848 several works had become institutionalized in repertory – most prominently *Don Giovanni, Le Nozze di Figaro, Der Freischütz,* and *Il Barbieri di Siviglia* – but idealistic critiques of the opera world kept such works in a canonic framework separate from that of instrumental music. The widespread survival of works by Donizetti, Bellini, and Meyerbeer on stage after midcentury reinforced that independence.

Opera selections, indeed opera overtures, comprise a third aspect of emerging opera canon. A much wider range of pieces, indeed operas, emerged in concerts than in the musical theatre. Many pieces were widely known among the general public, and others served as vehicles for critique of singers by aficionados. A loosely defined canon of selections can be identified by the 1860s (Ills. 25 and 26). Opera excerpts were roundly condemned for abridging the principle of the artwork, limiting their canonic status intellectually. But practices from the old order of opera life lived on in the nineteenth century, particularly the "insertion aria," a piece added to a work by another composer, two of which are cited in programs in this book (Exs. 4.5 and 5.2). Though aestheticians did not like to admit it, the insertion aria acquired an integrity as an artwork in its own terms, as

[46] Quoted in Johnson, *Listening in Paris*, p. 196.
[47] Jennifer Hall-Witt, *Fashionable Acts: Opera and Elite Culture in London, 1780–1880* (Lebanon, N.H.: University of New Hampshire Press, 2007), Ch. 5, "The Refashioning of Fashionable Society," pp. 185–226.
[48] John Rosselli, "Italy, The Decline of a Tradition," in *Late Romantic Era from the Mid-Nineteenth Century to World War One,* Jim Samson (ed.) (London: Macmillan, 1991), pp. 126–50; Katharine Ellis, "Systems Failure in Operatic Paris: The Acid Test of the Théâtre-Lyrique," in *Stage Music and Cultural Transfer: Paris, 1830–1914*, Mark Everist and Annegret Fauser (eds.) (Chicago: University of Chicago Press, forthcoming); Matthew L. Ringel, "Opera in 'The Donizettian Dark Ages': Management, Competition and Artistic Policy in London, 1861–70," unpublished Ph.D. thesis, King's College, University of London (1996).

Hilary Poriss has shown. The authority that such a piece could command is illustrated by a story written in the voice of an insertion aria, "An Aria Speaks," published in *Fraser's Magazine* in 1849. "I am an old song now, and have been often sung," declares the aria, because she can call up "the ruling passion of a multitude . . . an elevated feeling of enjoyment and delicious excitement."[49]

THE NEW MUSICAL INTELLIGENTSIA

High musical ideals could be established only if their principles were buttressed by intellectual and institutional authority. During the first half of the nineteenth century an intelligentsia arose within criticism, education, and concert management that assumed wide-ranging roles in the articulation of musical values and the interpretation of classics. Richard Sennett argued that during the nineteenth century audiences began to defer to higher intellectual authority, variously to the virtuoso, the critic, and the musicologist. "Those who were to witness the full, free, and active experience of a public performer prepared themselves by an act of self-suppression," Sennett declared. "The origin of this peculiar situation was a self-doubt which haunted the spectator." Sennett thus saw public musical experience becoming passive and barren of common expression. The rise of program notes meant that "people wanted to be told about what they were going to feel or what they ought to feel,"[50] different from Louis-Sébastien Mercier's 1785 depiction of "the public, which is dying to have its voice heard."[51]

Just how passive, or subject to "self-suppression," listeners became in the nineteenth century will not concern us here. Our concern is to determine the process whereby Romantic thinking endowed a higher realm of musical experience with an ability to discover truth. We have already noted that the Kantian "regulative" concept, as analyzed by Lydia Goehr, can usefully

---

49 Hilary Poriss, "An Insertion Aria Speaks," in Poriss, *Changing the Score: Aria Insertions, Opera Singers, and the Authority of Performance*, in progress; Poriss, "A Madwoman's Choice: Aria Substitution in *Lucia di Lammermoor*," *Cambridge Opera Journal* 13 (2001), 1–28 and "Making their Way through One-Hit Wonders," *19th Century Music* 24 (2001), 197–224; "An Aria Speaks," *Fraser's Magazine* 39 (1849), 17, 18; Emanuele Senice, "'Adapted to the Modern Stage': *La clemenza di Tito* in London," *Cambridge Opera Journal* 7 (1995), 1–2.

50 Richard Sennett, *Fall of Public Man: On the Social Psychology of Capitalism* (New York: Vintage, 1978), p. 209. See also Johnson, *Listening in Paris*, pp. 228–9.

51 Quoted in Ellen Russo, *Styles of Enlightenment: Taste, Politics and Authorship in Eighteenth-Century France* (Baltimore, Md.: Johns Hopkins University Press, 2007), p. 232.

define the authority invested in classical music and the "work concept." Goehr suggested how the concept of serious music and the museum-like repertory of classical works functioned within the epistemology of the art-work. A process of "aestheticizing" art arises, producing pure judgments of taste from the distinction between musical and nonmusical aspects.[52] I would argue that there occurred a change from one authoritative value system to another in the early nineteenth century, as the culture of miscellany was challenged by musical idealism. A journalist who attacked an opera fantasy as "trash" was arguing that the traditional concept be ousted in favor of a lofty new one. I would also argue that early forms of popular music – the *café-concert*, the music hall, and *Liedertafel* singing – arose as a further competing "regulative" concept in the second half of the century. We shall see that by the late 1860s popular songs performed in informal contexts had acquired a certain intellectual legitimacy, especially in France. Nevertheless, although the principle of miscellany was driven from some concert programs, some aspects of it remained in others. That is why, for example, solo vocal and instrumental numbers remained in the programs at the Gewandhaus throughout the nineteenth century (Exs. 8.12 and 8.13).

In the midst of all this, music critics took on a much deeper intellectual authority than that of eighteenth-century connoisseurs. On a certain plane, critics took for themselves some of the authority over musical taste earlier exerted by women in informal discourse and established a professional identity that women could not achieve.[53] In the 1840s critics had become fixtures in magazines and daily newspapers in the major cities, most prominently J. W. Davison and Henry Chorley in London, François Fétis and Hector Berlioz in Paris, Ludwig Rellstab and Robert Schumann in Leipzig, and August Schmidt and Alfred Julius Becher in Vienna. Music magazines flourished in large part because so many well-educated writers were ready to contribute pieces from cities all over Europe and in many cases were probably unpaid. Their authority nevertheless had distinct limits at this juncture. In 1842 a Viennese critic claimed that many reviewers were marginally competent and that concert-goers were still influenced chiefly by respected listeners in their midst, the traditional *Kenner*.[54]

---

[52] Lydia Goehr, *Imaginary Museum of Musical Works: An Essay in the Philosophy of Music* (Oxford: Clarendon Press, 1992), p. 103.

[53] Citron, *Gender and the Musical Canon*, p. 80; pianist Thérèse Wartel and author Louise Otto were among the few women critics.

[54] Ignaz Lewinsky, "Die moderne Musikkritik und ihre Repräsentanten," *AWMZ*, 13 May 1843, p. 237.

It is much too easy to write off the earlier style of music criticism as lacking in idealistic values. A review of a "monster" concert in London in 1840 illustrates a sophisticated assessment of performers, the critic taking pleasure in the concert's "plentiful entertainment":

Our musical season fairly commenced with the very good and plentiful enter-tainment offered by M. Benedict, yesterday week . . . Thalberg is the most perfect of executive artists; [we] admired, more enthusiastically than ever, his *Andante*, and his studies. Among the latter, a new one was introduced, in the form of a romance, supported, on repetition, by an odd, restless *tremolando*. Besides these, he played his *Don Juan Fantasia*; and, with M. Benedict, his fantasia on the Druid chorus in "Norma," arranged for two pianofortes. . . . Clara Novello has obviously returned, in her own estimation a *prima donna* – and, what is more, a Malibran. Her first song – the "Prendi," by De Beriot and Benedict – is one of the show-airs which were written expressly to display Malibran's magnificent compass of voice . . . [Novello's] voice is improved, being now a legitimate soprano of the rich-est and sweetest quality, . . . but to make Miss Novello a singer of the first class, almost as much is wanting as was required before she left England.[55]

This kind of critical commentary long remained central to the trade of many critics.

Critics tended to join the idealistic cause, in large part because that pos-ture helped shore up their newly claimed professional authority. Reviewers took particular aim at the miscellaneous program, its opera excerpts and *fantaisies*. In a series of reports on a tour through France and Germany in 1841, Chorley declared that "the selections of music would disappoint those who have conceived a high idea of German musical taste and cultivation." A program he heard in Mecklenburg-Schwerin featured "an air by Faccioli, Donizetti's sickly 'vivi tu,' Bellini's noisy duet, 'suoni la tromba,' and a flimsy bravura, with violin obligato, from Hérold's *Pré aux Clercs*." He urged "the perpetrators of our benefit concerts" to take as their model a program whose only vocal music was a well-known aria by Mozart.[56] The critique of virtuosity – indeed, the *battle* against it – also brought forth a set of tropes that entered permanently into the critical vocabulary. The "flood" of bad players every season was said to consist of "charlatans" who made ordinary technical tricks seem difficult, deafening listeners to good music.

[55] "Concerts of the Week," *ATH*, 15 February, 1840, p. 138; Robert Terrell Bledsoe, *Henry Fothergill Chorley: Victorian Journalist* (Aldershot, UK: Ashgate, 1998), pp. 28, 44–5, 67.
[56] Henry Chorley, *Music and Manners in France and Germany: A Series of Traveling Sketches of Art and Society*, 3 vols. (London: Longman, 1841), vol. 1, pp. 264–5, 272. Chorley cited the cavatina from Donizetti's *Anna Bolena* and "Suoni la tromba intrepido" from Bellini's *I Puritani*; Faccioli was probably a singer. For a satire on Chorley, see George Linley, *Musical Cynics of London, A Satire (Sketch the First)* (London: G. Bubb, 1862).

Critics used "symphonic values," as Dana Gooley put it, to discredit the preeminence of virtuosity in the mid-1840s.[57] Violinists remained closer to virtuosic tradition than pianists in the 1840s, and the leading performers of the rising generation – Henry Vieuxtemps, Joseph Joachim, and Wilhelm Molique, most prominently – were to confront the situation in contrasting ways during the next two decades.

The triumph of the "artist" over the "virtuoso" nonetheless came through a careful set of compromises between idealistic principle and traditional taste. Becher went through such a process while writing for the *Allgemeine Wiener Musik-Zeitung* in the 1840s. He drew on the vocabulary of philosophical idealism when, in a review of Munich pianist Sophie Bohrer, he declared that, "where music does not spring from expression of an inner life, it does not deserve its name," a quality he identified as distinctive to German music. He suggested the ever-present influence of Hegel in saying that "conquering the external demands of playing is a means by which to manifest an inner spirit . . . that indicates true art!"[58] But a month later Becher pulled back from privileging internality as he evaluated the playing of the Belgian Servais. After admitting that the cellist had not achieved a "subjective individuality" like that of Paganini, he conceded that Servais had made "the representation or the personification of a nationality, his fatherland in Belgium." Becher was willing to accept a performance exhibiting "not feeling, ardor, devotion, but rather sentiment, passion, abandon, etc., qualities found in Servais's playing by which his individuality and nationality interact with one another."[59] Thus did the idea of national character serve as a vehicle for forging a compromise in musical values.

What did the new forms of intellectual authority mean to the amateur listener? In German the words *Kenner* and *Liebhaber* had traditionally been used to distinguish between the connoisseur and the typical music-lover. Through the 1780s commentators such as Johann Mattheson spoke approvingly about the "natural capacities" of the *Liebhaber*.[60] But Johann Nikolaus Forkel lent greater ideological meaning to the distinction between the more or less learned publics, and in 1801 an author in the *Allgemeine musikalische*

---

[57] Dana Gooley, "The Battle against Instrumental Virtuosity in the Early Nineteenth Century," *Franz Liszt and His World*, Christopher Gibbs and Dana Gooley (eds.) (Princeton, N.J.: Princeton University Press, 2006), pp. 75–112.

[58] *AWMZ*, 6 January 1842, p. 11.

[59] *AWMZ*, 9 February 1842, pp. 86–87. See also on a concert by Anton Rubinstein, *AWMZ* 13 January 1842, pp. 23–24.

[60] Matthew Riley, "Johann Nikolaus Forkel on the Listening Practices of 'Kenner' and 'Liebhaber,'" *Music & Letters* 84 (2003), 421.

Zeitung spoke of "half-learned" amateurs trying without much success to play concertos by C. P. E. Bach.[61] By the 1840s commentators spoke even more harshly about untutored listeners. Eduard Krüger wrote that "when a collection of dilettantes get together for a little music, they tend to want chiefly just entertainment, rather than to dig deeper intellectually into the works they perform."[62]

Chorley extended the same criticism to the opera public, drawing sharp lines between good and bad listeners. In a piece called "Verdi-mania" (1846) he employed the word *popularity* negatively, arguing that Verdi's operas "contain certain elements of popularity" that the "select and sober" critic could not deem truly successful. He could not take seriously the taste of a "miscellaneous" public: "A theatrical audience is of necessity miscellaneous – made up of intelligences of every order; and the conditions of triumph within its sphere necessarily embrace effect to a degree which would be a degrading concession in music appealing to a more severe and select audience." Such people could not, he said, understand that Verdi's *Ernani* lacked originality and used simplistic tricks, piling one sentimental romance on another, "with hardly the sixth part of an idea!"[63] Professional critics approached their trade in part as educators but were not always sympathetic to the limited knowledge of their readers.[64] Shortly before he became head of the Brussels Conservatory and editor of the influential *Revue musicale,* François Fétis wrote what the New York edition called *Music Explained to the World; Or, How to Understand Music and Enjoy its Performance,* an early example of the many books on musical appreciation that would appear during the nineteenth century. He, like Chorley, spoke in disparaging terms about the less well-educated members of the public. "There is more than one degree of ignorance of art," he stated, "from the rare people who have a physical repugnance to it," to those "born in obscurity, and remote from cities," to those who regularly heard some music but absorbed only "a certain degree of unreflecting enjoyment."[65]

[61] "Bemerkungen über die Ausbildung der Tonkunst in Deutschland im achtzehnten Jahrhundert," *AMZ,* 28 January 1801, p. 300.

[62] Quoted in *AMZ,* 3 November 1847, p. 755. Leon Botstein contributed to this discussion in "Listening through Reading: Musical Literacy and the Concert Audience," *NCM* 16 (1992), 129–45.

[63] "Music and the Drama: The Verdi-mania," *ATH,* 17 January 1846, p. 73, quoted in Cooper, *House of Novello,* p. 132, and "Music and the Drama: The Verdi-mania," *ATH,* 2 January 1847, pp. 24, 51–2.

[64] Ellis, *Music Criticism in Nineteenth-Century France,* pp. 74–6 and *passim.*

[65] Francis James Fétis, *Music Explained to the World; Or, How to Understand Music and Enjoy Its Performance* (Boston, Mass.: B. Perkins, 1842; New York: Da Capo, 1987), pp. 272–3.

Commentators also sought to empower the classical music public as a source of learned taste. In 1831 the Viennese *Allgemeine musikalische Anzeiger* spoke of the public at the Concert Spirituel – individuals ranging from school teachers to lesser nobles – as "that elite which, year in and year out, is united at these classical productions, always worthy of the highest praise."[66] An aristocratic box-holder at the Kärtnertor Theater would probably have frowned when reading that statement, but musical life proceeded to change so rapidly that such a person would have accepted it three decades later.

CONTRASTING CONTEXTS

The movement favoring idealistic musical values contrasted in our four cities due to differences in political context, literary influence, and nature of the public. Leipzig led the way in the newer musical thinking, thanks to the early *Allgemeine musikalische Zeitung* and the idealistic challenge posed to it by Robert Schumann. The most sharply defined ideological movement developed in Vienna after 1815, driven by leaders of the Concert Spirituel. Musical politics were the most closely linked to national politics in London, where musical journalists borrowed language from the movement for parliamentary reform. Political vocabulary was the least evident in musical discourse in Paris, where the revolutionary experience made writers cautious and the literary community influenced musical commentary to a particular extent.

Leipzig

We begin with Leipzig because the Gewandhaus concerts began well before a repertory of classical music formed and accordingly carried practices of the old musical order into the new one. The centrality of the concerts to the life of the city's elite made the institution a rallying point for the community during the Napoleonic wars. August Eberhard Müller, the orchestra's first flute player and Cantor of the city, composed *Rise up, rejoice!* (Gerechte, frohlocket!) for New Year's Day 1807, set to a text calling for aid in time of public need:

> Rise up, rejoice! Rejoice all ye men!
> For justice give thy praise!
> Thank the harp for proclaiming its sound,
> Thank it for its yet unsung song!
> . . .

[66] *Allgemeine musikalische Anzeiger*, 17 February 1831, p. 27.

Hail, hail to the State, sing to the highest!
Hail, hail to the People, that holds it in trust!
Lend us peace mercifully, dear Lord, in these times.[67]

Because the city was small and the series faced little competition, the Gewandhaus continued to serve as the main meeting place for the city's elites, its sociability resembling an opera hall more than an orchestral series as we know it. The programs were therefore expected to satisfy a broader range of tastes among the subscribing elite than was the case at the other major orchestral series. The crisis surrounding the Napoleonic invasion brought such differences in taste to a head, as we can see vividly in reports on the concerts published in the *Journal des Luxus und der Moden*. A correspondent writing in 1800 damned the series with faint praise, saying that the balls were the main show to attend there, because one could see the latest modes in women's dress, hair, and jewelry. Fashion was just as much on display at the concerts, he said, because the same people, those "so-called listeners," were interested chiefly in the pastries sold at the break. He looked back sentimentally to the old days when the lively "Sebastian Bach" played in Richter's public house. He expressed doubt whether many subscribers could understand the many Italian texts and complained that opera selections were repeated too often, leaving little room for new ones.[68] The word *Kunst* did not appear once in this account.

The author of an 1807 report spoke a different language, one rich in aesthetic and political implication. The piece concerned the first Leipzig performance of Beethoven's Third Symphony, already known as the "Eroica." Warning that "the reader must understand what I say is partisan in nature," the correspondent posed an agenda for the concerts, demanding that the directing board apply its "vast knowledge, cultivated taste, and eager devotion to Art" to bring about "carefully advised repetition of the most impressive masterpieces we have already heard." The new symphony was a key case in point, in his view. Repeating works such as that would "satisfy the taste of the cultivated public," that is, "educated Leipzig."[69] The concepts of art and the artwork employed here reflected the new tendency to see music as a vehicle by which to discover aesthetic truth. That language empowered the new serious public that supported idealistic goals for the concerts. The

---

[67] Abonnenten Concerte, SGML, 1 January and 26 April 1807; "August Eberhard Müller," *Biographisch-bibliographisches Quellen-Lexicon der Musiker und Musikgelehrter*, 11 vols., 2nd. ed. (Leipzig, 1900–1904; Graz Akademisches Druck- und Verlangsanstalt, 1959), vol. 7, pp. 102–3.

[68] "Concerte in Leipzig," *JLM*, July 1800, pp. 351–3.

[69] "Ueber das stehende Concert in Leipzig, im vorigen Winterhalbjahre," *JLM*, July 1807, p. 442.

repetition of masterpieces laid the groundwork for canonic repertories at the Gewandhaus concerts, even though that was not the writer's intention.

A nervous compromise was maintained between competing factions under the guidance of the concert's directing board. Strong-minded though Leipzig's intellectuals were, they did not marshal attacks on the institution directly, as happened to the Philharmonic Society of London. We can see the compromise operating in a 1799 article in the *Allgemeine musikalische Zeitung* attacking the performance of opera excerpts, probably written by the editor Friedrich Rochlitz. Opera belongs only in the theatre, ran the argument, because concerts increasingly offered excerpts to pander to "the distressing taste for new, indeed only the very newest pieces, that is increasing so much in the opera world."[70] Yet the author did not criticize the Gewandhaus subscription series or its board directly, as seems to have been the magazine's policy. Indeed, in 1817 the orchestra joined the opera company established at the Rannstädter Theater, linking the concerts more closely with the opera world. The aggressive Berlin critic A. B. Marx was much less diplomatic than his Leipzig colleagues. In 1825 he condemned the city's central concert series, run by Karl Möser, for offering many opera excerpts, because the symphony and the cantata, he declared, were the only genres that allowed "justification for calling a concert *great*."[71]

Political crisis returned to Leipzig in the early 1830s, as long-standing disaffection over municipal taxation opened up political dispute more than ever before. Serious riots took place in the city in 1830 and 1831; journeymen blacksmiths led the first episode, and a more diverse set of agitators revived the unrest a year later. Members of the Young Germany movement made a liberal critique of the monarchy – *die Absolut* – and called into question the hereditary status of the city council. The journalist Ferdinand Stolle published a book on the riots, declaring that "People are complaining bitterly about the oppressive nature of the [Royal] bureaucracy, and about the inhumanity of the [City] police; and through this discontent object to the Monarchy."[72] Stolle extended his critique to the Direktorium of

[70] "Ueber das jetzt gewöhnliche Aufführen einzelner Opernscenen in Konzerten," *AMZ*, 1 May 1799, p. 481.

[71] Cited in Gramit, *Cultivating Music*, p. 129. See also Gooley, "Battle against Instrumental Virtuosity," p. 80; and Bernd Sponheuer, *Musik als Kunst und Nicht-Kunst* (Kassel: Bärenreiter, 1987), pp. 9–36.

[72] Ferdinand Stolle, *Die sächsische Revolution oder Dresden und Leipzig in den Jahren 1830 und 1831* (Leipzig: Wigand, 1835), p. vii. See Robert Beachy, *The Soul of Commerce*, pp. 197–221; Páll Björnsson, "Zwischen Ausflügen und Barrikadenkampf: Die Konstituierung des liberal-nationalen Netzwerkes in Leipig, 1843–49," *Leipziger Kalender 2001* (Leipzig: University of Leipzig, 2001), pp. 73–87; Steffen Sammler, "Protestkultur und politischer Wandel in Leipzig im 19. Jahrhundert," *Kulturpolitik und Stadtkultur in Leipzig und Lyon (18.-20. Jahrhundert)*, Thomas Höpel and Steffen Sammler (eds.)

the Gewandhaus concerts in a second book. Complaining about the high price of tickets, he stated that the board had "kept anyone in the lesser class of the *Bürgertum* from setting foot in the hall." He claimed that "the corrupt Ukases in the Subscription-Concert-Codex" had made "less wealthy people much embittered against the aristocratic atmosphere of the Gewandhaus."[73] The most distinguished German man of letters also came under fire: "Whoever wants to talk about revolution will name the city not Leipzig but rather Little Paris. It all hangs together: Goethe, the poetic Talleyrand, said it first."[74] The alienation of Leipzig's middling classes from their elite was even more forcefully expressed in a booklet published in 1848: *The People's Friend: Freedom, Equality, Brotherhood.* Citing the writings of Karl Marx and Friedrich Engels, the author derided Raymund Härtel – co-owner of the music firm Breitkopf & Härtel and a member of the city council – for toadying to the nobility out of fear for his property.[75]

The directing board of the Gewandhaus began to refashion the series somewhat in the 1830s, increasing the proportion of classics as compared to selections from recent operas. Still, the Leipzig series did that more gradually than the Concert Spirituel in Vienna or the Society of Concerts in Paris, where classics defined repertory from the start and little new music was performed by 1848. Neither the Gewandhaus board nor the press associated the concerts explicitly with classical music. In 1834 Stolle described the programs as mixed, offering "both classical pieces and ones of a varied nature." Although he claimed (incorrectly) that all nine Beethoven symphonies were done every season, he emphasized that the programs offered "pearly arias" by such fashionable composers as Auber, performed by top singers. The letter sent to subscribers at the start of the 1844–1845 season stressed the prominent pair of singers hired for the year; terms such as *classics* or *great works* were conspicuously absent from the document. As late as March 1848 the important new magazine *Die Grenzboten* remarked that "there is a larger public at the Gewandhaus that wants to hear pretty vocal numbers and dynamic virtuosos than prefer the symphonies."[76]

(Leipzig, Leipziger Universitätsverlag, 2004), pp. 55–68; *Saxony in German History: Culture, Society, and Politics, 1830–1933*, James Retallack (ed.) (Ann Arbor, Mich.: University of Michigan Press, 2000).

73 Ferdinand Stolle, *Das neue Leipzig nebst einer Kreuzthurminspiration über Dresden: Herausgegeben im Verein mehrer Freunde* (Leipzig: Wigand, 1834), p. 121.

74 Ibid., p. 3.

75 *Der Volksfreund: Freiheit, Gleichheit, Brüderlichkeit!* (Leipzig: C. V. Weller. 1848), p. 32.

76 Stolle, *Das neue Leipzig*, p. 122; *Einladung zu den Abonnement-Concerten im Winter 1844 bis 1845*, in Abonnenten-Concerte Programme, SGML; "Tagebuch: aus Leipzig," *Die Grenzboten* 1(8) (1848), 380. See also [J. J. Weber] *Ganz Leipzig für acht Groschen: Neuer und vollständiger Wegweiser durch*

Robert Schumann inaugurated the *Neue Zeitschrift für Musik* in close relationship with the literary movement Young Germany. In 1835 books by Heinrich Laube, Theodor Mundt, and Karl Gutzkow were banned by the German Confederation for questioning religious dogma and demanding constitutional government.[77] Though the magazine never spoke on political matters, Schumann was well acquainted with people in the movement. His "brotherhood" of writers functioned as a musical parallel to it, as Arnold Schering argued in 1917.[78] A politically outspoken periodical, *Unser Planet*, was put out by Schumann's publisher, C. H. F. Hauptmann, and included advertisements for the music magazine and for the music shop of Friedrich Wieck, whose daughter would marry Schumann.[79] Just as the German Confederation was about to take action against Laube, the *Neue Zeitschrift* published a striking aphorism, "Musical upheavals, like the political, are penetrating into the smallest village or profession."[80] During the 1840s, Schumann composed four-part songs for men's choruses that tended to be politically active.[81]

Influenced deeply by the literary radicalism of the 1830s, Schumann extended the idealistic viewpoint found in the *Allgemeine musikalische Zeitung* to a comprehensive critique of commercialized musical culture. The magazine occasionally offered articles on opera productions in Paris, and its lead articles made broad ideological attacks on international opera and opera *fantaisies*. Schumann frequently drew explicit boundaries between high and low taste. On one occasion he remarked that Rossini, Bellini, and Auber wanted nothing more than to be fashionable, recognized

Leipzig für Fremde und Einheimische (Leipzig: Weber, 1838), p. 56; and [Gottfried Wilhelm Becker], *Ein Blick auf das Jahr 1832 in Beziehung auf Leipzig* (Leipzig: A. Fest, 1833), pp. 33–7, which mentions the Gewandhaus only in regard to its visiting soloists.

[77] Hohendahl, *Building a National Literature*, pp. 104–22, 175–6, 274; *Das Junge Deutschland: Texte und Documenta*, Jost Hermand (ed.) (Stuttgart: Philipp Reclam, 1966); *Das Junge Deutschland: Kolloquium zum 150. Jahrestag des Verbots vom 10. Dezember 1835*, Joseph A. Kruse and Bernd Kortländer (eds.) (Hamburg: Hoffmann and Campe, 1987). James J. Sheehan, *German History, 1770–1866* (Oxford: Oxford University Press, 1989), pp. 572–87.

[78] Arnold Schering, "Aus den Jugendjahren der musikalischen Neuromantik," *Peters Jahrbuch* 24 (1917), 45–63. See also Gustav Wustmann, "Zur Entstehungsgeschichte der Schumannischen *Zeitschrift für Musik*," *Zeitschrift der Internationalen Musikgesellschaft* 8 (1907), 396–403; and Leon B. Plantinga, *Schumann as Critic* (New Haven, Conn.: Yale University Press, 1967), pp. 109–10.

[79] "Intelligenz-Blatt der Planet," *Unser Planet: Blätter für Unterhaltung, Zeitgeschichte, Literatur, Kunst und Theater*, 24 June 1834, p. 598 (FUCL).

[80] "Anzeiger: Kürzeres und Rhapsodisches für Pianoforte," *NZFM*, 12 May 1835, p. 153.

[81] John Daverio, "*Einheit-Freiheit-Vaterland*: Intimations of Utopia in Robert Schumann's Late Choral Music," in *Music and German National Identity*, Celia Applegate and Pamela Potter (eds.) (Cambridge, Mass.: Harvard University Press, 2003), pp. 59–77; Anthony Newcomb, "Schumann and the Marketplace: From Butterflies to Hausmusik," in *Nineteenth-Century Piano Music*, Larry Todd (ed.) (New York: Macmillan, 1990), pp. 258–315.

as a "genius *à la mode*," and he condemned the opera fantasy for "shameless vulgarity." The brotherhood of followers Schumann described in his writings was the basis for the comment that "we consider ourselves and our readers far too good to be burdened with such trash."[82] Schumann often drew a dichotomy between well-crafted German music and the shameless commercialism of Paris-based grand opera – for example, "[t]hat was written by Beethoven, it is a *German* work."[83] Thus did nationalism serve as an ideological vehicle for promoting the cause of serious music against decadent cosmopolitan music.

Schumann's *Collected Writings on Music and Musicians* (1854) eventually became the Bible of high musical values all across Europe. Published in a variety of editions and in many languages for the rest of the century, the book included pieces written almost entirely between 1834 and 1842, after which time his music tended to be less advanced in style. The most often-read section of the first edition was a set of aphorisms titled "Musical Rules for One's House and One's Life" (Musikalische Haus- und Lebens-Regeln) that served as an advice book for serious musicians. Franz Liszt made a French translation, *Conseils aux jeunes musiciens*.[84]

London

Idealistic musical principles evolved in London in the midst of the political and social upheaval that culminated in the Reform Act of 1832. The most important change brought by the legislation was not so much expansion of the electorate, but the opening up of political life to the public as a whole, taking discussion "out of doors," beyond the two Houses of Parliament. Strict party allegiance was born in this era, linked closely to new aspirations for social and political change. Musical life, opera in particular, was deeply involved with long-standing social issues central to the conflict over reform, leading musical commentators to adopt partisan vocabulary for their own purposes.[85]

Journalists often remarked that the three aristocracies of birth, wealth, and talent met at musical events, and concerts of note were now given in the

---

[82] Robert Schumann, *On Music and Musicians*, Paul Rosenfeld (trans.) (Berkeley: University of California Press, 1983), pp. 66, 70–1.

[83] Ibid., p. 100.

[84] *Conseils aux jeunes musiciens*, François Liszt (trans.) (Leipzig: J. Schuberth; Paris: Flaxland, 1878).

[85] John Phillips, *The Great Reform Bill in the Boroughs* (Oxford: Clarendon Press, 1992); Peter Mandler, *Aristocratic Government in the Age of Reform: Whigs and Liberals, 1830–1852* (Oxford: Clarendon Press, 1990); Arthur Burns and Joanna Innes, "Introduction," *Rethinking the Age of Reform*, Burns and Innes (eds.) (Cambridge: Cambridge University Press, 2003), pp. 1–70.

bourgeois City of London and points east. But the high nobility clung to leadership over musical life more tenaciously even than in Vienna, giving Italian opera an especially sharp class identity. In the 1820s aristocratic control of the King's Theatre was institutionalized even more formally than before.[86] Having lasted unnaturally long, aristocratic dominance of opera became an easy object of political attack from writers with a variety of partisan purposes. As early as 1813 Thomas Barnes, spokesman for the Opposition in the *Examiner*, found it useful to accuse the opera-going nobility of being musically ignorant. He complained that "these superb aristocrats are delighted with a style of performance which would disgust the lowest orders," because they were "worse educated than the inferior ranks of the middle portion of the community."[87] Conversely, in 1845 a conservative periodical, *The Connoisseur*, defended opera-rich benefit concerts against wild-eyed idealists as an honorable equivalent to rotten boroughs, "those bulwarks of the constitution, . . . now blotted from the page of English history."[88] Although such concerts must have drawn their public from a variety of political persuasions, any attack on traditional notions of prestige could threaten the government's authority.

Promoters of British music took advantage of idealistic slogans as well, attacking the "vulgar tastes" that kept the nobility from enjoying the works of local composers. The nationalistic movement begun at the end of the eighteenth century became vigorous again in the 1830s. A reviewer in the reform-oriented *Spectator* congratulated the Vocal Concerts – where one heard more English glees than Italian arias – for "making no subserviency to titled patrons, no truckling to noble directors, and no pandering to ignorant prejudices or vulgar tastes." Thanks to pieces by Handel's colleague Maurice Greene, late-sixteenth-century Luca Marenzio, and cathedral organist Charles Evans, the concert "upraised good music, and has also put down bad."[89] Yet conflict between social classes at that time had distinct limits. Aristocrats played important roles in parliamentary Reform and in the reshaping of cultural life.[90] Noblemen were an important part

---

[86] Weber, *Music and the Middle Class: Social Structure of Concert Life in London, Paris and Vienna, 1830–1848*, 2nd ed. (Aldershot, UK: Ashgate, 2003), pp. 8–10, 13–17, 35–59, 137–8, 140–1 and "L'institution et son public"; Hall-Witt, *Fashionable Acts*, pp. 3–139; and "Representing the Audience in the Age of Reform: Critics and the Elite at the Italian Opera in London," *Music and British Culture*, pp. 121–44.

[87] Quoted in Theodore Fenner, *Leigh Hunt and Opera Criticism* (Lawrence, Kans.: University of Kansas Press, 1972), p. 175 (9 May 1813).

[88] "The Past Concert Season," *Connoisseur: A Journal of Music and the Fine Arts*, 1 August 1845, p. 49.

[89] "Vocal Concert," *Spectator*, 23 March 1833, p. 260.

[90] Peter Mandler, *Fall and Rise of the Stately Home* (New Haven, Conn.: Yale University Press, 1997), pp. 64, 81, 111; and *Aristocratic Government in the Age of Reform: Whigs and Liberals, 1830–1852*

of the emerging public for self-consciously serious music, and the critique of opera was directed just as much against the music business as against the King's Theatre. Ultimately, bourgeois and aristocratic groups worked together in forming a community around classical music concerts.

Idealists spent as much venom against the Philharmonic Society as against the King's Theatre.[91] The Philharmonic came under heavy fire in part because a monopolistic professional organization was problematic in the metropolis where a free market had long existed in concert life. Resentment against the privileges given the Philharmonic's members, especially the frequent use of substitutes to play for them, fed the press campaign against it. Although the Society's leaders claimed to provide an alternative to the low taste and unrehearsed performances at benefit concerts, they quickly made major compromises with their lofty principles and brought in opera selections and virtuoso solos, because many of their subscribers held the virtuosic tradition dear. The institution was hoisted upon its own petard, one might say, when in 1827 a reviewer quoted the rule against opera excerpts in the founding document to denounce a program that offered just such music by Giovanni Pacini and Vincenzo Federici, composers admired by opera aficionados but despised by idealists. "All who possess any real knowledge of music, or a particle of genuine taste, must condemn [the program]. We will not waste a moment of the reader's or our own time in entering into any examination of such trash."[92]

The new and old modes of musical learning came into conflict in this discourse. The new thinking about instrumental music defined by Crotch and put into journalistic form by Davison rejected the traditional connoisseurship of singing in the Italian style or, for that matter, the mingling of vocal and instrumental virtuosity in concert. The Italianate tradition was nonetheless alive and well in the period, as the story "An Aria Speaks" suggests. Connoisseurs of opera followed Rossini in listening to his music "not as imitation or image or emotion, but as sheer music," as James Johnson suggested. Leigh Hunt made a legendary contrast between the music of Mozart and Rossini: "there is genius of many kinds; and of kinds very remote from one another," identifying Rossini as a "genius of sheer animal spirits."[93] The idealistic disillusionment with opera tradition came

(Oxford: Clarendon Press, 1990). See also Wahrman, *Imagining the Middle Class*, and Hall-Witt, *Fashionable Acts*.

91 See "Sketch of the State of Music in London," *QMMR* 5 (1823), 242.

92 "Philharmonic Society," *Harmonicon* 5 (1827), 145–6.

93 Johnson, *Listening in Paris*, p. 219; *Companion*, 16 January 1828, pp. 14–15. See also "Rossini in Perfection," *Spectator*, 4 May 1833, p. 404.

out with full force in an attack on Leigh Hunt. In a eulogy to Mme. Giuditta Pasta in his short-lived periodical *The Companion* (1828), Hunt compared her glorious musicality with the drab vocalizing he heard in oratorios: "In the concert-room, the audience expect little passion . . . They are themselves in a dull and formal state . . . All is quiet, mechanical, mediocre."[94] Then in 1843 a writer in the *Musical Examiner*, probably Davison, derided Hunt for intolerance toward new musical heroes: "He cannot decree Madame Pasta a triumph without having Handel, Mozart, and the mighty volume of their sacred music dragged at [Pasta's] chariot wheels while [Simon] Mayr and [Niccolò] Zingarelli!!!! sit beside her in the triumphal car."[95]

Endless dispute over the programming of the Philharmonic Society allowed chamber music concerts to become the main focal point of the classical music public. Violinist Henry Blagrove and his entrepreneurial colleagues built a large and socially diverse public for programs of quartets and classical opera selections that had few parallels anywhere but in America. A writer in *Blackwood's Edinburgh Magazine* in 1842 drew sharp ideological lines in defining his concerts as an "ideal school" as compared to promenade concerts focused on the quadrille, waltz, and polka:

The school of [Philippe] Musard and [Johann] Strauss is by no means an ideal school – and that is what we want. The quartet concerts of [Henry] Blagrove have done more for the popularization of music in this town than any other. We do not want mobs of musicians, with drums, trumpets, triangles and cymbals. . . . The musical quackery of the French school can do us no good: we wish to hear Beethoven, Mozart, Haydn, and Handel simply and elegantly treated.[96]

Vienna

A vacuum of leadership opened up in Viennese musical life after the Congress of Vienna in 1815. No member of the Imperial household picked up where Empress Marie Therese left off after her death in 1807, and the great noble families, threatened financially, ceased to exert their former leadership. The rapid expansion of the city's population and the turbulence of the economy brought both opportunity and uncertainty to a society in drift.[97] With little initiative remaining from court or nobility, opera productions at the Kärntnertor Theater became the focal point of musical life, linked to performances by singers and virtuosos in private homes, all caught

---

[94] "Madame Pasta: An Objection to Concerts and Oratorios," *Companion*, 6 February 1828, pp. 36–37.

[95] "Leigh Hunt," *Musical Examiner*, 25 November 1843, p. 327.

[96] "The World of London, Part XI: Music," *Blackwood's Edinburgh Magazine* 51 (1842), 429.

[97] Josef Karl Mayr, *Wien im Zeitalter Napoleons: Staatsfinanzen, Lebensverhältnisse, Beamte und Militär* (Vienna: Gottlieb Gistel, 1940).

up in the frenzy for Rossini's new operas. The very musical members of the "service" nobility stepped into the breach by founding the Society of the Friends of Music in 1814. The abrupt shift in the leadership of musical life at the time brought a special urgency to musical commentary, as can be seen in the magazine begun in 1818, the *Allgemeine musikalische Zeitung, mit besonderer Rücksicht auf den österreichischen Kaiserstaat.*

Nowhere else in Europe did titled gentlemen devote themselves so much to professional activities in musical life as in Austria. Habsburg Austria had placed a greater emphasis on music rather than literacy in primary education since the early eighteenth century, thereby stimulating an unusually wide population with considerable musical training.[98] A whole host of lesser nobles in state service spent most of their daily lives composing, performing, and helping run concerts, in the process lending prestige and political influence to the movement for classical music. Ignaz Ritter von Mosel (1772–1844) was Court Councillor, vice-director of the two court theatres, editor of the new magazine for two years, and composer of numerous religious and theatrical works. Heinrich Ritter von Lannoy (1787–1853), son of a Habsburg administrator of Jesuit lands in the Low Countries and owner of property south of Graz, was among the key leaders in both the Friends of Music and the Concert Spirituel.[99] Johann Vesque Graf von Puttlingen (1803–1883), likewise son of a Habsburg official, directed the office overseeing all foreigners while he developed a career in composition.[100] The ideology these gentlemen constructed for the reform of musical taste confirms the argument of Tia DeNora that aristocrats wished "to maintain status in the face of the loss of exclusive control over the traditional means of authority in musical affairs."[101]

The main early accomplishments of the Friends of Music were founding a conservatory in 1817 and opening a concert hall in 1831. But the growing fragmentation of taste in the musical community made the organization's activities go in different directions. The Society Concerts (Gesellschafts-Concerte) mingled classical overtures or symphonies with opera excerpts and opera *fantaisies*, performed strictly by amateurs. A series called the Evening Entertainments (Abendunterhaltungen) did include professional musicians, in programs offering an unusual miscellany of genres. The

98 Melton, "School, Stage, Salon."
99 Wolfgang Suppan, *Heinrich Eduard Josef von Lannoy (1787–1853), Leben und Werke* (Graz: Akademische Druck- und Verlagsanstalt, 1960).
100 Hertha Ibl, "*Johann Vesque von Püttlingen's Leben und Opernschaffen,*" unpublished Ph.D. dissertation, University of Vienna (1949).
101 Tia Denora, *Beethoven and the Construction of Genius: Musical Politics in Vienna, 1792–1803* (Berkeley: University of California Press, 1997), p. 49.

Concert Spirituel, founded in 1819 with loose ties to the Society, developed the most strictly defined canonic repertory in Europe in the 1820s. Despite all this, the Friends cannot be said have stood at the center of Viennese musical life until their new concert hall was built on the Ring in 1870.

Founding – indeed, *empowering* – a civic organization such as the Friends of Music carried deeper political implications in Vienna than in London or Paris. The organization reflected late eighteenth-century thinking about civic responsibility, public opinion, and constitutionalism. Mosel and Lannoy hinted at ideas of self-governance that must have been thought problematic in high quarters, leading the top noble families to keep their distance from the project.[102] Like the Philharmonic Society, the organization was endowed with an imposing but problematic set of goals for regenerating musical life. In 1828, for example, a writer in the *Theaterzeitung*, the city's main newspaper, kept tongue firmly in cheek, hailing the organization for trying to "raise music to a more lofty plane, . . . in quest of the Beautiful and the Good, without rivalries or factionalism."[103] Mosel went remarkably far out on a limb politically in the pieces he wrote for the magazine. At the very time when nationalist disturbances were occurring up and down the Rhine, he blamed the government – in effect, the high nobility – for the bad state of musical life. His argument typifies the political thinking surrounding voluntary organizations that Pieter Judson has identified in Austria during the *Vormärz*.[104] In "On the Decline of Music," Mosel declared that:

If the highest levels of the State are not ready to accept that it is they upon whom progress of the fine arts and improvement of taste depends, that will leave the middle class responsible for raising the young, people whose shoulders may not be strong enough for such a burden. All this threatens to bring further decline in music, poetry, and painting and to make our capital city rustic.[105]

In such a fashion did a member of the lesser nobility try to negotiate between the bourgeoisie and the governing high nobility. The extraordinary

---

[102] Erich Wolfgang Partsch, "Zur Geschichte, Struktur, Repertoirebildung und Publikum der Gesellschaft der Musikfreunde in Wien im Vormärz," *Les sociétés de musique en Europe*, pp. 157–78. On police, see Alice Hanson, *Musical Life in Biedermeier Vienna* (Cambridge: Cambridge University Press, 1985), pp. 34–60; and Rudolf Hofmann, *Der Wiener Männergesangverein: Chronik der Jahre 1843 bis 1893* (Vienna: Verlag des Wiener Männergesangvereinenes, 1893), pp. 6–7.

[103] "Concerte," *TZ*, 7 February 1828, p. 12.

[104] Pieter M. Judson, *Exclusive Revolutionaries: Liberal Politics, Social Experience, and National Identity in the Austrian Empire, 1848–1914* (Ann Arbor: University of Michigan Press, 1996), pp. 1–28 and *Wien Brennt. Die Revolution 1848 und ihre liberale Erbe* (Vienna: Böhlau, 1998), *passim*. On the decline of aristocratic patronage, see Wyn Jones, *Symphony in Beethoven's Vienna*, pp. 36–51.

[105] *AMZK*, 18 April 1818, p. 137.

patronage of chamber music by Austria's leading aristocratic families – indeed, by Archduke Rudolph, half brother of Emperor Franz – was disappearing.

Mosel wrote in a more colloquial and ideological style than was conventional in the Leipzig music magazine. He pressed the idea of decline a long way: "How can we tolerate a decay of music in a time when everyone is musical, when we hear nothing but that around us! Take account of this!" He stated darkly that "all you hear is mediocrity . . . only masterpieces of artistic clothiers and perfumers." In another piece, "A Sketch toward a much needed Discussion of the Wretched Present State of Affairs," Mosel called for a complete rethinking of what should be allowed in the concert hall, suggesting that leaders of the Friends of Music should take a firm hand in preventing bad programs by marginal musicians: "Who should give a public concert? What should be performed there? Where can it be given? How often should any one artist be allowed to give one?"[106] He declared war against facile virtuosity with notable vehemence: "A particular kind of fashionable music has become predominant in present-day taste," he said, "variations upon popular melodies that are nothing but gutter language."[107] The music offered at most benefit concerts, he said, was only frill when compared with the substance of Mozart's piano concertos and Beethoven's symphonies. Other writers followed in his path, speaking about taste as a matter of *Partei.* A letter published in 1820 stated that the many "republicans" favoring different factions in musical life needed to be restrained by "monarchy." The author claimed that a tiny party devoted itself exclusively to Beethoven, while Mozart no longer had many enthusiasts.[108] Frances Trollope found much the same when, during her visit to Vienna in 1835, she heard the upper classes favoring Thalberg and Strauss and ignoring Mozart and Haydn. She observed that "the people of Vienna are undergoing one of those fits of fashion to which all societies are occasionally subject."[109]

We shall see that Trollope was right, for by the mid-1840s the classical music public had grown in size and influence, enjoying the prominent Philharmonic concerts performed by members of the opera orchestra. Numerous leaders of the classical music world participated in the Viennese

---

[106] *AMZK,* 28 March 1818, p. 109.
[107] *AMZK,* 18 April 1818, pp. 135–36; *AMZK,* 26 December 1818, p. 473.
[108] Letter of October 31, 1820, W. C. Müller, *Briefe an deutsche Freunde,* 2 vols. (Altona: Hammerich, 1824), vol. I, pp. 142–3. A Baron Hager reported in 1815 that Beethoven was losing his supporters; see Buch, *Beethoven's Ninth,* pp. 80–1.
[109] Frances Trollope, *Vienna and the Austrians; with Some Account of a Journey through Swabia, Bavaria, the Tyrol, and the Salzbourg,* 2 vols. (London: Richard Bentley, 1838), vol. I, pp. 372.

Revolution of 1848. August Schmidt, for example, who began the *Allge-meine Wiener Musik-Zeitung*, served in the National Guard as captain of the 4th Company of the 6th District, and Vesque von Puttlingen supported Wagner after his expulsion from Dresden.[110] The magazine devoted a lot of attention to the revolution, publishing poetic tributes to the National Guard, discussions of press freedom, and an aphorism attributed to Schiller, "Do we need an Italian Opera? There is a moment in a man's life, when he stands apart from Italian opera more than usual."[111]

Paris

Ideas for reforming musical life tended to be less partisan in Paris than was the case in Leipzig or Vienna. The deep instability of the French state between 1789 and 1848 led commentators to hold back from couching their arguments in words comparable to "reform," "rotten boroughs," or *Partei*, and no polemicist emerged comparable to Schumann or Mosel. Leaders of the Conservatoire and the Society of Concerts exercised much sagacity in retaining government positions from regime to regime and welcoming both Legitimists and Orleanists to their concerts. "The post-revolutionary return to music of the past was rooted as much in justification for reaction as in the desire to found a new order," Sophie-Anne Leterrier suggested.[112] The administration of the Opéra likewise avoided political partisanship, even though it failed to find a satisfactory way to keep all parties happy under the July Monarchy.[113] Moreover, the importance of Paris in the music business – as the Los Angeles of the time – limited the critique of commercialism. Benefit concerts dominated by *fantaisies* and selections from recent *grands opéras* included few works by classical composers and not even many opera selections by Mozart. But major classical music concerts nonetheless took root on independent institutional bases. Pierre Baillot nurtured his chamber music concerts among an aristocratic public open to high aesthetic ideals. The Conservatoire concerts were established under the aegis of the state and built up a professional self-discipline that became a model for orchestras across Europe.

[110] Auguste Schmidt, "Selbstbiographie," in *Der Wiener Männergesangverein: Chronik der Jahre 1843 bis 1893*, Rudolph Hofmann (ed.) (Vienna: Verlag des Wiener Männergesangvereinenes, 1893), pp. xxv–xxix. Civil servants from the lower nobility similar to Mosel and Lannoy were central to the 1848 revolution; see Waltraud Heindl, *Gehorsame Rebellen: Bürokratie und Beamte in Österreich 1780 bis 1848* (Vienna: Böhlau, 1991).

[111] *AWMZ*, 6 April 1848, p. 65.

[112] Sophie-Anne Leterrier, *Le mélomane et l'historien* (Paris: Armand Colin, 2005), p. 59.

[113] Jane Fulcher, *Nation's Image: French Grand Opera as Politics and Politicized Art* (Cambridge: Cambridge University Press, 1987).

The city's music magazines, owned by Europe's most powerful music publishers, kept the lid on idealistic rhetoric in musical commentary. No French equivalent for the word *trash* emerged as the ultimate defamation of the miscellaneous program. Typical of the low-keyed Parisian prose was a comment in *France musicale* in 1842 that "the sonata and the concerto are proscribed in many concerts that follow fashion; Fontenelle's *bon mot* against the sonata still dictates vocal music in our day."[114] Songs written for the salon were not treated as derisively as was the case elsewhere. Indeed, in 1838 *France musicale* spoke in lofty terms about the "spiritual composer" Loïsa Puget, whose *romances* and *chansonnettes* "are now the rage in the salons."[115] If anything, a new genre of criticism appeared in reviews of concerts that catered to the general public.

Musical commentary went instead in a rather scholarly direction in Paris, for the heritage of *la musique ancienne* had endowed French musical culture with a firm historical consciousness. Interest in old music persisted among learned musicians and patrons, encouraged by the rejuvenation of the Catholic church. In the late 1820s Parisian music critics led by François Fétis mounted a campaign to establish an "aesthetic of reception" that would help listeners to appreciate music of the past independent of the pervasive influence of commercial music.[116] Fétis put on forward-looking "historical concerts" of pieces from the sixteenth and seventeenth centuries and in so doing helped Paris to replace London as the leader in performance of early music (Ex. 6.1).

Musical idealism assumed an unusually sectlike social character in Baillot's concerts. In the late 1790s Baillot held performances of chamber works in his rooms, drawing players and guests from *les grands*, families such as the Noailles, Louvois, Bondy, La Rochfoucauld, and Montalivet, joined by Austrian and Russian aristocrats from the Glitzine, Radziwill, and Razumovsky lines.[117] Musical idealism thus helped give some nobles a new musical home. Although his public became much more diverse socially and politically in the 1830s, the events never lost their aristocratic luster. In his subtle social history of the concerts, Joël-Marie Fauquet described the series as "an esoteric *musique réservé* that had departed from the patron's chamber to be founded, if problematically, upon passive listeners grouped around an

---

[114] "Concerts," *FM*, 15 May 1842, p. 186.

[115] "Soirée musicale de Mme Puget," *FM*, 28 January 1838, p. 4.

[116] Ellis, *Music Criticism*, pp. 3, 5.

[117] Joël-Marie Fauquet, *Les sociétés de musique de chambre à Paris de la Restauration à 1870* (Paris: Aux Amateurs de Livres, 1986), pp. 20, 71; Charles Guynemer, *Essay on Chamber Classical Music* (London: The Author, 1846), pp. 1–7.

idealized repertory, rather as those initiated into a sect tend to do."[118] The
Parisian concerts were thought to challenge the world of commercial music,
because "chamber music was perceived as an art defined in radical terms,
as the opposite of virtuosity and the lyric theatre, music then thought by
the bourgeoisie to represent musical 'progress.'"[119]

By 1848 the Society of Concerts came to exemplify the aesthetic ideals of
classical music more than any of the other major orchestras. That happened
thanks to the concerts' close links with the Conservatoire and the state, and
to the astute professionalism at work among its leaders. By achieving strong
institutional independence, the series was not expected to please a diverse
public and did not draw controversy such as wracked the Philharmonic
Society. Paris's intellectual elite flocked to the concerts and helped legitimate
the new musical ideals. "The concerts of the Conservatoire, today's haven
of art," wrote Joseph D'Ortique in 1833, "are not a place to get together
and chat, but a sanctuary to which the writer, the painter, all serious artists,
flock."[120] Yet *grand opéra* could not be completely excluded from those
hallowed walls. In 1838 the cavatina from Bellini's *Norma* was performed
on the same program with Beethoven's Symphony no. 9, leading the critic
of *France musicale* to grumble that the members of the orchestra had little
idea how to perform that kind of music.[121]

A WORLD OF ITS OWN?

A common language of idealistic musical values took root in the major
musical cities of Europe during the first half of the nineteenth century.
By the mid-1840s the concerts, periodicals, and a particular public had
begun to cohere as a musical world in its own right. By that time a person
traveling among these cities would keep hearing many of the same words –
allegiance to the "higher" taste of "classical" music, indeed "good" music,
possibly performed by "interpretive" artists. Our visitor would feel refreshed
to discover a certainty in these values, the sense that the knowledge acquired
about the music brought him or her musical truth. He or she would nonetheless be troubled by how foreign the elegant playing of Thalberg or
Servais (some of which he or she liked) seemed by the standard of the new
ideals and by the sense that the music of Meyerbeer had little to do with that

[118] Fauquet, *Sociétés de musique de chambre*, p. 33.   [119] Ibid., pp. 33, 29–30.
[120] Quoted in D. Kern Holoman, *Société des Concerts du Conservatoire, 1828–1967* (Berkeley: University
of California Press, 2004), p. 99.
[121] "Concert du Conservatoire," *FM*, 21 January 1838, p. 6.

of Mozart or Beethoven. The disconnection between these musical spheres bothered our traveler, who had been raised to assume that a symphony, a cavatina, and a set of piano variations would succeed one another at a concert seamlessly. Traditional tastes and assumptions were not gone from his or her mind, creating a nagging uncertainty about just what allegiance to "classical" music would mean.

CHAPTER 4

The rise of the chamber music concert

The first international repertory of old music – "classical" music – began to form just after 1800. What was previously called "ancient" music had remained a collection of local practices, because little other than Pergolesi's *Stabat Mater* and *La Serva Padrona* had become known in Europe as a whole. But during the 1770s performances of Handel's oratorios and odes began to move from Britain to Germany and Austria, followed by the founding of chamber music concerts in Vienna and Paris and the gradual growth of classical repertories at major orchestral series. By 1830 the terms *classic* and *classical music* were current in most parts of Europe, thanks to the burgeoning of printed musical commentary cutting across national boundaries. By the late 1840s it was conventional to speak in these terms about an area of concert life separate from opera and virtuoso concerts, even though it was not entirely clear just what that division meant.

The concept of classical music should be seen as pioneering rather than conservative during the first half of the nineteenth century. Endowing older works with canonic authority took two generations to accomplish because it made a fundamental break with musical tradition. The word *classical* took on a normative rather than a historical meaning in most musical commentary. During the late eighteenth century it was common to compare Handel to classical authors of Antiquity. By around 1820 the term *classical music* succeeded that vocabulary, used in ahistorical terms to denote music from a variety of periods, only occasionally made part of a distinction between Classic and Romantic composing styles.[1] Commentators tended to apply the term *classic* narrowly, most often to a quartet, symphony, or sacred work but usually not to an opera overture or

---

[1] Key studies of the term *classic* include Erich Reimer "Repertoirebildung und Kanonisierung zur Vorgeschichte des Klassikbegriffs," *Archiv für Musikwissenschaft* 43 (1986), 241–60; Ludwig Finscher, "Zum Begriff der Klassik in der Musik," *Deutsche Jahrbuch für Musik* 11 (1966), 9–34; and Klaus Kropfinger, "Klassik-Rezeption in Berlin, 1800–1835," in *Musikgeschichte Berlins im früen 19. Jahrhundert*, Carl Dahlhaus (ed.) (Regensburg: Bosse, 1980), pp. 301–80.

opera excerpt. Thus did the principle of the integral artwork come into play at an early date, though not spelled out systematically. The term *classical music* was applied more broadly than the term *classic*, for by 1840 it served as the headline for reviews of orchestral and quartet concerts, even when recent works predominated.[2] For that matter, in 1860 sacred works of François Boëly were called *classiques modernes* because they were composed on the model of "classiques anciens."[3] Still, the terms *chef-d'oeuvre* and *Meisterwerk* continued for some time to denote a recent work.

The chamber music concert and orchestral society had separate and contrasting histories. Concerts led by a quartet came first, begun by Ignaz Schuppanzigh in 1804 and Pierre Baillot in 1814, followed by series founded in London in 1835 and in Leipzig the following year. I use the term "quartet concert" as a synonym for "chamber music concert" because a quartet of string players almost always served as the core ensemble at these events. One cannot exaggerate how drastic a change quartet concerts brought to musical life. Although listeners today take for granted that such an event will offer no vocal music, doing so around 1800 amounted to a declaration of independence from a central principle of concert tradition. Save for the programs in London, chamber music concerts were more homogeneous in repertory than any other kind of concert, sometimes including only string quartets. Quartet concerts became focused on classical works – chiefly by the trinity of Haydn, Mozart, and Beethoven – earlier and more consistently than was the case with orchestral series. Nevertheless, orchestral and quartet concerts gradually grew closer to one another as the aesthetic and ideological bases of classical music became consolidated. By the mid-1840s the two kinds of concerts had come together to form a common world of classical music.

A curious mixture of introversion and extroversion became part of the world of chamber music that still lingers today. Quartet concerts had roots in the learning and cloistered socializing of the eighteenth-century musical society or collegium musicum. Although aesthetic writing rarely articulated the value of such music-making, it had long been common for instrumentalists to gather together for their musical and intellectual pleasure on their own, perhaps with no vocal music involved. Patrons were proud of the learning exhibited by their favorite groups of string players; the ensembles for which J. S. Bach wrote concertos in Cöthen, and with which he

[2] For example, "Nachrichten: Wiener Musikleben, Classische Concerte," *AMZ*, 1 March 1843, pp. 172–3.
[3] Ibid.; "Les classiques modernes," *FM*, 29 January 1860, p. 43; Leterrier, *Le mélomane et l'historien*, pp. 71–3, 86–7.

courted the Prussian King Frederick II, had that character.[4] Indeed, private performances with aristocratic amateurs preceded public concerts by the same players in Vienna and Paris. Such origins endowed the concerts with an image of aristocratic privacy that lasted well after they became public events with socially diverse audiences.[5] A quartet concert tended to gather a small, consistent public, for music critics often spoke about seeing the same faces year after year at such events. In 1834, for example, a Viennese journalist remarked that quartet concerts rarely attracted more than 150 people, "a small circle little known elsewhere."[6] The homogeneous nature of the programs, and the need to know a good deal about the music, inherently limited the size of a public at such events. In 1803 a Parisian journalist illustrated conventional wisdom on this matter, warning that a concert should not include too many instrumental pieces, because "its attractions will not be appreciated if they are not kept varied." Musicians must always, the reporter declared, "avoid the boredom born of uniformity."[7]

Yet quartet concerts gradually acquired a strong public identity, both musically and socially, during the first half of the nineteenth century. After Beethoven composed the "Razumovsky" Quartets (1808), Joseph Kerman argued, the genre became "symphonic" and ended up in "ensemble shouting." Robert Winter, for his part, suggested that composers found the string quartet a means to make four men sound like forty.[8] The quartet came into public prominence by stages. Originally such an ensemble existed to accompany a singer or virtuoso in a salon or small public concert. Antoine Elwart, the historian of Paris concerts, recalled how surprised he was to see the quartet becoming an ensemble in its own right at Baillot's series.[9] Furthermore, finding four players with similar ability and taste demanded that musicians seek one another out in a wide public sphere and subordinate their individual instincts to disciplined collegiality.[10] That

[4] Spitzer and Zaslaw, *Birth of the Orchestra*, pp. 238–62; Burchell, *Polite or Commercial Concerts*; and Charles Dill, "Ideological Noises: Opera Criticism in Early Eighteenth-Century France," *Operatic Migrations: Transforming Works and Crossing Boundaries*, Robert Marvin and Downing Thomas (eds.) (Aldershot, UK: Ashgate, 2006), pp. 65–84.

[5] Joseph Kerman, "Beethoven Quartet Audiences: Actual, Potential, Ideal," *Beethoven Quartet Companion*, Robert Winter and Robert Martin (eds.) (Berkeley: University of California Press, 1994), pp. 7–28; Fauquet, *Les sociétés de musique de chambre à Paris*, passim.

[6] *AMA*, 25 December 1834, p. 212.

[7] "Concert des amateurs, rue de Cléry," *CORR*, 1 January 1803, p. 2.

[8] Kerman, "Beethoven Quartet Audiences," *Beethoven Quartet Companion*, p. 15; Robert Winter, "Performing the Beethoven Quartets in their First Century," ibid., p. 34; "Miscellen," *AMZ*, 13 April 1825, p. 246. In Paris a critic called the string quartet "une symphonie en abrégé" (*RGM*, 1 November 1854, p. 254).

[9] Antoine Elwart, "Musique de chambre: Soirées de quatuors et quintetti," *RGM*, 5 August 1838, p. 310.

[10] Biba, "Beobachtungen zur Österreichischen Musikscenen," pp. 219–21.

social process led quartets to shift their performances from homes to public halls. The integration of nobles and bourgeois within a taste public developed to a particular extent at such concerts. It was usually presumed that nobles were attached principally to the opera, because that was the main public place where their social class tended to socialize. That is why it is productive to interpret each social class becoming "fractionalized," as Pierre Bourdieu put it, into groups who followed contrasting value systems.[11] In such a fashion class identities became blurred when aristocrats and bourgeois made common company at a quartet concert.

Ignaz Schuppanzigh established a "pure" program for the string quartet. His players would perform three or four pieces, with no vocal or solo virtuoso pieces, a practice that spread widely around Europe and indeed persists today. The main difference from present-day practices was that a program often included a trio, quartet, or quintet, sometimes including the piano, or for that matter a septet or nonet involving winds as well as strings, all enjoyed for the fullness of their sound. The quintet (including a bass, piano, or second viola or cello) was particularly common. Beethoven's Septet was often performed with quartets, as were the lively nonets composed by Louis Spohr, George Onslow, and Louise Farrenc. Sonatas for violin and piano, by contrast, were thought more appropriate for concerts aimed at the general public; Beethoven's "Kreutzer" Sonata, op. 47, was not performed with quartets very often. The piano trio likewise acquired a much wider public when musicians found such pieces useful for opening a concert focused on opera selections.

Programs of quartet concerts were strikingly similar throughout Europe. Not only did they all feature works by Haydn, Mozart, and Beethoven, they also included pieces by a common corps of highly respected composers. Several of these men were born around Beethoven's time: cousins Andreas Romberg (1767–1821) and Bernhard Romberg (1767–1841), Johann Nepomuk Hummel (1778–1837), Louis Spohr (1784–1859), and George Onslow (1784–1853).[12] Their works continued on programs through at least the 1850s and in some cases much longer. Felix Mendelssohn (1809–1847) and Robert Schumann (1810–1856) acquired similar status, although they received less unanimous or immediate praise as compared to their predecessors, and the chamber works of Franz Schubert (1797–1828) did not become standard repertory until at least the 1850s. Music by these composers was thought essential to a quartet's repertory even though they did not earn an iconic status as pronounced as the musical "trinity."

---

[11] Bourdieu, *Distinction*, pp. 260–67.
[12] See also Mara Parker, *String Quartet, 1750–1797: Four Types of Musical Conversation* (Aldershot, UK: Ashgate, 2002).

By 1830 few quartet concerts offered more than one piece by a living composer, at least a decade before that was the case at orchestral series. The only previous public concerts with as great a focus on old music had been London's Concert of Ancient Music (whose directors abandoned the anachronistic "t" in this period). It is remarkable how little criticism came from the press for performing little recent music, because the Ancient Concerts and almost all orchestral series came under such attack. Even Robert Schumann, the proponent of forward-looking music, acknowledged the hegemony of classical chamber works, after finding little merit in a new quartet that had won a coveted prize in 1842:

[T]he quartets of Haydn, Mozart, Beethoven, who does not know them and who dares cast a stone at them? It is abundantly clearly that these creations have an undying vitality, so much so that after the lapse of half a century they still delight all hearts, posing a challenge to the succeeding generation that in so long a period of time nothing comparable has been created.[13]

The very privacy and purity of quartet concerts spread their reputation and drew them into public life. As criticism of virtuoso concerts became more and more intense after 1830, commentators pointed to these events as the most notable place where the vision of "high" musical taste had been achieved. In 1830 a Viennese journalist wrote that he passed up a concert by Paganini to attend one by the Müller quartet, four brothers from Braunschweig in north central Germany. To his surprise, he found the music fascinating and the audience congenial, the audience including more women than he expected.[14] As chamber music took on canonic stature, so its public took on an authority in musical culture, being revered for its knowledge and disciplined listening habits. In London in 1844 Henry Chorley asserted in the *Athenaeum* that the increasing popularity of such concerts "argues the growth of a public whose pleasures are regulated by thought rather than by impulse, or mere vacant curiosity."[15]

VIENNA

Informal performances of Beethoven's quartets seem to have begun in 1795 – supposedly late Friday mornings, with a meal served at 4 PM – in the Viennese residence of Prince Karl von Lichnowsky and his wife, Princess Christine of the Thun line. The then twenty-year-old Schuppanzigh led in

---

[13] "Preisquartett von Julius Schapler," *NZFM*, 3 May 1842, p. 142.
[14] *AMA*, January 1830, p. 3.
[15] "Verdi-mania," *ATH*, 9 November 1844, p. 1028.

the expansion of these gatherings into public concerts in 1804. Schuppanzigh organized various series of quartet concerts until departing for Russia in 1816 and from his return in 1823 until his death in 1830.[16] His and other colleagues then put on similar concerts, and in 1849 Joseph Hellmesberger began a series that endured as Vienna's premier chamber concerts for the rest of the century.[17] Schuppanzigh followed a strict format in the series of six concerts that he presented twice a season between 1823 and 1825.[18] A third of the pieces performed at these concerts were by composers other than Haydn, Mozart, and Beethoven – Spohr and Onslow the most often.[19] A typical concert, including a quintet and a piano quartet, was held in 1826 in a public house where the Friends of Music often held events (Ex. 4.1).

4.1 *Quartett-Unterhaltung, Hôtel zum Rothem Igel, 12 March 1826*[20]

Quartet in C, op. 76, no. 3	†Haydn
Piano Quartet in E-flat, op. 16	Beethoven
Quintet in C Minor, K. 406	†Mozart

Other Viennese musicians nonetheless combined quartets freely with virtuoso pieces and even opera excerpts. In 1817, for example, violinist Josef Böhm, who played in Schuppanzigh's quartet and became a noted teacher, offered public concerts in the home of a patron where he led three quartets interspersed with an opera selection or a set of variations for violin, accompanied by the rest of his quartet.[21] For that matter, the resourceful Schuppanzigh regularly gave benefit concerts aimed at the general public. In 1827 he performed a rondo by Rodolphe Kreutzer and a set of variations by the fashionable pianist Léon de Saint-Lubin, along with an opera aria by the prominent Simon Mayr.[22] After his death quartet concerts were limited in number and did not always follow the pure format.

[16] *Thayer's Life of Beethoven*, pp. 170–2, 228, 262; Eduard Hanslick, *Geschichte des Konzertwesens in Wien* (Vienna: Braunmüller, 1869), pp. 202–3; Winter, "Performing the Beethoven Quartets in their First Century," *Beethoven Quartet Companion*, p. 34; Kerman, "Beethoven Quartet Audiences," ibid., pp. 10, 14, 22, 33.

[17] *Quartett Hellmesberger: Sämmtliche Programme vom 1. Quartett am 4. November 1849 biz zum 300. Quartett am 19. Dezember 1889* (Vienna: Wallishauser, 1889).

[18] PA/GMFV.   [19] PA/GMFV.

[20] PA/GMFV. I am indebted to Christopher Gibbs and John Gingerich for their transcription of chamber music programs in this period. The room in the public house was sometimes called a *Vereinsaal* (*Thayer's Life of Beethoven*, p. 938).

[21] "Kammermusik," *AMZK*, 23 January 1817, p. 27; *AMZK*, 27 February 1827, p. 69; and *AMZK*, 8 March 1817, p. 85; *Thayer's Life of Beethoven*, pp. 937–41.

[22] PA/GMFV.

The place where one could most regularly hear a quartet in Vienna was the Evening Entertainments, the series sponsored by the Friends of Music. Most of the performers were professors and students from the conservatory, and virtuosos occasionally visited the concerts, as Thalberg and Adolf Henselt did in the 1830s. A program always opened with a quartet or a quintet, somewhat less often by Haydn, Mozart, or Beethoven than at Schuppanzigh's series. The programs followed the tradition of miscellany to a fault, offering opera excerpts, virtuoso solos, and songs for solo voice or male quartet, with vocal and instrumental pieces alternating.[23] A program in 1825 included two interesting ensemble works: Johann Nepomuk Hummel's Septet for four winds and three strings, and a piece for harp, horn, and violins by Joseph Mayseder, the solo violinist of the Kärntnertor Theater whose music was performed across Europe (Ex. 4.2).

Schubert's songs, written either for a soloist or quartet, figured prominently at these concerts, and it was indeed in this context where his music was first treated in canonic terms, well before any of his symphonies or chamber works acquired such fame.[24] A wide variety of composers, including Mendelssohn and Robert Schumann, wrote songs for skilled amateur singers, either male or mixed, and they were often performed in convivial contexts. Mendelssohn and Schumann wrote songs for four male voices and piano similar to *Der Gondelfahrer*. In Germany music of this kind was usually called Liedertafel, a term supposed coined in Berlin shortly after 1800. Choruses singing such music sprang up all over Germany and Austria, and the music spread to Britain and North America; we shall see quartets for men sung on programs offered variously by Clara Wieck, the Leipzig Opera Chorus, and the Boosey Ballad Concerts (Exs. 5.11, 9.3, 9.5).[25] The relative similarity of this music to English glees, often called "part-songs,"

[23] PA/GMFV; Hanslick, *Geschichte des Concertwesens in Wien*, pp. 160–3; Otto Biba, "Franz Schubert in den musikalischen Abendunterhaltungen der Gesellschaft der Musikfreunde," *Schubert-Studien: Festgabe der Österreichischen Akademie der Wissenschaft zum Schubert-Jahr 1978*, Franz Grasberger and Othmar Wessely (eds.) (Vienna: Akademie der Wissenschaft, 1978), pp. 7–31; *Sammler*, 16 March 1840, p. 172; "Nachrichten," *AMZ*, 10 May 1826, pp. 313–15; *TZ*, 31 March 1835, p. 255.

[24] Christopher H. Gibbs, "Schubert in deutschsprachigen Lexica nach 1830," *Schubert durch die Brille* 13 (1994), 70–8; Ruth Solie, *Music in Other Words: Victorian Conversations* (Berkeley: University of California Press, 2004), pp. 118–52.

[25] Margaret Notley, "Schubert's Social Music: The 'Forgotten' Genres," *Cambridge Companion to Schubert*, Christopher H. Gibbs (ed.) (Cambridge: Cambridge University Press, 1997), pp. 138–54; Annegret Heemann, *Männergesangvereine im 19. und frühen 20. Jahrhundert: Ein Beitrag zur städtischen Musikgeschichte Münsters* (Frankfurt am Main: Peter Lang, 1992); John Daverio, "Einheit-Freiheit-Vaterland: Intimations of Utopia in Robert Schumann's Late Choral Music," in *Music and German National Identity*, Celia Applegate and Pamela Potter (eds.) (Cambridge, Mass.: Harvard University Press 2003), pp. 258–315; Applegate, *Bach in Berlin*, especially pp. 30–4.

encouraged export of the German repertory to Britain in the second half of the century.

4.2 *Abendunterhaltungen, Saal der nieder-österreichischen Landstände, 17 November 1825* [26]

Septet	Hummel
Aria, *Donna di Lago* (1819)	Rossini
Variations for guitar	
Male vocal quartet with piano, *Der Gondelfahrer*, D.809	Schubert
Introduction and Rondo for harp, horn and violins	Mayseder
Robbers' Chorus, with solo, *Almazinde* (1820)	Johann Peter Pixis

The string quartet thus mingled in the public marketplace with music of very different kinds, and Schubert scholars have made us aware of how vague social boundaries were between genres in that period.[27] Indeed, a title with the term *Unterhaltung* appeared not only for events given by Schuppanzigh's quartet but also by the Strauss-Kapelle and leading virtuosos. Admittedly, some essayists began to link the term with commercial entertainment in the 1820s, as research on Johann Strauss the Elder has shown.[28] Yet in both Leipzig and Vienna the term was used for quartet concerts through the 1860s, showing how gradually a linguistic differentiation between high and popular taste arrived in musical culture.[29] The word carried a more diverse set of connotations than "entertainment" does today, not necessarily implying a dichotomy between the light and the serious. Eduard Hanslick led the way in defining repertory in hierarchical terms. In his history of Viennese concert life, for example, he derided Böhm for the miscellany of his programs, declaring "How could one omit Mozart and not go beyond Beethoven's early works!"[30]

Schuppanzigh's concerts had direct influence on musical life in Berlin through Karl Möser, a member of his original quartet who took a position at

---

[26] PA/GMFV; *Franz Schubert: Dokumente, 1817–1830*, 2 vols., Till Gerrit Waidelich, Renate Hilmar-Voit, and Andreas Mayer (eds.) (Tutzing: Hans Schneider, 1993), vol. I, p. 255.

[27] *Cambridge Companion to Schubert*, especially chapters by Gibbs, Margaret Notley, and David Gramit.

[28] Norbert Linke, *Musik erobert die Welt; oder wie die Wiener Familie Strauss die 'Unterhaltungsmusik' revolutionirte* (Vienna: Herold, 1987).

[29] The term *Kammermusik* was used in Vienna in the 1810s but then dropped out of sight for a while. As late as 1868 a chamber music concert held at the Gewandhaus was called an *Abend-Unterhaltung für Kammermusik*, but in 1869 the program read *Erste Kammermusik*, Gewandhaus-Concerte, SBL.

[30] Hanslick, *Geschichte des Concertwesens in Wien*, p. 206.

the Prussian court. Möser directed a public concert series whose programs offered the usual mixture of opera overtures and excerpts, virtuoso pieces, symphonies, and sometimes quartets. Although he maintained such programs through the 1840s, he was giving chamber music programs following Schuppanzigh's model by 1830.[31] The change seems to have resulted from the "media campaign" mounted by A. B. Marx in the *Berliner allgemeine Musikzeitung*.[32] In 1832 a less dogmatic writer than Marx compared Möser's concerts with a less austere program given by a pair of visiting performers, outlining the dichotomy of taste between idealists and the general public:

Both concerts paid homage to the purer forms of art, in one way or another, for while Herr Möser selected quartets, quintets and symphonies from the classics, choosing among the higher forms of instrumental music, so the brothers [Adolf and Moritz] Ganz did the service of bringing the newest kinds of works before the public and in so doing helping ambitious young musicians to show their talents."[33]

The limited attention given to recent works at quartet concerts led musicians to put on programs devoted expressly to new works, a practice whose history we are tracing in this book. A series of four concerts given in Leipzig in 1847 included one program with pieces all by living composers: Mendelssohn's Quartet in E-flat, Onslow's Quintet in E, and a piano trio by Johann Ludwig Wolf. A reviewer dismissed Wolf's piece as "attractive and pleasing, but without any higher significance."[34] The demand that a piece must aspire to greatness grew out of idealistic aesthetics and the authority newly attributed to classics.

PARIS

The centrality of Schuppanzigh's "pure" concert format notwithstanding, it was in Paris where the longest lived series of quartet concerts was held before 1850. Pierre Baillot continued to lead concerts from 1814 until 1840, changing the programming only to a limited extent. It makes sense that similar quartet concerts appeared in Paris and Vienna, court cities that had a great deal in common socially and musically. Moreover, the most respected dynasty of violinists was based in Paris between 1770 and 1830 – Viotti, Baillot, Kreutzer, and Pierre Rode. Baillot's significance

[31] Mahling, "Zum 'Musikbetrieb' Berlins," pp. 40–2, 151.
[32] Applegate, *Bach in Berlin*, pp. 123, 159–74.
[33] "Nachrichten: Berlin," *AMZ*, 16 May 1832, p. 331.
[34] *AWMZ*, 7 December 1847, p. 580; ibid., 14 December 1847, p. 599; ibid., 21 December 1847, p. 611; ibid., 28 December 1847, p. 622. Johann Ludwig Wolf published a piano trio in 1840 that was played in Vienna in 1853; see *Quartett Hellmesberger*, p. 18.

in the history of chamber music concerts was thus comparable to that of Schuppanzigh.

Born in 1771, Baillot grew up within the learned nobility, the son of a lawyer for the Parlement of Paris; after the death of his father, he was raised by the titled governor of Corsica. Baillot studied the violin with noted teachers and traveled widely with the governor; after returning to Paris in 1794 he joined the faculty of the Conservatoire and expanded his contacts with aristocratic amateurs. A position in Napoleon's court took him to Moscow in 1805, where he put on sixteen *séances* of quartets and quintets for noble patrons.[35] Whereas members of the high aristocracy rarely attended public quartet concerts in Vienna after 1815, nobles such as the duc de Gramont (Antoine-Louis Marie de Gramont) and the duc de La Rochefoucauld (François Liancourt) continued to support Baillot's endeavor, from which he earned a substantial living.[36] Baillot brought together patrons from an interesting variety of social and political backgrounds under the July Monarchy (1830–1848). Though he originally was linked with Legitimists demanding return of the Bourbons, he also gained the patronage of Count Bondy (François-Marie Taillepied) and the Duke de Gramont, who moved in the world of high society; the Marquis de Louvois (Auguste-Marie Le Tellier de Souvre), who built mills and blast furnaces in the Yonne; and the banker André Leroux, who provided his grand *hôtel* in the 9th arrondissement for concerts.[37] The bourgeois and the aristocrat thus worked together to refashion the cultural life of Orleanist France. In his book on the nineteenth-century French nobility, David Higgs remarked that "Having realized that they could no longer aspire to be a ruling caste, nobles sought to permeate the new ruling body with their old ideas."[38] We might say that in musical life the nobility developed new tastes to bring back their old privileges.

Baillot's programs resembled those of Schuppanzigh in the complete absence of vocal music and in their focus upon works by Haydn, Mozart,

35 Charles Guynemer, *Essay on Chamber Classical Music* (London: The Author, 1846), p. 5; Fauquet, *Les sociétés de musique de chambre*, p. 20. See Anne Penesco, "Baillot et l'école franco-belge de violon," *Le Conservatoire de Paris, 1795–1995*, Anne Bongrain and Alain Poirier (eds.) (Paris: Buchet, 1999), pp. 91–100.

36 Fauquet, *Les sociétés de musique de chambre*, pp. 69–79.

37 Ibid., pp. 19, 48–9, 71; David Higgs, *Nobles in Nineteenth-Century France: The Practice of Inegalitarianism* (Baltimore, Md.: Johns Hopkins University Press, 1987), pp. 4, 11, 41, 17, 110, 120; Gustave Vapereau, *Dictionnaire universel des contemporains*, 2 vols., 2nd ed. (Paris: Hachette, 1861), vol. 1, p. 229; vol. 2, p. 1028.

38 Higgs, *Nobles in Nineteenth-Century France*, p. xiii. See also Leterrier, *Le mélomane et l'historien*, pp. 73–4.

and Beethoven. But Baillot adhered to older practices in programming more than did Schuppanzigh. His programs included five or six pieces rather than three or four, and the pieces came from a variety of countries. A program given in 1815 offered a pair of quintets by Boccherini before and after quartets by Haydn, Mozart, and Beethoven and ended with a piece of his own similar to what we saw Böhm perform – a set of variations on a folk air that he played with accompaniment by the rest of the quartet (Ex. 4.3). Baillot thus maintained the tradition of solo virtuosity in his concerts, as Schuppanzigh did not.

4.3 *"Séances Baillot," rue Bergère, no. 16, 6 March 1815*[39]

Quintet no. 2, op. 18, no. 4, G. 286 (2 cellos)	†Boccherini
Quartet in F Minor, op. 9, no. 4	†Haydn
Quartet in F, K.590	†Mozart
Quartet in D, op. 18, no. 3	Beethoven
Quintet no. 41, op. 46, no. 4, G. 362 (2 cellos)	†Boccherini
Air "Charmante Gabrielle" varié, op. 25	Baillot

Nevertheless, Baillot departed from local practices more noticeably than did Schuppanzigh. Parisian programs still tended to follow standard formats fairly strictly after the revolution, compared with the free-market-like experiments going on in London and Vienna. In fact, for some time Baillot limited the number of works led by the piano on his programs, because musical idealists thought the fast-selling instrument smacked of commercialism in the city that led the music business internationally. Putting on a concert without vocal music or the piano amounted to an even more drastic break with tradition in that context than it did in Vienna, and the quartet concerts were therefore unusually sequestered from the rest of the musical world. Baillot's series influenced German and English musicians significantly. Violinist Charles Guynemer, who left Paris for a career in London, expressed his debt to Baillot in his astute *Essay on Chamber Classical Music* (1846). John Ella, who led a major series of quartet concerts in London, got to know chamber music chiefly at Baillot's concerts.[40]

Practices became freer in Paris during the 1830s, when experimentation in the programming at benefit concerts (see Chapter 5) led a few musicians

---

[39] Fauquet, *Les sociétés de musique de chambre*, p. 295. See also Kerman, "Beethoven Quartet Audiences: Actual, Potential, Ideal."

[40] Guynemer, *Essay on Chamber Classical Music*; Christina Bashford, "The Late Beethoven Quartets and the London Press, 1836–ca. 1850," *Musical Quarterly* 84 (2000), 90–1; and "John Ella and the Making of the Musical Union," *Music and British Culture*, pp. 193–214.

to include quartets in miscellaneous programs. In 1831 a Munich quartet led by the violinist Anton Bohrer and his brother Max, a cellist, performed Beethoven's Quartet, op. 132 and a quartet Onslow dedicated to them, along with their own duo *fantaisie* and a popular selection from *Der Freischütz* (Ex. 4.4).

4.4 *Violinist Anton and Cellist Max Bohrer, 3 March 1831, Salons de Pape* [41]

Quartet no. 12, in E-flat, op. 23	Onslow
Piano Trio	†Beethoven
Quartet in A Minor, op. 132	†Beethoven
Duo-Fantaisie, violin and cello	A. & M. Bohrer
Adelaide, op. 46	†Beethoven
Prayer, *Der Freischütz*	†Weber

In 1844 the *Revue et Gazette musicale* went so far as to combine a Beethoven string quartet with the cavatina from Bellini's *Beatrice di tenda* (1833) and an *air* from Fromental Halévy's *Reine de Chypre* (1841).[42] Although this kind of programming did not continue in Paris, it demonstrates how much chamber music concerts had come into the public eye. The "cult" for "music classical and severe," as the reviewer of that 1844 concert put it, was no longer a sequestered cultural event. Parisian musicians ended up following Schuppanzigh more than Baillot in planning concerts and playing Beethoven rather than Boccherini. Beethoven's late quartets did not find as strong an audience in Paris as in Vienna or London, however. Alexandre Chevillard had limited success with his Society for the Last Quartets of Beethoven but led a series focused on Beethoven's early and middle works for many years.[43]

LEIPZIG

Leipzig lacked a courtly tradition of violin playing, and the Gewandhaus monopoly may have delayed formation of a chamber music series. But quartets were performed in private and at concerts by visiting ensembles. In 1832, for example, the four Müller brothers presented concerts at the Hôtel de Pologne as well as at the Gewandhaus, offering a program on

[41] Fauquet, *Les sociétés de musique de chambre*, p. 118.
[42] "Premier Concert de la *Gazette musicale,*" *RGM*, 29 December 1844, p. 435. Identified as "No. 9 en ut," the work was probably op. 9, no. 3, in C minor. See also discussion of Franz Liszt's concerts of 1837 that included Beethoven's piano trios in Chapter 5.
[43] Fauquet, *Les sociétés de musique de chambre*, pp. 80–145.

the Schuppanzigh model of pieces by Haydn, Mozart, and Beethoven.[44] Ferdinand David started a chamber series immediately after his appointment as concertmaster of the orchestra in 1836, applying his experience with performing quartets with Mendelssohn in Berlin. Because the subscription concerts still included many virtuoso pieces and opera excerpts, the quartet concerts acquired a special reputation as the meeting place for the city's most learned listeners. Their title, "Abendunterhaltung," was used to suggest a more intimate gathering than the subscription concerts.

The works played at Leipzig's quartet concerts tended to be more recent than those in Vienna or Paris, thanks to the presence of Mendelssohn and to the gradual shift to classics in the Gewandhaus series. The first concert led by David in 1836 followed tradition by offering a mixed program, including pieces from Mendelssohn's *Lieder ohne Worte* for piano. But the vocal numbers and instrumental solos soon fell by the wayside; in 1844, for example, a program offered just a quartet each by Haydn, Mozart, and Beethoven, the latter represented by Op. 127. Mendelssohn's works in a variety of genres became central to the repertory; one program offered a violin sonata and his Octet with a quartet by Mozart and a piano trio by Beethoven.[45] Pieces by Ignaz Moscheles became frequent at the Gewandhaus once he became professor at the Conservatorium in 1847. Works by young foreign composers also appeared on the programs – quintets by Niels Gade and Félicien David at a concert in 1845, for example. Yet this tendency did not persist long, for the programs had become severely canonic by the early 1860s.[46]

LONDON

London musicians departed the farthest from the Schuppanzigh format in designing chamber music concerts, and they opened up their concerts to the widest audience. Although the Beethoven Quartet Society followed Schuppanzigh's pure model, most other London concerts offered several instrumental solos, songs, or opera excerpts, usually by canonic composers, along with two or three quartets or quintets. Such programming was intended to draw listeners of diverse interests; as the program notes of the Musical Union stated in 1845, the pieces were "purposely selected to please

[44] Dörffel, *Geschichte der Gewandhausconcerte*, vol. 2, p. 209; Winter, "Performing the Beethoven Quartets in their First Century," *Beethoven Quartet Companion*, pp. 44–5.
[45] Abendunterhaltungen, 14 December 1844 and 18 November 1843, in Abonnenten-Concerte, 1842–48, SGML.
[46] Programme im Saale des Gewandhaus zu Leipzig, 1840–1881, SBL.

persons of various tastes."[47] Just as string quartets had appeared fairly often at London's subscription concerts in the 1780s (Ex. 2.4), so did the Philharmonic Society offer one or two on almost all programs in its first fifteen seasons. Haydn was represented as often as Beethoven thanks to his visits to the city, and a particular number of composers were represented – Viotti, Bernhard Romberg, Ignaz Pleyel, Frédéric Kalkbrenner, and Ferdinand Ries, for example.

But although the tradition of long, varied programs in London encouraged quartets to use diverse genres, the egalitarian political mood may also have given musicians the idea of opening up chamber music to a broad public socially. A significantly wider range of the middle classes went to quartet concerts than in any of the other cities. Violinist Henry Blagrove began organizing such events in 1835, calling his main series the "Quartett Concerts." Some ten ensembles gave performances over the next fifteen years, attracting audiences as large as 600 people.[48] The programs could be challenging, because all the ensembles took advantage of Beethoven's five late quartets, most often op. 127 and op. 130. A critic of the *Morning Chronicle* depicted the public as modest in status but lofty in taste, listeners who did not want "English ballads or the airs of the last new opera" and came from "the large and rapidly increasing body of amateurs, of both sexes, who are conversant with the higher branches of instrumental music"[49]

A program offered at the Quartett Concerts in 1841 typified these events, with two vocal pieces between two major works in each half (Ex. 4.5). The program illustrates how opera, salons, and quartet concerts could be linked in a serious miscellaneous concert. Weber had written the aria "Was sag' ich?" for insertion in a production of Cherubini's *Lodoïska* in Berlin, and Jacques Burgmüller, a founder of the Lower Rhine Festival in Düsseldorf, produced elegant songs for the salon that were often included in operas.[50] A trio by Henri Reber illustrates the many close links between French and British musical life. Visitors from Vienna must have been amazed to hear such music with string quartets.

47 "Synopsis Analytique," *Record of the Musical Union*, 24 June 1845, p. 2.
48 Christina Bashford, "The Late Beethoven Quartets and the London Press"; "John Ella and the Making of the Musical Union"; "Learning to Listen: Audiences for Chamber Music in Early Victorian London, *Journal of Victorian Culture*, 4 (2000), 25–51; "Public Chamber-Music Concerts in London, 1835–1850: Aspects of History, Repertory and Reception," 2 vols., unpublished Ph.D. thesis, King's College, University of London (1996); and *John Ella, Chamber Music, and Victorian London*, forthcoming.
49 Quoted in Bashford, "Public Chamber-Music Concerts in London," vol. 1, p. 45.
50 J. Palgrove Simpson, *Carl Maria von Weber: Life of an Artist*, 2 vols. (London, 1865), vol. 1, p. 401.

4.5 Quartett Concerts, Hanover Square Rooms, 25 February 1841[51]

Quartet in B-flat, op. 18, no. 6	†Beethoven
Aria, "Was sag' ich?" in Cherubini's *Lodoïska* (1816)	†Weber
Song, "O beauteous daughter of the starry races,"	
new words, *Sechs Lieder*, op. 48, no. 6	†Beethoven
Piano Trio in E-flat, op. 12	Reber

—

Quartet in C, op. 59 (1819)	†Andreas
	Romberg
Duet, "Ah, Perdona," *La Clemenza di Tito* (1791)	†Mozart
Spanish Serenade, *Chi godere* (1840)	Burgmüller
Quintet for strings, K. 516 (1787)	†Mozart

Few nobles went to the Philharmonic Society, or attended the Quartett Concerts, but a remarkable number went to the Musical Union, an entrepreneurial chamber music series run by John Ella from 1845 to 1888. Taking advantage of the decline of the Concert of Ancient Music, Ella used his wide social network to attract the most prestigious audience in London concert life.[52] He normally combined two quartets or quintets with several songs or virtuoso solos, often by star performers. In 1847, for example, the fashionable young violinist Henry Vieuxtemps not only led quartets by Mozart and Beethoven but also played a *boléro* by Auguste-Joseph Franchomme and a *morceau de salon* of his own. Ella knew how to please his public. A critic admitted that "we can pardon Mr. Ella the anomaly of solos at classical quartet meetings, when the solos in question are [performed with] such unexceptionable specimens of taste and skill as these."[53] Yet Ella also occasionally deferred to the Viennese model by offering programs of three major chamber works.

London's most learned chamber music series, the Beethoven Quartet Society, almost always followed Schuppanzigh's model of programming. The Society was founded in 1845 under the leadership of Thomas Alsager, a part-owner of *The Times*, who invited fifty high-level amateurs and professionals to concerts at his house on Harley Street. London's musical intelligentsia often gathered at these concerts, the Earl of Falmouth becoming

[51] Chamber-Music Concerts, RCM/CHP.
[52] Bashford, "John Ella and the Making of the Musical Union"; Weber, *Music and the Middle Class*, pp. 61, 64, 71–6, 85 113, 141.
[53] *MW*, 22 May 1847, p. 336.

the organization's first president.[54] The Society acquired a lofty reputation throughout Europe; the *Neue Zeitschrift für Musik* was awed by the "careful study" of Beethoven's late quartets found at the concerts.[55] Indeed, the programs might include a piece from each of Beethoven's style periods, a scheme probably influenced by writings of Fétis and Anton Schindler published in 1839 and 1841.[56] The programs included extensive notes, one of the earliest examples of the practice, introducing a pedagogical goal that went contrary to the tradition of informal learning in concert life. A program in 1846 (Ill. 9) was designed to illustrate the evolution of the string quartet in works by Haydn (seemingly op. 20, no. 2, and op. 76, no. 4), Mozart (in D Minor, probably K.421), and Beethoven (op. 131). The young violinist Charles Lucas offered equally strict programs in a series of Musical Evenings at his home in the West End for several seasons.[57]

Virtuosos and string quartets joined forces much more extensively in London than anywhere else. Pianist Louise Dulcken, who gave some of the splashiest benefit concerts in the city (Ill. 4), blended the repertories of quartet and virtuoso concerts with great skill in *soirées musicales* at her home. In one instance she combined quartets by Haydn and Onslow, familiar arias by Mozart, a tarantella by Chopin, and a dashing fantasia on Swedish national airs by Ferdinand Ries. Thus did Dulcken expose how the supposedly austere string quartet could fit nicely with fashionable virtuosity and the growing fascination with Chopin. Composers likewise used the growing interest in chamber music to their advantage. In 1844, for example, George Macfarren, whose overture *Chevy Chase* (1837) had just been performed by the Gewandaus orchestra, put on a concert of his own songs and those of the critic Davison, framed by chamber works of Mendelssohn.[58] Indeed, British song remained integral to chamber music programs for the rest of the century.

Moreover, an unusual amount of recent music appeared in London's quartet concerts, thanks to their mixed format. Christina Bashford's comprehensive study of chamber music concerts between 1835 and 1850 indicates that composers other than the musical trinity represented well over half of the pieces performed at all events in that period, and most of those

---

[54] Guynemer, *Essay on Chamber Classical Music*, pp. 11, 13; Christine Bashford, "The Late Beethoven Quartets," pp. 90–1.
[55] Quoted in Winter, "The Quartets in Their First Century," *Beethoven Quartet Companion*, pp. 53–4.
[56] Bashford, "The Late Beethoven Quartets," p. 89.
[57] Chamber-Music Concerts, CHP/RCM. [58] Ibid.

pieces were by living composers.[59] Music by Mendelssohn ended up second only to Beethoven (192 pieces versus 271), considerably more than was performed in comparable concerts in Leipzig. As with the Philharmonic concerts, pieces by British composers amounted to around twelve percent of the total repertory, primarily by William Sterndale Bennett, George Macfarren, and George Osborne. Bennett ranked sixth among all composers in chamber music programs given between 1845 and 1850, his forty-three pieces outnumbering Bach's thirty-seven and Handel's twenty.[60] Although represented chiefly by songs, British composers at least had a foothold in the most learned area of musical life.

The origin of the most common type of "new music" concert can be seen in chamber music concerts before 1850, because a "mixed" chamber music program has served as the principal format for such events ever since that time. As composers found it increasingly difficult to place works with orchestras – not to speak of opera companies – they began organizing programs for voice, solo instruments, and small ensembles in order to showcase their works. Early attempts at a new music concert would often include a piece or two by canonic composers, either foreign or domestic. In 1843, for example, the Society of British Musicians offered five British works and ended with well-known pieces by Spohr and Beethoven (Ex. 4.6). Henry Smart, then thirty years old, would see his songs performed widely throughout the century; Frederick Jewson became a prominent professor at the Royal Academy of Music. The British canon was represented only by Callcott's ballad, interestingly enough. Founded in 1834, the Society was the first organization ideologically defined to promote a nation's music. Comparable organizations arose in the Allgemeine Deutsche Musikverein (1861) and the Société Nationale de Musique (1871). The Society grew out of the late-eighteenth-century movement for the support of British composers active in the Vocal Concerts in the 1790s and British Concerts held from 1823. Although it originally offered orchestral pieces, first heard in "trials" as at the Philharmonic Society, financial exigencies led the officers to shift to chamber concerts in the early 1840s.[61] At that time British composers were finding themselves deeply affected by changes in aesthetic expectations brought by Romanticism and musical idealism. The glee was falling out of favor because sociability and high-level composition

[59] Bashford, "Public Chamber-Music Concerts in London, 1835–1850," vol 2, pp. 231–2.
[60] Ibid., p. 232; Nicholas Temperley, "Zenophilia in British Musical History," *Nineteenth-Century British Music Studies* (Aldershot, UK: Ashgate, 1999), vol. 1, pp. 3–29.
[61] Simon McVeigh, "The Society of British Musicians (1834–1865), and the Campaign for Native Talent," in *Music and British Culture*, pp. 145–68, a key discussion of the evolution of British music.

ceased to seem compatible professionally. Although glees and other songs were still performed, indeed composed, for the rest of the century, a serious composer was now asked to focus on "serious" instrumental works.

4.6 Society of British Musicians, Erap's Harp Rooms, 20 January 1843 [62]

Trio in G Minor, violin, cello & piano	George Lambert
Ballad, "They Told me her Heart"	†Callcott
Septet in E-flat (fl, ob, hn, 2 cl, 2 bn)	Lucas
Song	Henry Smart
Trio in F, violin, cello, piano	Jewson
Song, from *Sechs deutsche Lieder*, op. 25	Spohr
Septet in E-flat	†Beethoven

Chamber music concerts in Boston closely resembled those in Britain. For example, in 1848 the Brighton Musical Union offered a cello solo performed by Alfredo Piatti and Weber's *Concert-Stück* along with Beethoven's Quartet, op. 18, no. 1, and a quintet by Onslow.[63] On other occasions, of course, the Brighton musicians followed the pure format of quartet concerts. The Harvard Musical Association of Boston offered a similar contrast in programs when it offered the city's first chamber music concerts in 1844. Whereas one program combined Beethoven's Piano Trio in E-flat, op. 1, no. 1, with quartets by Mozart and Haydn, another in the series included a polonaise by Herz and a violin solo (*La Mélancholie*) by Canadian François Prume, with a Mozart quartet in D minor and Beethoven's Piano Trio in C Minor.[64] By the early 1850s American-born musicians were being educated abroad, in Leipzig and Weimar most of all, along with musicians from many countries. A product of such a visit can be seen in a program that pianist William Mason (1829–1908) presented in 1855 with players of the Mendelssohn Quintette Club (Ill. 10). Having met Brahms in Weimar, Mason stayed in touch with the German musical scene. Whereas the ensemble performed works by Mozart and Beethoven, he led Brahms's Piano Trio in B, Op. 8, two months after its première in Danzig and played an impromptu and a *Valse de Salon* of his own composition.[65] Though a permanent orchestral series had not been established in Boston, a classical music scene was alive and well in the New World city.

---

[62] Chamber-Music Concerts, CHP/RCM.   [63] Provincial Concerts, BLO/JJ.

[64] Program collection, HMLA.

[65] Program Collection, BPL; William Mason, *Memories of a Musical Life* (New York: Century, 1901), pp. 127–8; Broyles, *"Music of the Highest Class,"* pp. 28–31, 88, 261–4.

STRING QUARTETS ON THEIR OWN

String quartets came into public prominence by stages. First they accompanied singers and participated in mixed programs, then performed with high-ranking amateurs in private, and finally initiated a major new kind of public concert. We today have a hard time realizing how drastic an innovation such concerts were in their early period. Quartet concerts stood apart from the mainstream of musical life for several decades while setting a new standard for high-level music-making. Schuppanzigh, Baillot, and their successors should be credited with imaginative and determined leadership. Their events greatly influenced later innovations in concert design. As musical life broke up into separate spheres in the 1850s, the idealism inherent in the quartet concert served as a model for the solo recital and for the New Music concert, and indeed for programming as a whole. The quartet concert created a practical and welcoming context where music-making that did not command a large public could be appreciated in its own terms.

CHAPTER 5

Convention and experiment in benefit and virtuoso concerts

The traditional benefit concert underwent deep change and fragmentation between 1815 and 1848. The traveling virtuoso and the local performer usually organized more or less the same kinds of events for their personal profit or loss. Both types of musicians made experiments in program design that ended up reshaping conventional practices or abandoning them altogether. The alternation of vocal and instrumental pieces and the balancing of genres began to give way to more homogeneous programming. Some concerts were devoted chiefly to ballads, opera selections, classical works, or a composer's own music, and a few pianists performed entirely alone. A program might manifest an identity of serious or light taste, reflecting the tension between idealism and commercialism. Yet traditional formats still predominated for the most part in the "flood" of concerts, as journalists liked to call it. By the mid-1840s opinion in many quarters turned against the virtuoso program of *fantaisies* and selections from recent operas, finding the music poorly crafted and overly commercialized. An angry disillusionment set in, a sense that self-serving musicians had lost the public's trust. In this chapter we will first sketch out basic program formats and then explore the experiments that eventually broke up this area of concert life into separate musical spheres.

The collegiality of the traditional benefit concert weakened as institutional monopolies gave way to something of a free-market condition almost everywhere in Europe during the 1830s. Grand opera, virtuoso concerts, and the printed media worked closely together to exploit the public's thirst for cultural stimulation, making this kind of capitalism no longer "petty." Periodicals followed performances by Thalberg, Liszt, and Jenny Lind just as closely as they did the premières of Bellini's *Norma* or Meyerbeer's *Le Prophète*. However widely Beethoven's fame spread after his death, his symphonies became much less widely known than melodies of those two operas and the *fantaisies* written on them. Nicolò Paganini and Franz Liszt used concert tours to build personal capital, and local musicians required the families they served to buy tickets to their annual concerts. Musical commercialism influenced the music itself. The competitiveness essential to the virtuoso was "performative" in nature, intensifying the theatricality of virtuoso showmanship.[1] Distaste for the "flood" aside, concert-goers were intrigued by the competitive process among virtuosos that magazines narrated in reports from large and small towns all across Europe and North America.

The fragmentation of concert life was related to deep, long-term changes in the social structure of elites in the major cities of Europe. The unity and the influence of the older *beau monde* as a functioning group began to decline as urban populations grew, the numbers of people in the upper classes increasing too much for them to function as a community. There were simply too many people one ought to know and to gossip about. The explosion of periodicals and the opening-up of politics to a wider public weakened the ability of elite social networks to control urban culture. The formerly tightly bound upper-class world became increasingly subdivided as to taste for different kinds of entertainment. Moreover, as social disturbances became more common throughout Europe, some members of the elites began trying to retreat from public into private contexts. Thus a concert series requiring payment for a subscription was called "private" in such cities as Birmingham, Bremen, and Berlin, differentiating it from benefit concerts open to any paying customer. For that matter, the initial announcement of the Viennese Evening Entertainments assured listeners that only members of the "educated classes" would be admitted to its events.[2]

Virtuoso concerts differed to a certain extent in the key four cities under study. Paris was the most important city for virtuoso performance due to the presence of the main piano and publishing firms, but programming moved slowly away from traditional models, and classical works were infrequent. Vienna rivaled Paris as a center of virtuoso playing, its programs achieving an influential compromise between virtuosity and idealistic values. London's virtuoso concerts were important as well, for the solo recital originated there, and classical works became unusually common at benefit concerts. Although Leipzig lacked a court-based virtuoso tradition,

[1] On commercialism, see Cormac Newark, "Metaphors for Meyerbeer," *JRMA* 127 (2002), 33–42, and Heinrich W. Schwab, "Kopenhagen als Reiseziel ausländischer Virtuosen," *Le musicien et ses voyages*, pp. 143–67.
[2] Programs, BCL and FUSB; *Kurze Nachtricht über Zweck und Verfassung der Anstalt der wochentlichen musikalischen Abend-Unterhaltungen* (Vienna: Anton Strauss, 1818), pp. 12–13.

the leadership of Robert and Clara Schumann and Ferdinand David stimulated widespread performance of classics in the 1840s.

The main change in virtuoso and benefit concerts from the 1810s onward was the overriding focus on opera. Not only were opera selections still a necessary component of every benefit concert, but also the *fantaisie* on music from an opera emerged as the main virtuoso genre at such events. If Paganini played one in a Viennese concert in 1828 (Ill. 3), Thalberg focused his repertory on them in 1836 (Ex. 5.3). Virtuosos avoided the public's distaste for abstraction by drawing on what listeners had seen on stage to present brilliant new sonic pictures. Music performed at benefit concerts was chiefly what can be called the *performer's* as opposed to the *composer's* music. Players focused on the performative process – the *fantaisie*, variations, transcription, and improvisation – and pianists were accustomed to "preluding," making an ad hoc introduction to a piece.[3] Singers adapted pieces freely, too, stating on a program that a well-known aria would be done "with variations," an extended process of ornamentation.[4] Virtuoso compositions were so far from being fixed that periodicals, programs still less, rarely indicated the first performance of a piece, even for so major a figure as Liszt.[5] For the same reason, music in abstract genres – Beethoven's sonatas or Schumann's experimental pieces of the 1830s – was not thought appropriate for the public concert until at least the 1840s.

A canonic repertory of opera overtures and vocal selections took root all across Europe during the first half of the nineteenth century. A few works by Cimarosa, Mozart, Rossini, and Weber were still put on stage by the 1840s with extensive adaptation, but excerpts represented a far wider range of works.[6] By then selections from operas by Italian, German, Austrian, and French composers remained in use on a long-term basis throughout Europe.

[3] David Ferris, "Public Performance and Private Understanding: Clara Wieck's Concerts in Berlin," *JAMS* 2 (2003), 354–55; Kenneth Hamilton, *After the Golden Age: The Decline of Romantic Pianism and the Dawn of Modern Performance* (Oxford: Oxford University Press, forthcoming), Ch. 4, "A Suitable Prelude."

[4] For example, Mme. Dorus-Gras sang an air from Auber's *Sirène* "with variations" at the 1844 "monster concert" (Queen's Theatre Concert Hall, CPH/RCM). Mme Margareta Stockhausen (mother of Julius) sang a Spanish song "with Variations" at the same venue on 9 June 1835. A concert held at the Gewandhaus on 17 December 1821 included Catharina Canzi singing Peter von Winter's "Mich fliehen alle Freuden," from his opera *Die schöne Müllerin*, "mit Variationen" (Leipziger Concert-Programme 1820–24, SGML). See Valerie Woodring Goertzen, "By Way of Introduction: Preluding by Eighteenth- and Early Nineteenth-Century Pianists," *Journal of Musicology* 4 (1996), 299–337.

[5] Geraldine Keeling, "Concert Announcements, Programs and Reviews as Evidence for First or Early Performances by Liszt of his Keyboard Works to 1847," *Studia Musicologica Academiae Scientiarum Hungaricae* 34 (1992), 397–404.

[6] On Parisian productions, see Mark Everist's detailed discussion in *Music Drama at the Paris Odéon, 1824–1828* (Berkeley: University of California Press, 2002).

The earliest cohort of favored opera composers included Hasse (b. 1699), Pergolesi (1710), and Gluck (1714), followed by Sarti (1729) and Sacchini (1730), but the largest group was born around midcentury: Paisiello (1740), André-Ernest Grétry (1741), Jean-Paul-Édige Martini (1741), Cimarosa (1749), Niccolò Zingarelli (1749), Antonio Salieri (1750), Martin y Soler (1754), Mozart (1756), Cherubini (1760), and Méhul (1763). Names not familiar today were common for much of the nineteenth century: Ferdinando Paër (b. 1771), Pietro Carlo Guglielmi (1772), Nicolas Isouard (aka Nicolo, 1773), Gaspare Spontini (1774), D.-F.-E. Auber (1782), and Ferdinand Hérold (1791). Pieces by Weber (b. 1786) and Rossini (1792) dominated concert programs to a particular extent.[7]

Opera overtures and selections acquired multiple canonic identities in contrasting musical contexts. Pieces from the best known operas – Mozart's *Don Giovanni*, Weber's *Der Freischütz*, and Auber's *La Muette de Portici*, for example – were performed in band concerts, street ensembles, and eventually music halls and *cafés-concerts*; as such they became known by virtually the entire society. Benefit concerts and orchestral series offered pieces from many of the same works, chiefly by Paisiello, Cimarosa, and Mozart. Most people probably associated the pieces chiefly with the theatre or with benefit concerts rather than with classical music orchestral series, where the pieces acquired a more explicitly historical identity. Moreover, the piano-vocal scores published for every major work brought a "republicanization" of opera, its possession by the public as a whole rather than by the elite audience that governed its original performance.[8]

An opera selection possessed a cosmopolitan as well as a national identity. Weber's opera style has been interpreted in such a light, as music that evoked contrasting national traits within an essentially cosmopolitan style.[9] Mozart's music behaved like a chameleon in taking on diverse national identities. Although listeners at an orchestral concert identified his symphonies as German music along with that of Beethoven, people at a benefit concert would associate excerpts from his operas with Italian opera repertory, works by Cimarosa and Paisiello most of all. In London *Die Zauberflöte* was often performed as *Il flauto magico*, and excerpts were incorporated into

[7] For perspective on these figures, see David Kimbell, *Italian Opera* (Cambridge: Cambridge University Press, 1991) and Albert Cler, *Physiologie du musicien* (Paris: Aubert, 1843), pp. 88–95.
[8] Thomas Christensen, "Public Music in Private Spaces: Piano-Vocal Scores and the Domestification of Opera," in *Music and the Cultures of Print*, Kate van Orden (ed.) (New York: Garland, 2000), pp. 67–94.
[9] Michael Tusa, "Cosmopolitanism and National Opera: The Case of Weber's *Der Freischütz*," *Journal of Interdisciplinary History*, 36 (2006), 483–506.

Concert
des
Herrn Campagnoli.

Im Saale des Gewandhauses.
Donnerstags, den 29 December, 1785.

Erster Theil.

Sinfonie.
Scene, von Paisiello. (Madem. Balthasarin.)

Dove, ahi, dove son io?
Misero padre! Agli adorati congedi
Chi restàr potrà? Queste, ch'io sento
Mormorarmi d'intorno aure funeste,
Aure sono di morte. Ah, che fù mai
Di me, de'regni miei, di te, cor mio,
Che fra gli affetti miei fei l'affetto primiero?
Inumano Alessandro! è questo un pegno
Della clemenza tua? barbaro! Jo chiamo
Tutti i Numi a vendetta. Amico,
In questo funesturio momento
Alla rea cura affido
I miei tuneri pegni, e l'onor mio.
Patria, Figli, Consorte, io parto, addio!

Mentre ti lascio, oh figlia!
In sen mi trema il core.
Già, che parvenza amara!
Provo nel mio dolore
Le tsanie ed il terror.

Parto, tu piangi, oh Dio!
Ti chiedo un sol momento;
Oh Dio, che fier tormento!
Ah, mi si spezza il cor.

Concert auf der Violine. (Herr Campagnoli)
Arie aus Creso, von Sacchini.

Quest' alma innamorata
Vacilla in mille affanni:
E'lo (germana ingrata)
Che palpitar mi fà.

Zweyter Theil.

Sinfonie.
Arie aus Sinfonie, mit concertirender Violine und Flöte, von Naumann.

Seit du sanft, sicher ich mein Leben,
Wollte ich dir mein ganzes Herz;
Ganz bleib ich dir ergeben:
Götterfreuden sind kein Schmerz.

Menschenwohl ist dein Vertrauen;
Alles zauchzt dir frohen Dank,
Liebe schwebt auf deinem Lauter;
Herzen schmiegen, sie verschönen
Kann dein mächtiger Gesang.

Concert auf der Violine. (Fr. Campagnoli)
Sinfonie.

Der Anfang ist um Fünf Uhr.

Endliche Billets sind bey dem Billetverkäuffer Meyer und am Eingange des Saals zu 16 Groschen zu haben.

Illustration 1. Concert of Bartolomeo Campagnoli, Gewandhaus, Leipzig, 29 December 1785: Stadtgeschichtliches Museum, Leipzig.

Great Room, King's-Theatre,
HAY-MARKET.

..

Mr. DRAGONETTI'S
BENEFIT.

..

On MONDAY, APRIL 20th, 1801.

Will be performed,

A CONCERT
OF

VOCAL and Instrumental MUSIC.

PART I.

OVERTURE	Mozart.
Duetto—Meffrs. VIGANONI and ROVEDINO	Mozart.
Chorus	Mozart.
Aria	Madame Duffek.
Concerto Fiano-Forte	Mr. Field.
Duetto—Meffrs. VIGANONI and CIMADOR	Mozart.
Favorite Air, " Now vanifh before thy holy beams," and Chorus from Creation	Haydn.

PART II.

SYMPHONY (M.S.)	Haydn.
Trio—Madame DUSSEK, Signora ROVEDINO, and CIMADOR	Mozart.
The favorite Air in Alzira -	Madame Banti.
Accompanied by Meffrs. Leanders	Bianchi.
Concerto - - - -	Mr. Dragonetti

Marcello's celebrated Duetto, by Meffrs. VIGANONI and CIMADOR.
Grand Chorus, " *The Heavens are telling the Glory of God,*" from Creation—*Haydn*

To begin precisely at Eight o'Clock.

TICKETS to be had of Mr. DRAGONETTI, No. 6, Sherrard-Street, Golden-Square; Meffrs. BRODERI and WILKINSON's Mufic Warehoufe, No. 13, Hay-Market; CLEMENTI and Co's. do. No. 26, Cheapfide and at the Office of the Theatre.

W. GLINDON, Printer, No 48, RUPERT-STREET, Coventry-Street.

Illustration 2. Concert of Domenico Dragonetti, King's Theatre, London, 20 April 1801: Centre for Performance History, Royal College of Music.

27. Junŋ 1628.

K. K. Hoftheater nächst dem Kärnthnerthore.

Mit hoher Bewilligung wird

Herr

NICOLO PAGANINI,

Kammer-Virtuos Sr. Majestät des Kaisers von Oesterreich,
ein

Concert

zu geben die Ehre haben.

Vorkommende Stücke

1) Ouverture aus der Oper: Faniska, von Cherubini.
2) Concert für die Violine, von Rode, bestehend aus einem Allegro maestoso, (Adagio religioso in Doppelgriffen von Paganini), und einer Polacca, vorgetragen vom Concertgeber.
3) Neue Arie von Balducci, (Gli affanni tuoi cor mio), gesungen von Sigra. BIANCHI.
4) Ouverture aus der Oper: Die Blinden von Toledo, von Mehul.
5) Capriccio über das Thema: Là ci darem la mano, aus der Oper: Don Juan, von Mozart, und andere Variationen, componirt und vorgetragen vom Concertgeber.
6) Ouverture aus der Oper: Semiramis, von Catel.
7) Arie (Due vite a me sì caro), von Pavesi, gesungen von Sigra. BIANCHI.
8) Neueste Composition von Paganini, bestehend aus einer maestosa Sonata sentimentale mit Variationen, über das Thema von J. Haydn: Gott erhalte Franz den Kaiser, mit Begleitung des Orchesters, auf der G-Saite allein vorgetragen vom Concertgeber.

Eintrittspreise in Conventions-Münze:

Eine Loge zu ebener Erde, im 1. u. 2. Stock	14 fl.	Ein gesperrter Sitz im vierten Stock . . . 2 fl. 30 kr.
Eine Loge im dritten Stock	8 fl.	Eintritt in das Parterre oder die Gallerie 1 fl. 30 kr.
Ein gesperrter Sitz im ersten Parterre oder Gallerie	2 fl.	— in den vierten Stock . . . 48 kr.
		— in den fünften Stock . . . 30 kr.

Die Logen und gesperrten Sitze sind Vor- und Nachmittags zu den gewöhnlichen Amtsstunden der Stadt im Steinmetzischen Hause Nr. 1032, zu ebener Erde, nächst dem Eingange in das Kärnthnerthortheater, zu haben.

Der Anfang ist um 7 Uhr.

Illustration 3. Concert of Nicolò Paganini, Hoftheater, Vienna, 27 June 1828: Archiv der Gesellschaft der Musikfreunde in Wien.

GREAT CONCERT ROOM,

HER MAJESTY'S THEATRE.

PROGRAMME
OF
MADAME DULCKEN'S
(PIANISTE TO HER MAJESTY THE QUEEN)
ANNUAL GRAND MORNING CONCERT,
MONDAY, MAY 31, 1841,
TO COMMENCE AT TWO O'CLOCK PRECISELY.

PART I.

TERZETTO, Signori TAMBURINI, F. LABLACHE, and LABLACHE,
"Pensa e guarda." .... *Meyerbeer.*
ARIA, Madame PERSIANI, "Come provar.". .... *Pacini.*
DUETTO, Mlle. LOEWE and Signor TAMBURINI, "Dunque io son."
(*Il Barbiere di Seviglia.*) .... *Rossini.*
ARIA, Signor RUBINI, "Fra nembi crudeli." ......(*I Briganti.*) ......*Mercadante.*
(Corno Obligato, Signor PUZZI.)
GRAND FANTASIA, Pianoforte, Madame DULCKEN.
(*La Donna del Lago.*) .... *Thalberg.*
ARIA, Madame G. GRISI, "Come è bello." ......(*Lucrezia Borgia.*) .....*Donizetti.*
FANTASIA, Violin, on a Theme by *Schubert,* Herr DAVID ....*David.*
GRAND AIR, Madame DORUS GRAS ...... (*Le Cheval de Bronze.*) ......*Auber.*
BALLAD, Mlle. MEERTI, "Ave Maria." ....*Schubert.*
FANTASIA, Harp, Mons. GODEFROID, ... *Godefroid.*
GRAND DUETTO, Mesdames PERSIANI and VIARDOT GARCIA,
"Lasciami, non t'ascolto." ....(*Tancredi.*) ....*Rossini.*
ROMANZA, Signor MARIO, "Tristo e fuor d'ogni speranza." .... *Schira.*
(Corno Obligato, Signor PUZZI.)
GRAND DUET, for Two Pianofortes (first time of performance),
Madame DULCKEN and Mr. LISZT .... (*Hexameron.*) ....*Liszt.*

PART II.

PREGHIERA, "Dal tuo stellato soglio," Mesdames G. GRISI, PERSIANI,
VIARDOT GARCIA, DORUS GRAS, and SCHRŒDER DEVRIENT;
Mlles. LOEWE, and MEERTI; Sig. RUBINI, MARIO, TAMBURINI,
LABLACHE, F. LABLACHE, and Mr. J. PARRY. Pianoforte, Madame
DULCKEN, Messrs. LISZT and BENEDICT; Harp, M. GODEFROID;
Violin, Herr DAVID; French Horn, Signor PUZZI.
(*Il Mosè in Egitto.*) .... *Rossini.*
RONDO FINALE, Madame VIARDOT GARCIA........(*Nina.*) ....*Coppola.*
GRAND ARIA, Mlle. LOEWE. Violin Obligato, Herr-DAVID.
(*Le Pré aux Clercs*—first time of performance.).......................*Herold.*
TRIO, Mesdames GRISI, PERSIANI, and VIARDOT GARCIA,
"Le faccio un inchino." ....(*Il Matrimonio Segreto.*)..........*Cimarosa.*
DUETTO BUFFO, Madame DORUS GRAS and Signor LABLACHE,
"Son qual tenero agnelletto." ....*Mosca.*
DUO CONCERTANTE, on Themes of *Oberon,* Pianoforte and Violin,
Madame DULCKEN and Herr DAVID .... *Benedict and David.*
DUETTO, Madame GRISI and Signor RUBINI, "Va menzogner."
(*Gli Arabi.*)...*Paccini.*
A FAVORITE ENGLISH SONG, Mr. JOHN PARRY, "Singing Lesson." *J. Parry.*
DUETTO BUFFO, Signori LABLACHE and F. LABLACHE (by desire),
"Se fiato in corpo avete." ....(*Il Matrimonio Segreto.*) ....*Cimarosa.*
FINALE, "Ridiamo, cantiamo." ....*Rossini.*

Illustration 4. Concert of Louise Dulcken, Concert Room, King's Theatre, London, 31 May
1841: Centre for Performance History, Royal College of Music.

ASSEMBLY ROOMS, STAMFORD.

GRAND
MORNING CONCERT,

On Wednesday, Sept. 16, 1840,

To commence at 1 o'clock precisely.

M. LISZT,

First appearance this Season of this Extraordinary Pianist.

Mr. LAVENU, has the honor to inform the Nobility, Gentry and his Friends, that he has succeeded in engaging

M. LISZT

Who will, on this occasion, perform his Grand Marche Hongroise, and his Grand Galop Chromatique; also a Grand Duet with

Mr. MORI.

Mr. RICHARDSON,

(The celebrated Flutist) will perform some of his most favorite Fantasias.

Mlle. DE VARNY,

Prima Donna of La Scala, Italian, Opera, Paris, and Her Majesty's Theatre, London, will sing some of her most popular Arias and Duet.

Miss LOUISA BASSANO

Of the Nobility's Concerts, will sing some of her admired Airs & Ballads

Mr. J. PARRY,

Will sing some of his latest and most desired Compositions.

Mr. LAVENU,

will preside at the Piano Forte.

Family Tickets, to admit four, 21s.—Single Tickets 5s. to be had of Messrs. ROSE, MORTLOCK & JOHNSON.

PART 1.

TRIO—"L'usato ardir il mio," (Semiramide) Mlle. De Varny, Miss Bassano and Mr. J. Parry....Rossini.

ARIA—"Alfin son tua," (Lucia di Lammermoor) Miss Bassano....Donizetti.

MARCHE HONGROISE—Grand Piano Forte—M. LISZT....Liszt.

DUETTO—"Suppi che un rio dovere," (Bianca e Faliero) Mlle. De Varny and Miss Bassano....Rossini.

BALLAD—"The Inchcape Bell," Mr. J. Parry....Parry.

FANTASIA—Flute—Mr. Richardson.

ARIA—"L'Amor suo mi fa beato," (Roberto Devereux) Mlle. De Varny....Donizetti.

FANTASIA ON FAVORITE AIRS—M. LISZT....Liszt.
Grand Piano Forte—M. LISZT

LYRIC LEGEND—"Edinburgh to Eskdale," Miss Bassano....Wade.

Mr. J. Parry will sing his new Song of "The Musical Husband."

PART 2.

DUETTO—"Colei Sofronio," (Torquato Tasso) Mlle. De Varny and Mr. J. Parry....Donizetti.

BALLAD—"Memory's Dream," Miss Bassano....Lavenu.

GRAND DUETT—Piano forte—Introducing the favorite QUARTETT from Lucia di Lammermoor, and GRAND GALOP CHROMATIQUE, Messrs. LISZT and MORI....Liszt.

ROMANCE—"I'm with thee," Mlle. De Varny....Wade.

VARIATIONS—Flute—Mr. Richardson.

NEW DUETT—"The Sisters," Mlle. De Varny and Miss Bassano.

MORCEAUX CHOISIS—from his celebrated Recital, Piano Forte, M. LISZT....Liszt.

SONG—"Wanted a Governess," Mr. J. Parry....Parry.

TRIO—"Soave sia il vento," Mlle. De Varny, Miss Bassano and Mr. J. Parry....Mozart.

Conductor, Mr. LAVENU.

The Piano Forte is one of Erard's new patent, and is brought expressly from London for the occasion.

Illustration 5. Concert of Franz Liszt, Assembly Rooms, Stamford (UK), 16 September 1840: Centre for Performance History, Royal College of Music.

Zweites
CONCERT

von

Franz
Liszt

Donnerstag den 5. März 1846,

Mittags um halb 1 Uhr,

im Saale der Gesellschaft der Musikfreunde.

Programm.

1. **Ouverture** aus Wilhelm Tell, arrangirt von Liszt

2. a) **Le Lac de Wallenstadt.**) Aus dem Album d'un
   b) **Au bord d'une source.**) voyageur.

3. **Fantasie in C,** von Fr. Schubert,

4. **Zwei Etuden** von Chopin,

5. **Fantasie** aus Norma, von Liszt

gespielt
von
LISZT.

Illustration 6. Concert of Franz Liszt, Vienna, Saal der Gesellschaft der Musikfreunde, Vienna, 5 March 1846: Archiv der Gesellschaft der Musikfreunde in Wien.

SALONS ÉRARD, 13, RUE DU MAIL

Samedi 29 Mars, à huit heures et demie précises

2ᵐᵉ CONCERT

DE MADAME

CLARA SCHUMANN

PROGRAMME

1° **Sonate** en *la mineur*, pour piano et violon . . . . R. SCHUMANN.
Mᵐᵉ CLARA SCHUMANN et M. ARMINGAUD.

2° Air de **Jules César**. . . . . HAENDEL.
Mˡˡᵉ ORWIL.

3° A **Andante et presto**. . . . . D. SCARLATTI.
B **Sarabande et gavotte** . . . . J-S. BACH.
Mᵐᵉ C. SCHUMANN.

4° **Le Roi des Aulnes** . . . . SCHUBERT.
M. MARCHESI.

5° **Sonate** en *ut majeur* (op. 53) . . . . BEETHOVEN.
A Allegro.
B Adagio.
C Rondo.
Mᵐᵉ C. SCHUMANN.

6° **Adélaïde**. . . . . BEETHOVEN.
Mˡˡᵉ ORWIL.

7° **Carnaval**. (Les masques.) Scènes mignonnes. (Op. 9) . . . . . R. SCHUMANN.
Préambule. — Pierrot. — Arlequin. — Valse noble. — Papillons. — Lettres dansantes. — Chiarina. — Chopin. — Reconnaissance. — Pantalon et Colombine. — Valse allemande et Paganini. — Aveu. — Promenade. — Pause. — Marche des Davidsbündlers (1) contre les Philistins.

STALLE RÉSERVÉE, 10 FR. — ENTRÉE, 5 FR.

(1) Les Davidsbündler (compagnons de David) étaient une société de jeunes artistes qui s'était formée à Leipzig sous l'inspiration de Robert SCHUMANN, contre le *philistinisme*, c'est-à-dire contre la pédanterie et le mauvais goût des FAUX admirateurs qui profanaient les grands maîtres par une imitation fade et servile.

Illustration 7. Concert of Clara Schumann, Salons Érard, Paris, 29 March 1862: Bibliothèque Nationale de France.

Zweites
CONCERT

Johannes Brahms und Julius Stockhausen

unter gefälliger Mitwirkung

des Fräulein Helene Magnus

Dienstag den 2. März 1869,

Abends halb 8 Uhr,

im k. k. kleinen Redouten-Saale.

PROGRAMM:

1. **Sonate** in C-moll (op. 111) . . . . von **Beethoven.**

2. **Arie** aus der Oper „Rothkäppchen" („Enfin me
   voilà seul") . . . . von **Boieldieu.**

3. **Variationen** über ein eigenes Thema (op. 21,
   Nr. 1, in D-dur) . . . . von **Brahms.**

4. **Duett** aus der Oper „Figaro's Hochzeit" „Perchè
   crudel finora") . . . . von **Mozart.**

5. **„Die zürnende Diana"** . . . . von **Schubert.**

6. a) **Gigue** und **Vivace** . . . . von **Rameau.**
   b) **Ungarische Tänze.**

7. **Lieder** aus dem Eichendorff'schen Liederkreise . . von **Schumann.**

Concertflügel: Streicher.

Cerclesitze à 3 fl., Parterresitze à 2 fl., Eintrittskarten à 1 fl.

sind in der k. k. Hof-Kunst- und Musikalienhandlung des Herrn C. A. SPINA
am Graben, in der Musikalienhandlung des Herrn J. P. GOTTHARD am
Kohlmarkt und am Abend des Concertes an der Cassa zu haben.

Illustration 8. Concert of Johannes Brahms and Julius Stockhausen, Saal der Gesellschaft der Musikfreunde, Vienna, 2 March 1869: Centre for Performance History, Royal College of Music.

HONOR TO BEETHOVEN.

SEASON 1846.

THE BEETHOVEN QUARTETT SOCIETY,

76, HARLEY STREET.

SIXTH MEETING, MONDAY, MAY 25,

At Eight o'clock. Quartetts to commence at Half-past Eight.

PROGRAMME.

QUARTETT in C, No. 2, Op. 16,   (Paris Ed. No. 32,)   **HAYDN.**

Moderato.	Adagio.
Minuetto & Trio.	Fuga Allegro ⁶⁄₈ a quattro soggetti.

QUARTETT in D Minor, No. 2,   **Dedicated to HAYDN—MOZART.**

Allegro Moderato.	Andante.
Minuetto & Trio.	Allegro ma non troppo.

QUARTETT in B Flat, No. 4, Op. 76,   (Paris Ed. 78,)   **HAYDN.**

Allegro con spirito.	Adagio.
Minuetto & Trio.	Finale.

QUARTETT in C ♯ Minor, Op 131,   **BEETHOVEN.**

Adagio ma non troppo e molto expressivo.		Allegro Molto Vivace.
Allegro Moderato.		Andante ma non troppo.
Andante Moderato.		Allegretto.
Adagio ma non troppo.	Adagio.	Presto.
Adagio quasi Andante.	Allegretto.	Allegro.

The Members of this Society will not fail to perceive that the principle of selection in the three concluding programmes is entirely in harmony with the original design. Having presented in the five fixed programmes the progress of *Beethoven* in this class of composition in his youth, his maturity, and in his parting glory, we now show the progress of the Quartett itself, from the early efforts of its inventor, *Haydn*, taken up in the midway of his career with an increased energy by *Mozart*, which *Haydn's* later productions prove that he himself was influenced by ; and closing each evening with one of the great *"Posthumous Quartetts"* when the system had reached the greatest elevation and grandeur that it is probably destined to attain.

The selection for the next Meeting on the 8th June, will be *Mozart's* Quartett in B♭ Op. 18; his first Quartett in G, dedicated to *Haydn*; *Haydn* in D minor, Op. 76 ; and the Posthumous of *Beethoven* in A minor.

Haydn's first Quartett for two Violins, Tenor and Violoncello, (in real parts for each instrument,) his Op. 1. in B flat, 6-8 time, was written in 1750, when he was eighteen years of age, and arose from the following circumstances :—One of his friends, *Baron Furenberg*, who had an estate a few miles from Vienna, was in the habit of inviting *Haydn*, with the parish priest, his intendant, and *Albrechtsberger*, a brother of the celebrated contrapun-

[VOLTI.

Illustration 9. Concert of Beethoven Quartet Society, 76 Harley Street, London, 25 May 1846: Centre for Performance History, Royal College of Music.

WILLIAM MASON'S
MUSICAL SOIRÉE,

AT THE

Warerooms of Messrs. Chickering,

On Wednesday, Dec'r 26th, at 7½ o'clock, P. M.,

ASSISTED BY THE

1855

MENDELSSOHN QUINTETTE CLUB.

PROGRAMME.

1. QUARTET in B Flat, No. 6, Op. 18.—1. Allegro.
   2. Adagio. 3. Scherzo. 4. Finale; La malinconia, Adagio and Allegro.   L. VAN BEETHOVEN.

2. A. Fantasie Impromptu. Œuvre posthume.   F. CHOPIN.
   B. Preludes, Op. 24.   STEPHEN HELLER.

3. ANDANTE and FINALE from the Fifth Quintet in
   E Flat,   MOZART.

4. A. 'Toujours,' Valse de Salon, }
   B. 'Silver Spring,' Impromptu, }   WILLIAM MASON.

5. GRAND TRIO, in B major, Opus 8: for Piano-
   Forte, Violin and Violoncello.—1. Allegro moderato. 2. Scherzo. 3. Adagio. 4. Allegro
   agitato.   JOHANNES BRAHMS.

Single Tickets, $1.00: Tickets to admit a Gentleman and Lady, $1.50:
For sale at RICHARDSON's Musical Exchange, 282 Washington
Street, and at Messrs. CHICKERING's Warerooms.

E. L. Balch, Printer, 21 School St.

Illustration 10. Concert of William Mason and Mendelssohn Quintette Club, Chickering
Rooms, Boston, 26 December 1855: Boston Public Library.

Concert

Im Saale des Gewandhauses.

Donnerstags, den 15. Februar 1787.

Erster Theil.

Sinfonie, von Naumann.

Scene, aus Giulio Sabino, von Sarti. (Mad. Schick.)

Non dubitar, verrò, dono più grato
Offrir non mi potevi, al grande invito
Sento l'alma avvampar, vedrai, qual uso
Farò di quest' acciar, chi fa se mai
Più funesto vedesti
Di questa spada balenare il lampo,
So quei che dico, e lo vedrai nel campo.
Là tu vedrai chi fono,
No, non ti parlo in vano,
Fatale è questa mano,
Forte chi men la teme,
Più ne dovrà tremar.
E della tromba il fuono,
Ch' oggetto è di fpavento,
Precederò contento,
La morte ad incontrar.

Terzett auf der Violine. (Herr Berger.)

Terzett, aus Il Rè Teodoro, von Paifiello.

Belifa. Mio caro Sandrino!
    Quel cor dunque m'ama?
Sandrino. Ti cerco, ti brama,
    Per te tutto è ardor.
Lifetta. Suo caro lo chiama
    Si parla d'amor.
Bel. Il vago mio volto
Lif. Conquiste fa ognor.
    Che vedo! che ascolto!
    M'infultano ancor!
Sand. Non far la tiranna
    Col nuovo amator.
Lif. L'infido m'inganna,
    E finfe finor.
Bel. } a 2. La gioja, il diletto,
Sand. } La rabbia, il difpetto
a 3. Da questo momento
Lif. Mi fento nel cor.

Zweyter Theil.

Sinfonie, von Rofetti.

Rondo, von Cimarofa. (Mad. Schick.)

Care donne giovinette,
Che gelofi fpofi avete:
Voi per prova dir potete,
Se contenta poffo ftar.
Mà fe mi fa lo-fpofo
Un fegno d'allegria,
La mia malinconia
Mi voglio far paffar;
Canzoni vò cantare,
Vò ridere, e ballar.

Chor, aus Il Moftro, von Seydelmann.

Grazie fi rendano
Al Dio del giorno!
Di lieti cantici
Le valli intorno
Nel noftro giubilo
Facciam rifuonar.
Sal. Se nella Reggia
    Vogliam guidarlo,
    Bifogna ifcuoterlo,
    Convien deftarlo.
Stip. Eccomi fubito
    Che brutta faccia!
Fag. La mia borraccia
    Lafciala là.
Stip. Quai calci!
Sal. Sogna.
Stip. Ah fenza fallo
    Or fua Maeftà

Sal. D'effer cavallo
    Sognando va.
Stip. Sù via rifveglifi!
Sal. Lo tento in vano.
Sal. Di terra levifi
Stip. Dunque pian pinno.
    Pian piano alziamolo.
    Che brutta faccia!
Fag. La mia borraccia ——
    Lafciala là.
Stip. Quai calci!
Sal. Sogna.
Stip. Ah fenza fallo
    Or fua Maeftà
    D'effer cavallo
    Sognando va.

CORO. Grazie fi rendano &c.

Sinfonie, von Stamitz.

Illustration 11. Abonnenten-Concert (Subscription Concert), Gewandhaus, 15 February 1787: Stadtgeschichtliches Museum, Leipzig.

His Majesty.

PHILHARMONIC SOCIETY.

FIFTH CONCERT, MONDAY, MAY 1, 1826.

ACT I.

Sinfonia, Letter T. - - - - - - -	*Haydn*
Quartetto, " " Madame Pasta, Signor Curioni,	
Mr. Phillips, and Signor De Begnis - - - -	*Wiegl.*
Concerto Flute, Mr. Fürstenau (First Flute to the King of Saxony) -	*Fürstenau*
Terzetto, " O nume benefico," Madame Pasta, Mr. Phillips, and	
Signor De Begnis (La Gazza Ladra) - - - -	*Rossini*
Overture, Oberon - - - - - - -	*C.M. Von Weber*

ACT II.

Sinfonia in C Minor - - - - - - -	*Beethoven*
Recit. ed Aria, Madame Pasta, " Ombra adorata aspetta" (Romeo e	
Giulietta) - - - - - - - -	*Zingarelli*
Concerto Violin, Mr. De Beriot (Violin de la Chambre de S. M. le	
Roi de France) - - - - - - -	*Rode & De Beriot*
Duetto, " O Statua gentilissima," Signor Curioni and Signor De	
Begnis (Il Don Giovanni) - - - - - -	*Mozart*
Overture in D. - - - - - - -	*A. Romberg*

Leader, Mr. Loder.—Conductor, Sir G. Smart.

To commence at Eight o'clock precisely.

The Subscribers are most earnestly entreated to observe that the Tickets are not transferable, and that any violation of this rule will incur a total forfeiture of the subscription.

It is requested that the Coachmen may be directed to *set down* and *take up* with their horses' heads towards Piccadilly.

The door in Little Argyll street will be open after the Concert, for the egress of the Company.

The next Concert will be on Monday, *May* 15.

TERZETTO.—Mad. Pasta, Mr. Phillips, and Signor De Begnis.

		Pod. L' istante è propizio
		Amore discendi,
		Se il core gli accendi
Ninetta.	Respiro	Che gioja sarà.
Podesta.	Mia cara	
Fer.	Signora	**Nin.** O Nume benefico
P.	Partite, udite,	Che ect.
	Uscite di qua	**Pod.** Siamo soli, amor seconda
Fer.	O Nume benefico	La mia fiamma, i voti miei
	Che il giusto difendi	Ah se barbara non sei
	Propizio ti rendi	Fammi parte del tuo cor
	Soccorso pietà.	

Illustration 12. Concert of Philharmonic Society, Hanover Square Rooms, London, 1 May 1826: Centre for Performance History, Royal College of Music.

Grand Miscellaneous Concert.

PART I.

The First four Movements of the *Dettingen Te Deum*. .... Handel.

SONG—Mr. TAYLOR. " The Fall of Zion." .... Paesiello.

GLEE. " Blest pair of Sirens." .... S. Smith.
Mrs. KNYVETT, Messrs. KNYVETT, BRAHAM, PHILLIPS, and E. TAYLOR

RECIT. and AIR—Mr. BRAHAM. " Deeper, and deeper still." *(Jephtha.)* } Handel.
RECIT. and AIR—Mrs. KNYVETT. " Farewell, ye limpid streams."
ARIA—Madame PASTA. *Ho perduto.* *"Suoi frequenti palpiti" - Paccini* ~~Paesiello.~~

QUINTETTO. " Sento o Dio." *(Così fan tutte.)* .... Mozart.
Madame CARADORI ALLAN, Mrs. KNYVETT, Messrs. BRAHAM,
E. TAYLOR, and Signor DE BEGNIS.

CONCERTO, VIOLONCELLO—Mr. LINDLEY. .... Lindley.

SONG—Madame CARADORI ALLAN. " Let the bright Seraphim."
(Trumpet obligato—Mr. HARPER.) } Handel.
And CHORUS. " Let their celestial concerts all unite." ....

SONG (MS.)—Mr. PHILLIPS. " The Sea."
(For whom it was expressly composed by the Chevalier Neukomm, who will direct the performance.)

DUETTO—Madame PASTA and Signor DE BEGNIS. . " Io di tutto." Mosca.

CHORUS. " To Rome's immortal Hero." *(La Clemenza di Tito.)* ... Mozart.
(Arranged and adapted to English Words by Mr. E. TAYLOR.)

PART II.

OVERTURE, *Anacreon*. .... Cherubini.

GLEE. " Deh dove senza mi." .... Dr. Cooke.
Mrs. KNYVETT, Messrs. KNYVETT, BRAHAM, and PHILLIPS.

RECIT. ed ARIA—Madame PASTA. " Ombra adorata." *(Rome e Giulietta.)* Zingarelli.

~~DUETT—Mr. BRAHAM & Mr. PHILLIPS. "I, my dear, was born to-day." Travers.~~

SONG—Mrs. KNYVETT. " Lo ! here the gentle lark." .... Bishop.
(Flute obligato, Mr. NICHOLSON.)

DUETTO. · " All' idea." *(Il Barbiere.)* ... Rossini
Mr. BRAHAM and Signor DE BEGNIS.

MADRIGAL. " Let me careless." .... Linley.
Mrs. KNYVETT, Messrs. KNYVETT, BRAHAM, PHILLIPS,
and E. TAYLOR.

SONG and CHORUS—Mr. PHILLIPS. " Haste thee, Nymph." *(L'Allegro.)* Handel.

ARIA—Madame CARADORI ALLAN. " Batti, batti." .... Mozart.
(Violoncello obligato, Mr. LINDLEY.)
BALLAD—Mr. BRAHAM. *"The Rover's Bride."* ~~"There was once a golden time."~~ ~~Mrs. Hill Wilson.~~
(Accompanied by himself on the Piano-Forte.)

SCENA—Signor DE BEGNIS. " I Violini." .... Sacchini.
(In which Signor DE BEGNIS will perform the part of " Il Fanatico," at the rehearsal of his New Overture.)

DUETTO. " Ravvisa." *(Il Crociato.)* .... Mayerbeer.
Madame PASTA and Madame CARADORI ALLAN.

GRAND CHORUS. " The arm of the Lord."
(From the Oratorio of Judah, arranged by Gardner.)

Illustration 13. Concert in University Musical Festival, Holywell Music Room, Oxford, 16
June 1832: Centre for Performance History, Royal College of Music.

III.

CONCERT SPIRITUEL.

Sonntag den 10. *März* 1833.

1. Sinfonie in B, von Beethoven.

2. Credo aus der Pastoralmesse von Abbé Vogler.

3. Jubel-Ouverture von C. M. Weber.

4. Kyrie aus Beethovens letzter grosser Messe in D.

Illustration 14. Concert Spirituel, Saal der Gesellschaft der Musikfreunde, Vienna, 10 March 1833: Universität der Musik und Darstellende Kunst, Vienna.

Tonkünstler-Versammlung
zu Hannover.

FÜNFTES CONCERT
des
Allgemeinen Deutschen Musikvereins,

Mittwoch, den 23. Mai, Abends 7 Uhr

im königlichen Theater

unter Direction des königlichen Hofkapellmeisters
Carl Ludwig Fischer.

Orchester: Königl. Kapelle in Hannover, verstärkt durch Mitglieder der herzogl. Dessau'schen Hofkapelle, sowie durch auswärtige Mitglieder des Allgemeinen deutschen Musikvereins.

Erster Theil.

1. **Richard Metzdorff** (Vereinsmitglied in Braunschweig) Erster Satz („König Lear") aus Op. 17: „König Lear," grosse tragische Symphonie (Dmoll) in 4 Abtheilungen für Orchester, unter Direction des Componisten.

2. **Johann Svendsen** (Vrnsm. in Christiania), Andante und Finale aus dem Adur-Concert, Op. 6, für Violine solo und Orchester, das Solo vorgetragen von Herrn Kammervirtuos Robert Heckmann (Vrnsm. aus Cöln).

3. **Robert Franz** (in Halle), Lieder mit Pianofortebegleitung, gesungen von Herrn Arnold Senfft v. Pilsach (Vrnsm. in Berlin), am Pianoforte begleitet von Herrn Musikdirector Julius Kniese (Vrnsm. in Frankfurt a. M.

Zweiter Theil.

4. **Felix Dräseoke** (Vrnsm. in Dresden), Scherzo für Orchester, zweiter Satz aus der Gdur-Symphonie Op. 12.

5. **Otto Lessmann** (Vrnsm. in Berlin), Lieder mit Pianofortebegleitung, gesungen von Fräulein M. Breidenstein (Vrnsm. in Erfurt), begleitet vom Componisten.

6. **Xaver Scharwenka** (Vrnsm. in Berlin), Concert in Bmoll für das Pianoforte mit Begleitung des Orchesters, Op. 32. Franz Liszt verehrungsvoll zugeeignet. Die Solopartie vorgetragen vom Componisten (in drei Sätzen.)

Dritter Theil.

Dante-Symphonie
für Orchester und Schlusschor

von

Franz Liszt
(Vereinsmitglied).

Der Schlusschor ausgeführt von Mitgliedern des Engel'-schen Gesangvereins, das Sopran-Solo gesungen von Fräulein M. Breidenstein.

Illustration 15. Annual Meeting, Allgemeine Deutsche Musikverein, Königliches Theater, Hannover, 24 May 1876: Deutsche Staatsbiblithek, Berlin.

THE CONCERT COMPANION.

No. II.]   [PRICE 1d.

Theatre Royal Lyceum and English Opera House.
PROMENADE CONCERTS
A LA MUSARD.

PROGRAMME FOR THIS EVENING.

PART I.			PART II.		
Overture, "*Anacreon*"	... ...	Cherubini	Overture, "*Guillaume Tell*"	... ...	Rossini
Quadrille, "*Venise*"	... ...	Musard	Quadrille, "*La Prison d'Edinburgh*"		Musard
Overture, "*Oberon*"	... ...	Weber	Overture, "*Zampa*"	... ...	Herold
Quadrille, "*Le Danois*" (by desire)	...	Musard	Quadrille, "*Les Echos*"	... ...	Musard
Overture, "*Les Aveugles de Tolède*"	...	Mehul	Overture "*Gustavus*"	... ...	Auber
Waltz, "*Le Duc de Reichstadt*"	...	Strauss	Waltz, "*Hommage à la Reine d'Angleterre*"	Strauss

Wednesday and Saturday, December 26 and 29, a Solo on the Clarionet by Mr. Lazarus.
Thursday and Friday, December 27 and 28, a Solo on the Violin by Mr. Willy.

NAMES OF PERFORMERS.

Conductor.				Oboes.	Cornets à Piston.	Tromboni.
Signor Negri.	Mr. Blagrove,	Mr. Gibbs,	Mr. Pigott,	Mr. G. Cooke.	Mr. C. E. Laurent,	Mr. Smythies, sen.
Leader.	C. Betts,	Elsmore,	White,	Keating.	Jarrett.	Smythies,
Mr. Willy.	Wood,	Streather.	Acraman.		Horns.	Healy.
	Case.		*Double Basses.*	*Clarionets.*	Mr. Platt,	
Deputy Leader.		*Tenors.*	Mr. Edgar,	Mr. Lazarus,	Rae,	*Kettle Drum.*
Mr. Patey.	*Second Violins.*	Mr. Hill,	Griffiths,	Mc. Donald.	C. Harper,	Mr. Goodwin.
	Mr. Watkins.	Calkin,	G. Cubitt,		Horn.	*Side Drum.*
First Violins.	G. Richards,	Alsept,	Severn,	*Bassoons.*	Mr. Harper.	Mr. Hortop.
Mr. W. Cramer,	Hope,	Eastcott,	Griffiths, jun.	Mr. Baumann,	*Trumpets.*	*Big Drum.*
Bannister,	Ireland,	Barnett.	*Flutes.*	Keating, jun.	Mr. Harper,	Mr. Dumont.
Dunsford,	Smith,	*Violoncellos.*	Mr. Richardson,		Harper, jun.	*Triangle.*
Shalichon,	Jacobs,	Mr. Hatton,	Roe, sen.	*Flageolet.*	*Ophycleide.*	Mr. Bernard.
Payton,	Brooks,	Goodban.	Saynor.	Mr. J. Streather.	Mr. Ellison.	

THE SOLOS WILL BE PERFORMED BY
Messrs. WILLY, HARPER, PLATT, G. COOKE, HATTON, BAUMANN, RICHARDSON, LAZARUS, C. E. LAURENT,
HILL, EDGAR, J. STREATHER, PATEY, SAYNOR, HARPER, Jun., RICHARDS, &c.

Admission One Shilling.—Doors open at Half-past Seven.—The Concert commences at Eight, and terminates by Eleven.
Stalls for the Balcony, and Seats in the Dress Circle, to be had on Payment of 1s. extra.
Private Boxes, £1 1s. and 10s. 6d each, may be obtained at the Theatre; also of Messrs. SEGUIN, 12, Regent Street;
MITCHELL, Bond Street; SAMS, St. James' Street; ANDREWS, Bond Street, and all the Principal Libraries.
The Quadrilles to be had at Messrs. Boosey's, Holles Street, Oxford Street.

CAUTION.—The only correct Bill of the Evening is sold within the Theatre, price One Penny. Those sold at the Doors are incorrect.

Printed by J. Brimmer, Mornington Place, and Published EVERY MONDAY by J. Onwhyn, 4, Catherine Street, Strand, where all Communications are requested to be sent Free of Expence.

Illustration 16. Promenade Concert, Royal Lyceum Theatre, London, 26–29 December 1838: British Library.

Montag, den 11. October 1852.

Grosses
Abschieds-Concert
des
Kapellmeisters Strauss
mit seiner
eigenen Kapelle aus Wien.

PROGRAMM.
I. Theil.
1. Ouverture zur Oper: *„Der Freischütz"* v. C. M. von Weber.
2. Windsor=Klänge, Walzer von Joh. Strauss.
3. Nocturne=Quadrille von Joh. Strauss.
4. Annen=Polka von Joh. Strauss.

II. Theil.
5. Der Carneval von Venedig, Grosse Fantasie von weiland Joh. Strauss.
6. Attaque=Quadrille von Joh. Strauss.
7. Gambrinus=Tänze, Walzer von Joh. Strauss.
8. Nebelbilder, Grosses Potpourri von Joh. Strauss.

III. Theil.
9. Liebeslieder, Walzer von Joh. Strauss.
10. Krönungs=Marsch a. d. Op.: *„Der Prophet"* v. Meyerbeer.
11. Loreley=Rhein=Klänge, Walzer von weiland Joh. Strauss.
12. Heiligenstädter Rendez=vous=Polka von J. Strauss.

Druck von **Oskar Leiner** in Leipzig.

Illustration 17. Concert of Strauss-Kapelle, led by Johann Strauss, Jun., Centralhalle, Leipzig, 11 October 1852: Musikabteilung, Wiener Stadt- und Landesbibliothek.

FOR TWO NIGHTS ONLY!

GRAND

INSTRUMENTAL CONCERT

AT THE CITY HALL.

The Germania

MUSICAL SOCIETY,

Beg leave to announce to the Citizens of

WORCESTER AND VICINITY,

That they will give a

GRAND INSTRUMENTAL

CONCERT,

AT THE CITY HALL,

On Tuesday Evening, June 5th.

PROGRAMME.

PART I.

1—OVERTURE TO STRADELLA · · · · · FLOTOW
2—WALTZ—The Villagers · · · · · · LANNER
3—GRAND VARIATIONS FOR THE TRUMPET—
executed by Mr. HAASE · · · · · GRANTZ
4—STEVAN'S FAVORITE POLKA · · · · LENSCHOW

PART II.

5—OVERTURE TO MIDSUMMER NIGHT'S DREAM, MENDELSSOHN
6—VARIATIONS FOR THE VIOLIN—Executed by
Mr. SCHULTZE · · · · · · PAGANINI
7—FINALE—From the Symphony No. 5, in C Minor · BEETHOVEN

PART III.

8—OVERTURE TO ZANETTA · · · · · AUBER
9—WALTZ—The Tremolo · · · · · · LABITZKY
10—GRAND POT POURRI—The Musical Telegraph · STRAUSS

TICKETS 50 CENTS EACH,

To be had at the Hotels, Music Stores, and at the Door.

DOORS OPEN AT 7.   CONCERT TO COMMENCE AT 8.

V. E. HICKCOX, PRINTER.

Illustration 18. Concert of Germania Musical Society, City Hall, Worcester, Mass., 5 June 1849: Courtesy of the American Antiquarian Society, Worcester.

VILLA GARDENS.

THE Annual BREAKFAST CONCERT for the BAND of HORNS and CLARIONETS, Meſſrs. WHITEHEAD, WEST, HOLLOWAY, and STARUP, is fixed for Wedneſday the 25th of April 1787.

Principal Vocal Performers. Miſs WILLIAMS, Maſter TAYLOR, Mr. JACKSON, and Mr. INCLEDON.

Firſt Violin, Mr. ROGERS jun. Violoncello, Mr. HERSCHELL; and Oboe, Mr. ASHLEY.

Act I. Overture. Cantata Maſter Taylor; (being his firſt performance in public) "The banks of the Tweed." Glee, "Harpy the man." Hunting Song, Miſs Williams, "The welkin reſounds." Epitaph, "Wind, gentle evergreens." Song Mr. Incledon, "Ma chere amie." Full Piece.

Act II. Symphony. Comic Song, Mr. Jackſon, "Zooks that an old man can't keep a chicken." Glee, "Come live with me, and be my love." Song, Miſs Williams, "The ſoldier tired." Catch, "Joan ſaid to John." The laſt new favourite Hunting Song, ſung at the Theatre with univerſal applauſe, Mr. Incledon. Concerto Oboe, Mr. Aſhley.

Breakfaſt at ten, and the Concert to begin at half páſt eleven.

☞ Tickets 3s. 6d. each, to be had at Mr. Whitehead's, Orchardſtreet; Mr. Weſt's, Pump-Room-Paſſage; the Pump-Room; Lintern's Muſic-Shop; York-Houſe; Mr. Marrett's, Milſom-ſtreet; and at the Villa Gardens.

Horns and Clarionets during Breakfaſt, as uſual.

Illustration 19. "Breakfast Concert," Villa Gardens, Bath, 25 April 1787: British Library.

SELECT ORATORIO,

BY the Handel & Haydn Society, and the 4th of a regular course for the season. Gentlemen holding season tickets to the performances of the above Society, are respectfully informed that the fourth regular Oratorio for the season will take place THIS EVENING, at 7 o'clock precisely.

March 12.   JOS. LEWIS, Sec'ry.

MISS DAVIS'S CONCERT.

MISS DAVIS respectfully informs her friends and the public, that she intends giving a CONCERT on FRIDAY EVENING, the 15th inst. at Boylston Hall, with the aid and assistance of several amatuers. Dr. G. K. Jackson has kindly offered his services on this occasion to preside at the Piano Forte; and the Government of the Handel and Haydn Society have generously tendered the use of Boylston Hall.

PART I.

O say not Woman's love is bought, - Whitaker.
Di Tanti Palpiti, - - - - - - - - - - - - Rossini.
Glee, - - - - - - - - - - - - - - - - - - (Amatuers)
The Shamrock, - - - - - - - - - - - . Irish.
A Highland Lad, - - - - - - - - . - - - Phipps.

PART II.

Love and Time, - - - - - - - Moore and Kelly.
Di Piacer, - - - - - - - - - - - - - - - - Rossini.
Auld Robin Grey, - - - - - - - - - - - Hook.
Glee, - - - - - - - - - - - - - - - - - (Amatuers.)
The Mocking Bird, (*accompanied on a Flute by an Amatuer.*) - - - - - - - - - - - - - Bishop.

Tickets at one dollar each, to be had at the Franklin Music Warehouse, No. 2, Milk-street, at S. H. Parker's, No. 12, Cornhill, at Mr Forster's Concert Hall, at the Exchange Coffee House, and at the Marlboro' Hotel.

Illustration 20. Concert of Miss Helen Davis, Boylston Hall, Boston, 15 May 1822: Huntington Library, San Marino, California.

Musical Melange.

On friday Evening Aug
At the George Inn precisely at 9
Tickets 1/ea

Hull 1834

Mr. SHAW,

THE CELEBRATED BASS SINGER,

FROM THE ROYAL GARDENS, VAUXHALL,

Will have the honor of introducing to the Nobility, Gentry, and Inhabitants of this Town and its Vicinity, a

Miscellaneous Entertainment

IN TWO PARTS, CONSISTING OF

POPULAR SONGS,

INTERSPERSED WITH

COMIC RECITATIONS, &c.

In the course of the Evening Mr. Shaw will sing the celebrated Hunting Song of

"The Death of Tom Moody."

PART I.	PART II.
INTRODUCTORY ADDRESS.	SONG, "The Sea,"—*Neukomm*
RECITATION, ..." The Origin of Music,"	COMIC STORY, "The Doctor, Nurse, Blacksmith,
RECITATIVE and SONG, "Friend of the Brave,"	and Tailor."
(*Callcott.*)	A POPULAR OLD BALLAD, "The Old English
COMIC "*A la Francaise*," and " A Dancing Mas-	Gentleman."
ter's Description of a Battle."	COMIC SONG, "Pity the sorrows of a poor old man.
AN ADMIRED BASS SONG, " Follow him."	THE CELEBRATED BASS SONG, " The Wolf,
COMIC STORY, "The Jew and Monk."	(*Shield.*)
SONG. "The holy Friar."	COMIC STORY, " Frenchman and Landlord."
BALLAD, "The Bloom is on the Rye."—*Wade*	BALLAD, " O, Green were the Groves.
COMIC STORY, "The Yorkshireman and his family."	SONG........" The Land,"—*Neukomm.*
COMIC SONG, " The great Sea Snake."	COMIC TALE, "Two Frenchmen "
A PATRIOTIC SONG, " Old England for ever shall	COMIC SONG, " The King and the Sailor."
weather the Storm."	FINALE,............"The King ! God bless him ! "

☞ Admission, 2s 6d. each ; the younger branches of Families and Seminaries at half price. One Ticket will admit Two Children. Tickets to be had of Mr. Shaw. The performance will commence precisely at eight o'clock, which will not be protracted beyond ten.

"MR. SHAW, the celebrated Bass Singer, whose several performances at the Hoop Hotel Assembly Room, have given satisfaction. His voice is of great compass, clear, and brilliant, his selection of Songs, (with recital,) and the manner of Singing, are highly calculated to please; and his powerful and tasteful execution of several energetic Songs, have been hailed with rapturous plaudits" *Cambridge Independent Press.*

The Nobility, Gentry, and Seminaries are respectfully informed that a Private Performance may be obtained, on giving timely notice ; and Mr. Shaw begs to state, that he will attend either Public or Private Dinner or Supper Parties.

F. SISSONS, PRINTER, WORKSOP.

Illustration 21. Concert of Mr. Shaw, Hull, 1834: John Johnson Collection of Ephemera: Bodleian Library, Oxford.

Hôtel de Saxe.

Singspiel-Halle (Salon variété)

unter Leitung

des Directors Herrn Otto Weiss.

2. Debut des Gesang-Komikers Herrn Engels vom Stadttheater zu Erfurt.

3. Auftreten der Opernsängerin Frl. Marie Bennôt von der deutschen Oper zu Brüssel.

PROGRAMM.

I. Theil.

1. **La cascade** von Pauer, vorgetragen von dem Kapellmeister Hrn. Klahre.
2. **In den Augen liegt das Herz!** Lied von Hölzel, gesungen von Frl. Troll.
3. **Der dumme Peter.** Komische Scene mit Gesang, vorgetr. von Hrn. Herrmann.
4. **Arie und Rondo** a. d. Op.: „Die Nachtwandlerin", ges. von Frl. Bennôt.
5. **Die Waisenkinder.** Couplet, vorgetr. von Hrn. Engels.

II. Theil.

1. **Ein Pensionskind.** Komische Scene mit Gesang aus „Bei Wasser und Brod", vorgetr. von Frl. Brüning.
2. **1. Walzer-Rondo** von Gumbert, ges. von Frl. Troll.
3. **Narziss im Frack.** Soloscherz mit Gesang, vorgetragen von Hrn. Herrmann.
4. **Duett** a. d. Op.: „Figaros Hochzeit", ges. von Frl. Bennôt und Hrn. Carlo.
5. **Ein politischer Hausknecht.** Komische Scene mit Gesang, vorgetragen von Hrn. Engels.

III. Theil.

1. **Rondo brillante** von C. W. v. Weber, vorgetragen von dem Kapellmstr. Hrn. Klahre.
2. **Arie des Seneschall** a. d. Op.: „Johann von Paris", ges. von Hrn. Carlo.
3. **Die stille Wasserrose.** Lied von Kücken, gesungen von Frl. Bennôt.
4. **Der guate Bu'a.** Oestreich. Lied, ges. von Frl. Troll.
5. **Das Liebesgeständniss einer Köchin.** Komische Scene mit Gesang, vorgetr. von Frl. Brüning und Hrn. Engels.

Druck von A. Th. Engelhardt in Leipzig.

Illustration 22. Singspiel-Halle (Salon Variété), Hôtel de Saxe, Leipzig, 4 December 1866: Stadtgeschichtliches Museum, Leipzig.

GRAND CASINO DE PARIS

12, rue de Lyon (ancien théâtre Parisien).
Le plus vaste Café-Concert de la capitale.
Tous les soirs à 7 heures

SPECTACLE-CONCERT

Orchestre de 30 Musiciens. — **M. HUOT**, chef d'orchestre.

Représentation de :

M. RATEL, ex-1er danseur comique de la Porte-St-Martin.
Mmes JULIE, ALEXANDRINE, AUGUSTINE, 1res danseuses.
M. VINOY, gymnasiarque extraordinaire,

PREMIÈRE PARTIE :

Mmes EMÉLIE. — Le petit Collégien, le Tisserand, l'Arlésienne.
PERRA. — Herculanum, le Trouvère, le Brindisis.
ERNESTINE. — Ma Lispeth, Sautez monacos, Servante d'auberge.
AUGUSTINE. — La Gitane, Amour et Vin, les Violettes.

MM. VANDRENESSE. — Ous qu'est ma guitare, Ce dont on est ben aise.
DONEVAL. — Soldat du roi, Ne nous aimons plus.
GUILLOT. — Tribulations d'un troupier, la Fête à mon parrain.
FROMENT. — Petit grillon, le Jour du repos.
CALVAT. — Faust, Ivon, roi des forêts.

DEUXIÈME PARTIE :

LES MEUNIERS

ballet pantomime en 1 acte.

M. Ratel jouera Nicaise. — Les autres rôles par M. Barrois,
Mlles Julie, Alexandrine, Augustine.

LE TAMBOUR AÉRIEN

par M. Vinoy, gymnasiarque extraordinaire.

DUOS

Le Châlet.	Les Dragons de Villars.
Le Trouvère.	L'Institutrice.
La Reine de Chypre.	La Perle de l'Alsace.
Les Mousquetaires.	Le Retour d'Ulysse.
Le Pré aux Clercs.	Le beau Paris.
Cabaret de Suzon.	Les deux Lutteurs.
Mlle J'ordonne.	Marjolaine.
Une Bonne pour tout faire.	M. et Mme Denis.
La jolie Fille de Perth.	S. P.

Illustration 23. *Café-Concert*, Casino de Paris, February 1868: Bibliothèque Nationale de France.

MR. JACQUES BLUMENTHAL'S

ANNUAL MATINÉE MUSICALE,

AT

The Dudley Gallery,

BY THE KIND PERMISSION OF

THE RIGHT HON. LORD WARD,

ON

THURSDAY, JUNE 25, 1857,

TO COMMENCE AT THREE O'CLOCK.

PROGRAMME.

PREMIÈRE PARTIE

BARCAROLE, "Le Gondolier du Lido" (nouveau), ...*Muaini.*
Mr. BLUMENTHAL.

DUO, "Les Muletiers." ....
MM. SOLIERI et LEFORT.

ARIA, "Ah no la ruai." .....(*La Festa della Rosa.*) ... *Coppola.*
Miss LOUISA PYNE
(Her first appearance since her return from America.)

MELODIE, "Une Larme" (nouveau), et } Mr. BLUMENTHAL.
CAPRICE, "La Caressante," ....

STORNELLI, { "Il primo amore," } Sig. SOLIERI ....*Biletta.*
{ "La Marinarella," }

DUO des "Voluntés Verdes." ....*Bordaleium.*
Miss LOUISA PYNE et Mons. LEFORT.

SECONDE PARTIE

NOUVELLE ROMANCE, "Les Etoiles." ....*Blumenthal.*
Mons. JULES LEFORT.

DUO, "Da quel dì," ....(*Linda di Chamounaix.*).....*Donizetti.*
Miss LOUISA PYNE et Signor SOLIERI

"UNE PETITE HISTOIRE," racontée par } Mr. BLUMENTHAL.
et
"LE VIRTUEL," Rondo Galop (nouveau), }

ROMANCE, "Que je voudrais avoir vos ailes." ....*Henrion.*
Mons. LEFORT.

SICILIENNE, "Merci, jeunes amies." ...(*Vêpres Siciliennes.*).*Verdi.*
Miss LOUISA PYNE

IDYLLE, "Un Sourire" (nouveau), et
CHANSON NAPOLITAIRE, "La Luvibella" (by desire).
Mr. BLUMENTHAL.

TRIO FINAL, "Vadasi via di quà." ....*Marfini.*
Miss LOUISA PYNE, MM. SOLIERI et LEFORT.

Le Piano sera tenu par MM. BILETTA et VERA.

Illustration 24. Concert of Jacques Blumenthal, Dudley Gallery, Piccadilly, London, 25 June 1857: Centre for Performance History, Royal College of Music.

Salle Herz, 48 rue de la Victoire

Matinée musicale annuelle

donnée par

Madame RONZI, née Scalese

Professeur de Chant.

Le Lundi 3 Mai 1869, à 2 heures précises

avec le concours de M. BAGIER, par les Artistes de son Théâtre.

Programme.

__ Première Partie. __ | __ Deuxième Partie. __

Première Partie.

1. Duo Cenerentola (Un Segreto)... Rossini.
   chanté par Mr Scalese & Agnesi

2. Duo de D. Pasquale (Tornami a dir)... Donizetti.
   chanté par Mme Ronzi et M. Palermi.

3. Air de la Favorite (O mio Fernando)... Donizetti.
   chanté par Mlle de Rosello

4. Duo de Rigoletto, ... Verdi.
   chanté par Mr Krauss et M. Delle Sedie.

5. Romance (Senza Speranza)... Lucantoni.
   chanté par Mr Palermi.

6. Romance de Maria di Rudenz. Donizetti.
   chanté par Mr Delle Sedie.

7. Grand Duo pour Piano & Clarinette, Weber.
   exécuté par Mr Mme Busoni.

8. Air de Semiramide (Bel raggio). Rossini.
   chanté par Mlle Krauss.

Deuxième Partie.

1. Trio dell' Italiana in Algieri (Pappataci) Rossini.
   chanté par Mrs Palermi, Scalese & Agnesi

2. Air de Beatrice Tenda ...... Bellini.
   chanté par Mme Ronzi.

3. A. Canzone Napolitana | pour piano { Blumental.
   B. Pendule .... { Fumagalli.
   exécuté par M. Wais Busoni.

4. Romance dell' Nozze di Figaro (Non so più) Mozart.
   chanté par Mme Krauss.

5. Romance de Faust....... Gounod.
   chanté par Mr Nicolini.

6. Solo pour Clarinette (Il Trovatore) Cavallini.
   exécuté par M. Busoni.

7. Air de Vêpres Siciliennes Verdi.
   chanté par M. Agnesi.

8. Quatuor de Rigoletto .... Verdi.
   chanté par Mme Krauss & Rosello
   Mrs Palermi & Delle Sedie

Le Piano sera tenu par M.M. Alary, Lucantoni & Fossi.

Les Pianos sortent des ateliers de M. Henry Herz.

Illustration 25. Concert of Mme Ronzi, née Scalese, Salle Herz, Paris, 3 May 1869: Bibliothèque Nationale de France.

Illustration 26. Cover of edition, *Potpourris sur les motifs d'Opéras favoris pour le Piano*, by Henri Cramer, c. 1860–1870: Getty Research Institute, Los Angeles, California.

pasticcios made up mostly of British ballads, taking on a distinctly plebian air when translated into English for lower middle-class audiences. Musical polemicist Thomas Worgan complained, "toujours Mozart, Rossini, and Meyerbeer; and Rossini, Meyerbeer, and Mozart; and Meyerbeer, Mozart, and Rossini, is a trespass on our patience," the repertory buoyed up by "a fresh importation of Signori and Signore."[10] The special prominence of Mozart's Italian operas limited interest in him within the movement for German opera. The argument made by some commentators that the operas of Mozart and Weber were essentially German did not convince the many German opera-goers who associated them more with music of Meyerbeer than with classical symphonies.

Beethoven was represented on benefit concerts by early works written for the general public where he aimed, as Lewis Lockwood suggested, "to inaugurate an independent career but not to shock patrons or listeners too radically."[11] The song *Adelaide*, op. 46 (1795), was performed by far the most frequently (sometimes translated into Italian), and was rivaled in some contexts by the divertimento-like Septet in E-flat, op. 20, for clarinet, horn, bassoon, violin, viola, cell, and bass (1799). According to a reviewer in the Viennese *Der Freimüthige* in 1805, listeners impatient with the complexity of Beethoven's style wished he would compose more pieces like the "ingratiating" Septet.[12] In 1843 a character in a novel by Jules Janin declared *Adelaide* "the most touching and affectionate complaint which ever sprang from the heart of a lover or a poet."[13]

STANDARD FORMATS IN CONCERT DESIGN

Concert life experienced its own Restoration after 1815, as traditional patterns – most of all alternation between vocal and instrumental pieces – came back as the norm in most benefit concerts. The experimentation widespread in Vienna and London during the 1780s and 1790s began to subside during the Napoleonic Wars, and musicians followed traditional formats for the most part when they resumed their tours after 1815. The main new tendency was the primacy of the *fantaisie* or a set of variations among the instrumental works. Programs became suffused with music from the theatre, all the more

---

[10] Worgan, *Musical Reformer*, p. 25; Cowgill, "'Wise Men from the East.'"
[11] Lewis Lockwood, *Beethoven: Music and the Life* (New York: Norton, 2003), p. 176.
[12] Quoted in Morrow, *Concert Life in Haydn's London*, p. 208. On the dedication of the Septet to Empress Therese, see Rice, *Empress Marie Therese*, pp. 244–8.
[13] Quoted in David Tunley, *Salons, Singers and Songs: A Background to Romantic French Song, 1830–1870* (Aldershot: Ashgate, 2002), p. 273.

because opera overtures supplanted symphonies as the opening number. Concerts offered by local musicians and traveling virtuosos tended to be similar in this regard, with pieces backed up by an orchestra in both cases. The symbiosis of vocal and instrumental virtuosity remained as strong as ever as the fundamental principle of the benefit concert.

A program adhering closely to long-standing convention was presented in Paris in 1818 by the Bohrer brothers – violinist Anton and cellist Max – visiting from Munich (Ex. 5.1). Tradition asserted itself not only in the alternation between vocal and instrumental genres but also in the choice of a symphony to open the first half, a practice that was about to disappear. Symmetry lived on in program design here: the first half included two old arias and a concerto by each player, and the second offered parallel solos and opera selections. The brothers also led "mixed" chamber music concerts in Paris in 1831 (Ex. 4.4).

5.1 *Violinist Anton and Cellist Max Bohrer, 9 March 1818, Académie Royale de Musique, Paris*[14]

Symphony	†Haydn
Aria, "Pria che spunti," *Il Matrimonio Segreto*	
(1792)	†Cimarosa
New Concerto for violin	*Anton Bohrer*
Aria, "Non più andrai," *Le Nozze di Figaro*	
(1786)	†Mozart
New Concerto for cello	*Max Bohrer*
–	
Overture, *Timoléon* (1794)	†Méhul
Opera Scene	Felice Blangini
Duo for violin and cello on a French melody,	
with *boléro*	*A. & M. Bohrer*
Vocal trio	Paër
Variations on a Swedish Air	*Max Bohrer*

Mme Anna Kraus-Wranitzky, a leading singer from Vienna contracted for two seasons at the Gewandhaus, advertised a program with a similar balance of genres in 1823 (Ex. 5.2). That an instrumental rondo was the only piece by a composer from the German states illustrates the power of

---

[14] "Affiches typographiques de l'Opéra," BNF. I am indebted to Olivier Morand for this program; see his article "Vie et mort d'une redevance: le droit de l'Opéra, 1811–1831," *Revue de musicologie* 93 (2007), 99–122.

cosmopolitan opera in Germany's "Paris." Indeed, Mme Kraus-Wranitzky aimed her selections at Leipzig's operatic specialists, singing a cavatina from *Alzira* (1810) by the much-admired, short-lived Nicola Manfroce, a piece that had been inserted, with new text, in Rossini's *Tancredi* (1813) in Bologna.[15] She also sang a cavatina from a comic opera written by Joseph Weigl for La Scala and an aria by Zingarelli, Manfroce's teacher in Naples. Although the overtures by Beethoven and Mozart carried canonic implications by that time, Kraus-Wranitzky presented herself as a sophisticated singer, not as an interpreter of classics such as Julius Stockhausen would do forty years later (Ill. 8).

5.2 *Singer Mme Anna Kraus-Wranitzky, Gewandhaus, 1 February 1823*[16]

Overture, *Leonore*	Beethoven
Scene/Aria, "Tancredi, idolo mia," violin obbligato	†Manfroce
New Concertino for 2 flutes	Benoît Berbiguier
Cavatina, "Deh mi lascia in abbandono," *Il rivale de se stesso* (1808)	Weigl
—	
Overture, *Nozze di Figaro*	†Mozart
Scene/Aria, *Romeo und Julia* (1796)	Zingarelli
Rondo for orchestra	Peter Lindpaintner
Lieder	

A concert Thalberg gave in London in 1836, though traditional in sequence of genres, demonstrates particularly well how recent opera now permeated virtuoso concerts (Ex. 5.3). The triumvirate of Rossini, Bellini, and Donizetti dominated many programs, to which Thalberg added the aging Vincenzo Pucitta, who was famous for accompanying the famous singer Angelica Catalani on tour. The creativity in performance practice found in the period appears in the cadenza from Giuseppe Tartini's "Devil's Trill" Sonata performed by Charles de Bériot with Mme Maria Malibran. As this program suggests, a concert would not normally include a piece from the same opera as the one on which a virtuoso performed a *fantaisie*.

---

[15] *Tancredi: Melodramma eroico in due atti di Gaetano Rossi, musica di Gioachino Rossini*, 3 vols., Philip Gossett (ed.) (Fondazione Rossini: Pesaro, 1984), vol 3, pp. 33, 131. I am grateful to Professor Gossett for this information.

[16] Benefiz und Extra-Concerte, 1823–24, SGML; Dörffel, *Geschichte der Gewandhausconcerte*, vol. 1, pp. 47–51; David Wyn Jones examines the Wranitzky family in *Symphony in Beethoven's Vienna*, pp. 44–6, 74–97.

5.3 *"Mr. Thalberg's Morning Concert," King's Theatre Concert Room, London, 21 May 1836* [17]

Duo, "Se pur giungi," *Marina Faliero* (1835)	Donizetti
Air	Pucitta
Second Caprice in E-flat, op. 19	*Thalberg*
Duo, "Dunque io son," *Il Barbiere di Siviglia* (1816)	Rossini
Aria	Rossini
Fantaisie on themes from *Les Huguenots*, op. 20	*Thalberg*
Duo, "In mia man alfin tu sei," *Norma* (1831)	†Bellini
Air, "Udite o rustici," *L'Elisir d'amore* (1832)	Donizetti
Duo, "Se inclinasse," *L'Italiana in Algeri* (1813)	Rossini
Cadenza from the "Devil's Trill" Sonata	
(Mme Malibran and M. de Bériot)	†Tartini
Fantaisie on themes from *Guillaume Tell*, op. 22	*Thalberg*

Thalberg established a mainstream of pianistic virtuosity in the mid-1830s. Projecting a singing melody above rich harmony and texture, he wrote for the taste of the general public without alienating many idealists. His performing style, Dana Gooley has written, "conjured up an operatic singing voice" that "tapped into a strong, already existing aesthetic predilection of the Parisian publics, while Liszt asked his audiences to listen in new ways."[18] A critic praised one of his concerts for offering fewer and better pieces than the "crowd" of musicians who offered fifteen to eighteen undistinguished numbers. Another critic declared that Thalberg "brought a revolution to the art of the piano" by turning technical prowess to new artistic purposes, and Fétis called him "the creator of a new school."[19] Thalberg's reputation would live on; in 1898 a Leipzig commentator spoke warmly of "that beloved virtuoso" who had "cultivated a very special art."[20]

For all the expansion of the upper-middle-class concert public, leading virtuosos still made their mark most definitively through private performances in aristocratic homes. That tendency was the strongest in Vienna. In 1835 the English writer Frances Trollope visited the city's most prestigious private concerts, including one given by the Queen of Two Sicilies, finding Thalberg and Henry Vieuxtemps treated with great respect. Because she

[17] *MC*, 6 May 1836, p. 1; *MC*, 16 May 1838, p. 1; *MC*, 23 May 1836, p. 3; *MW*, 27 May 1836, p. 171; *TL*, 23 May 1826, p. 4.
[18] Dana Gooley, *Virtuoso Liszt* (Cambridge: Cambridge University Press, 2004), pp. 22–3.
[19] "Concert de Thalberg," *FM*, 25 March 1838, pp. 5–6; "Thalberg," *FM*, 18 March 1838, p. 1; Hamilton, *After the Golden Age*, Ch. 1, "Great Tradition – Grand Manner – Golden Age."
[20] Unsigned book review, *Die Gesellschaft*, 14 (1898), 421.

was accustomed to London's rich classical fare, Trollope was surprised to see that "Handel, Mozart, Haydn, and the like, are banished from 'ears polite.'"[21] By that she meant their instrumental music, because she must have heard some Mozart at the Kärntnertor Theater. The court awarded the title "k. k. Kammervirtuoso/in" to Thalberg, Paganini, and Clara Wieck, but not Liszt.[22]

Virtuosos needed to balance self-promotion with collegiality to a certain extent. It had long been standard practice for a visiting performer to include pieces by local composers on programs, and deference to one's hosts became even more important as virtuosos focused their programs on themselves to a greater extent in the 1830s. If Paganini performed variations on a theme by Haydn in Vienna in 1828 (Ill. 3), Liszt balanced six songs in British idioms with six excerpts from Italian opera when he visited Stamford, Lincolnshire, in September 1840 (Ill. 5). Five of the songs were by British composers, most prominently the Irishman John Orlando Parry, who sang comic songs at many of London's most prestigious benefit concerts. The program followed the eighteenth-century symmetrical ordering of genres, Liszt playing his own music at four intervals. Thalberg gave longer programs than Liszt when he toured England and devoted more attention to his own music. Indeed, the practice of performing almost entirely one's own music, done only occasionally in the 1780s, became more common after 1820 among aspiring virtuosos. In 1821 a bassoon player from Dresden gave a program like that typical at the Gewandhaus with his ten-year-old son. Johann Nepomuk Hummel offered such programs widely; he advertised only his own works for a concert at the Gewandhaus that same year and focused on his own music in London in 1830. Critics warned against the practice, arguing that it made a program too homogeneous, with too much old repertory.[23]

The updated benefit concert – almost all fairly recent music, focused on opera selections and *fantaisies* – became widespread during the late 1830s and the 1840s. Although a significant number of pianists moved toward classical repertory, violinists and cellists usually used a conventional format aimed at the general public. In Vienna in 1843 Vieuxtemps gave a pair of concerts like that in the Grosser Redoutensaal, a large hall where massive productions of Handel's oratorios were produced. The leaders of the Vienna Philharmonic went so far as to ask cellist Adrien Servais to perform a *romanesca* at the

[21] Trollope, *Vienna and the Austrians*, vol 1, pp. 130–2, 372, 367–8.
[22] Christopher Gibbs, "Just Two Words, Enormous Success," *Franz Liszt and His World*, Christopher Gibbs and Dana Gooley (eds.) (Princeton, N.J.: Princeton University Press, 2006), p. 191.
[23] Leipziger Concert-Programme 1820–24, SGML; Joel Sachs, *Kapellmeister Hummel in England and France* (Detroit: Information Coordinators, 1977), p. 69.

inaugural concert of the orchestra in 1842. A critic compared Servais to Liszt, saying that he "could struggle with titans to bat them away like gnats."[24] Vieuxtemps and Servais continued giving concerts together with *fantaisies* and opera excerpts through the 1860s. Young musicians who later became internationally known leaders of classical music usually did not perform classical works in their early concerts. In 1844 Viennese violinist Joseph Hellmesberger, who founded his city's central quartet series five years later, played a concert with his brother, Georg (they were fourteen and fifteen years old, respectively), that included violin solos by Vieuxtemps and Johann Kalliwoda and a concertino for two violins by a local colleague. Arias by Saverio Mercadante and Otto Nicolai, conductor at the Kärntnertor Theater, came between the instrumental pieces.[25] The thirteen-year-old Theodor Leschetizky, later the dean of Vienna's piano teachers, offered a similar program the next year, including two *fantaisies* and vocal pieces by Donizetti and Mercadante.[26]

London musicians took miscellany about as far as it might go in mingling classics, British songs, and Italian opera selections. The unusual length of London programs gave the almost seventy-year-old John Cramer the opportunity to mingle genres and eras at his annual concert in 1840 (Ex. 5.4), bringing to mind programs of the Viennese Society of Musicians or Evening Entertainments (Ex. 4.2). Cramer offered the London *cognescenti* older works not often performed at virtuoso concerts – a trio by Corelli, a wind quintet by Mozart, and a duet by Pietro Carlo Guglielmi, who had worked at the King's Theatre before his death in 1817. Cramer maintained a repertory of songs by British composers that were to disappear in the new order of serious benefit concerts – pieces by Henry Bishop, Michael Balfe, the young singer Maria Billington Hawes, and the omnipresent John Parry.

5.4 *"Mr. Cramer's Morning Concert," Hanover Square Rooms, 3 July 1840* [27]

Overture, *Fidelio*	†Beethoven
Duet, "Oh guardate che figura," *La Capricciosa corretta* (1805)	†Guglielmi
Aria, "Che farò senza Euridice," *Orfeo ed Euridice* (1764/1774)	†Gluck
Concerto for Piano in D Minor	*Cramer*

---

[24] "Nachrichten: Wien," *AMZ*, 10 June 1846, p. 386.
[25] "Nachrichten," *AWMZ*, 13 February 1843, p. 74.   [26] PA/GMFV, 17 April 1844.
[27] Hanover Square Rooms, CPH/RCM. He had published an edition of Mozart's Andante and Rondo in C Minor.

Aria, "Non v'è donna," *Falstaff* (1838)	Balfe
Ballad, "As I Walked by Myself"	Hawes
Quintet in E-flat, op. 452 (pf, ob, cl, bn, hn)	†Mozart
–	
Trio	†Corelli
Ballad, "John Anderson, my Jo"	
Song, "Forlorn I Track," *The Wanderer*	†Schubert
Aria, "Ave Maria," clarinet obligato	Cherubini
Andante and Rondo in C Minor	†Mozart/ *Cramer*
Duet, "Meet again"	Bishop
New Song, "Wanted, a Governess"	Parry
Finale, *La Clemenza di Tito* (1791)	†Mozart

The concerts held at court in England, France, and Austria in the 1840s almost always adhered to the model of the virtuoso program. Queen Victoria, King Louis-Philippe, and Austrian Emperor Ferdinand I all sponsored concerts combining virtuoso pieces with opera selections. A concert in 1846 at Buckingham Palace, for example, offered six opera numbers, two songs, two virtuoso pieces, two overtures, and a waltz by Johann Strauss, the Elder. The only trace of classical repertory at these events appeared in a concert at Schönbrunn in 1847 – the Andante from Beethoven's Seventh Symphony, music of the sort not found in that context a decade earlier. Like the Evening Entertainments, the *Hofkonzert* included a piece for male voices, "Unser Ziel," by the evening's conductor Ludwig Weiss, as well as an aria and chorus from Bellini's *Beatrice di Tenda* (1833).[28] Royalty thus embraced the general taste of the upper classes. In the British case that also involved deference to middle-class musical taste, for Henry Bishop was knighted in 1842 at the instigation of Prince Albert.

The crisis that overwhelmed virtuosos in the 1840s resulted from musicians putting on too many concerts too fast, stars listed on concert bills failing to show, and the lure of wealth bringing professionals to write music for the lowest possible denominator. Some virtuosos turned into little more than arrangers, Léopold de Meyer leading the pack (Ex. 5.7). Publishers found marketing tools to package editions that teachers thought would attract more students, leading to demands that teachers be required to take professional licenses. Yet it must be recognized that idealists making this

[28] "Court Circular," *LT*, 20 May 1846, p. 5; PA/GMFV; Beate Kraus, *Beethoven–Rezeption in Frankreich: von ihren Angangen bis zum Untergang des Second Empire* (Bonn: Beethoven-Haus, 2001), pp. 201–12; Jennifer Caines, "In Consort: Queen Victoria, Her Court and Women Musicians, 1837–61," unpublished Ph.D. thesis, University of Alberta (2007).

critique posed a set of aesthetic principles that went against major aspects
of the virtuoso tradition. Most important of all, the idea of the integral
artwork posed a serious threat to the musician skilled in improvisation and
preluding. For that matter, only part of the music public was ready to accept
the new ideals. Either compromise had to be reached between virtuosity
and idealism or proponents of the two points of view would have to go
their separate ways.[29]

TOWARD THE OPERA GALA AND CONCERTS OF POPULAR SONG

Musicians began taking liberties with the traditional benefit concert in the
1830s by offering programs made up almost entirely of vocal music. To be
sure, opera companies had occasionally offered benefit concerts of that kind
by major singers, sometimes with an act from an opera as the second half.
But that tended to be an institutional rather than an individual concert,
linked to the company's repertory. In some cases, experiments derived from
the practice of giving homogeneous programs of vocal pieces in private gatherings, endowing a public event with the aura of elite socializing. Practical
factors worked toward more vocal pieces. The cost and the complexity of
hiring an orchestra and trying to rehearse with soloists led musicians to turn
to the piano for accompaniment. The new vocal programs took quite different directions. Some musicians began concentrating on opera excerpts,
prefiguring what in the twentieth century would be called the opera "gala."
Others began developing popular repertory of songs and ballads, drawn
in part from the theatre, music that ended up central to music halls and
cafés-concerts. In the 1850s singers such as Julius Stockhausen inaugurated
the song concert or what was eventually called the *Liederabend*.

A drastic break with convention can be seen in a concert given in Paris
in 1838 by the pianist/entrepreneur Henri Herz and the distinguished violinist Charles Lafont (Ex. 5.5). The program offered three vocal pieces
in a row and then three instrumental ones together, followed by such
novelties as a *symphonie concertante* for four violins by Lafont and the
overture to Rossini's *Semiramide* performed on eight pianos. One senses
popular music concerts in the offing; not only did Lafont offer one of his
own *ballades*, but also the whole second half was devoted to a *comédie-
vaudeville*, a genre entirely foreign to concert life. By that time traditional
vaudeville melodies were being replaced by newly composed theatre music,

[29] Gramit, *Cultivating Music*, pp. 125–60 and *passim*; Gooley, "Battle against Instrumental Virtuosity
in the Early Nineteenth Century," *Franz Liszt and His World*, pp. 75–112.

arousing sentimentality about the fading genre that helped bring about the *café-concert*.[30]

5.5 *Pianist Henri Herz and Violinist Charles Lafont, Théâtre Ventadour, March 1838*[31]

Overture, *Obéron*	†Weber
Aria, *Semiramide* (1823)	Rossini
Concerto no. 3 for piano	*Herz*
Trio, *Stradella* (1837)	Niedermeyer
Solo Air	*Lafont*
Ballade, "Départ du jeune marin"	Lafont
Fantaisie on Donizetti's *Lucia di Lammermoor* (1835)	*Herz*
Overture, *Semiramide*, arranged for 8 pianos[32]	Rossini
Solo for harp	*Mlle Beltz*
Symphonie Concertante for 4 violins	*Lafont*

—

La Marquise de Prétintailles, comédie-vaudeville, a "comédie melées de chants" (1836)

Another kind of idiosyncratic program was offered at London's "monster" concerts, directed by the fabulously successful German expatriate Jules Benedict. Designed to attract the *crème de la crème* of London's singers and patrons, the events displayed a sophisticated knowledge of the expanding horizons of French and Italian opera. Benedict's 1844 extravaganza offered thirty-nine pieces by thirty composers, only eight of them deceased; all the music came from opera save for four songs and seven instrumental numbers. The program opened with the quintet from *Così fan Tutte* and concluded with a *terzetto buffa* composed by Martin y Soler in 1795. Listeners were treated to pieces by Chopin, Hippolyte Monpou, Giuseppi Verdi, Giuseppe Persiani, and Jacques Offenbach, the latter himself playing the cello solo in his *Musette, Air de ballet du 17ième siècle* (op.24). [33] Louise Dulcken indulged herself in similar experimentation at her benefit concert in 1841, opening it

---

[30] Alf. D-s., "Les airs de Vaudeville," *RGM*, 20 June 1839, pp. 201–2.

[31] "Concerts," *FM*, 25 March 1838, p. 7; *FM*, 8 April 1838, p. 5.

[32] The pianists were an impressive group: "Mmes Wartel, Lottin; Mlles De Crécieux, Loveday, Cordel, Forest, Barault et Ousèze; MM Jacques Herz, Rosenhain, Osborn, Alkan, Sowinski, Billard, Rosellen, and Herz," *FM*, 25 March 1838, p. 7.

[33] See transcription in W. Weber, "From Miscellany to Homogeneity in Concert Programming," *Poetics* 29 (2001), 131–2.

with a terzet, "Pensa e guarda" from Meyerbeer's *Margherita d'Anjou*, and offering only four instrumental pieces out of a total of twenty-three (Ill. 4).

A few Viennese concerts were devoted almost entirely to opera excerpts, sung to piano accompaniment, during the 1840s. One offered in 1842 surprised a critic, who was forced to admit that piano accompaniment added "a certain distinction" to a performance.[34] Two years later the noted tenor Giovanni Davide (son of Giacomo Davide, Ex. 2.4) advertised a program focused on Donizetti that opened with the first movement of a piano trio, as would often occur in later decades (Ex. 5.6). Not only was Donizetti the leading opera composer at this time, he was about to direct the Italian repertory at the Kärntnertor Theater that season. Strikingly, the only instrumental solo scheduled was by the Viennese Franz Pecháček, born eighty years before. Davide nonetheless followed tradition by performing in only three pieces on the printed program. Similar concerts occurred in Leipzig at the Hôtel de Pologne, bringing competition to the Gewandhaus.[35] One given in 1839 balanced French and Italian music in selections from Rossini's *Tancredi* (1813), Bellini's *La Sonnambula* (1831), Hérold's *La médecine sans médecin* (1832), and Auber's *Lestocq ou L'intrigue et l'amour* (1834). For that matter, performance of a set of variations by Léon Herz (Henri's brother) illustrates how much cosmopolitan repertory still dominated the taste of many German concert-goers. The program nonetheless deferred to local composers by including an octet for male voices by Ignaz von Seyfried.

5.6 *Singer Giovanni Davide, Friends of Music Hall, Vienna, 1 January 1844* [36]

Piano Trio in B-flat, 1st movement	Joseph Mayseder
Romanza, *Linda di Chamounix* (1842, Reichard)	Donizetti
Duet, *Marino Faliero* (1835, Dlle Corridori and Davide)	Donizetti
Variations brillantes in C for violin	†Pecháček
Cavatina, *Barbiere di Siviglia* (1816, Dlle Corridori)	Rossini
Poetic Declamation	
Duet, *Don Pasquale* (1843, female dilettante and Davide)	Donizetti
Terzet, *Donna Carieta* (1826, Corridori, Reichard and Davide)	Mercadante

[34] "Nachrichten," *AWMZ*, 15 March 1842, p. 139.
[35] Hôtel de Pologne, SGML. See Léon Herz, *Souvenir de l'opera, Lucia di Lammermoor, de Donizetti: Fantaisie pour le violon avec accompt. de piano-forte: Oeuvre 6* (Vienna: Diabelli, 1837).
[36] PA/GMFV.

A profitable new career opened up for composers specializing in song in this period. The Viennese musician Heinrich Proch, for example, established himself first as a solo violinist but became known primarily as a singer and song composer.[37] At his 1836 benefit concert he performed a concertino and a set of variations, and two of his lieder were sung, one for the unusual combination of two voices and two cellos. As his concerts shifted mostly to songs in the 1850s he organized prestigious private concerts, including one given by the Duke of Coburg for the Crown Prince of Brazil. In 1867 he gave a splashy charity concert whose miscellaneous format looked back to the kind of format offered forty years before. By then his music had taken on the status we might call "middle-brow."[38] The Parisian composer and singer Loïsa Puget built a career similar to Proch's, composing *romances* and *chansonnettes* that must have made their way into the *cafés-concerts*.[39] We will see a whole host of such composers from many countries prospering in the 1850s.

Instrumentalists likewise identified a well-heeled public of "middle-brow" taste, people who wanted brilliant but not challenging music on a program. Thus the Austrian pianist Léopold de Meyer gave several concerts every season in Vienna in the 1840s devoted to arrangements of tunes for piano and orchestra, along with the simpler kind of songs (Ex. 5.7).

5.7 *Pianist Léopold de Meyer, Friends of Music Hall, 16 April 1844* [40]

Overture, *Oberon*	†Weber
Russian Songs arr. for piano	Meyer
Lied, "Der Bursch und sein Liedchen"	Gustav Hölzel
Concerto in E-flat, 1st movement	Meyer
Duet for two bass voices, accompanied by piano	Hackel
Arrangement of Turkish song, "Bajazett"	Meyer
Arrangement of Paganini's *Nocturne* and	
Il carnevale di Venezia	Paganini *Meyer*

The press made Meyer a particular object of scorn as concern mounted about a decline in taste at virtuoso concerts. A writer for the *Theaterzeitung* that year had Meyer in mind, as well as virtuosos performing idiosyncratic new instruments in a satirical piece:

---

[37] PA/GMFV.

[38] The term *high-brow* arose in the 1880s, *low-brow* around 1900, and *middle-brow* in the 1960s; Levine, *Highbrow/Lowbrow*, pp. 221–2.

[39] "Soirée musicale de Mme Puget," *FM*, 28 January 1838, p. 4.

[40] "Nachrichten," *AWMZ*, 16 April 1844, pp. 181–82; *AWMZ*, 11 May 1843, p. 235. Hölzel created the role of Beckmesser in *Die Meistersänger von Nürnberg* in 1868.

A Peep-Show seen with strong Lighting, or a Concert Program for the Year 1844:

1. Wedding-Party-Bash, Nocturne for Night-Watchman for 8 pipes, 6 rattles, and 4 party horns.
2. Chromatic Galop, done on several beer cans.
3. Brilliant concerto on the bass drum, with accompaniment by 4 ugly mermaids.
4. Variations on "Beautiful Minka," for the carriage horn.
5. Symphony by Beethoven, transcribed for the varnishing stone.
6. Torments of Hell Galop, for 6 flails and 24 bootjacks.[41]

Vocal-music concerts in Britain and North America began moving away from cosmopolitan repertory in this period. The song, the glee, and the ballad became central components of British provincial concerts around the turn of the nineteenth century. In Edinburgh a "Scotch song" was standard at most concerts by the 1780s, and such pieces by Shield and Callcott were regularly offered at Oxford's Holywell Music Room twenty years later.[42] A program at Birmingham's Private Concerts in 1801 included a glee, "Hark! the hollow woods resounding" by John Stafford Smith, and a song, "My lodging is on the cold ground, love" by harpist Robert Bochsa, along with pieces of "ancient" music by Handel and Geminiani and "modern" works by Mozart and Pleyel.[43] An 1815 concert given by a harp teacher, Mrs Bury, ignored Italian opera completely, presenting just music by British composers, most prominently Hook and Bishop, save for a piece each by Mozart and Handel.[44] Although the concert took place away from the prestigious West End, at the Free Masons' Hall in Lincoln's-Inn Fields, the charge of 10s 6d for a ticket indicates a wealthy audience. Musicians in provincial cities had even greater freedom to redefine their music in "popular" terms. A bass soloist from Vauxhall Gardens brazenly entitled a concert in Hull in 1834 a "Musical Melange" and "Miscellaneous Entertainment" (Ill. 21). The program announced "Popular Songs" ("The Jew and the Monk") and *vaudeville*-like "comic recitations" ("The Frenchmen and the Landlord") in proudly plebeian terms. Yet, as was the case with the 1787 concert in Bath (Ill. 19), most of the songs were by quite distinguished English composers: "The Wolf" by Shield, which had been inserted in Samuel Arnold's opera

---

[41] "Guckkasten-Bilder in heiterer Beleuchtung," *TZ*, 15 November 1844, p. 1124.
[42] Concert advertisements, *Caledonian Mercury*, 2 February 1786, p. 1; Oxford Musical Society programs, BLO.
[43] Programs, BCL.   [44] *Mrs Bury's Concert & Ball, Freemasons' Hall, Holborn*, BLJJ.

Castle of Andalusia (1782), and "Friend of the Brave," set by Callcott to Thomas Campbell's poem *Pleasures of Hope* (1801).

The ballad and the song increased so much in importance that they dominated the annual concert that Birmingham singer Benjamin Pearsall gave in 1844 (Ex. 5.8). A leading soloist at the Birmingham Festival, Pearsall included pieces by Auber and the balladeer Friedrich Kücken but no Italian opera save for a violin solo on music from Bellini's *Norma*. Cosmopolitan and national canons stand out in the program: arias by Handel, Haydn, and Weber at the start and theatre songs by Dibdin and Arne at the end. The program listed both aristocratic and bourgeois patrons, illustrating the interaction between the two elites that was common in provincial towns, even though industrial families took the lead in the city's government.

5.8 *"Mr. Pearsall's Grand Concert," Town Hall, Birmingham, 28 November 1844* [45]

Overture, *Prometheus*	†Beethoven
Glee, *With Sighs, sweet Rose* (1798)	†Callcott
Rec./Air, "In native Worth," *Creation*	†Haydn
Air, "Holy, holy" ("Dove sei"), *Rodelinda*, text from Samuel Arnold's *Redemption* (1786)	†Handel
Duet, *I Know a Bank*	C. E. Horn
Recitative and Air, *The Tempest* (1817)	William Horsley
Fantasia for violin	*Henry Hayward*
Scena, "Softly Sighs the Voice of Evening," *Freischütz* (1821)	†Weber
Song, *Up to the Forest hie!*	John Barnett
Song, *Rocked in the Cradle of the Deep*	Joseph Knight
Ballad, *I'll Speak of Thee*	Hawes
Glee, "Blow, gentle Gales," *The Slave* (1816)	Bishop
Overture, *Fra Diavolo* (1830)	Auber
Song, "I'm a poor Shepherd Maid," *La bergère chatelaine* (1820)	Auber
Ballad, *The Harp is Now Silent*	Kücken
Glee, 4 v., *By Celia's Arbour* (1808)	Horsley
Solo for cello, on Bellini's *Norma*	*Heinemeier*

[45] Ibid.; *Birmingham Musical Examiner & Dramatic Review*, 20 October 1844, p. 95. Joseph Mazzinghi was British born. Similar programs were given by the York Philharmonic Society in that period; see David Griffiths, *A Musical Place of the First Quality: A History of Institutional Music-Making in York, c.1550–1990* (York, UK: York Settlement Trust, 1990), pp. 155–8.

Ballad, "Then you'll Remember Me," *Bohemian Girl* (1843)	Balfe
Ballad, *Tom Starboard* (1845)	†Joseph Mazzinghi
Duet, "The Brigand Chief," *Les Diamants de la Couronne* (1841)	Auber
Ballad, "The Sailor's Journal," *Will o' the Wisp* (1796)	†Dibdin
Song, "Where the Bee Sucks," *The Tempest* (1789, after Purcell)	†Arne
Finale, *God Save the Queen*	†Arne

Concert repertory and editions of ballads moved back and forth between Britain and North America in this period, rivaling cosmopolitan opera and learned classical music. As we saw in the program presented in Portsmouth, New Hampshire, in 1796, a singer might put on a concert with limited backup by other performers. We find a more firmly rooted musical world in 1822, in the advertisement placed by Miss Helen Davis for a concert in Boston that the "Government" of the Handel and Haydn Society permitted her to hold in Boylston Hall (Ill. 20). Known to have one of the best voices in the city's church choirs, Davis obtained the services of the venerable, Oxford-born George K. Jackson as accompanist.[46] She balanced arias from Rossini's *Tancredi* (1813) and *La Gazza Ladra* (1817) with ballads from Bishop's *The Slave* (1816) and John Whitaker's *Heir of Veroni* (1817). Hook's 1785 *Death of Auld Robin Gray* served as a canonic reference point to these songs and to equally recent ballads by Michael Kelly and Thomas Phipps. The only backup was seemingly the amateurs who sang glees.

One could, indeed, argue that the "ballad concert" came into existence in Boston earlier than in Britain. The Scottish singer William Richardson Dempster took advantage of that development; a leading song composer, he was known particularly for "The Blind Boy" (1842), set to a poem of Helen Selina, Lady Dufferin. When on tour in Boston in 1839, Dempster advertised a concert offering his own pieces and those of Bishop, John Braham, Henry Loder, and Robert Linley.[47] An edition of songs he published there in 1847 included pieces on texts by Robert Burns – "Oh! Poortith Cauld," "Highland Mary," and "Duncan Gray."[48] His attempt to set cantos

---

[46] Broyles, *"Music of the Highest Class,"* pp. 187–8.

[47] *Concert of Mr. Dempster, the Temple, April 27, 1839*, Collection of Concert Programs, BPL.

[48] "Mr. Dempster's Ballad Soirées," *ATH*, 10 December 1846, p. 13–5; *Dempster's Original Ballad Soirées* (Boston: Dutton & Wentworth, 1847). See Derek Carew, "The Consumption of Music," *Cambridge History of Nineteenth-Century Music*, Jim Samson (ed.) (Cambridge: Cambridge University Press, 1992), pp. 237–58.

of Tennyson to music nonetheless led a local critic to regret that "his songs are all alike."[49] In London the year before, he presented "Mr. Dempster's Original Ballad *Soirées*" in the Princess Theatre near Oxford Street. Shows at that theatre were aimed at a modest middle-class public, but Dempster took it upon himself to advertise the series in the influential *Athenaeum*. During one of their long American tours in 1841, an English couple, Joseph and Mary Ann Wood, née Patton, gave a program made up entirely of ballads and songs save for arias from *Così fan Tutte* and *La Gazza Ladra*.[50] Most of the pieces were composed by Britons who spent much of their careers in America – Henry Russell, William Brough, and James Gaspard Maeder. As we have seen so often, pieces by canonic composers (Attwood, Mozart, and Dibdin) served as book ends to the program.

THE RECITAL AND OTHER EXPERIMENTS

Concerts devoted to self-consciously serious repertories arose during the 1840s in response to concern that benefit concerts had become crudely commercial.[51] Recital, unprecedented before Liszt's experiments of the late 1830s, appeared on only a few occasions, chiefly in London, before the mid-1850s. Most of the solo recitals in this period were performed by virtuosos and focused chiefly on recent music. Examples of the collegial chamber concert were more common, taking a variety of forms. It could involve two musicians – most often a pianist with a violinist or a singer – who performed both individually and jointly, a format that remained common in London and Paris until the eve of World War I.[52] Or a pianist might invite a singer and several instrumentalists onto a program, possibly to perform a trio or a quintet at the start. The programs of chamber music concerts, with their strict choice of classical and modern works, provided a model for collegial concerts. Musicians nonetheless had to try different strategies to make sure they could attract substantial audiences.

Pianists led the movement to reform musical taste, embracing the principles discussed in Chapter 3: performance of classical works; exclusion of lesser genres; replacement of opera excerpts with serious songs; and the perception of the concert-giver as interpreter. But rarely did a performer follow all these precepts. Eliminating the orchestra was an important first step,

---

[49] "Music in Boston," *Harbinger*, 10 January 1846, p. 76.
[50] Advertisement, *Boston Evening Transcript*, 1 January 1841, p. 3.
[51] For sophisticated discussion of programming, see Ferris, "Public Performance and Private Understanding"; and Gibbs, "'Just Two Words, Enormous Success.'"
[52] "Salle Pleyel," BOP; Archive, Wigmore Hall.

done originally by the best known virtuosos. Thalberg ceased hiring an orchestra so that he could focus on his own pieces within a homogeneous, opera-rich program. Presenting several pieces in the same genres together arrived at the same time, but it was rare before the mid-1830s. Liszt adopted the practice during his visit to Vienna in 1838. Liszt also took leadership in performing pieces by classical composers, chiefly Handel, Scarlatti, and Beethoven, and his arrangements of Schubert's songs began to give such status to Schubert.[53] Including a trio or a quintet began to provide a vigorous new way for a collaborative concert to begin. Liszt tried that in a series of four concerts he ran in Paris in 1837 – a Beethoven piano trio followed by opera excerpts, songs, and pieces for solo piano, echoing the variety of the Viennese Evening Entertainments (Ex. 4.2). Though this format seemed utterly bizarre at the time, elements of it were common by the 1860s.[54]

The solo recital amounted to a declaration of independence by the performer from the traditional benefit concert.[55] Liszt's famous quip to Countess Belgiojoso that he played alone, as if he were the Sun King, captures the motivation behind his early effort. The term *recital* entered musical vocabulary with a complex set of meanings when he gave two concerts alone in London in 1840. Because reading a poem in public by heart had been called a "recital," advertisements for Liszt's concerts stated that he would offer "recitals" of his recent *fantaisies* at each concert.[56] By the time he left London the press had applied the term to concerts themselves, even when he included other musicians on the program. In November 1840 *Jackson's Oxford Journal* spoke of Liszt's mixed program in the Star Assembly Room as "one of his piano-forte recitals."[57] The term may have been used chiefly when a pianist played from memory rather than from scores, but in any event it came to have iconic significance in denoting serious musical purpose.

[53] Gibbs, "'Just Two Words, Enormous Success,'" pp. 216–18. Clara Wieck offered unusually little vocal music there just before Liszt appeared; see pp. 213–15.
[54] Dana Gooley, "Franz Liszt: The Virtuoso as Strategist," in *Musician as Entrepreneur and Opportunist, 1700–1914: Managers, Charlatans and Idealists*, William Weber (ed.) (Bloomington, IN: Indiana University Press, 2004), p. 148.
[55] See further in Janet Ritterman and W. Weber, "Origins of the Piano Recital in England, 1830–1870," in *The Piano in Nineteenth-Century British Culture: Essays on Instruments, Performers and Repertoire*, Susan Wollenberg and Therese Ellsworth (eds.) (Aldershot, UK: Ashgate, 2007), pp. 171–92. Violinist Ole Bull reported giving a concert alone in Norway because he found local musicians so bad: Sara C. Bull, *Ole Bull: A Memoir* (Boston: Houghton Mifflin, 1883), p. 147.
[56] *Morning Herald*, 10 June 1840, p. 1; *TL*, 2 July 1840, p. 6.
[57] Quoted in Susan Wollenberg, "Pianos and Pianists in Nineteenth-Century Oxford," *Nineteenth-Century Music Review* 2 (2005), 116.

The solo recital occurred only occasionally until the mid-1850s, limited entirely to pianists before then. Marie Pleyel, née Moke (legally separated from publisher Camille Pleyel in 1835), followed Liszt's example on arriving in London in 1846; she advertised a series of three concerts as "recitals" but played alone only at the first one (Ex. 5.9). One critic called her effort an "experiment" whose "great variety of styles... put the capabilities of the pianist to an unusually severe test."[58] Although the program began with the Hummel Adagio, a traditional opening in an older style, all three of Pleyel's recitals focused on operatic *fantaisies*, and this program included three transcriptions of vocal pieces. Yet she continued Liszt's treatment of Schubert canonically well before many quartets or orchestras had thought of doing so, at a time when Schubert was still associated with the parlor or the singing club.[59] The hegemony of classical repertories had been so well established in London by the time of Pleyel's concerts that critic Davison expressed disappointment in the *Musical World* that she focused on the "modern 'romantic' school" and thereby "rejected" the great names of Beethoven, Mozart, Bach, Weber, and Mendelssohn.[60] Davison's comment indicates that he was open to a woman focusing her repertory on classics, perhaps as a moral alternative to commercial virtuosity. Because composition in the more highly valued genres was thought improper for women, playing Beethoven was to provide an important niche for ambitious women pianists, as Clara Schumann had already demonstrated.

5.9 *Pianist Marie Pleyel, Willis's Rooms, 18 May 1846*[61]

Adagio, *Grande fantaisie*	†Hummel
Fantaisie on themes from *Guillaume Tell*	Theodor Döhler
L'Inquiétude, morceau de concert	Alexander Dreyschock
Quartet, *Don Pasquale*, transcription	Donizetti/Emile Prudent
Fantaisie on Bellini's *La Sonnambula*	Thalberg
Marguerite au rouet (*Gretchen am Spinnrade*, D.564), transcription	†Schubert/Liszt
"La Danza, Tarantella Napoletana," *Soirées musicales*, transcription	Rossini/Liszt

---

[58] *TL*, 20 May 1846, p. 5. See Beatrix Borchard, "Die Regel und die Ausnahmen, Reisende Musikerinnen im 19. Jahrhundert," *Le musicien et ses voyages*, pp. 173–202.

[59] Gibbs, "Schubert in deutschsprachigen Lexica nach 1830."

[60] "Madame Pleyel," *MW*, 23 May 1846, p. 237.

[61] "Reception of Madame Pleyel by the English Press," *MW*, 23 May 1846, pp. 237, 251–2; Ellsworth, "Women Soloists and the Piano Concerto in Nineteenth-Century London," *Ad Parnassum: A Journal of Eighteenth- and Nineteenth-Century Instrumental Music* 2 (2004), pp. 21–49.

The ten-year-old Camille Saint-Saëns made a key experiment in devoting a virtuoso concert to classical works in his debut in Paris on 26 May 1846 (Ex. 5.10). Playing a program designed by his teacher Camille Stamaty, Saint-Saëns performed four solo pieces between concertos by Mozart and Beethoven, accompanied by a large orchestra. Clearly influenced by the Society of Concerts, the event illustrates how a virtuoso and an orchestra featuring classical music could have common repertory in pieces by Hummel and Frédéric Kalkbrenner. Yet precious little music by Handel, Mozart, or Beethoven had been performed at benefit concerts in Paris since around 1830. Commentary on virtuosity went in a new direction in a piece on his debut by a Viennese critic who used the term *interpretation*, arguing that Saint-Saëns had performed "the most challenging pieces by Bach, Beethoven, Weber, and Hummel with as much grace as proper interpretation."[62] A new vocabulary and a new artistic goal are evident in this statement. The closest Parisian parallel to the program was one presented by the idiosyncratic pianist Charles Alkan in 1844. Opening with his Concertino no. 1, accompanied by string quartet, Alkan offered five items of classical music: pieces by Bach and Scarlatti; a transcription of the minuet from Mozart's Symphony in G Minor, K. 550; one of Beethoven's rondos for piano; and Weber's *Mouvement perpetuel.* Paul Blanchard spoke for tradition in declaring his surprise that a pianist would play five classical pieces in a row.[63]

5.10 *Pianist Camille Saint-Saëns, Salle Pleyel, 6 May 1846*[64]

Concerto for piano in B-flat, K.450	†Mozart
Air varié and Fugue	†Handel
Toccata	Kalkbrenner
Sonata	†Hummel
Prelude and Fugue	†Bach
Concerto no. 1 in C Minor, op. 15	†Beethoven

Clara Wieck Schumann exercised major leadership in shaping the repertory and the aesthetic significance of the recital. Guided by her father,

62 "Saint-Saëns," *NGD*, vol. 22, p. 124; "Geschwind, was gibt's in Wien Neues?" *TZ*, 28 April 1847, p. 400.
63 "Concert de C. V. Alkan," *FM*, 14 April 1844, p. 119; *FM*, 26 April 1844, pp. 131–32.
64 Jean Bonnerot, *C. Saint-Saëns, 1835–1921, La vie et son oeuvre* (Paris: Durand, 1922), pp. 21–22. The Kalkbrenner Toccata might have been the *Trois études en forme de toccata*, op. 182 (Paris, 1847).

Friedrich Wieck, she began her career playing a standard repertory of opera *fantaisies* and other pieces in fashionable idioms, along with Italian opera numbers.[65] Her early programs also included a diverse array of songs and instrumental pieces by German composers – from keyboard works by Bach to male vocal solos and quartets written for sociable music-making. Putting on an Extra-Concert in the Gewandhaus when she was twelve, Clara and her father deferred to Parisian cosmopolitanism by offering a set of variations by Henri Herz and two operatic selections by Paër (Ex. 5.11). She also performed a concerto by the highly respected German pianist Johann Peter Pixis, then resident in Paris, and variations by the still little-known Frédéric Chopin. Perhaps the most telling name on the program was that of the organist Adolf Hesse of Breslau, who had done important work in reviving Bach's music. Yet the Wiecks also reached out to *Liedertafel* music-making by offering a Notturno for six male voices by Carl Ludwig Blum, head of the Berlin opera and a student of Salieri.[66]

5.11 *Pianist Clara Wieck, Gewandhaus, 9 July 1832* [67]

Symphony no. 2	Hesse
Aria	Paër
Concerto, op. 100	Pixis
Notturno, *Singet der Nacht ein stilles Lied,*	
for six male voices	Blum
Variations on "La ci darem la mano,"	
Nozze di Figaro	Chopin
Duet	Paër
Bravour-Variations, op. 20	Herz

[65] Nancy B. Reich, *Clara Schumann: The Artist and the Woman* (Ithaca, N.Y.: Cornell University Press, rev. ed., 2001), pp. 212–13; Pamela Susskind, "Clara Schumann's Recitals, 1832–50," *NCM* 4 (1980), 70–6. Herr Wieck came under harsh criticism in the Berlin press for manipulating his daughter's career toward his social and financial benefit more than was thought appropriate; see "Zeitung," *Der Freimüthige oder Berliner Conversations-Blatt,* 7 March 1835, p. 195; 22 April 1835, p. 320.

[66] Jon W. Finson, "Schumann, Popularity and the Ouverture, Scherzo, and Finale, Opus 52," *Musical Quarterly* 59 (1983), 1–25; Daverio, "Einheit-Freiheit-Vaterland," in *Music and German National Identity*, pp. 258–315; Heemann, *Männergesangvereine im 19. und frühen 20. Jahrhundert*; Carola Lipp, "Eine Mikroanalyse sozialpolitischer Differenzierung und verwandtschaftlicher Substrukturen in württembergischen Gesangvereinen des Vormärz und der Revolution 1848/49," *Les sociétés de musique in Europe*, pp. 431–54.

[67] Dörffel, *Geschichte der Gewandhausconcerte*, vol. 2, p. 209. She also included *Liedertafel* songs and an overture by Conradin Kreutzer, one of the most prominent *Liedertafel* composers, at a concert she gave in Vienna in 1837 (21 December 1837, PA/GMF).

Clara and Robert Schumann put on particularly pure examples of idealistic programming in the 1840s, marking a major change in her programming. The cabal of free-thinking intellectuals who wrote for the *Neue Zeitschrift für Musik* sought what David Ferris has described as an "idealized and frankly elitist conception of musical performance." Private performance could be purer than public performance in their eyes, contrary to the usual assumption that salon music was focused on fashionable kinds of music.[68] The couple put on regular concerts together at the Gewandhaus in the 1840s, including a "Morning Musical Entertainment" (musikalische Morgenunterhaltung) that was announced on the program as open only to "invited listeners" (Ex. 5.12). The concert began and ended with chamber works Robert had written and blended piano works by Bach and Beethoven with his songs, which were thus defined as art works different from the vocal quartets just discussed. The performance of the Beethoven Sonata Op. 101 in this context was one of the relatively few instances where the sonatas were given in public before 1850. Ironically, Robert began to compose more music for the general public – the Piano Concerto in A Minor and choruses for student groups, for example – at the very time when Clara began to narrow her attention to discriminating listeners.

5.12 *Clara and Robert Schumann, Gewandhaus, 8 January 1843* [69]

String Quartet in A Minor, op. 41, no. 1	R. Schumann
Prelude and Fugue	†Bach
"Warum willst du Andre fragen," *Gedichte aus Friedrich Rückert's "Liebesfrühling,"* op. 12	C. Schumann
"Du meine Seele, du mein Hertz," *Myrthen,* op. 25/1	R. Schumann
Sonata in A, op. 101	†Beethoven
Chaconne for violin	†Bach
"Wachst du noch, Liebchen?" & "Wer ist vor meiner Kammerthür" for soprano & tenor, *Vier Duette,* op. 34/2-3	R. Schumann
"Liebeszauber," *Sechs Lieder,* op. 13	C. Schumann
Piano Quintet in E-flat, op. 44	R. Schumann

In her own concerts, Clara moved toward a middle ground between the highly specialized program of 1843 and what most piano virtuosos were offering. A concert in Leipzig in 1841 included Liszt's *fantaisie* on *Lucia di Lammermoor* and the four-hand version of *Hexaméron* (the collaborative variations on Bellini's *I Puritani*). But in 1846 she gave a concert that included neither *fantaisies* nor classics, playing instead Mendelssohn's Concerto in G Minor, a barcarolle by Chopin, a *Lied ohne Worte* by Fanny Hensel, and her own *Scherzo.*[70] Thus did she display special talent as she negotiated between new musical ideals and music the general public could appreciate.

William Sterndale Bennett developed influential "collegial" programs, setting the standard for that kind of concert in London. Recognized for his gifts as a pianist, Bennett gained an early reputation as a composer in the mid-1830s and was warmly regarded by the circle around Robert Schumann while he lived in Leipzig. He designed his annual benefit concert as an idealistic alternative to the cosmopolitan norm, once offering Beethoven's still little-performed Violin Concerto and Spohr's poignantly chromatic Symphony no. 2 in D Minor. Then in 1843 he presented an annual series without orchestra called "Classical Subscription Concerts," first in private and then in the Hanover Square Rooms.[71] His first concert in 1843 included Beethoven's Sonata Op. 57 and a piano duet by Mozart. In 1851 *The Times* identified Bennett as "the first to influence the public mind in favor of the pianoforte works of the great masters."[72] Nevertheless, a ballad by Benedict, *The Cottage Door*, maintained the repertory of English vocal idioms, as we saw in the 1840 concerts of Liszt and Cramer (Ill. 5, Ex. 5.4).

The authority of Italian opera and the virtuoso *fantaisie* remained stronger in Vienna than in London or Leipzig. Until the mid-1840s it was uncommon for more than two of the eight to ten pieces at a benefit concert to be by classical composers. Liszt led the way in 1838 by performing Beethoven's sonatas in A-flat (op. 26) and C# Minor ("Moonlight," op. 27, no. 2). Other pianists followed his example during the following decade; Theodor Döhler, who was thought to imitate Thalberg, surprised the critics by performing the "Kreutzer" Violin Sonata (op. 47), followed by three of his own etudes together. Jenny Lind, who usually offered standard programs of opera selections and virtuosic *fantaisies*, invited Mendelssohn to perform the "Moonlight" Sonata at a concert she presented in

---

[70] Ibid., vol. 2, pp. 214, 217.

[71] CPH/RCM; Nicholas Temperley, "Schumann and Sterndale Bennett," *NCM*, 12 (1989), 207–20; Peter Horton, "William Sterndale Bennett: Composer and Pianist," in *Piano in Nineteenth-Century British Culture*, pp. 119–48.

[72] *TL*, 3 June 1851, p. 6. See also *MW*, 27 March 1852, p. 194.

1846.[73] But the first concerts devoted almost entirely to classics were performed by French musicians, pianist Thérèse Wartel and her husband Pierre, a tenor engaged at the opera in 1842–1843 (Ex. 5.13). At their two concerts all but a couple of songs were by Mozart, Beethoven, Weber, and Schubert; she performed Beethoven's "Pathétique" Sonata, and he sang from the six *Gellert Lieder*, op. 48. A local critic portrayed them as a model of the "German Spirit" and grumbled that Viennese taste was so bad that it took "fanatically German" French musicians to produce such a program. Yet the review also complained that a theatre song by Albert Grisar – "which pleased everyone and has been the rage in the salons" – was performed with a Beethoven sonata.[74] The Wartels organized no such serious programs in Paris, however. She gave few concerts on her own but became known, it was said, for "dedicating herself to the cult for severe classical music."[75]

5.13 *Pianist Thérèse Wartel and Singer Pierre Wartel, Friends of Music Hall, 15 January 1843*[76]

Overture, *Nozze di Figaro*	†Mozart
Adelaide	†Beethoven
Sonata in C Minor, op. 13, "Pathétique"	†Beethoven
Lied, *La Prière* (*Das Gebet*), *Gellert Lieder*, op. 48 (1802)	†Beethoven
Lied, *Le Printemps* (*Der Frühling*)	†Schubert
Concerto for piano	†Weber
Songs:	
a) *Le Secret* (*Das Geheimnis*)	†Schubert
b) *L'arrivée du régiment*	Albert Grisar

Nevertheless, a great deal of Beethoven's music was performed in private homes in Vienna, chiefly under the auspices of publisher Carl Haslinger. Henry Vieuxtemps, who seems never to have performed Beethoven publicly in Vienna, led performance of three Beethoven quartets – including op. 130 – at a private soirée at the company's show rooms in 1844.[77] That

---

73 Gibbs, "Just Two Words, Enormous Success," pp. 217–18; PA/GMF; "Theodore Döhler," *AWMZ*, 26 March 1842, p. 150; *AWMZ*, 12 May 1842, pp. 234–35.
74 "Nachrichten, Wien," *AMZ*, 1 March 1843, p. 177; "Concert," *AWMZ*, 15 November 1842, p. 550; Fauquet, *Dictionnaire*, p. 538.
75 "Premier Concert de la *Gazette musicale*," *RGM*, 10 November 1844, pp. 374–76.
76 PA/GMFV. Wartel was one of the few women who published reviews in music magazines; see Katherine Ellis, "Female Pianists and their Male Critics in Nineteenth-Century Paris," *JAMS* 50 (1997), 353.
77 PA/GMFV. The Quartets op. 18, no. 1, op. 59, no. 3, and op. 130 were performed.

same season Haslinger held a *soirée* at his residence to offer pieces little known today, such as the "Trauer-Marsch" from Beethoven's Sonata Op. 26 arranged for physharmonika and piano, and the Chorus of the Dervishes from the incidental music *Ruins of Athens* (op. 113).

Composers who were not well known as virtuosos increasingly turned to the benefit concert to promote their music. Such musicians were at a serious disadvantage in the time, for not only had court and church positions declined in number, but also concert repertories were shifting toward classics. In 1823 the young Saxon composer Carl Reissiger conducted a program at the Gewandhaus focused on scenes from *Didone abbandonate*, an opera he was setting for Weber to produce in Dresden. Whereas the first half was devoted to Germanic music (by Beethoven, Hummel, and Spohr), the second concluded with the composer's piano trio and an aria by Paër. Yet Reissiger ended up better known for his melodramas and light operas (Ex. 7.11 and Ill. 26).[78] French pianist Louise Farrenc had greater success with concerts of her own music, for in 1838 she performed her own piano works and conducted *Hymne à l'éternel* for four voices, a *ballade* for piano and orchestra, and *Didone abbandonata* for chorus and solo voice. The reviewer of *France musicale* was enthusiastic about what he heard but made clear that it was the "composer's" rather than the "performer's" music and that he found her etudes severe.[79] Hector Berlioz set the standard for the composer's concert in Vienna as well as in Paris. In 1846 he conducted a program in the Grosser Redoutensaal, offering movements from the *Symphonie Fantastique, Roméo et Juliette*, and *Harold en Italie*. One can gauge the high repute in which he was held in Vienna by his ability to gain court approval to appear in the Grosser Redoutensaal and indeed to have a poem written in his honor.[80]

VIRTUOSITY IN CRISIS

The virtuoso concert gradually slipped into crisis during the 1840s. Its legitimacy was being called into question among the fans of virtuosos as much as among idealists. In 1842 a Viennese critic showed no signs of worry when he praised a young violinist for playing effortless staccatos, pizzicatos, and triple-stops, displaying "the precision, purity, and elegance of an artist potentially of the first rank."[81] But four years later a writer in the

---

[78] Extra-Concerts, 1823–24, SGML.   [79] *FM*, 27 May 1838, pp. 5–6.   [80] PA/GMF.
[81] "Musikalischer Telegraf," *TZ*, 1 July 1842, p. 700.

same periodical expressed deep disillusionment with the state of virtuoso playing:

Lord knows, what an army of concert-givers we face this season! The writing of music has no living Mozart or Beethoven of whose praises we sing, and least of all does any performing musician come close to that. Too many pianists try to make themselves into virtuosos. How many pianists can attain any real artistry? Very few indeed, Liszt first among them, a musician about whom so many Viennese went into raptures. . . . It is a bitter fate to have to listen to so many crummy piano-players who do nothing but pound their fingers on those keys.[82]

A severe decline in the European economy in the late 1840s, caused by unusually bad harvests, meant that fewer and fewer performers could make tours, and the upheaval in the winter and spring of 1848 wreaked havoc in most musicians' lives. Sigismond Thalberg bravely put on a concert in the Friends of Music Hall in Vienna on 3 May 1848. Performers must have spent time meditating on the problem the Viennese critic described in 1846 – the demand by the public that a firmer order be given to musical life and the "army of concert-givers." Something of that kind was in fact done, willy-nilly, once the upheaval came to an end.

[82] B. Thenmann, "Spiegelbilder aus Wien," *TZ*, 18 July 1846, p. 682.

CHAPTER 6

Toward classical repertory in orchestral concerts

A fundamental change occurred in concert life when professional orchestras moved to the center of musical life and thereby rivaled opera. Although benefit concerts, and eventually recitals, were more numerous, and chamber music concerts acquired the most learned public, elite orchestral concerts came to enjoy a major role within musical life and European culture generally. Orchestral series established themselves on a more permanent basis than any other major type of concert; by 1870 subscribers were passing their seats down through wills. The orchestras of which we speak – the Leipzig Gewandhaus (1781), the Philharmonic Society of London (1813), the Society of Concerts of the Conservatoire in Paris (1828), and the Vienna Philharmonic Orchestra (1842) – still exist today. Their concerts evolved into civic institutions that became central to city life and to their nation.[1] By the 1860s their concerts had achieved wide influence over taste, education, and criticism, giving them an authority within musical culture equal to that of opera.

The repertory performed by orchestras underwent a massive shift to classical music in the course of two generations. As Charts 6.1 and 6.2 demonstrate, during the 1780s only eleven percent of the pieces performed at the Gewandhaus subscription concerts were by deceased composers. Although the percentage at the Gewandhaus went up to forty-eight percent by the mid-1840s, the newer series in Paris and Vienna, having begun at a higher level, reached seventy-five and seventy-four percent, respectively, by that time. In 1870 the Gewandhaus and Philharmonic Society as well as the Parisian Society of Concerts and the Vienna Philharmonic had comparable numbers, all between seventy-four and eighty-five percent.[2] We have seen

---

[1] See also William Weber, "The Great Orchestras: Institutions of Monopoly and Hegemony," in *Sociétés de concert en Europe, 1700–1920*, pp. 243–65.

[2] Programs are to be found in Dörffel, *Geschichte der Gewandhausconcerte*, vol. 1; Myles Birket Foster, *History of the Philharmonic Society of London: 1813–1912* (London: John Lane, 1912); D. Kern Holoman, "Société des Concerts: Chronology," http://hector.ucdavis.edu/sdc/MainFrame.htm; Richard von

that principles of musical idealism drove this change, bringing a new vocabulary to musical discourse. In the 1780s a piece could be praised for being a *well-crafted* and *affecting* work by a *master composer*, but it eventually would be superseded by something new. By 1870 a composition soon had to be deemed a *great* work – indeed, an *artwork* – by a *classical* composer, to be selected for a major orchestral series. Such language would have been thought strange in Mozart's time. Did he and his colleagues not entertain the public by making the masters before them seem out of date?

During the first half of the nineteenth century orchestral programs served to some extent as staging grounds for vocal and instrumental soloists and occasionally chamber ensembles. In more cases than not, opera selections and solo – even unaccompanied – instrumental numbers continued in the orchestras' programs for the rest of the century. The professional self-interest of individual musicians came into play in some respects. At the Society of Concerts in Paris, for example, Conservatoire professors made sure they performed solos despite rising criticism of that genre. As that suggests, the public at orchestral concerts was more diverse in taste than was the case at chamber music concerts. Each orchestra worked out a set of compromises among conflicting pressures regarding programming. Controversies arose from efforts to satisfy different groups and sometimes became feverish culture wars over what was performed or what was not. Significantly, the earliest homogeneous classical repertory was built by a transitional ensemble, Vienna's Concert Spirituel (1819–1848), where a narrowly defined repertory was offered to a small and loyal public. We therefore need to examine programs carefully, comparing the sequence of genres chosen by each orchestra and finding how they differed in profile.

Did the great orchestras bear the stamp of any social class in their early histories? We have seen that quartet concerts carried an aristocratic identity even though they built up diverse publics early in their history. It is best to interpret the social orientation of the orchestral societies as defined by the *professional* as opposed to *commercial* component of the middle classes.

Perger, *Denkschrift aus Anlass der Feier des fünfzigjährigen ununterbrochenen Bestandes des Philharmonischen Konzerte in Wien, 1860–1910* (Vienna: Fromme, 1910); and Clemens Hellsberg, *Demokratie der Könige: Die Geschichte der Wiener Philharmoniker* (Zürich: Schweizer Verlagshaus, 1993), pp. 40–1. Because periodicals did not identify many pieces on programs before 1850, the proportion of living and dead composers is the best measure of the age or a repertory. To be sure, death of a musician at an early age – as happened to Bellini and Mendelssohn, for example – can bring about quantitative imbalance. But composers who ceased producing actively – such as Rossini and Meyerbeer – can correct such distortion. Calculating the average date of birth of composers represented, in relationship to pieces performed, is another useful criterion, and the standard deviation of that figure can also be enlightening.

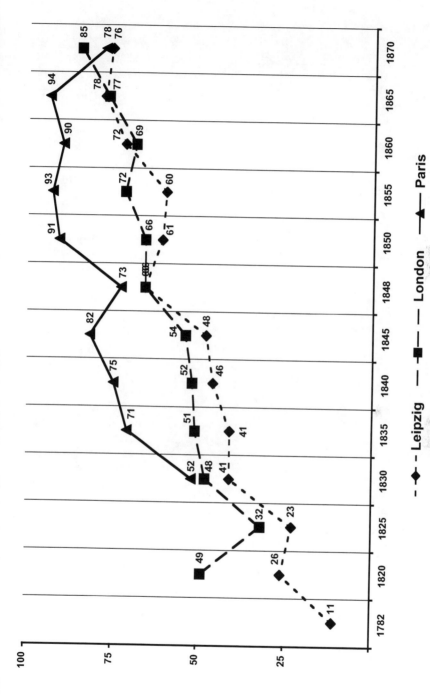

Chart 6.1. Percentage of Dead Composers, Leipzig, London, Paris, 1782–1870.

Legend: Leipzig ◆ — ◆ London ■ - - ■ Paris ▲——▲

171

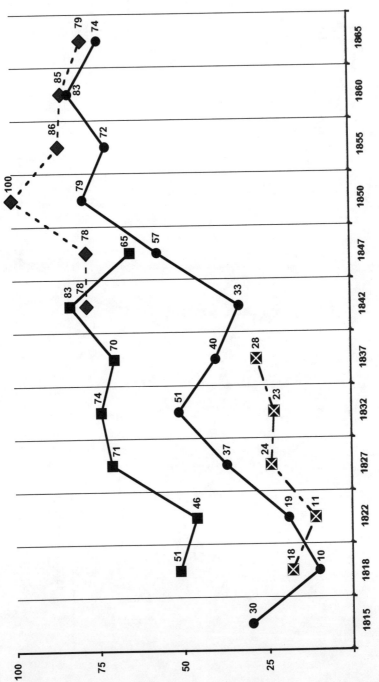

Chart 6.2. Percentage of Dead Composers in Vienna, 1815–1870.

- - - ◆ - - - Philharmonic ━━■━━ Concert Spirituel ━━●━━ Society Concerts ━ ⊠ ━ Abend-Unterhaltungen

Social historians have found major differences between the world of business and that of the liberal professions and the civil service during the nineteenth century.[3] The orchestras were prime examples of the successful ways in which musicians, like doctors, lawyers, university professors, and civil servants, used professional organizations to enhance their power and social standing.[4] More men in the *Direktorium* of the Gewandhaus were from the professions (especially the law) than from business.[5] By contrast, benefit concerts possessed a distinct commercial identity, because the musicians organized them as entrepreneurs and in so doing worked closely with publishers and piano manufacturers. Many musicians thus ultimately connected to both aspects of bourgeois identity. Nevertheless, the elite orchestras in Paris, Leipzig, and Vienna drew some aristocrats to their performances and participated within aristocratic musical traditions. Indeed, in the eighteenth century orchestral concerts emerged with a close relationship with court music-making and thereby endowed public concerts with a certain social distinction. Musicians leading music halls, ballad concerts, and *cafés-concerts* were to break with that tradition by giving their events flagrantly commercial and populist identities.

THE COMMON REPERTORY

Orchestral programs remained traditional in makeup as compared to quartet concerts, because both vocal and instrumental music were basic to their repertories. Only at a few concerts of the Vienna Philharmonic could one hear a program with no music for voice or chorus. The orchestras in our four major cities also shared a good deal of common repertory during this period. One would always find opera overtures, opera selections, symphonic works, and accompanied instrumental solos on their programs. But the frequency of choral pieces and songs varied to a greater extent.

Although the symphonies of Beethoven were universal to all orchestras, opera overtures rivaled those great works for popularity among most concert-goers. An overture had a life of its own independent of the opera for which it was written, probably associated with benefit concerts more than any other context in listeners' minds. At orchestral concerts

---

[3] Preface, Weber, *MMC*, 2nd. ed., pp. xi–xxxxiv. David Gramit confirms the key role played by families from the professions in "Unremarkable Musical Lives: Autobiographical Narratives, Music, and the Shaping of the Self," in *Musical Biography: Towards New Paradigms*, Jolanta T. Pekacz (ed.) (Aldershot UK: Ashgate, 2006), pp. 159–78.

[4] Penelope Corfield, *Power and the Professions in Britain, 1700–1850* (London: Routledge, 1995).

[5] Menninger, "The Serious Matter of True Joy."

overtures might serve as "bookends" that opened and closed each half of a program, providing a framework of universally-known music for the concert as a whole. Cherubini's overture to *Anacréon, ou L'amour fugitive* (1803), for example, was performed more often than any other piece in the first fifty years of the London Philharmonic Society; audiences were captivated by the contrast between its heavily sensuous main theme and several boisterous climaxes, one of which anticipates the storm at the end of Act I.[6] By the 1840s a few "concert" overtures – for example, Beethoven's *Consecration of the House* and Mendelssohn's introduction to *Midsummer Night's Dream* – enjoyed a similar prominence in many kinds of concerts.

The performance of operatic vocal selections also constituted a common culture in musical life. Such pieces held just as important canonic roles at orchestral series as at benefit concerts. Although we will not try to compare which pieces were performed in the two contexts, it is clear that almost all the same composers were represented, from Gluck, Sarti, and Sacchini to Cimarosa, Paeisiello, and Mozart and finally to Spontini, Méhul, and Rossini (see list in Chapter 5, pages 143–4). The public's wide knowledge of these selections must have aided the orchestras in establishing canonic repertories as a whole, even though this music did not receive the scrutiny that critics and aestheticians gave the symphony. The performance of music from a recent opera was another matter, however. Suspicion of the commodification of opera stimulated intense criticism of an orchestra that performed selections from new works, especially selections from operas by Donizetti, Bellini, and Meyerbeer. Such pieces were not performed often by the orchestras in Paris and Vienna – court cities where major new operas were being initiated. Compromise with aesthetic principle seems to have come easier in London and Leipzig, where operas were imported. That the two pairs of cities were Catholic and Protestant, respectively, may also have contributed to this difference, given the intellectual hegemony exerted by Catholicism traditionally. Yet the Gewandhaus concerts and the Philharmonic Society kept performing pieces by Donizetti, Bellini, and quite a variety of other opera composers for much of the century, and the London concerts suffered particularly from the ire its programming drew from the idealist press. Performance of *fantaisies* on the music of recent operas came under similar critical attack. In Vienna the Concert Spirituel and the Philharmonic concerts abstained completely from performance of such pieces, but the Conservatoire concerts did offer quite a few in its early seasons.

---

[6] Foster, *History of the Philharmonic Society*, p. 540. David Wyn Jones identifies a significant decline in the symphony in Vienna in the early nineteenth century; see *Symphony in Beethoven's Vienna*, pp. 155–80.

Orchestral societies divided along similar lines in the performance of sacred works or oratorios. The two orchestras in Catholic cities – the Conservatoire concerts and the Viennese Concert Spirituel – included a religious work at over two-thirds of their programs, but such music appeared only occasionally in the two Protestant locales. Sacred music began to decline at the Gewandhaus by around 1815, and the Philharmonic Society avoided such pieces, due in part to its rivalry with the Concerts of Ancient Music. The royal chapels in Vienna and Paris maintained their traditions of high musical craft through at least the 1810s, encouraging the Conservatoire concerts and the Viennese Concert Spirituel to perform liturgical works frequently. Movements for liturgical or theological reform were more vigorous at the time among Catholics than Protestants, calling for the church to return to the ideas of the ancient church fathers and to reach out to the society as a whole. Close links developed between the reform movements in religion and music in France and northern Germany, focused on revival of the music of Palestrina.[7] There were nonetheless limits to the spiritual character of orchestral concerts. Although the Viennese Concert Spirituel began in a church and never completely lost that identity when it shifted to public halls, the Vienna Philharmonic, which in effect replaced it, possessed a secular tone from the start. The Conservatoire concerts balanced the secular and the sacred, thanks to the careful programming of its leaders.

Although the term *symphony orchestra* is not appropriate for concerts held before the late nineteenth century, the symphony became a genre special to orchestral series by the 1830s. Symphonies gave way to overtures at benefit concerts and were performed complete only occasionally at promenade concerts, except for a short-lived experiment in Paris in 1837–1840. A special iconic significance developed around the genre when orchestras began performing only a symphony after intermission. The Gewandhaus began that practice with its first performance of Beethoven's "Eroica" Symphony in 1807 (Ex. 6.4), and the London Philharmonic Society treated the Ninth Symphony similarly in 1825. The practice constituted a fundamental break with traditional programming and established a serious new kind of music-making. The Beethoven symphonies acquired a unique status by being offered systematically on a regular basis. By 1818 the Gewandhaus series was the first to perform all of his first eight symphonies, and by 1830 offered each

[7] Franklin, *Nineteenth-Century Churches*; Ellis, *Interpreting Music of the Past*, pp. 21, 71–72, 173–74, 191; Leterrier, *Le mélomane et l'historien*, Ch. 6–9; Garratt, *Palestrina*, pp. 48–52, 61, 83; Applegate, *Bach in Berlin*, pp. 198–200; Rémy Campos, *La Renaissance introuvable? La Société de musique vocale religieuse et classique du prince de la Moskowa* (Paris: Klincksieck, 2000).

work at least once every third year.[8] Such pride was taken in the practice that journalists claimed inaccurately that all nine works were played annually.[9] Similar schedules for the Beethoven symphonies were set up at the Philharmonic Society, the Conservatoire concerts, and the Vienna Philharmonic soon after their founding. Significant but less iconic roles emerged for Mozart's last four symphonies and some of the twelve symphonies Haydn composed in London. Another major innovation was the dedication of a program to a single canonic composer. The first and only example of such a practice in the eighteenth century took place in the many Handelian programs in Britain, especially those presented at the 1784 Commemoration in the composer's honor. The Viennese Concert Spirituel made a major innovation in 1824 by devoting an entire program to Haydn, Mozart, and Beethoven in succession, and other institutions soon often honored Mozart's birth and death days.

The orchestral concerts presented a much wider selection of composers than the musical trinity of Haydn, Mozart, and Beethoven. A collegial tradition persisted from the eighteenth century whereby a moderate number of composers were honored in common, even though one or two might be viewed with particular respect. For example, in 1776 Carl Junker, a writer and composer in southwest Germany, published *Twenty Composers: A Sketch* to identify the leading musicians of his time, admiring Haydn particulary but raising doubts about the music of Luigi Boccherini.[10] Likewise, in 1804 a Parisian music magazine invoked the importance of "Graun, [C. P. E.] Bach, Gluck, Haydn, Mozart, Salieri, and other great figures" while belittling an overture by the Austrian Joseph Wölfl.[11] Although Haydn, Mozart, and Beethoven held special prominence in musical commentary, they played quite different roles in orchestral programs, a complex subject we will not discuss here. One cannot understand what went on in the orchestral concerts without confronting the music of a wider group of composers. The orchestras we are studying all included pieces by nine musicians born between 1760 and 1784, three of them French and two Italian. Overtures, vocal selections, and, in some cases, symphonies by Luigi Cherubini (1760–1842) and Étienne Méhul (1763–1817) were performed in all four cities. Concertos by the Paris-based violinists Giovanni Viotti (1755–1824) and Pierre Rode (1774–1830) were often heard at the same

[8] Reimer, "Repertoirebildung und Kanonisierung."   [9] Stolle, *Das neue Leipzig,* p. 22.
[10] Carl Ludwig Junker, *Zwanzig Componisten: eine Skizze* (Bern: Typographische Gesellschaft, 1776). See William Weber, "Canonicity and Collegiality: 'Other' Composers, 1790–1850," *Common Knowledge* 14 (2008), 105–23.
[11] "Concert de la rue de Grenelle," *CORR,* 24 January 1804, p. 58.

institutions. Four German virtuosos had similarly wide exposure: the pianist Hummel (1778–1837), violinists Spohr and Andreas Romberg (1767–1721), and the latter's cousin, cellist Bernhard Romberg (1767–1841). Finally, pieces by George Onslow, a Frenchman who lived in England at intervals, were performed at chamber music concerts throughout Europe.

Spohr became the most distinguished of these figures. His concertos, symphonies, operas, quartets, and oratorios were performed all over Europe; critics thought that his music approached the greatness of Mozart or Beethoven more than did that of any other composer in the time. He came to the fore as a violinist who took virtuosity in a new direction, developing svelte melodies with sophisticated harmonic activity. His symphonies prefigured the shift toward the rhapsody or the suite; he, in effect, experimented with neoclassicism in ways that became common during the 1860s. In 1843 Davison declared in the *Musical World* that Spohr would be admitted "into the realms of classical immortality" because his works would "take their station among the master-pieces of Bach, Handel, Gluck, Haydn, Mozart, Beethoven, Weber and Cherubini."[12] Although his music came under fire in the 1840s, it retained a significant place in orchestral concerts throughout the century.[13] A similar respect was accorded to Onslow for the vitality and color in his symphonies, quartets, and indeed his nonet for winds and strings. When his Symphony in A was performed at the Gewandhaus in 1845 a critic stated that the orchestra's leaders saw it "standing right beside the symphonies of the classical composers."[14]

Music written in the Classic style continued to influence composers deeply for several generations after Romantic tendencies appeared. Kenneth DeLong has argued that composers often identified as "Biedermeier" took advantage of the Romantic style's open textures, regular metric periods, and chromatic inflection of harmony. Use of such features along with new techniques afforded a continuity with the past in a time of flux in composing practices. This could also afford the composer a certain artistic respectability, acknowledging the authority accorded to classical repertories.[15] Although there are many precedents for an old style remaining in play after a new one arose, the Classic style played unusually important roles within

---

[12] Quoted by Clive Brown in his perceptive "Heinrich Spohr," *NGD*, vol 24, pp. 198–211, and *Louis Spohr: A Critical Biography* (Cambridge: Cambridge University Press, 1984).

[13] See the extensive collection of programs, chiefly from Germany and the United States, 1860–1920, in FUSB.

[14] "Nachrichten," *AMZ*, 31 December 1845, pp. 932–3; "Onslow," *NGD*, vol.18, pp. 413–14.

[15] Kenneth DeLong, "Conventions of Musical Biedermeier," *Convention in Eighteenth- and Nineteenth-century Music: Essays in Honor of Leonard G. Ratner*, Wye J. Allanbrook, Janet M. Levy, and William P. Mahrt (eds.) (Stuyvesant, N.Y.: Pendragon Press, 1992).

both the compositional process and concert programs. Thus although the *stile antico* was employed chiefly as an academic exercise in the 1600s, remnants of the Classic style persisted in music written for public performance. The problem deserves much further discussion, especially regarding composers outside Germany and Austria.

A special form of historical program was inaugurated by François Fétis in a series of "Concerts Historiques" he presented in 1832–1833. The first program, made up almost entirely of vocal pieces, went much farther back in time than any orchestral concert attempted before the 1870s (Ex. 6.1). The main precedent was the Academy of Ancient Music in mid-eighteenth-century London, focused on sacred music rather than opera (Ex. 2.10).

6.1 *Concert Historique #1, Sunday, 8 April 1832, Salle du Conservatoire*[16]

Excerpts from:
Ballet comique de la Reine (1581)
Euridice (1600)   †Jacopo Peri & Giulio Caccini
Orfeo (1607)   †Claudio Monteverdi
Xerxes (1654)   †Francesco Cavalli

—

Monologue, *Armide*, "Enfin il est en
    ma puissance" (1686)   †Lully
Chorus, *Persée* (1682)   †Lully
Aria, *Basilius* (1694)   †Reinhard Keiser
Aria, *Laodicea e Berenice* (1701)   †Alessandro Scarlatti
Duo, *Berenice* (1737)   †Handel
Buffo duo, *La Serva Padrona* (1733)   †Pergolesi
Chorus, *Zoroastre* (1749)   †Rameau

Systematic historical programs remained foreign to orchestral societies, however. For all the effort to define concerts as serious, the goal of entertaining the audience persisted in muted form in classical music life. An orchestra might occasionally design a "historical" program, however, as the Gewandhaus series did in 1847 to celebrate its past. An announcement drew on the emerging canonic vocabulary by telling subscribers that "[t]he next three concerts are works by the Great Masters of the last 100 Years."

---

16 "Concerts Historiques," *Revue Musicale*, 31 March, p. 71, 9 April, p. 80, and 14 April, pp. 81–85, 1832. Baillot also presented similar concerts; see Ellis, *Music Criticism*, pp. 14–15. On the Scarlatti aria, see Robert Wangermée, *Correspondance de François-Joseph Fétis*, Robert Wangermée (ed.) (Sprimont: Mardaga, 2006), p. 83.

The programs drew from the concerts' former repertory and followed the traditional format (Ex. 6.2).

6.2 *Abonnenten-Concerte, Gewandhaus, 18 February 1847*[17]

Suite	†J. S. Bach
Aria, *Jephtha* (1752)	†Handel
Adagio and Fugue for violin (Joseph Joachim)	†Bach
Duet, *Stabat Mater* (1736)	†Pergolesi
—	
Overture, *Samson* (1743)	†Handel
Aria, Miserere	†Jommelli
Chaconne for violin (Joachim)	†Bach
Aria, *Richard Coeur de Lion* (1784)	†Grétry
Overture, *Iphigénie in Aulis* (1774)	†Gluck

Charts 6.1 and 6.2 provide a historical outline for our comparison of repertories in the four major cities. Because the four orchestral institutions began anywhere from 1781 to 1842, their histories varied according to the time they began. Because Leipzig was so small a city, and the founding of the Gewandhaus in 1781 predated the movement toward classical music, its programs remained the most firmly rooted in traditional practices, lagging behind the other three orchestras until the 1860s. Although fifty percent of the pieces offered by the London Philharmonic Society in its early years were by dead composers, that number declined to thirty-two percent by 1825 before rising again at about the same rate as that at the Gewandhaus. The Conservatoire and the Vienna Philharmonic concerts, founded later, offered significantly more classical pieces from the start. In 1828 the Parisian concerts started at a level higher than the Leipzig and London orchestras, moving up from fifty-two percent in 1830 to eighty-two percent in 1845. Chart 6.2 presents contrasting patterns found for four Viennese concert series between 1815 and 1870.[18] Two series did not depart far from the tradition of presenting recent music. The percentage of pieces by dead composers at the Evening Entertainments never went beyond twenty-eight percent, which was reached when they ended in 1840, and the figure for

---

[17] Abonnenten-Concerte, SGML.

[18] Due to the unusually wide numerical variations among seasons displayed by the Viennese concerts, Chart 6.2 indicates the average percentage from a group of seasons, the first of which is cited. The seasons employed are 1822/23–1826/27; 1827/28–1831/32; 1832/33–1836/37; 1837/38–1841/42; 1842/43–1846/47; 1847/48–1849/50; 1850/51–1854/55; 1855/56–1859/60; 1860/61–1864/65; 1865/66–1869/70. The seasons of the Concert Spirituel were usually only in the winter and spring.

the organization's main series, the Society Concerts, never went beyond the fifty-one percent reached in 1830. Much more consistent classical repertories developed with the Viennese Concert Spirituel, which reached seventy-four percent in the mid-1830s, and the Vienna Philharmonic, whose programs began in 1842 at a level almost as high as that at the Paris Conservatoire. After 1848 the percentages of all four orchestras continued to rise, ending up between seventy-four and eight-five percent in 1870.

LEIPZIG

Because the Gewandhaus was a social center for Leipzig's upper classes, its governing board had to design programs that accommodated different tastes within the public. Although the presence of a contentious intelligentsia in the city made that task challenging, the board successfully guided the concerts through major changes in programming by 1870.[19] The most extreme voices in the satirical press attacked the concerts as elitist, but the climate of musical opinion did not become as disputatious as the one surrounding the Philharmonic Society in London. Writers in the *Allgemeine musikalische Zeitung* and the *Neue Zeitschrift für Musik* aimed their critique of bad taste more at the music itself than at the concert series where it was performed.

Innovations in concert programming came in the wake of the 1806 French invasion and the ensuing turmoil. A correspondent of the *Journal des Luxus und der Moden* spoke of "the threatening, thunderous storms of the war" that had troubled the city that season, forcing cancellation of several concerts and "make us yearn to taste the arts of peace." He hoped that "through the fearful emotions of music we will be once more upright and free."[20] The political situation heightened divisions of taste within the musical community and brought about the first major change in the program format that had been followed rigidly at the subscription concerts (Ex. 2.1, Ills. I and II). The local première of Beethoven's "Eroica" Symphony had long-term consequences for the subscription concerts. First performed in Vienna on 7 April 1805, the "Grand Heroic Symphony" was offered at the Gewandhaus on 29 January 1807, in the conventional spot at the start of the concert, followed by a scene from a recent opera (Ex. 6.3).

[19] Grotjahn, *Die Sinfonie*, pp. 102–7 and *passim*; Hans-Joachim Nösselt, *Das Gewandhausorchester: Entstehung und Entwicklung eines Orchesters* (Leipzig: Köhler & Amelang, 1943), especially pp. 129–67; Friedrich Schmidt, *Das Musikleben der bürgerlichen Gesellschaft Leipzigs im Vormärz, 1815–48* (Langensalza: Beyer, 1912).

[20] "Ueber das stehende Concert in Leipzig, im vorigen Winterhalbjahre," *JLM*, July 1807, p. 443.

6.3 *Abonnenten-Concerte, Gewandhaus, 29 January 1807*[21]

Symphony no. 3 in E-flat, op. 55, "Eroica"	Beethoven
Scene with Chorus, "Ah padre Mio!" *Zaira*	
(1799)	Francesco or Vincenzo Federici
—	
Concerto for viola	*A. Schneider*
Finale, *Aci e Galatea* (1801)	†Johann Naumann

The symphony had such a profound impact upon the public that it was brought back the next week, "By Demand," as the only piece after intermission, accompanied only by operatic pieces by Mozart (Ex. 6.4).

6.4 *Abonnenten-Concerte, Gewandhaus, 5 February 1807*[22]

Overture	Beethoven
Concerto for piano	†Mozart
Terzet, "Vengo – aspettate-Sesto!"	
La Clemenzo di Tito (1791)	†Mozart
—	
Symphony no. 3 in E-flat, op. 55	Beethoven

The scale of the symphony, indeed its extraordinary Romantic ambition, reshaped the miscellaneous concert program significantly. A new practice was established for granting a privileged place on a program to an unusually important work. The "Eroica" was subsequently offered every year or two, sometimes twice in a season, acquiring a special place in the repertory. Not only symphonies by Beethoven but also long works by composers such as Spohr and Peter Winter enjoyed this privilege. It is indeed likely that composers such as they wrote challenging pieces in the hope that one might be made the focal point of a concert. Traditional practices nonetheless remained largely intact in the next twenty-five years. Even though a major symphony might come alone after intermission, the subscription concerts continued to offer a standard format of opera selections and virtuoso numbers. For all that commentators criticized opera excerpts, a substantial part of the audience wanted to hear virtuosic opera and instrumental pieces back to back. Almost every program included one or two

---

[21] Abonnenten-Concerte, SGML. Though *Zaire* was attributed to Vincenzo Federici, it may have been composed by Francesco Federici; see "Federici," *NGD*, vol. 8, p. 639–40. Schneider seems to have been a visitor.
[22] Abonnenten-Concerte, SGML.

instrumental solos with orchestral accompaniment, most often variations
or *fantaisies* on music from a prominent opera. A program in 1830 (Ex. 6.5)
was typical for the time in balancing symphonic, operatic, and virtuosic
pieces, framed by pieces of Haydn, Mozart, and Beethoven. Four selections
by Rossini (including *Zelmira*, his last work in Naples) were the focus of
the program, but attention must have been paid to the variations played
by Anna Caroline Oury, a twenty-two-year-old Franco-German aristocrat
who had studied with Carl Czerny.

6.5 Abonnenten-Concerte, Gewandhaus, 15 October 1830[23]

Symphony   †Haydn
Aria and Chorus, *Zelmira* (1822)   Rossini
Concerto for Piano in A Minor   Hummel
—
Overture, *Coriolanus*, op. 62   †Beethoven
Terzett, *Zelmira* (1822)   Rossini
Variazioni brillanti for piano   *Anna Caroline Oury (née Belleville)*
Chorus, *Idomeneo* (1781)   †Mozart
Encores: two numbers from Rossini's *Guillaume Tell* (1829)

Perhaps influenced by political crisis, the Gewandhaus board reshaped
its policies in the 1830s, upgrading performing standards and giving more
classical works and somewhat fewer opera selections. Although Felix
Mendelssohn provided important leadership as music director (1835–1840
and 1843–1847), the directing board tended to know what it wanted to
do, trying to bolster the institution in troubled times. The two parts
of a concert in 1846 illustrate old and new programming at the series
(Ex. 6.6).

6.6 Abonnenten-Concerte, Gewandhaus, 12 November 1846[24]

Overture, *The Wood Nymphs* (1838)   William Sterndale
                                            Bennett

Aria, "Al desio di chi t'adora," *Le Nozze di
  Figaro* (his substitute aria, Vienna, 1789)   †Mozart
Concerto for violin   *Ferdinand David*
Cavatina, *Robert le Diable* (1831)   Meyerbeer

[23] *AMZ*, 27 October 1830, pp. 705–7.
[24] Abonnenten-Concerte, SGML; *AMZ*, 18 April 1847, pp. 768–69. The solo was not cited on the
printed program. See Applegate, *Bach in Berlin*, pp. 240–1, 253. On the aria, see "Two Mozart
Replacement Arias for Figaro," in www.mozartforum.com.

Lieder ohne Worte (or *Romances sans paroles*)
 for violin (1845), piano acc. by Niels Gade Henry Vieuxtemps
—

Solo for violin   †J. S. Bach
Symphony no. 3 in E-flat, op. 55   †Beethoven

The first half followed the traditional succession of genres, focusing on a well-known opera selection and a piece Vieuxtemps had written there the year before. But the second half took the innovation of 1807 a step further by including a violin solo by Johann Sebastian Bach, probably the Chaconne in D Minor, with the "Eroica" Symphony. That an instrumental solo was now the oldest piece on the program demonstrates a major change in the nature of virtuosity at these concerts.

 The Gewandhaus programs became a key model – the "Gewandhaus-Typus," as Rebecca Grotjahn has identified it – for German concert societies.[25] Still, in the early 1840s its classical repertory was limited compared with what the Paris Conservatoire concerts and the Vienna Philharmonic provided. The proportion of pieces by dead composers grew from twenty-three to forty-six percent between the seasons 1824–1825 and 1845–1846, much less than what the Conservatoire concerts offered by that time. One could still hear a succession of vocal and virtuosic pieces by living composers on one program, as happened on 4 February 1847: a new concerto by de Bériot, a set of variations by David, a symphony by the Lübeck-born violinist Ludwig Pape, and a song by the Swede Adolf Lindblad that had been widely performed by Jenny Lind.[26]

 Just as the Gewandhaus concerts arose well before the other orchestral series, so they were the first to acquire a competitor (Ex. 6.7). Begun as a private ensemble, the Euterpe Society offered public concerts from 1834 to 1886, after which it was replaced by a series directed by Hans Winderstein. By the 1840s its players were chiefly professionals employed in the theaters, though some also worked in the Gewandhaus.[27] Although isolating the symphony after intermission followed the Gewandhaus format, the program opened with an aria, not an instrumental work, and included pieces by Berlioz and by an amateur (***) that would not appear at the elite series. Pieces by local composers and foreigners such as Berlioz were heard alongside *fantaisies* on *grands opéras*. The division between the two institutions reflects division within the Leipzig *Bürgertum*. The Euterpe

[25] Grotjahn, *Die Sinfonie*, pp. 102–9.   [26] Abonnenten-Concerte, SGML.
[27] Euterpe Concerte, SGML; Manfred Würzbacher, *Die Konzertätigkeit des Musikvereins Euterpe und des Winterstein–Orchesters im 19. Jh.* (Leipzig: Breitkopf und Härtel, 1966); [K. W. Whistling], *Der Musikverein Euterpe zu Leipzig, 1824–74, Ein Gedenkblatt* (Leipzig: Kahnt, 1874).

was the earliest orchestral series in our four cities to serve a public separate from the established elite. As Schumann's journal put it bluntly in 1835, the concerts were "bringing classical music directly to the middling classes."[28]

6.7 Euterpe-Verein, Saal der Buchhändlerbörse, 23 February 1847[29]

Aria, "Ich grausam," *Don Juan*	†Mozart
Variations on a Russian Song for violin	David
Lied for cello and piano	Franz Lachner
Song	K***
Overture, *Les Francs-Juges* (1826)	Berlioz
–	
Symphony no. 5 in C Minor	†Beethoven

LONDON

London musical life was being torn every which way just after the turn of the nineteenth century, as was soon to happen in politics. The repertory of "ancient" music, unique in Europe, came under attack for its weak intellectual rationale, and those who followed Continental musical life were unhappy because the symphonies of Haydn and Beethoven lacked a proper home since the Professional Concerts ended in 1793. However popular the glee and the catch had become among prestigious gentlemen, that music seemed increasingly out of place when performed with works of Mozart and Beethoven. The idealists began objecting to the convivial musical genres and to Italian opera selections taking greater prominence than symphonies. It was for good reason that leaders of various organizations stepped into the breach to try to bring order to the chaos they saw in the musical world.

A long-standing institutional myth to the contrary, the Philharmonic Society did not inaugurate performance of Austro-German classics. The Beethoven symphonies were first performed in Britain at the revived Vocal Concerts in 1801, as Ian Taylor has demonstrated.[30] The repertory brought British and Germanic works together, with a limited deference to Italian opera (Ex. 6.8). A program given in 1806 featured a Beethoven symphony (either the First or the Second) and a canzonet Haydn composed in London, along with vocal pieces by leading British composers since Arne and opera selections by Paisiello and Naumann. The preponderance of British composers was implicitly nationalistic, and the predominance of vocal

[28] *NZFM*, 15 April 1835, p. 123.   [29] Euterpe Concerte, SGML.
[30] Ian Taylor, "'A Period of Orchestral Destitution'? Symphonic Performance in London, 1795–1813," *NCMR* 2 (2005), 139–168.

music hard to find elsewhere in European concert life. A subscription concert located in the City of London in 1819 separated musical units more systematically: Handel and Haydn in the first half, contrasted with recent British and Italian vocal music in the second half.[31]

6.8 *Vocal Concert, Willis's Rooms, 14 February 1806*[32]

Overture and Dead March in *Saul*	†Handel
Elegy, *O'er Nelson's Tomb*, 4 voices	†Thomas Norris
Scene, "Hark! my Daridcar," incidental music,	
Tyrannic Love or the Royal Martyr (1694)	†Purcell
Nocturne, "All' amor mio," 3v	†Johann Naumann
New Glee, 4v	John Clarke-Whitfield
New Concerto for flute	*Andrew Ashe*
Duet, "As I saw fair Flora"	Haydn
Recitative and Aria, "Farewell, ye limpid	
Springs and Floods," *Jephtha*	†Handel
"Military Symphony," Air, and Chorus,	
"Come if you Dare," *King Arthur* (1691)	†Purcell
—	
"New Grand Sinfonie (MS)"	Beethoven
Song, *The Soldier's Dream*, acc. organ	Thomas Attwood
"Glee" "My Mother Bids me Bind my Hair,"	
from *six Original Canzonets* (1794), arr. for 4v	
by Greatorex	Haydn
Song & Chorus, *Trafalgar* (1806)	Callcott
Trio (vn, vc, bc) by "Handel & Martini"	[? movements by Handel & G.-B. Sammartini]
Aria, "Ah fate, O Dio dipianto"	Paisiello
Glee, "Peace to the Souls of the Heroes"	Callcott
Song, "From rosy Bowers," incidental music to	
Don Quixote (1694)	†Purcell
Song, *The wooden Walls of England for*	
Ever, 3v and chorus (1804)	†Arne

---

[31] *London Subscription Concerts, London Tavern, 8 March 1819*, George Smart Papers, BL.
[32] *TL*, 12 February 1806, p. 1; quoted in Taylor, "A Period of Orchestral Destitution?" pp. 150–1. "As I saw fair Flora" may have been "As I saw fair Clora" by George Hayden, published c. 1710 (as Chloe in 1760), David Wyn Jones advises me. The Paisiello piece was probably an insertion aria for *L'inganno amoroso* (1786) set by P. A. Guglielmi.

Miscellaneous concerts like that one combining British and Continental music flourished throughout the nineteenth century, both in the metropolis and in provincial cities. A particularly imposing program was heared at the 1832 Oxford University Musical Festival, a "Grand Miscellaneous Concert" of twenty-six pieces, made up of Handelian selections, opera excerpts from Sacchini to Meyerbeer, the overture to *Anacréon*, a pair of glees, a concerto by Thomas Lindley, and recent songs by Bishop and John Braham (Ill. 13). Thus did the "domesticated" music of Handel unify cosmopolitan and national repertory. The Birmingham Private Concerts offered similar fare, with ballads particularly prominent. A program in 1841 included both recent and canonic British songs (by Purcell, Arne, Bishop, and J. P. Knight) and opera arias by Zingarelli and Nicola Vaccaj.[33] As a rule, overtures (in this case by Auber and Beethoven) figured more centrally in the concerts than did symphonies. The bourgeois in East London did something similar. The Eastern Institution in Whitechapel, for example, put on "Dress Concerts" that featured singers of note singing pieces by Pergolesi, Rossini, Balfe, and James Howard Tully, conductor at Drury Lane.[34]

Officers of the Philharmonic Society attempted to bring a new focus and discipline to its programs. The subscribers were made up largely of high-level musicians and their patrons, different from the general upper-class public found at the Gewandhaus concerts. As one music journal declared in 1822, "The audience at the Philharmonic are neither 'the great vulgar [i.e. nobles] nor the small [bourgeois]' – they are the cognoscenti."[35] Cyril Ehrlich characterized well the claim to authority made by the society's officers: "they needed 'patronage' from people who were then described as 'amateurs,' but had every intention of running their own show."[36] Indeed, the Society provided a model of professional musicians directing a concert series, which must have influenced the Conservatoire concerts and the Vienna Philharmonic at their inception.

Yet the Society's First Prospectus set up unattainable idealistic goals for the programming. The "laws" stated in the founding document directed the concerts to "promote the performance, in the most perfect manner possible, of the best and most approved instrumental music."[37] That would make opera excerpts and virtuoso solos, perhaps even concertos, inappropriate. But from the start, a program of ten pieces would offer two to four operatic

[33] Birmingham Private Concerts, BCL.   [34] Eastern Institution, CPH/RCM.
[35] *QMMR* 4 (1822), 433.   [36] Ehrlich, *First Philharmonic*, p. 1.
[37] Ibid., pp. 2–7; Foster, *History of the Philharmonic Society*, 4; Therese Ellsworth, "Women Soloists and the Piano Concerto in Nineteenth-Century London," *Ad Parnassum: A Journal of Eighteenth- and Nineteenth-Century Instrumental Music* 2 (2004), 21–2, 27–9.

vocal numbers, and one or two opera overtures would also be included. Moreover, solo instrumental numbers were standard repertory by 1820, and opera *fantaisies* followed. Still, by limiting the performance of British works, banning glees and related songs almost completely, the Philharmonic's programs became significantly less mixed than those of the Vocal Concerts (Ex. 6.8). Offering one or two string quartets at each concert in the first ten years also made the concerts quite austere, and the growing classical reportory had the same effect once quartets were gone. Sociability and serious music-making were now seen as incompatible; the Catch Club, Glee Club, and Madrigal Society now had limited influence on public musical life. This framework of programming lasted until the 1890s, when a militant generation of composers turned the Society's repertory back to British music.

The Philharmonic was not founded to construct a canonic repertory. Indeed, it began in part in reaction to the static repertory and aristocratic dominance of the Concert of Ancient Music (that was about to abandon the anachronistic "antient"). The Philharmonic Society selected only a few elements from ancient music, chiefly trios by Corelli, opera arias by Jommelli, and selections from Handel's operas and oratorios. Nevertheless, by the mid-1830s the ideal proposed for its new concerts, "the best and most approved" sorts of music, led to repertory that featured pieces by classical composers. From the start the programs favored a relatively small number of composers, mainly Haydn, Mozart, Cherubini, Beethoven, and Viotti. The Society's procedures for deciding on repertory tended to slow down the addition of works to repertory. In 1814 a general meeting of members voted £200 a year for "further improvement of musical composition," but the procedure by which that was done institutionalized tension between composers and the orchestra. This is the first known instance of a practice that would be followed by the Paris Conservatoire concerts, the Vienna Philharmonic, and other orchestras during the nineteenth century: "trial" performance of manuscript pieces in private, after which the directing board would vote on whether to add the piece to the repertory.[38]

By the early 1820s Philharmonic programs followed a standard sequence of genres for each half of a concert, with occasional variations: Symphony – Opera number – Concerto or Chamber work – Opera number – Overture. The format resembled that of the Gewandhaus in its alternation of vocal and instrumental works and its focus on operatic music. Although scholars have linked these London concerts chiefly with classical symphonies, some

---

[38] Meeting of Directors, 20 January 1815 and 5 January 1817, Papers of the Royal Philharmonic Society, BL.

subscribers probably went largely to hear the opera selections, which often amounted to half of a program. A concert in 1826 offered four such pieces, where all but one were three decades old, by Mozart, Zingarelli, Weigl, and Rossini, as well as overtures by Weber and Andreas Romberg (Ill. 12).[39]

During the 1830s and 1840s the Philharmonic drew the wrath of the idealistic press by performing more recent opera pieces than did any of the other major orchestras. The Philharmonic was responding to the growing passion for international opera among England's "middling" classes. As the voice portrayed in "An Aria Speaks" declared, "I have been introduced into many operas, and have made my appearance at the Philharmonic . . . Ah! it is a fine thing to be a popular song."[40] In 1836, for example, a program was packed with numbers by Mercadante (*I Normanni a Parigi*, 1832), Bellini (*Norma*, 1831), and Rossini (*Maometto Secondo*, 1820, and *Zelmira*, 1822). Idealists would have nothing to do with this music. The reviewer for the *Musical World* declared that there was no justification for putting excerpts like that on the same program with Beethoven's Second Symphony, and asserted that Italian singers were "incapable of [singing] such classic music as alone should be performed at these concerts."[41] Another critic defined musical knowledge ideologically by condemning excerpts by Giovanni Pacini and Vincenzo Federici as "trash," music that "all who possess any real knowledge of music, or a particle of genuine taste, must condemn."[42] Performance of opera *fantaisies* created similar dispute between views beholden to tradition and idealism. By the mid-1840s the only recent instrumental piece on many programs was usually a virtuosic piece, often an opera *fantaisie*. The Philharmonic presented some of the most well-known virtuosos of the time – pianists Thalberg, Meyer, and Alexander Dreyschock and the violinist Camille Sivori. In 1843 the reviewer for the *Musical Examiner* defied tradition by demanding that Dreyschock be prevented from performing his own music at the Philharmonic concerts and instead be told to play a Mozart concerto.[43] The author declared that "we strongly object to [performers] being allowed to play their own music, in the shape of trivial fantasias . . . [among] a grave and classically-included body of artists."

Much to its credit, the Philharmonic offered an impressive variety of composers and pieces, more wide-ranging and less repetitive than was presented at the Conservatoire concerts. One finds the leaders exploring

39 Foster, *History of the Philharmonic Society*, p. 79. The Weigl excerpt, "Stupefatto," was probably from his popular *L'amor marinaro* (1797) and that by Romberg from *Die Ruinen von Paluzzi* (1811).
40 "An Aria Speaks," *Fraser's Magazine*, 39 (1849), 20; Poriss, "An Aria Speaks."
41 *MW*, 27 March 1836, p. 26.   42 *Harmonicon* 5 (1827), 145–6.
43 "Fair Play to All Parties," *Musical Examiner*, 11 March 1843, pp. 133–34.

new areas of repertory in an 1840 program (Ex. 6.9) that offered pieces written early in the careers of three composers – the first concerto published by Rode (1794), an aria from a *melodramma tragico* by Mercadante (1821), and a song by Franz Lachner, the German who tried to start professional orchestral concerts in Vienna in 1831.[44] For all the Italian opera on these programs, one also heard pieces by such dramatic craftsmen as Auber and Heinrich Marschner. Indeed, one could hear much more recent French opera at the concerts of the Philharmonic than at the Conservatoire.

6.9 *Philharmonic Society, Hanover Square Rooms, 9 March 1840*[45]

Symphony no. 5 in C Minor	Spohr
Duet, "La Serenata," *Soirées musicales*, piano	
accompaniment	Rossini
Concerto no.3 for piano in C Minor, op. 37	†Beethoven
Lied, "The Sea hath pearly Treasures"	
(Nachts in der Kajüte), *Gedichte*, op. 34, no. 5,	
for voice, horn, piano,	Franz Lachner
Overture, *Euryanthe* (1823)	†Weber
—	
Symphony no. 1, in C, op. 21	†Beethoven
Duet, "Vanne se alberghi," *Andronico* (1821)	Mercadante
Concerto for Violin in D Minor (1794)	†Pierre Rode
Trio, "Night's lingering Shades," *Zemira and Azor* (1819)	Spohr

The Philharmonic board also greatly limited performance of pieces by British composers, as the subscription concerts of the late eighteenth century had done before. Such music formed about ten to fifteen percent of all pieces performed from the 1820s through the 1840s but figured more prominently in the later period, thanks to the reputations of William Sterndale Bennett and Cipriani Potter, the latter known for his post-Beethovenian instrumental works.[46] Henry Bishop also obtained performance of a cantata and several songs because he conducted many of the concerts. In this regard the Philharmonic's offerings were a bit better than the Conservatoire concerts, though both institutions greatly limited pieces by indigenous composers. By contrast, the Philharmonic ignored its nation's eighteenth-century music more completely than did the Conservatoire series. Arne was absent from the programs until 1864, and Purcell until 1887; even the

[44] Künstler-Verein, 1830, PA/GMFV; Hanslick, *Geschichte des Concertwesens in Wien*, pp. 315–16.
[45] Foster, *History of the Philharmonic Society*, pp. 200–1.   [46] Ibid., pp. 59, 116–17, 174–5.

Ancient Concerts presented a piece from Arne's *Artaxerxes* and a glee by Samuel Webbe, the Elder, in the 1840s.[47]

Bostonians enjoyed the musical populism brought by three orchestras competing for public attention during the 1840s, none becoming predominant.[48] Here again we find a Protestant city keeping sacred and secular music separate. Religious works remained the province of the Handel and Haydn Society, opera selections were provided by touring companies, and the orchestras focused their attention on symphonies, overtures, and virtuoso pieces of different kinds. A strictness of taste is evident in the performance of a Beethoven symphony alone after intermission more often than was done by the London Philharmonic. The Boston Academy of Music sometimes included no vocal pieces, as was rare in Europe. But in 1846 it followed international practice in offering a pair of arias by Donizetti and Bellini along with Beethoven's Seventh Symphony, the overtures to *Freischütz* and Auber's *Le Duc d'Olonne* (1842), a horn concerto by Lindpaintner, and a duet for flute and piano by Lafont and Herz. The Boston Musical Fund Society likewise added "O ruddier than the Cherry" from Handel's *Acis and Galatea* to a program of symphonic and virtuosic pieces.[49] But the amateur Philharmonic Society appealed to a broader public by putting the most popular of songs – Balfe's "I Dreamt I Dwelt in marble Halls" and Thomas Moore's "Believe Me, if All these endearing young Charms" – between movements of Beethoven's Fifth Symphony, on a program also including a concerto by Hummel and an aria from Auber's *Fra Diavolo* (1830).[50]

PARIS

French musical life experienced a deep discontinuity dating from the major changes that occurred at the Opéra in the 1770s. Although *la musique ancienne* was gone from the repertory by 1785, it left behind a historical awareness that aided in the building of a new repertory of old works after 1800, culminating in the founding of the Society of Concerts in 1828. Like Baillot's chamber music series, the society's concerts were based in a more self-contained institution than the Gewandhaus series or the Viennese Society of the Friends of Music. That kind of institution made it possible for Baillot and leaders of the orchestras to be unhindered in conceiving

---

47 Concert of Ancient Music, CPH/RCM.
48 Broyles, "Music of the Highest Class," pp. 195–203, 236–42, 332.   49 Concert programs, BPL.
50 "Boston Philharmonic Society" and "Boston Academy of Music," *Harbinger*, 27 February 1847, pp. 185–6.

of canonic repertories systematically and building repertory smoothly. The presence of nobles, high civil servants, and major *gens de lettres* among the subscribers also helped, giving the series both intellectual and political legitimacy. A "classical consensus" was therefore achieved in France by the early 1850s with less dispute than that surrounding the orchestras in London or Leipzig.[51]

A canonic repertory began to coalesce at the student concerts of the Paris Conservatoire, the *exercices des élèves*, which after 1800 attracted sophisticated listeners from outside the school.[52] Even though the concerts were never intended to present a repertory of old works, pieces survived from widely spaced points in the eighteenth century, such as by Pergolesi (1730s), Jommelli (1750s), Mozart (1780s), and Cherubini, as a program of 1807 suggests (Ex. 6.10). It is striking to see the Offertorium, probably written for the Papal chapel in 1751 or 1752, performed just after a revolution concerned with both ecclesiastical and political issues.[53] The first performance of Beethoven's music in Paris, his Symphony no. 1, occurred at these concerts earlier that year.

6.10 *Exercices des élèves, Saal du Conservatoire, 26 April 1807*[54]

Symphony in G Minor [K. 550?]	†Mozart
Air, *Sémiramis* (1802)	Charles Catel
Concertante for flute, horn, and bassoon	Catel
Duet, *Stabat Mater*	†Pergolesi
Offertorium	†Jommelli
Overture, *Faniska* (1806)	Cherubini

When the Concert Spirituel was reborn under the Restoration, it held no monopoly such as it had under the *ancien régime* but played an important role in extending this repertory. Major portions of Mozart's *Requiem*, Haydn's *Creation*, or Handel's *Messiah* might appear alone on the second half of a program, similarly to the focus on a symphony at the Gewandhaus.

[51] Leterrier, *Le mélomane et l'historien*, pp. 164–73. See also Samson, "The Great Composer," pp. 264–5.
[52] Jean Mongrédien,"Les premiers exercices publics d'élèves (1800–15), d'après la presse contemporaine," in *Le Conservatoire de Paris, 1795–1995*, A. Bongrain, Y. Gérard, and M. H. Courdroy-Saghai (eds.) (Paris: Buchet, 1996), pp. 15–37; Laurence Ardouin, "La musique ancienne au Conservatoire: évocations de la Pratique d'un répertoire," in E. Hondré (ed.), *Le Conservatoire de Musique de Paris* (Paris: Conservatoire national supérieur de musique de Paris, 1995), pp. 173–84.
[53] Timothy Tackett, *Religion, Revolution, and Regional Culture in Eighteenth-Century France: The Ecclesiastical Oath of 1791* (Princeton, N.J.: Princeton University Press, 1986).
[54] Constant Pierre, "Exercices des élèves (concerts et représentations), Programmes," *Le Conservatoire national de musique et de declamation: Documents administratifs recueillis ou reconstitués* (Paris: Imprimérie nationale, 1900), pp. 484–85.

The most recent music at the series tended to be accompanied instrumental solos, four of which, for as many instruments, we see in a program
from 1827 (Ex. 6.11). This program was as symmetrical as those prior to the
Revolution; canonic works by Mozart and Beethoven served as "bookends"
for each half, and selections by Rossini and Cherubini came between the
solos.

6.11 *Concert Spirituel, Académie Royale de Musique, 14 April 1827*[55]

Symphony	†Beethoven
Aria, *La Donna del Lago* (1819)	Rossini
Air varié for trombone	*Félix Vobaron*
Ave Maria, soprano & English horn (?1816)	Cherubini
Fantasy for piano	Herz
Hymn, *Thamos, King of Egypt* (K. 345)	†Mozart
—	
Overture, *Don Juan* (1787)	†Mozart
Air, *Les Abencérages* (1813)	Cherubini
Fantaisie for violin	*Pantaléon Battu*
Duo, *Sémiramide* (1823)	Rossini
L'Angélus, fantaisie for flute	*Jean-Louis Tulou*
Création, excerpts	†Haydn

The Society of Concerts was more closely linked to the state than the
other orchestral concerts we are studying. The Philharmonic Society of
London had no relations with any parliamentary body, the cities of London or Westminster, or the court in Windsor; the Gewandhaus stood close
to the Leipzig city government but not to the Saxon monarchy. The Paris
concerts, though incorporated privately, were linked to the state-supported
Conservatoire and owed privileges for use of the Salle du Conservatoire
to the Office of Fine Arts and the Ministry of Commerce. Yet the orchestra performed few ceremonial functions in this period, save for giving a
concert in the Tuileries Palace in 1845 that was not widely noticed. Its concerts remained an enclosed world among the *cognescenti*, attracting more
intellectuals than did the Philharmonic Society.[56] Here again we find a
state-subsidized concert series devoted extensively to sacred music. Conflict over Church authority flared up in 1830, after mobs sacked seminaries
and bishops' houses, even targeting the royal Église St. Germain-l'Auxerrois

55 "Affiches typographiques de l'Opéra," BNF. I am indebted to Olivier Morand for this source.
56 Holoman, *Société des Concerts*, p. 105.

in Paris. Perhaps for that very reason, the series held a "Concert Spirituel" on Palm Sunday and Easter Day and often chose liturgical settings for these occasions: masses by Mozart, Haydn, and Cherubini; Mozart's *Requiem*, *Ne pulvis et civis*, and *Ave Verum*; Beethoven's *Missa Solemnis*; Jomelli's *Confirma loc*; and Gossec's *O Salutaris*. Major parts of oratorios – Handel's *Samson* and *Judas Maccabaeus* and Haydn's *Creation*, for example – took on a heightened religious meaning when included with liturgical works. A program in 1839 typical of the early seasons included a motet by Cherubini and excerpts from Haydn's *Creation* (Ex. 6.12). (Movements from Beethoven's quartets were also orchestrated, as was done with his Septet in this instance.) The series appealed directly to Catholic tradition by occasionally performing an *a capella* piece in Renaissance style, most often a setting of the text "O filii et felice Rex" by the early seventeenth-century composer Volckmar Leisring. In the mid-1840s a group of male and female singers, many of them aristocrats, performed in concerts of the Society for Religious and Classical Music, whose programs included music as far back as Palestrina. It was led by Joseph-Napoléon Ney, Prince de la Moskowa, who was married to a daughter of the banker Jacques Lafitte.[57]

6.12 *Société des Concerts, Salle du Conservatoire, 29 March 1839*[58]

Symphony no. 7 in A, op. 92	†Beethoven
Fantaisie for piano on Halévy's *Guido et Ginevra*	
(1838)	*Theodore Döhler*
Motet, *Inclina, Domine*	Cherubini
Septet, excerpts, arranged for orchestra	†Beethoven
Création, excerpts	†Haydn

Leaders of the Society of Concerts sought a political middle-ground after the 1830 revolution. Two programs in 1828–1829 were said to come "by order of Her Royal Highness the Duchess of Berry," a leader of the reactionary Bourbon Ultras who fled Paris in July 1830. The first extant list of subscribers (1837) included people with a wide range of political positions, from Legitimists to reforming Orleanists. Interestingly, subscriber Charles-Forbes de Montalembert, from an old Poitou family, supported the movement let by Félicité Lamennais for rejuvenating the church along quasisocialist lines. Some subscribers also attended Baillot's concerts, among them the liberal duc François de La Rochefoucauld and a

[57] Campos, *La Renaissance introuvable?*
[58] Holoman, http://hector.ucdavis.edu/sdc/MainFrame.htm.

member of the Legitimist Noailles family.[59] Nonetheless, the directing committee had to pressure the new government to keep paying for the royal box, and all support for music at the royal chapel ended permanently in 1831.[60]

By 1835 the Paris series performed half as many pieces by dead composers as the Philharmonic Society then did, offering few recent orchestral pieces and concentrating particularly on Haydn, Mozart, Beethoven, and Weber (see Chart 6.1).[61] Moreover, it performed only five or six pieces per concert, compared with the nine or ten offered in London and the six to eight in Leipzig. The programs were forward looking in that they did not follow a standard sequence of genres; even though a symphony usually opened a program, genres were arranged in a variety of ways on different occasions. The Conservatoire concerts adhered closely to idealistic principle by performing few vocal numbers from recent operas. Between 1835 and 1850 pieces by Bellini appeared on the programs only twice, Meyerbeer once, and Donizetti not at all. Rossini was often represented in the first two decades, though in large part because he had ended his career as an opera composer in 1829. The excerpts came largely from works institutionalized at the Opéra, chiefly *Le Siège de Corinthe* (1826) and *Guillaume Tell* (1829). Meyerbeer in effect succeeded Rossini in this role in the mid-1850s, by which time he had ceased to compose regularly. Nevertheless, opera *fantaisies* were fairly frequent at the concerts through the mid-1840s; after all, the Conservatoire was teaching instrumentalists to work in the world of commercial music. If Theodore Döhler performed his *fantaisie* on music by Halévy (Ex. 6.12), Jean Rémusat treated a theme by Giovanni Pacini, and the ever-touring Léopold de Meyer offered pieces based on *Norma* and *Der Freischütz.*

No other major European orchestra performed Beethoven as often as the Conservatoire did; indeed, a piece by him appeared at all but a few concerts through the 1860s. All nine symphonies were introduced in the first five seasons, and seven or eight were offered every season. The repetitive programming did not explore Beethoven's oeuvre as widely did the

59 Abonnés, 1838, Société des Concerts, Fond Conservatoire, BNF; Elisabeth Bernard, "Les abonnés à la Société des Concerts du Conservatoire en 1837," in *Music in Paris in the Eighteen-Thirties*, Peter Bloom (ed.) (Stuyvesant, N.Y.: Pendragon, 1987), pp. 41–52; Vapereau, *Dictionnaire universel*, vol. 2, pp. 1028, 1306; Higgs, *Nobles in Nineteenth-Century France*, pp. 63, 110, 134; Fauquet, *Sociétés de musique de chambre*, p. 71.
60 Holoman, *Société des Concerts*, pp. 85, 147–50; Jo Burr Margadant, "The Duchesse de Berry and Royalist Political Culture in Post-Revolutionary France," *The New Biography: Performing Feminity in Nineteenth-Century France*, Margadant (ed.) (Berkeley: University of California Press, 2000), pp. 33–71.
61 Holoman, *Société des Concerts*, pp. 103–116, 135–6, 141–3, 152–5, 166–70, 181–3.

Viennese Concert Spirituel or the Gewandhaus concerts.[62] Concertos –
even those by Beethoven – were particularly uncommon, because for some
time Conservatoire professors found the accompanied solo or the *fantaisie*
more advantageous for their careers. The programs offered one or two
instrumental solos at almost every concert through the mid-1840s, usually performed by a professor. A concert on 29 March 1829, for example,
included a solo for horn by the orchestra's principal Jean-Baptiste Mengal
and one for cello by Auguste Franchomme. But the *fantaisie* fell into such
disrepute for its commercialism that in 1840 Cherubini dictated that a list of
"classical composers" for the piano be drawn up for the piano examinations
at the Conservatoire and that no *airs variés* be included.[63] The concerto,
having classical precedents, then emerged as the premier virtuoso vehicle
at the concerts.

   Although the Paris orchestra's directing committee made no policy limiting new works, it offered fewer pieces by living composers than all the
other orchestras under study. Cherubini enjoyed a special place on the
programs because he was director of the Conservatoire and honorary president of the concerts. The strikingly influential Ambroise Thomas – whose
operas became widely known – succeeded to that privilege even before
taking over as director in 1871. But nothing by Boieldieu was performed
in this period, or by Auber after he became head of the Conservatoire in
1842. Indeed, a "curious stagnation" arose in the repertory in the 1840s, as
D. Kern Holoman has noted.[64] The "trial" performances for projected
new works, called *répétitions d'essai*, were governed by stricter rules than at
the Philharmonic Society because the Conservatoire maintained a complex
system for evaluating students and applicants for the Prix de Rome. A committee, determined by lot, could accept or reject a piece, ask for changes,
or propose a second hearing.[65] Although the board paid little attention to
living French composers, it did offer a surprising amount of French music
from Lully to Méhul. Even though eighteenth-century French music was
widely disparaged in the press, Méhul was featured with a wide range of
symphonies, overtures, and opera selections, and a concert was named in his
honor in 1830.[66] Music by Grétry and Rameau was played in 1840, the latter
having almost completely disappeared from performance in Paris after 1785.

---

[62] For a comprehensive analysis of its Beethoven repertory, see Kraus, *Beethoven–Rezeption*.
[63] Luigi Cherubini, "Désignation des morceaux de concours, 1er juin 1840," in Pierre, *Le Conservatoire*,
    p. 308.
[64] Holoman, *Société des Concerts*, p. 177.
[65] Committee Reports, 30 December 1841, "Société des Concerts, Statutes Règlementaires," Holoman,
    http://hector.ucdavis.edu/sdc/ and *Société des Concerts*, pp. 57, 112, 167.
[66] Ellis, *Interpreting Music of the Past*, pp. xiv, 16–17, and *passim*.

Opera excerpts by Gluck also became standard repertory, as was not always the case elsewhere in Europe. The first piece by Lully on the series appeared on a program in 1845 that typified programs by that time for its uniformly canonic contents (Ex. 6.13).

6.13 *Société des Concerts, Salle du Conservatoire, 26 January 1845*[67]

Symphony no. 3, in E-flat, op. 55	†Beethoven
Hymn [? *Opferlied* for soprano and chorus, op. 121]	†Beethoven
Concerto for piano in C	†Mozart
Scene of Caron, *Alceste* (1674)	†Lully
Overture, *Coriolanus*, op. 62	†Beethoven
Final chorus, *Christ on the Mount of Olives*, op. 85	†Beethoven

For all their distinction, the Conservatoire concerts were not widely known outside the specialized world of classical music. The institution "cultivated exclusivity," as Beate Kraus put it.[68] It is hard to find a travel guide or a memoir published in the 1840s that mentioned the series, as such publications always did for the Opéra and leading virtuosos. A well-informed book titled *Physiologie du musicien* (1843) cited Mozart and Beethoven but not the Paris concerts where their music was most notably performed.[69] A memoir by a German inveighed against prejudiced juries at the Conservatoire but failed to mention the concerts.[70]

A much wider public attended the remarkable *Concerts de la rue St. Honoré* that were presented at intervals between 1837 and 1840. The experienced conductor Henri Valentino attempted to marry orchestral classics with the dance music made popular by Philippe Musard, whose concerts had formerly occurred in the same hall. Whereas the first half of the three-hour program offered overtures and dance pieces, the second half would focus on a symphony, often by Mozart or Beethoven, and include instrumental solos and more dance pieces. A recent composition – a nonet by Félicien David, for example – might also be included. No promenade concert anywhere in Europe is known to have offered as many complete performances of symphonic works before the Crystal Palace Concerts began

[67] Holoman, http://hector.ucdavis.edu/sdc/MainFrame.htm.
[68] Kraus, *Beethoven-Rezeption*, p. 159, and pp. 107, 332.
[69] Cler, *Physiologie du musicien*, pp. 109, 114.
[70] Charles de Forster, *Quinze ans à Paris (1832–1848): Paris et les parisiens*, 2 vols. (Paris: Didot, 1848–49), vol. 1, pp. 269–75. Nor are the concerts cited in Charles de Kock, *La Grande Ville: Nouveau tableau de Paris* (Paris: Bureau central des publications nouvelles, 1842) or *Paris actuel ou 12 dans un: Janvier 1842* (Paris: Martinon, 1842).

in 1855. Though the tickets were cheap, musical and literary notables were much in attendance, specially invited on some occasions. The experiment did not work because the dance and the symphony proved aesthetically incompatible. Reviewers praised the high performing standards at the concerts and admired them for aiding the "progress" of musical taste, but opinion grew increasingly unhappy about the number of quadrilles and waltzes. Hector Berlioz grumbled about Valentino using "using dance music to appeal to the masses" (la contredanse... pour attirer la foule), and correspondents from Schumann's magazine wrote that audiences might be unruly.[71] All of which pointed ahead to the division between "light" and "serious" music-making at midcentury.

VIENNA

A complex blend of tradition and innovation governed orchestral concerts in Vienna during the first half of the nineteenth century. Culture wars broke out in the press between these conflicting tendencies, especially when concert directors tried to satisfy different groups. On the one hand, miscellaneous programs that focused on recent music – brilliant new wine in sturdy old bottles – persisted at the Society Concerts (Gesellschafts-Concerte) and Evening Entertainments (Abendunterhaltungen) sponsored by the Society for the Friends of Music. On the other hand, an uncompromisingly pure repertory of classical music emerged in the local Concert Spirituel, and the Philharmonic concerts reshaped that repertory for a broader public in the 1840s. Although the Philharmonic orchestra was a resounding success, the classical music world was still small and very much in transition in Vienna when revolution broke out in March 1848.

Though the *Evening Entertainments* never had an orchestra, its figures for dead and living composers suggest a baseline for traditional programming. If we look once more at Chart 6.2, we find that the proportion of pieces by dead composers at this series began as low as eleven percent in the mid-1820s and grew only to twenty-eight percent by the late 1830s. A few of the concerts were focused on composers thought classical (notably Beethoven, J. S. Bach, or Georg Vogler), but the increase in the percentage came chiefly from performance of convivial part-songs by Schubert (1828) and opera

[71] Hector Berlioz, "Concerts de la rue Saint-Honoré," *RGM*, 29 October (1837), 470–1; lead article, *MW*, 17 October (1839), 381–2; "Concert St. Honoré," *NZFM*, 15 January (1839), 20 (noting "schlechten Geschmack"); 15 September (1840), 2. See also Kraus, *Beethoven-Rezeption*, pp. 151–9; Fauquet, *Dictionnaire*, p. 1251; *Le Ménestrel*, 15 October (1837), 4.

selections by Bellini (d. 1835). The number of concerts declined steeply during the 1830s, as it became evident that the string quartet and the opera excerpt were no longer compatible on the same program.

Leaders of the Friends of Music hoped that the *Society Concerts* would be the centerpiece of the city's musical life, like the subscription concerts at the Gewandhaus. But the city was too big and socially diverse for that to happen, especially because the organization excluded professional musicians from performing at the series until after mid-century. Although journalists called the audience "select" – including members of the lesser nobility – press reports were often hostile because virtuoso concerts were so much more professional and in touch with general taste. The number of works by living or dead composers performed at the Society Concerts fluctuated from season to season to an unusual extent, indicating serious division in the organization over priorities for programming. The percentage of pieces by dead composers fluctuated by as much as twenty percent from one season to another, sinking to ten percent in the early 1820s, rising to as high as fifty-one percent after the deaths of Beethoven and Weber, and settling back to thirty-three percent by the mid-1840s.

Competition between major musical alternatives was apparent from the start of the Society Concerts in 1814. Iconic names – Handel, the recently deceased Haydn, and the vigorous if deaf Beethoven – dominated programs in the society's first concerts, much as was the case with the Philharmonic Society in London. Leaders of the two organizations seem to have chosen particularly imposing works around the time of the Congress of Vienna and the Revolution of 1848 to deal with the crises then faced. But in the late 1810s musical taste swung giddily toward recent operas by Rossini, Mercadante, and Simon Mayr and away from music by Mozart or Beethoven. The Society Concerts offered more varied opera selections than the Evening Entertainments – pieces by Salieri, Spontini, Cherubini, and Méhul, indeed, a soprano aria from Sarti's *Giulio Sabino* of 1781. Yet the programs also included local composers of distinction, often represented by choral pieces. A concert in May 1819, for example, offered cantatas on Christmas and May Day, framed by overtures by Cherubini and Beethoven (Ex. 6.14). Even though court music was in decline, a talented group of musicians was still in charge. The Bohemian clarinetist Antonio Cartellieri had played for Empress Marie Therese; Joseph Eybler succeeded Salieri as Kapellmeister in 1824; and the 67-year-old Johann Schenck was a leading theorist in the tradition of Johann Fux.[72]

---

[72] Rice, *Empress Marie Therese*, pp. 28, 54–5, 59, 203, 252–3.

6.14 *Gesellschafts-Concerte, 9 May 1819*[73]

Overture, *Die Tage der Gefahr*	
(*Les Deux Journées*, 1800)	Cherubini
Cantata, *Die Hirten bei der Krippe*	
(The Sheep at the Manger)	Joseph Eybler
Andante and Variations for clarinet	†Antonio Cartellieri
Cantata, *Der Mai* (On May Day)	Johann Schenk
Overture to ballet music *Prometheus*, op. 43	Beethoven

Pieces earning the new title "classical music" became more common at the Society Concerts by the late 1820s, making concerts more homogeneous for a time. Handel's *Judas Maccabaeus* and *Israel in Egypt* were performed more or less completely in 1834 and 1836; all-Beethoven programs took place in 1838, 1840, and 1844. Many of the works performed are not well known today, particularly Beethoven's incidental music to Goethe's *Egmont* and to Kotzebue's *Ruins of Athens*. The programs also honored the deaths of other distinguished Austrians – Eybler, Vogler, Maximilian Stadler, and Joseph Weigl. Yet by the late 1830s the concerts were swept up in the craze for Donizetti and Bellini, most of all when Donizetti visited Vienna to conduct the première of *Linda di Chamounix* in 1842. One Society Concert presented an aria from his *Gemma di Vergy* and a fantasy on his *Lucrezia Borgia*, with pieces by Haydn and Mozart coming fore and aft (Ex. 6.15). Moreover, by this time local composers began to act as an interest group, stimulating demands in the press that their music be performed more often.[74] A Society Concert given in 1846 offered pieces by four living composers, including an oratorio by Emil Titl, Kapellmeister at the Theater an der Josefstadt, as well as Mendelssohn's Symphony no. 3.

6.15 *Gesellschafts-Concerte, Grosser Redoutensaal, 11 April 1844*[75]

Symphony in B	†Haydn
Variations for violin	de Bériot
Aria for soprano, *Gemma di Vergy* (1834)	Donizetti
Introduction and Variations on Drinking Song	
from Donizetti's *Lucrezia Borgia*	Léopold de Meyer

[73] Richard von Perger, *Geschichte der k. k. Gesellschaft der Musikfreunde in Wien*, 2 vols. (Vienna: Gesellschaft der Musikfreunde, 1912), vol. 1, p. 286. The concerts took place variously in the Hôtel zum römischen Kaiser and the Hall of the Lower Austrian Estates.
[74] See a composer writing in the *Wiener Sonntags-Blätter*, 23 January 1842, p. 1.
[75] Perger, *Geschichte der k. k. Gesellschaft der Musikfreunde*, vol. 2, p. 295.

Overture, *Die Genueserin* (1839)   Peter Lindpaintner
Chorus, "Die Erde erzittert," *Die Zauberflöte* (1791)   †Mozart

The culture wars that engulfed musical life in the 1840s brought the
Society Concerts under heavy fire from proponents variously of classics,
grand opera, and the less prominent local composers. The crisis made clear
that "miscellaneous" programming could no longer contain its divisive
parts. One critic attacked the Society for giving all-Beethoven programs that
pleased only his fans.[76] An idealist writing for the satirical *Neue komische
Briefe des Hans-Jürgels von Gumpoldskirchen* complained that the Society
Concerts played only individual movements from major symphonies.[77]
A nonpartisan journalist threw up his hands, suggesting that the Society
was foolish "to give every part of the public a corresponding gift in every
program." A French visitor claimed that people were fleeing the Society
Concerts to hear the Strauss-Kapelle in suburban Hietzing.[78]

By contrast, the *Concert Spirituel* followed a straight classical path from
its inception in 1819. The series went farther than any series in the four
cities in replacing miscellany with a strictly defined canonic repertory.[79]
Commentators repeatedly said that a concert-goer had to know a lot about
serious music to enjoy the repertory and that the concerts gathered together
an educated milieu separate from the general public. A Viennese journalist noted in 1832 that at the Concert Spirituel "the musical intelligentsia
[*Intelligenz*] grows in size and expands in its influence, helping make its
great works become ever better known and revered."[80] The contrasts drawn
between the Concert Spirituel and the Strauss-Kapelle thus manifested an
early form of the "polarization between supposedly serious and entertaining
music," as Martha Handlos has stated it.[81]

The series was initiated by Franz Xaver Gebauer, choral director of
the Augustinian Hofpfarrkirche, a chapel that was linked to the court
but received no funding for music. Called *Übungskonzerten* ("practice ses-
sions"), the meetings entailed sight-readings by the church's musicians and
other interested players. Religious language was often used to extol the

76 *Sammler*, 12 December 1840, p. 780.
77 *Neue komische Briefe des Hans-Jürgels* (1842), vol. 1, pp. 14, 30–1.
78 *Zuschauer*, 9 February 1846, p. 177; *RGM*, 4 December 1842, p. 483.
79 Martha Handlos, "Die Wiener Concerts Spirituels (1819–1848)," in *Österreichische Musik/Musik
in Österreich: Beiträge zur Musikgeschichte Mitteleuropas, Theophil Antonicek zum 60. Geburtstag*,
Elisabeth Hilscher (ed.) (Tutzing: Hans Schneider, 1998), pp. 283–319; and "Studien zum Wiener
Konzertleben im Vormärz," unpublished Ph.D. dissertation, University of Vienna (1985); Wyn
Jones, *Symphony in Beethoven's Vienna*, pp. 184–91. Though the series was not officially linked to the
Friends of Music, its leaders contributed funds to its library; see *Monatsbericht der Gesellschaft der
Musikfreunde* 2 (1830), p. 88.
80 *AWMZ*, 29 March 1832, p. 51.   81 Handlos, "Die Wiener Concerts Spirituels," p. 288.

series for its "piety," as opposed to the "profane" nature of benefit and charity concerts.[82] A handwritten memorandum about the series in 1820 stated that although both old and new works would be performed, "only the very best works in each genre" would be admitted.[83] That same year Ignaz Mosel wrote an article hailing the concerts as a force to protect the music of "classical masters" that was being driven out of concerts and the opera. Invoking a principle similar to one claimed for the London Philharmonic Society, he encouraged Gebauer to exclude "all concertizing pieces or bravura singing" from his programs in favor of symphonies and sacred choruses. Mosel saw the Concert Spirituel as "a dam built by holders of high musical taste against the rule of tasteless music distorted by excessive ornamentation."[84] The correspondent to the Leipzig *Allgemeine musikalische Zeitung* declared that Gebauer had banned "all modern jingles [*Kling-Klang*]" from the series' programs.[85]

The early programs of the Concert Spirituel usually combined a major symphony with several choral-orchestral works, both secular and sacred. The sacred pieces tended to be in a more polyphonic style than those at the Paris Conservatoire concerts, even though only a small public existed for that kind of music in Vienna. Pieces by living and dead composers were carefully balanced during these years. In 1819, for example, a symphony in C by Haydn was paired with the Mass in E-flat that Hummel had composed in Vienna in 1804.[86] By the same token, in 1821 a Mozart symphony in D was combined with sacred music by five living composers, from a motet by Bonifazio Asioli to a *Loblied* by Maximilian Stadler. But two weeks later, in the fairly small Hall of the Lower Austrian Estates, music by a quintessentially canonic group of composers was performed, including Beethoven's Seventh Symphony and a chorus composed by Haydn to words by Peter Pindar while in London in 1792 (Ex. 6.16).

6.16 *Concert Spirituel, Saal der nieder-österreichischen Landstände,*
     12 January 1821 [87]

Symphony no. 7 in A, op. 92	Beethoven
Alleluja	†Johann Albrechtsberger
Requiem, "De profondis"	†Gluck
Motet, "Lasset uns aufsehen"	†C.P.E. Bach
Chorus, *Der Sturm: Hört! Die Winde*	
furchtbar heulen (1792/1798)	†Haydn

[82] *Sontagsblätter,* 27 March 1842, p. 224; *TZ,* 28 February 1846, p. 203
[83] Handlos, "Die Wiener Concerts Spirituels," p. 284.   [84] *AMZK,* 5 April 1820, p. 217.
[85] "Nachrichten: Wien," *AMZ,* 17 May 1820, p. 333.
[86] Hanslick, *Geschichte des Concertwesens,* p. 187.   [87] Ibid., p. 188, and PA/GMFV.

After Gebauer died in 1822, leadership of the Concerts Spirit(u)el passed to Eduard von Lannoy, who revived them after a year's respite with a more formal, public structure. Paid professional musicians made up about a third of the orchestra, but limited rehearsal time hurt performing standards. Lannoy made a major innovation in March 1824 by designing a series of concerts devoted separately to music by Haydn, Mozart, and Beethoven, in that order. The Haydn program offered a symphony and parts of his oratorio *Last Seven Words* (1796). The Mozart concert included the Litany *Heiliger sieh gnädig hernieder* ("Mercy upon us, Lord," K. 125), the Symphony in G Minor, K. 550, and his Fantasy for Piano in C Minor arranged for orchestra by Seyfried.[88] Beethoven, who had grumbled about the concerts, was represented by one of his settings of the Credo (probably an early mass), the first half of *Christ on the Mount of Olives*, the "Pastoral" Symphony, and the overture to *Coriolanus*. The printed programs at the series were as austere as the music performed; the one handed out on 10 March 1833, for example, was elegant in its simplicity (Ill. 14).

From 1824 the Concert Spirituel was devoted to classical works more consistently than was the case with any other orchestral concerts across Europe for a decade. The 1833 program was typical, balancing an overture and a symphony with two movements from masses, all by deceased great composers. Returning to Chart 6.2, we see that the proportion of pieces by dead composers began at fifty-one percent, moved up to seventy-four percent by the mid-1830s, and, after a slight drop, ended up as high as eighty-three percent in the mid-1840s.

A decline in the percentage to sixty-five percent occurred in the years 1847–1848 as the series, by now outshone by the Philharmonic concerts, offered more pieces by local composers. The mass of abbé Vogler, composed in 1767, was unusually old for this repertory, save for the famed *Miserere* (a nine-part *falsobordone* chant for two choirs) that Gregorio Allegri wrote for the Papal chapel around 1640.[89] What Viennese listeners regarded as antiquated tended to be more recent than what their colleagues were hearing at the Concert of Ancient Music in London or at Parisian concerts influenced by the rich historical discussion of music in that city. The belief that old music was inferior to the new persisted in Vienna, as is apparent in a remark made in 1827 about a Christmas oratorio by Eybler given at the concerts: "[E]ven though this music was written over thirty years ago, its style and texture still make for a first-class piece, attesting to Eybler's mastery in the smallest detail."[90]

[88] "Nachrichten: Wien," *AMZ*, 29 April 1824, p. 283.   [89] "Concert Spirituel," PA/GMFV.
[90] "Nachrichten: Wien," *AMZ*, 23 April 1827, p. 284.

Lannoy and his colleagues imposed stricter limitations on operatic and virtuosic pieces in their repertory than did the committee running the Paris Conservatoire concerts. In the twenty-five seasons from 1824 only twelve vocal selections from operas were performed at the Viennese concerts; remarkably enough, only two were by Mozart, and ten were written for the Paris Opéra, mostly choral pieces by Cherubini. One Mozart selection was from *Ahasverus* (1824), a pasticcio of his music by Ignaz von Seyfried. Leaders of the Viennese concerts thus ignored Italian – indeed, Austro-Italian – opera but yet deferred to the cosmopolitan authority of the Paris Opéra. The only recent Austrian operatic number came from Seyfried's melodrama *Moses* (1802). Still, the concerts did take note of the opera world in the early 1840s, performing an Ave Maria composed by Donizetti and an aria from Handel's *Rinaldo* as arranged by Meyerbeer.[91]

The Viennese Concert Spirituel was equally uncompromising in regard to the concerto. The series contributed significantly to establishing a canon of classical concertos and indeed to severing the formerly intimate relationship between composer and performer. No composer seems to have performed his own concerto at the series. The great majority of concertos were by Mozart and Beethoven; the latter's Violin Concerto, only recently popular in Europe generally, was offered as many as three times in the 1830s. Leading virtuosos came to play Beethoven concertos rather than their own – Vieuxtemps in 1834, Thalberg in 1839, and Liszt in 1840. Only a few concertos by living composers were presented, most prominently those by Hummel in 1833, Spohr in 1836, and Mendelssohn and Molique in 1841. Thus did an old concert tradition weaken greatly.

The Concert Spirituel became more closely linked with the larger musical world in the 1840s, influenced by the newly founded Philharmonic concerts. Not only did its directors offer pieces by Donizetti and Meyerbeer, but they also usually included a piece by a living composer, increasingly from outside Vienna. In February 1847 they offered a recent setting of the "Salve regina" by Otto Nicolai, the north German who was about to end his triumphant but brief career as conductor at the Kärntnertor Theater (Ex. 6.17). Though best known for his operas, Nicolai was deeply involved in the revival of Palestrina's music and wrote church music extensively in Rome and Bologna. The series began exploring little-played pieces by major composers – in the 1847 program Mozart's Clarinet Concerto and an early symphony by Haydn, and in 1844 Spohr's unusual Double Concerto for String Quartet.

---

[91] *AWMZ*, 11 March 1848, pp. 121–2; Giacomo Meyerbeer (arr.), *Recitativo ed aria dell' opera Rinaldo* (Berlin: Schlesinger, c1840).

6.17 *Concert Spirituel, Saal der Musikfreunde, 18 February 1847*[92]

Symphony in C [claimed as an early work]	†Haydn
Salve regina (1846)	Otto Nicolai
Concerto for Clarinet, op. 622	†Mozart
Overture, incidental music to *Egmont*, op. 84	†Beethoven

Like the Concert Spirituel, the grand choral concerts of the *Society of Musicians* held in the Grosser Redoutensaal turned abruptly toward canonic repertory during the mid-1820s. Two or three concerts occurred each season, offering Haydn's two oratorios in full performance from the late 1790s, but not full versions of Handel's works. Beginning in 1824 not only *Messiah* but also *Jephtha, Samson, Solomon*, and *Athalia* were regularly performed at the monumental concerts. By the 1830s works by living composers appeared on only one out of four programs, and even less after that; Mendelssohn's works appeared there infrequently.[93] By contrast, Boston's Handel and Haydn Society kept recent works in play through the 1850s, offering new works by Spohr, Mendelssohn, Rossini, Charles Edward Horn, and Sigismund Neukomm. Rossini's *Stabat Mater* (1832/1841) and Neukomm's *David* (London, 1834) remained standard repertory long after midcentury in both Britain and North America.[94]

The *Philharmonic Concerts*, as early productions of the Vienna Philharmonic Orchestra were called, broadened the public for classical music with its forward-looking programs. The first one took place in the Grosser Redoutensaal at 1 P.M. on Easter Monday, 3 March 1842, before the Royal family, Prince Metternich, leading nobles and literati, and an audience of 1,500 people. None of the concert societies in Leipzig, London, or Paris had ever performed before so large, august, or politically influential a public. The social status of classical music rose to a new level at this event. Planning for the first concerts involved a wide range of government officials and intellectuals; a concert honoring the Kaiser's birthday in the second season also drew the Royal family, with numerous eulogies written for the occasion.[95]

---

[92] *AWMZ*, 20 February 1848, p. 90. The *Salve regina* was probably composed in 1846 for the Bishop of Raab; see Ulrich Konrad, "Otto Nicolai und die Palestrina Renaissance," in *Palestrina und die Kirchenmusik im 19 Jahrhundert*, 2 vols., Winfried Kirsch (ed.) (Regensburg: Bosse, 1989–1999), vol 1, p. 131.

[93] Pohl, *Denkschrift... Tonkünstler-Societät*, pp. 62–79.

[94] Charles C. Perkins and John S. Dwight, *History of the Handel and Haydn Society* (Boston: Mudge, 1883–1913; New York: Da Capo, 1977), Appendix, pp. i–xxiii.

[95] Ulrich Konrad, "Die Philharmonischen Konzerte unter Otto Nicolai: Die Gründungszeit (1842–47)," in *Klang und Komponist: Ein Symposion der Wiener Philharmoniker, Kongressbericht*, Otto Biba

The orchestra assembled for the Philharmonic in 1842 was linked contractually to the opera orchestra and thereby to the court. This was the first time classical music was performed on a regular basis by a fully professional orchestra in that city.[96] The initial concert had the trappings of a miscellaneous program – two overtures, a cello solo (the Servais *Romanesca*), and Beethoven's concert aria "Ah perfido, spergiuro" (op. 65) as well as his Seventh Symphony. Thereafter the Philharmonic Concerts offered fewer works and excluded virtuoso solos completely. Remarkably enough, six of the twelve programs given by the Philharmonic between 1842 and 1847 offered only three works, and no program had more than five. In all, eighty-four percent of the pieces performed were by dead composers. The flyer announcing the concerts warned that the new concerts would "give something special, something great, something extraordinary, . . . Hear! Hear! it will give only what is classical and of significance."[97] That statement made explicit a fundamentally new conception of a concert: to be included on a program, a piece had to be deemed "great," that is, actually or potentially canonic in stature. Vienna's Philharmonic concerts thus followed the London Philharmonic Society and the Conservatoire concerts in making classical repertory cosmopolitan in nature. Still, the Viennese orchestra bowed to *grand opéra* by performing the overture to Meyerbeer's incidental music to the play *Struensee* in 1847.

The Philharmonic programs were the earliest examples of the "pure" format of three pieces followed by major orchestras at the end of the nineteenth century. An 1844 program separated well-known symphonies by Mozart and Beethoven with an aria for bass from *Acis and Galatea* (Ex. 6.18), and another avoided vocal music, putting Meyerbeer's overture between Mozart's K. 550 and Beethoven's Second Symphony.

6.18 *Philharmonische Concerte, Grosser Redoutensaal, 10 March 1844*[98]

Symphony in C, K. 551, "Jupiter"   †Mozart
Aria for bass, *Acis and Galatea*   †Handel
Symphony no. 6, op. 68, "Pastorale"   †Beethoven

and Wolfgang Schuster (eds.) (Tutzing: Hans Schneider, 1992), pp. 27–36; *Perger, Denkschrift zur Feier*, pp. 1, 9; Hanslick, *Geschichte des Concertwesens in Wien*, pp. 314–18.
[96] For an early effort, see note 44.
[97] Cristl Schönfeldt, *Die Wiener Philharmoniker* (Wien: Bergland, 1956), p. 24; Hellsberg, *Demokratie der Könige*, pp. 22–4.
[98] Hellsberg, *Demokratie der König*, p. 41; Perger, *Denkschrift*, p. 55.

As these programs suggest, leaders of the Vienna Philharmonic Concerts developed a more approachable, less specialized, repertory than was found at the local Concert Spirituel. They offered fewer sacred pieces, preferring oratorios to polyphonic liturgical works, and, for that matter, gave their concerts a secular tone. An opera overture or selection by a classical composer appeared on almost all the programs in this 1840s, reviving the long-standing links between theatre and concert hall. Because the orchestra formed part of the Court Opera, the concerts were able to draw on soloists from the Kärntnertor Theater, which the Concert Spirituel could not often afford to do. The programs offered numbers not only from Mozart's operas but also from Sacchini's *Oedipe à Colone* (1786), Vogler's *Samori* (1804), and Spohr's *Faust* (1813). An increasing number of older operas were also being offered at the Kärntnertor theatre at that time; in 1846, for example, the repertory at the theatre included pieces from Gluck's *Alceste* (1767/1776) and *Armide* (1777), Winter's *Das unterbrochene Opferfest* (1796), and Beethoven's *Fidelio* (1805).[99] Classical music concerts were drawing a larger and more prestigious public than previously, as a journalist pointed out in 1845.[100] The proliferation of piano arrangements for domestic use enabled those who could not attend concerts hear arrangements of the "Jupiter" or "Pastorale" symphonies for two or four hands. The symphonies and concertos written between 1775 and 1810 that had seemed esoteric in 1825 now acquired an expanding public that leaders of the Philharmonic concerts exploited successfully.

One is not surprised to find a rich history in Viennese orchestral concert programs during the first half of the nineteenth century. Less to be expected are the variety and uncertainty of direction taken by concert institutions and the tensions apparent within the public. The city's Concert Spirituel stands out as by far the most important early force for performing classical music. But by 1848 the Philharmonic Concerts were taking place only once or twice a year, and it was not until 1860 that the orchestra mounted a full season of eight concerts comparable to what had long been done by the Leipzig Gewandhaus, the London Philharmonic Society, and the Paris Society of Concerts. Looking at the 120 concerts reported to have been held in Vienna during the season 1842–1843, no more than 17 were focused on classical music.[101] The broad public drawn to the early concerts of the Vienna Philharmonic nonetheless boded well for the future of this kind of music-making.

99 "Nachrichten: Wien," *AMZ*, 11 July (1846), 486–8.   100 *Wiener Zeitung*, 8 February 1845, p. 66.
101 "Allgemeine Uebersicht der Musikaufführungen," *AWMZ*, 27 June 1843, pp. 319–20.

UNTERHALTUNGSMUSIK VERSUS CLASSISCHE MUSIK

By 1848 orchestral concerts and quartet concerts had opened up an unprecedented set of listening opportunities. In the four major cities under study one could hear works by master composers much longer after their deaths than had ever been possible before – for starters, Handel's *Judas Maccabaeus* (1747), Mozart's "Paris" Symphony (1778), and selections from Cherubini's *Lodoïska* (1791). Virtuosos were still playing concertos by Mozart and Beethoven, and singers kept pieces by Gluck, Cimarosa, and Méhul in repertory. An international movement had brought this about; a variety of regions contributed to the new repertory in contrasting ways. Yet the new classical music world had an anxious mood. A gap had been growing between "light" and "serious" music – *Unterhaltungsmusik* versus *classische Musik* – and tension between them was becoming institutionalized. Though composers such as Mendelssohn and Schubert wrote a great deal for the general public, that would become much more difficult after midcentury. In 1843 the Viennese correspondent for the *Allgemeine musikalische Zeitung* deplored the "sins of taste" among those who obeyed the "Strauss-Lanner dictatorship" over the city's musical life.[102] The composers' lobby was equally vocal. A Viennese journalist asked why Handel's *Judas Maccabaeus* rather than a new work by Spohr had been given yet again at the annual festival of the Friends of Music:

Hats off to the worthy old master; who is greater, more formidable, than he? ... Yet the public has got to stay in touch with music of its time, with the best that is arising, for otherwise people will gradually come to mistrust music claimed to be the best. It is vital to the interests of this grand festival to be regenerated by the lure of what is new, since otherwise, alas, the whole institution will slip into indifference.[103]

That issue, the status of new music, would become a major source of dispute throughout Europe during the second half of the nineteenth century.

---

[102] "Nachrichten: Wiener Musikleben," *AMZ*, 5 July 1843, p. 496.
[103] "Nachrichten: Wiener Musikleben," *AMZ*, 1 March 1843, p. 173.

CHAPTER 7

Promenade concerts: rise of the "pops"

Until recently, histories of promenade concerts have tended to be chronicles of any commendable rise, or much regretted fall, in the number of classics included in their programs. Just as the illustrious conductor and entrepreneur Louis Jullien has been applauded for having performed a few movements of Beethoven in London, so the period after his death in 1860 was deplored as a "dangerous interim," in contrast to the classical taste attributed to Sir Henry Wood at the Promenades from 1895.[1] This interpretation reveals little, however, about the main kinds of music people heard at these concerts – the dance pieces and opera medleys that framed most programs. The promenade concert provided a major new direction in concertizing; the "pops" concert was born in this context. It identified a critical middle ground of taste and sociability within the expansion and reorganization of the musical world in the middle of the nineteenth century. This chapter pays special attention to the work of Philippe Musard and Louis Jullien in Paris and London and to that of Johann Strauss the Elder and Johann Strauss the Younger in Vienna. Though the term *promenade concert* was used most often in Britain, similar notions influenced the events in all three cities. We will continue discussion of this subject through the year 1875.

Concerts became differentiated from one another in the middle of the nineteenth century in several respects: seriousness of repertory, breadth of public, and extent of formality in etiquette. The quartet concert defined one extreme point by 1820, thanks to its strictness in genres and listening and its association with a public of aristocrats and educated bourgeois.

---

[1] Adam Carse, *The Life of Jullien* (London: W. Heffer, 1951), p. 2. See Simon McVeigh, "'An Audience for High-Class Music': Concert Promoters and Entrepreneurs in Nineteenth-century London," in *Musician as Entrepreneur*, pp. 162–82; and *The Proms: A New History*, Jenny Doctor and David Wright (eds.) (London: Thames and Hudson, 2007).

The *café-concert* and the music hall set up the opposite standard during the 1850s, having the widest publics, the most informal sociability, and repertories far from the now-recognizable classical music world. The promenade concert ended up in the middle, linked with both classical music orchestras and music halls or *cafés-concerts*. Although it relied on commercial theatricality, it was also an outgrowth of orchestral ensembles originating in court musical life. The promenade concert established itself firmly in its own right, whereas the virtuoso concert of the 1830s did not. Indeed, once virtuosos abandoned the potpourri and *fantaisie*, the two genres found a new home in promenade concerts.

The promenade concert resembled the benefit concert in important respects. For one thing, as a speculative venture, led by an "entrepreneur-conductor" (as John Spitzer has put it), it depended on drawing audiences consistently large enough to break even.[2] Moreover, its programs were suffused with the common musical culture of opera – overtures, selections, and medleys. Musical entrepreneurs blended aspects of the eighteenth-century pleasure gardens with public balls and industrial show palaces to forge a cultural synthesis with an identity all its own. Promenade concerts differed from orchestral concerts in their construction as a visual as much as a musical show. Promoters aimed to engage listeners' eyes just as much as their ears. Different from the grave neoclassicism predominant in new concert halls, the spaces fitted out for promenade concerts were showplaces lavishly decorated with eye-catching décor and bright lighting. An advertisement for a Jullien concert in 1841 promised "a profusion of green-house plants, fountains of real water, groups of sculpture" and bragged about offering gasoline lighting.[3] The conductors often applied a theme to a piece or to a concert as a whole, giving listeners a means to visualize the music. They might highlight an appealing place (Venice or the Alps), new technology (the train ride), or an event (coronation of the Austrian Emperor). Concert spaces usually provided areas or passageways where people could walk about freely. That informality differentiated the promenade concert from fully seated orchestral events, but it is doubtful that most people were mingling while the orchestra was playing. A large bank of seats usually faced the orchestra, making moving about less easy than among the boxes in a traditional opera house. A drawing of a concert by Jullien's ensemble in Covent Garden in 1843 (see cover) shows promenade

---

[2] John Spitzer, "The Entrepreneur-Conductors and their Orchestras," *NCMR*, forthcoming.
[3] Carse, *Life of Jullien*, p. 43; advertisement for Strauss-Kapelle, *Wiener Zeitung*, 7 March 1846, p. 1.

areas on either side of the orchestral platform, but otherwise a seated audience.[4]

The conductors, held in high esteem for the high-level players they assembled, had a shrewd sense of concert programming. The director of such a series was responsible for an elaborate process of arranging varied pieces of music for the program, a craft that grew out of the musical theatre and looked ahead to movie music. Just as a theatre conductor was expected to arrange songs and intermission music for the shows, so the conductor would compose medleys of opera tunes or tableaux on recent topics, in the process defining the musical and social ambience at the venue. Opera was as central to promenade concerts as it was to benefit concerts, contributing a visual element to instrumental music. A conductor would often arrange to have a medley published well before the première of an opera.[5] Well-known overtures framed programs at promenade concerts, and the first piece after intermission gradually came to be a long potpourri based on an opera (Ex. 7.3). Instrumental soloists also performed opera *fantaisies*, a genre that found refuge in this context. From the 1830s through the 1860s dance pieces framed the programs at all leading promenade concerts, defining the events in musical and social terms. Still, as we shall see in the case of Leipzig, operatic music did sometimes serve the same purpose.

Promenade concerts presented programs made up entirely of instrumental music well before that became common at classical music orchestras. Although eighteenth-century English pleasure gardens had alternated between songs and orchestral numbers, the rising cost of major singers limited vocal music and forced the conductors to seek out new strategies for providing contrast. A program would normally alternate between dance pieces and overtures, and the dances would rotate among the quadrille, the polka, and the waltz. Moreover, conductors featured the principal players in the orchestra as soloists in medleys and in accompanied solo pieces. The public came to know the players well, seeing their names on the program. An early promenade concert in London, for example, listed names of everyone in the orchestra (Ill. 16).

Promenade concerts acquired a cosmopolitan identity by 1850. Entrepreneur-conductors gained international prominence in a whole host of cities – not only Jullien and Musard in Paris and London and Strauss and Lanner in Vienna but also Josef Gung'l in Berlin, Hans-Christian Plumbye

4 *Illustrated London News*, 23 December 1843, p. 413.
5 Jules Rivière, *My Musical Life and Recollections* (London: Sampson, 1893), p. 44.

in Copenhagen, Joseph Labitzky in Karlsbad, near Prague, and Charles Lenschow in the United States.[6] They all performed each others' pieces regularly and often combined forces when on tour; the centrality of opera selections on their programs blurred national differences among them. We shall see nonetheless that programs became more nationally specific after 1850.

A subtle framework of commonalities, differences, and exchanges existed between promenade and classical music concerts. The promenade concert absorbed genres that disappeared from classical music concerts (the opera fantasy and certain opera selections), and it also stimulated new ones (orchestrated dance music and topical tableaux). Canonic repertory developed within these concerts at an early date, because conductors drew on opera overtures and selections that had survived for some time in the theatre and in benefit concerts. The most common opera overtures included not only those by Mozart but also those from Méhul's *Le Jeune Henri* (1797) in 1838, Cherubini's *Anacréon* in 1844 (1803, Ex. 7.3), and Rossini's *Semiramide* in 1874 (1823, Ex 7.2). Promenade concerts gave such pieces an identity linked more closely to the benefit concert than to the classical music orchestral series. But when a promenade conductor performed music from a symphony by Beethoven or Spohr, the audience would identify it chiefly with a classical music institution, lending the informal concert a certain aesthetic stature. Musical influence flowed in both directions. Arguably, the symphonic idioms that emerged in the 1860s – the suite, the serenade, the rhapsody – were influenced by music composed for promenade concerts. The suitelike quality of Spohr's symphonies may in fact explain why excerpts from them appeared at these concerts. During the 1840s it was unusual for a promenade concert to offer more than one or two movements from a symphony, for entrepreneurs must have watched closely the collapse of the Concerts St. Honoré in Paris in 1840. But by the mid-1850s the first half of a promenade concert was sometimes devoted to classical music selections thought approachable to the general public. The Strauss-Kapelle did not follow that practice, however. Because its chief goal was to promote its own music, the ensemble maintained a rigorously up-to-date repertory save for an introductory overture in an older style.

The performance of opera overtures and symphonic movements at promenade concerts sparked dispute over who "owned" this music, and in what

---

[6] See *Marienbader Elegien*, Capriccio recordings, WDR Rundfunkorchester Cologne (2000) and Lumbye's music on *Strauss of Scandinavia: Waltzes & Polkas*, Regis Records, Odense Symphony Orchestra.

terms, as we have already seen in the Concerts St. Honoré. The viewpoint was often expressed in the idealistic press that such pieces were "classics" that should be performed only in serious gatherings with comparable repertory, thus not recognizing a growing public for such music-making. In 1840 Henry Chorley declared that that "these entertainments have a tendency to lead their managers downwards towards the vulgar, rather than the many upwards, to a discernment of what is true, beautiful and permanent." He worried that such performances of overtures by Beethoven, Mendelssohn, and Cherubini would mean that "these fine works were desecrated, under pretense of popularizing them."[7] By the same token, a critic in the *Neue Zeitschrift für Musik* – the author Louise Otto – admitted that playing a Beethoven symphony in a garden before people drinking and talking "has cast my liberalism into a harsh dilemma."[8] Idealists feared that the new mass audience would spurn the classics. In 1845 a Viennese commentator declared that, "For the masses it is Strauss, for the elite Beethoven, at least that's how I see it, and how it shall be, because it never was any different."[9] By "elite" he meant an intellectual elite, not a social class; within "the masses" he included the (philistine) rich he saw listening to the Strauss ensemble in the Prater.

The differentiation between promenade and classical music concerts became less strict after 1850, as music halls and *cafés-concerts* set a new standard for informal music-making and low-priced concerts of classical music enlarged the public for orchestral music generally. Some promenade concerts began offering more classical works than before, though usually just in the first half. Connections between formal and informal concerts went the furthest in Berlin, where the ensemble begun by Benjamin Bilse during the 1860s evolved into the Berlin Philharmonic Orchestra in 1882.[10] *Cafés-concerts* and music halls likewise performed opera overtures and vocal selections, as we shall note in Chapter 9. Interactions among concert settings thus became freer; organizers of informal concerts began defining works shared with classical music series in their own terms ideologically. Pieces by Mendelssohn became particularly important in that

7 *ATH*, July 18, 1840, p. 579.
8 Louise Otto, "Polemische Blätter, Ein Beitrag dazu: Garten Concerte," *NZFM*, 8 August 1846, p. 46. She published novels and *Das Recht der Frauen* (Hamburg, 1866).
9 *AMZ*, 1 April 1845, pp. 154–5.
10 Rebecca Grotjahn, "Die Entdeckung der *Terra incognita* – Benjamin Bilse und sein reisendes Orchester," *Le musicien et ses voyages*, pp. 253–82; Jochen George Güntzel, "Benjamin Bilse als Kapellmeister in Liegnitz," in *Deutsche Musik im Osten: Beiträge zur Musikgeschichte Schlesiens, Tagesgericht Liegnitz 1991* (Bonn: Schröder, 1994), pp. 183–200. I am indebted to John Spitzer on this subject.

context due to the popular touch inherent in many areas of his music. Nevertheless, dance pieces and opera medleys continued to frame the programs at most promenade concerts.

A second major development after 1850 was the linkage of national identities to the music played in promenade concerts. Although the medley of music from a French or Italian opera continued in most programs, more of the pieces selected were composed in the home country, in some cases tinged with nationalist implications. Stronger national identities can be seen in promenade concert programs in Britain, Germany, and Austria; in France that tendency had already existed in Musard's programs of the 1830s. After the early "dance kings" had established international reputations, their successors began to include an increasing amount of music from their own nations or regions. We shall see that listeners turned to music halls and *cafés-concerts* for a similar reason. This change came about partly because some composers used nationalist slogans as a way to compete with classics in gaining access to programs. Still, promenade concerts did not become hotbeds of nationalism. Themes related to national culture found in musical contexts were usually not linked to the politics of the nation-state or nationalistic movements. *Liedertafel* choruses were a special case, as has been shown for the choruses in Münster.[11]

Celia Applegate has defined the distinction between musical and political nationalism carefully, showing that the rediscovery of Bach's St. Matthew Passion in 1829 awakened "currents of national awareness," a sense of German community, but "did not follow the same trajectory as that of the coalescence of German states into a national union."[12] This approach to regional identities enables us to distinguish between national and nationalistic assumptions or movements. The growing repertory of German opera at promenade concerts was more national than nationalistic. For that matter, the dance pieces performed at promenade concerts can be seen to carry a *central* European identity because the entrepreneur-conductors came from a variety of countries in that region – Austria, Hungary, Bohemia, Denmark, as well as the German states. The main reason for national identities growing in these concerts derived from the widespread ideological critique of cosmopolitan opera and its elite public. The diatribes of Richard Wagner against the Italian operatic tradition represented a widespread disillusionment with the musical and social hegemony of cosmopolitan opera. Listeners from a variety of social classes,

---

[11] Heemann, *Männergesangvereine im 19. und frühen 20. Jahrhundert.*
[12] Applegate, *Bach in Berlin*, p. 255; Heemann, *Männergesangvereine im 19. und frühen 20. Jahrhundert.*

free-thinking intellectuals especially, were looking for a musical culture less pretentious than *grand opéra* – music that evoked an earthy, popular character.

The tradition of miscellany took new form in promenade concerts. Whereas in 1800 the miscellaneous program was virtually universal, it now amounted to a special format drawing together a certain variety of genres and tastes. In 1865 a London journalist remarked that an unusual variety of music could be heard on one promenade program, an "extraordinary mélange" that made sure that "something is provided for people of all tastes; every kind of music is represented."[13] A remarkable miscellany was heard at an 1865 concert where Josef Strauss, the middle brother (1827–1870), directed the Kapelle, the Vienna Men's Singing Society, and a military band in excerpts from Meyerbeer's *l'Africaine*, Wagner's *Tristan und Isolde*, and the chorus "What Girls do to Logic" (Ex. 7.8). Still, entrepreneur-conductors, like North American glee club directors long since, imposed both social and musical unity on disparate styles, skillfully manipulating the distinctive sound of his ensemble.

PARIS

In Paris promenade concerts were originally oriented toward a fairly well-off public. Philippe Musard focused his career on directing balls, both privately and for the court; rumor said that he earned fifty thousand francs a year by the late 1830s. The concerts he began in 1832, first open-air and then indoors, drew a public that an English visitor characterized as "the fashionable west-end Lounge of Paris."[14] Directing an orchestra of eighty players, mostly students from the Conservatoire, he created an international model for the promenade concert; imitations of his enterprise cropped up all over Europe with his illustrious name in the title. A program reported by an English visitor contained four opera overtures, six dance pieces (three on opera tunes), and an arrangement of a piece from an opera, as well as a movement from Beethoven's First Symphony (Ex. 7.1). Musard favored national over cosmopolitan repertory, rather as the Opéra did but benefit concerts did not. Yet this program was atypical of his concerts in its inclusion of two pieces by classical composers.[15]

13 "Promenade Concerts," *MW*, 2 September 1865, p. 544, originally in *The Reader*.
14 "Musard en 1832," article from unnamed periodical, Fonds Montpensier, BNF; "Musard's Concerts at Paris," *MW*, 16 June 1837, pp. 5–6.
15 See Ch. 6, note 71.

7.1 *Concert of Philippe Musard, Salle Valentino, rue St. Honoré, June 1837*[16]

Part I:

Overture, *La Flûte Enchantée* (1791)	†Mozart
Quadrille	*Musard*
Overture, *Le Maçon* (1825)	Auber
Quadrille Romantique	*Musard*
"La Tyrolienne," *Guillaume Tell* (1829), arranged	Rossini/*Musard*
Quadrille on the *romance Les Laveuses*	
du Couvent (Albert Grisar, 1836)	*Musard*

Part II:

Overture, *Margherite d'Anjou* (1820)	Meyerbeer
Quadrille on *Les Chaperons Blancs* (Auber, 1836)	*Musard*
Andante, Symphony no. 1 in C	†Beethoven
Quadrille, *Le Samois*	*Musard*
Overture, *Les Deux Aveugles de Tolède* (1806)	†Méhul
Tarentella, *La Muette de Portici* (1828), arr.	Auber/*Musard*

The Revolution of 1848 triggered two decades of sweeping change in the rules governing Parisian entertainments. Monopolies evaporated for a time, new genres and formats appeared, and promenade concerts began offering elaborate programs of vocal music closely related to the emerging *café-concert*. Isaac Strauss, Musard's successor as director of court balls in the mid-1840s, put on a program at the Jardin d'Hiver that offered a wealth of selections from the musical theatre, discussed below in reference to *cafés-concerts* (Ex. 9.7). The growth of the *café-concert* in Paris during the 1850s limited attendance at promenade concerts, leading conductors to shift from dance pieces to opera overtures and selections as the focus of programs. Interestingly enough, the generic term *popular music* was adopted for a series called "Concerts of Popular Music" given at the Elysée Montmartre in 1869 under the direction of Olivier Métra, who later conducted at the Folies Bergères (Ex. 7.2). Most of the operas involved were over twenty years old, and the program included a "hymn" by Haydn, probably an arrangement of a chorus from *Creation*. Pieces from French opera, by Ambroise Thomas and the ever-present Gounod, occupied important spots as penultimate pieces in each half.

---

[16] "Musard's Concerts at Paris." Samois is a city southeast of Paris.

7.2 "*4e Concert de la Musique Populaire*," *Elysée Montmartre, 21 November 1869* [17]

Overture to *Merry Wives of Windsor* (1849)	†Nicolai
Orchestral *Fantaisie* on *Anna Bolena* (1830)	†Donizetti/ *Fessy*
Overture to *Der Freischütz* (1821)	†Weber
Fantaisie for flute on *Carnaval de Venise* (1857)	Ambroise Thomas/ ***
La nuit	*Olivier Métra*

—

Overture to *Semiramide* (1823)	†Rossini
Orchestral Fantasy on *Il Trovatore* (1853)	Verdi/*Métra*
Austrian Hymn, for strings	†Haydn
March and Chorus of Soldiers, *Faust* (1859)	Gounod
Waltz, *Tour du Monde*	*Métra*

LONDON

The "Promenade Concerts à la Musard" begun in London in 1838 followed a similar alternation between overtures and dance pieces but with an increasingly international profile. A program given by the Theatre Royal Lyceum (also known as the English Opera House) offered six dance pieces by Musard and Strauss, one by the latter on Napoleon's deceased son, and six overtures, those by Cherubini and Rossini written for Paris (Ill. 16). Pieces by Lanner and Labitzsky appeared on later programs. A repertory of canonic overtures quickly emerged. This program followed the convention of opening with an overture in an older style, Cherubini's *Anacréon*, and also offered Méhul's overture for *Les Aveugles de Tolède* (1806). That the Philharmonic also performed overtures by Méhul illustrates the common culture developing between the otherwise so different types of concerts. Louis Jullien broadened the programming at promenade concerts after crossing the Channel in 1840 to direct concerts at a variety of venues. Bringing experience at concerts competing with Musard's, he saw that the London public was ready for adventurous new musical entertainment, and he proceeded to attract a broader middle-class public than Musard had done in Paris. Maintaining unity with quadrilles and polkas, he gradually introduced a variety of genres from Italy, Germany, and Britain and gave special attention

[17] Program collection, MM; Fauquet, *Dictionnaire*, p. 795. The characters *** indicated an amateur performer.

to instrumental solos. A program in 1844 included an *English Quadrille, Highland Quadrille,* and *Irish Echoes* and included solos by Apollon Marie Barret, the French first oboist at the King's Theatre (Ex. 7.3). Hermann-Louis Koenig, the most prominent trumpeter internationally, often visited the concerts. The *Adieu Romance* illustrates how the *cornet-à-pistons* (a small trumpet with valves) was to become a central component of British musical life, flourishing in both middle- and working-class communities.[18]

7.3 *Promenade Concert, Covent Garden Theatre, 12 February 1844* [19]

Overture, *Anacréon* (1803)	†Cherubini
Highland Quadrille	*Jullien*
Cornet solo, *Adieu Romance*	Roch-Albert [*Jullien*]
Valse à deux Temps	*Jullien*
Descriptive Fantasia, *The Destruction of Pompeii*	Roch-Albert
—	
Fantasia on *Don Juan,* solos for oboe & bassoon	†Mozart/*Jullien*
Quadrille, *The Irish Echoes*	*Jullien*
Solo for oboe	Apollon Marie Barret
Waltz, *Mecklenburger Strelitz*	Koenig
English Quadrille	*Jullien*

Jullien treated classical music as an important secondary component of his repertory, sometimes doing a single movement from a Beethoven symphony. A concert in Manchester in 1848 was unusual for the time, offering not only several classical pieces but also solo vocal numbers featuring the young Sims Reeves.[20] Jullien placed the classics ironically: the Allegretto from Beethoven's Seventh Symphony came between two ballads by Michael Balfe, and the Andante from Haydn's "Surprise" Symphony fell between arias by Donizetti and Rossini. Dance pieces surrounded such disparate music as the overture to Mozart's *Die Zauberflöte* and "Sound an alarm" from Handel's *Judas Maccabaeus.* In 1856 Jullien made an early example of devoting the first half of a concert to music by one composer, in this case Mendelssohn. The "Scottish" Symphony, the Violin Concerto, and the overture to *Ruy Blas* contrasted with a quadrille on *Il Trovatore*

---

[18] Dave Russell, *Popular Music in England, 1840–1914: A Social History* (Montreal: McGill-Queen's University Press, 1987).
[19] Carse, *Life of Jullien,* pp. 48–9.   [20] Manchester, CPH/RCM.

and a fantasy on *La Traviata*, as well as six dance pieces and a cornet solo by Angelina Goetz, whose music he issued through his publishing firm.[21] Jullien's attempt to produce opera seems to have led to his final financial collapse. Alfred Mellon, Jullien's main successor after his suicide in 1860, occasionally devoted the first half of a program to classics. In 1866 he did so for Beethoven, offering *Adelaide*, the Septet, the song *Der Kuss* (op. 128), and the supposedly complete "Eroica" Symphony. A medley on Gounod's *Faust* opened the second half, and a descriptive quadrille on taking the train to Paris closed it. Still, the highlight of the evening was the star Adelina Patti singing "variations" on music from Benedict's opera *Brides of Venice* (1844).[22]

The great majority of British promenade concerts nonetheless stuck to Jullien's format of dance pieces, overtures, and medleys. In 1870, for example, Jules Rivière offered a program at the grandiose Alhambra Palace on Leicester Square that included no music usually thought classical. He focused instead on French music – the overtures to Auber's *La Muette de Portici* (1828) and Hérold's *Le Pré aux Clercs* (1832) and *Galop Express Train* by the long deceased pianist Frédéric Kalkbrenner.[23] Promenade concerts of this kind spread quickly to North America. A contingent of musicians who had left Berlin toured widely as the Germania Musical Society, offering programs modeled on those given by Josef Gung'l in Berlin.[24] Their program in Worcester, Massachusetts, in 1849 added the Finale of Beethoven's Fifth Symphony to the usual fare, including a dance piece by Charles Lenschow, the ensemble's leader (Ill. 18). The ensemble offered several classical pieces on some occasions and attempted unsuccessfully to hold a series of concerts in Boston devoted entirely to classical works. Louis Jullien seems to have presented significantly more classical music in North America than in England. Still, the Germania program just cited illustrates the standard repertory in promenade concerts as a whole in this period.[25]

[21] Carse, *Life of Jullien*, p. 91. See "A Sketch from the Life of Jullien," *MW*, 14 May 1853, p. 307 and subsequent issues.

[22] "Covent Garden," CPH/RCM. The Benedict piece was cited as *Il Carnovale di Venezia*.

[23] Theatres, CPH/RCM. See Rivière, *My Musical Life and Recollections*, pp. 126–30. He probably adapted Kalkbrenner's *Galop brillant sur un motif de l'opéra* Le Proscrit *de A. Adam* (Paris, 1834). Promenade concert programs are also found at BLO/JJ and at the University of Kent at Canterbury.

[24] Nancy Newman, "Good Music for a Free People: The Germania Musical Society and Transatlantic Musical Culture of the Mid-Nineteenth Century," unpublished Ph.D. dissertation, Brown University (2002); "'Gleiche Rechte, gleiche Pflichten, und gleiche Genüsse': Henry Albrecht's Utopian Vision of the Germania Musical Society," *Yearbook of German–American Studies* 34 (1999), 83–111.

[25] Newman, "Good Music for a Free People," pp. 347–52; Joseph Horowitz, *Classical Music in America: A History of its Rise and Fall* (New York: W. W. Norton, 2005), pp. 15–93.

The tendency toward nationally focused repertories became common at British promenade concerts after 1850. The term *promenade* was used for an outdoor event given at New College, Oxford, by a freemasons lodge in 1857, drawing some 1,500 people to hear the local Glee Union in a program principally of British songs.[26] A not dissimilar "garden concert" was given in 1874 in Folkestone, on the south coast (Ex. 7.4). Here we see how the glee and the part-song (probably accompanied) remained prominent in repertory, in pieces by such British composers as Arne, Balfe, Lord Mornington, and both George and Walter Macfarren, mingled with medleys of operas by Donizetti and Nicolai. The madrigal supposedly by Constanzo Festa (d.1545) illustrates the continuing English interest in Elizabethan music. For that matter, the time had come when two-thirds of the pieces at a promenade concert could be by dead composers.

7.4 *Garden Concert, Band of the 23rd Royal Welsh Fusiliers, Lawn Pavilion, Folkestone, 5 September 1874*[27]

Overture, *Semiramide* (1823)	†Rossini
Part-song, "The Sands of the Dee"	George Macfarren
Duet, "Take this Ring," *The Talisman* (1874)	†Balfe
Waltz, *Sounds of the Hesperus*	Gung'l
Song, "The Rose Song," *The Talisman*	†Balfe
Trumpet Solo, *The Soldier Tir'd* (Thomas Harper)	†Arne
Madrigal, "Down in a flowery Vale"	†Constanzo Festa
Medley	†Donizetti/*arr.?*
Part-song, "You stole my Love"	Walter Macfarren
Aria, "Let the bright Seraphim," *Samson*	†Handel
Part-song, "In this Hour of softened Splendor"	Ciro Pinsuti
Quadrille, "Les Amazones"	Jean-Baptiste Arban
Irish Song, "Robin Adair"	
Glee, "Here in cool Grot"	†Lord Mornington
Medley, *Merry Wives of Windsor*	†Otto Nicolai

VIENNA

Johann Strauss the Elder followed many of the same practices as Musard, Jullien, or Gung'l – concerts in vividly decorated spaces, programs framed by dance numbers, and a heroic posture as conductor and entrepreneur.

[26] *TL*, 23 June 1857, p. 5.   [27] Thomas Harper Concert Programs, CPH/RCM.

He offered quadrilles and polkas almost as often as waltzes, and the great majority of his pieces were medleys or potpourris on recent operas or events. Strauss originally played in the intimate venue of the public house (possibly involving two violins, a bass, and a flute) and gradually expanded the Strauss-Kapelle to a twelve-piece ensemble and finally to almost thirty instruments by his death in 1849. The press treated Strauss in special terms, reporting his concert in *Neuigkeiten* ("What's New") rather than *Musik*. Strauss found a niche for the ensemble around which he built his wide-ranging enterprises of publishing, marketing, and touring. Under his influence the term *Unterhaltungsmusik*, entertainment for the general public, began to be cited as the opposite of serious concerts focused on classical music.[28]

As early as 1828 the influential *Theaterzeitung* declared that Strauss had transformed the music in public houses, driving out tedious Alpine singers and capturing public attention adroitly.[29] Almost every piece touched on something that interested the public – a new opera, the crowning of Emperor Ferdinand, or the invention of the telegraph. Among his most often-performed pieces was *A Bouquet by Strauss* (Ein Strauss von Strauss), a medley of tunes by composers as diverse as Haydn, Beethoven, Auber, Bellini, Hérold, and Lanner. The potpourri *A Musical Word Game* (1833) challenged listeners to name his most famous tunes in rapid succession. Thus his programs avoided seeming monochromatic, even while offering only instrumental music. Strauss nonetheless harked back to Austrian tradition in planning concerts for religious feast days and at carnival time, writing the *Katharina-Fest-Waltz* for a particularly important Austrian holy day.

In Vienna the Strauss-Kapelle announced pieces informally, by voice or on a blackboard, but produced programs while on tour. One printed in Mannheim listed many pieces on topical themes and included a Bellini cavatina, probably to involve a local performer in the proceedings (Ex. 7.5). Quite a few other overtures and instrumental solos were certainly performed, mostly by composers other than Strauss. Its program for a concert in London in 1838 included *fantaisies* for flute and harp by English players, the former called *Reminiscences of Hérold*.[30]

---

[28] Norbert Linke, *Musik erobert die Welt, passim.* I am indebted to Ingomar Rainer for information.
[29] "Neuigkeiten," *TZ*, 20 July 1828, p. 350; *TZ*, 16 November 1833, p. 923; database, http://www.johann-strauss-gesellschaft.at/.
[30] "Strauss-Kapelle Programme," SLBV.

7.5 *"Evening Entertainment by Johann Strauss and his 26-Member Orchestra, in the Great Hall of the Theater, Mannheim," 11 November 1835*[31]

Overture to *The Forgers (Le serment, ou Les faux-monnoyeurs*, 1832)	Auber
Ovation Waltz (coronation of Emperor Ferdinand I, 1835)	*Strauss*
Cavatina, *Norma*	†Bellini
Grand Potpourri, Ein Strauss von Strauss (1832)	*Strauss*
—	
Philomelen-Waltz (dedicated to Princess of Baden, 1835)	*Strauss*
Venetian and *Fortuna Galop* (1834)	*Strauss*
Grand Potpourri, *A Musical Word Game* (1833)	*Strauss*
Garland Waltz, medley of famous waltzes (1834)	*Strauss*

Strauss won greater renown within fashionable society internationally than any other entrepreneur-conductor. Viennese periodicals indicated that aristocrats were regularly seen at his concerts, and, like Musard, Strauss was director of court balls. This fame carried over to the tours: while in London in 1838, the Kapelle performed at the prestigious annual benefit concert given by harpist Robert Bochsa, opening and closing the second half with the *Fireworks Waltz* and *Paris Carnival Galop*. The rest of the program consisted of opera excerpts by Cimarosa, Rossini, Mercadante, and Bellini, performed by a different ensemble.[32]

As for classical repertory, the Strauss-Kapelle did not go beyond performing overtures and including melodies by Mozart or Beethoven in potpourris. Promoting and selling their music motivated them to keep their own programs contemporary. One could argue that Strauss distanced himself from Mozart and Beethoven for the same reason that the Parisian Conservatoire concerts and the Viennese Concert Spirituel abstained from offering excerpts from recent *grands opéras*. Press reports make clear that an overture would open each half of a program by the Kapelle and that one or two might come in the middle of each half. The main overtures were those to Weber's *Oberon*, Beethoven's *Egmont*, Mozart's *Don Giovanni*, and Mendelssohn's *Midsummer Night's Dream*. Just as often represented, however, were overtures by composers marginal to the usual definition of "classical" music:

[31] Linke, *Musik erobert die Welt*, p. 124.
[32] Ibid., *passim*; Ludwig Scheyrer, *Johann Strauss's musikalische Wanderung durch das Leben* (Vienna: Auf Kosten des Verfassers, 1851), pp. 54–6.

Auber's *Muette de Portici* or *Le Serment*, Hérold's *Pré des Clercs*, and Rossini's *Barbiere di Siviglia* or *Guillaume Tell*.

By limiting the range of his repertory and carefully managing his public and professional relations, Strauss remained more or less immune to the accusations of commercialism or bad taste heaped on Jullien or Gung'l. Such musical idealists as Berlioz and Schumann spoke highly of the professionalism and musicality of his ensemble. Yet criticism did surface in the press. In 1833 the column *Neuigkeiten* in the *Theaterzeitung* suggested that Strauss was all things to all men, "the Mozart of the Waltz, the Beethoven of the Cotillon, the Paganini of the Galop, the Rossini of the Potpourri."[33] Shortly after Johann Strauss the Younger began directing concerts in 1844, a reviewer complained that the ensemble had serious difficulties making its way through the overture to *Midsummer Night's Dream*, and another derided the "autocratic rule" exerted by Strauss and Lanner locally.[34] The *Theaterzeitung* sought the center in such discussion. In 1844 it published a thoughtful assessment of the elder Strauss, praising him for knowing what the public wanted to hear and also – borrowing language from the idealists – "raising dance music to a high plane it has never reached before."[35]

After the elder Johann Strauss died of scarlet fever on 25 September 1849, leadership of the Strauss-Kapelle passed without a break to his twenty-four-year-old son Johann, who had caused a considerable sensation with his first performances in 1844. Although the father avoided identification with the 1848 revolution, the son linked himself so closely to it – writing waltzes called *Freedom Song* and *Revolution March* – that it took fifteen years of diplomatic efforts with the new Emperor before he could direct at court balls. During July 1851, as constitutional issues were fought out between the Habsburg government and the weak Assembly of the German Confederation, Strauss advertised that he would hold a "Grand Festival to the Centralization of Nationalities, with a Ball, whose mood will be every bit as exciting as this venue is accustomed."[36] "Centralization" might have referred either to the empire or to the diverse national origins of composers often on his programs. The next year Strauss began borrowing techniques from Richard Wagner and composed a medley of music from

[33] "Neuigkeiten," *TZ*, 16 November 1833, p. 923.
[34] "Localzeitung: Casino in Hietzing," *Oesterreichisches Morgenblatt*, 23 November 1844, p. 564; "Nachrichten," *NZFM*, 5 July, 1845, p. 495.
[35] "Denkwürdigkeiten," *TZ*, 14 November 1844, p. 1123.
[36] Advertisement, "Ein Grosses Nationalitäten-Centralisations-Fest mit Ball, dessen Tendenz eine besonders heitere und dieser grossen Lokalität angemessene ist," *Fremden-Blatt*, 6 July 1851, p. 1.

Lohengrin, thereby drawing a vicious condemnation from critic Eduard Hanslick.[37]

Programs given on the Strauss-Kapelle's 1852 tour, seen in one from Leipzig, resembled closely those of the 1840s, using genres common to all promenade concerts – potpourri, *fantaisie*, and the usual dance forms (Ill. 17). The Leipzig Centralhalle, constructed in 1849 (shown on the program), opened up Leipzig concert life significantly. The program included two famous pieces by the elder Strauss ("von weiland Joh. Strauss"), and several other overtures and instrumental solos were no doubt done between the dances. A concert in the Teatro San Carlo in Naples in 1874 (Ex. 7.6) illustrates the links between the Strauss-Kapelle and benefit concerts (note the cello solo by Servais) and German promenade concerts (note the solo for valved trumpet), as well as the music of Johann's youngest brother, Eduard Strauss (1835–1916). Here, as always, few pieces save the overtures were more than a dozen years old, quite different from British or German promenade concerts. The Polka-Galop on *Indigo and the Forty Thieves*, Strauss's operetta of 1871, illustrates how he began to shift from concerts to musical theatre prior to the stunning success of *Die Fledermaus* in 1877.

7.6 *Concert of Strauss-Kapelle, Teatro San Carlo, Naples, 21 May 1874*[38]

Overture, *Si j'étais roi* (1852)	†Adolphe Adam
Waltz, *Wine, Women & Song* (1869)	J. Strauss, Jun.
Fantaisie for cello on a Hungarian theme	†Servais
Polka, *Make the Way Free!* (1869)	Eduard Strauss
Paraphrase on Mendelssohn's *Lorelei* of 1847	Neswabda
Waltz, *Bella Italia* (1874)	J. Strauss, Jun.
Solo for valved trumpet on themes of Weber	Theodor Hoch
Polka-Galop on *Indigo und die vierzig Räuber* (1871)	J. Strauss, Jun.
March, *La Reine de Saba* (1862)	Gounod

The first major change in the makeup of the Strauss family's concerts came in joint ventures with military bands and men's choruses. In 1847 the father undertook such a concert in a "Grand Ball in the Outdoors," held in the Volksgarten, tripling the number of performers at his command.[39] Like the Strauss-Kapelle, *Liedertafel* clubs also maintained a distance from

---

[37] Linke, *Musik erobert die Welt*, pp. 175–7.   [38] Strauss-Kapelle Programme, 1836–1929, SLBV.
[39] Max Schönherr and Karl Reinöhl, *Das Jahrhundert des Walzers*, vol. 1, *Johann Strauss Vater, Ein Werkverzeichnis* (London: Universal Edition, 1954), p. 295; Rudolf Hofmann, *Der Wiener Männergesangverein: Chronik der Jahre 1843 bis 1893* (Vienna: Verlag des Wiener Männergesangvereines, 1893); Heemann, *Männergesangvereine im 19. und frühen 20. Jahrhundert*.

the classical music world. They occasionally shared classical programs with orchestral societies but at their own concerts concentrated on music written by *Liedertafel* conductors. Pieces by Schubert, Mendelssohn, or Schumann sung at their events had been written directly for *Liedertafel* use and were not perceived as being like these composers' "classical" symphonies. The clubs preserved the long tradition of convivial music-making that the classical music world had abandoned. Indeed, some critics expressed doubt that *Liedertafel* music stood on the same plane as the great works of art. In 1864 a Viennese reviewer objected to a program at the Men's Singing Society (*Männergesangverein*) that called Johann Herbeck's "Was uns liebt und was wir lieben" a "new" piece, because the music seemed banal and insipid. By that time the Wagnerian movement had endowed the term *new music* with a high aesthetic meaning. Another critic used the words *philistines* and *student lads* in referring to the city's main male choruses.[40]

Names of leading *Liedertafel* composers predominated in a program that the Men's Singing Society performed on the Vienna Prater in 1865 – Franz Abt, Conradin Kreutzer, Julius Otto, and Anton Storch (Ex. 7.7).[41] Choral songs like Schubert's "At Night," such as we saw at the Viennese Evening Entertainments, were performed widely in Britain and America by this time. Here we find an extreme in the homogeneity of programming; the pieces represented had almost entirely the same musical forces and national origin. The lyrics and the comic element linked *Liedertafel* to German concerts resembling *cafés-concerts* (Ill. 22).

7.7 *"Volkskonzert," Vienna Männergesangverein, Prater, 5 June 1865*[42]

"The Shoemaker's Sunday," chorus and solo	†Conradin Kreutzer
"The Blacksmith's Darling"	Vinzenz Lachner
"Spring is Near"	†Kreutzer
Prize Song	Julius Otto, Jun.
"Song of the Wanderer," solo	W. Fischer, Jun.
Song	August Schäffer
–	
"At Night"	†Schubert
Swabian Volkslied, "Three Little Roses"	

40 "Concerte," *Recensionen und Mittheilungen über Theater und Musik*, 17 December (1864), 814; "Berichte: Wien," *AMZ*, 10 March (1869), 77–8 (*Philister* and *Burschen*).
41 Hofmann, *Wiener Männergesangverein*, pp. 529–32.   42 PA/GMF.

Swabian Dance Songs
"Welcome," chorus and four horns   Anton Storch
Comic Quartet, "Such a Disgrace"
"Forest Prayer," solo   Franz Abt
"Chorus of the Dervishes"   Beethoven/Johann
                                                Kalliwoda

In the 1850s and 1860s Johann Strauss the Younger collaborated extensively with the Men's Singing Society. Programs for joint concerts normally
also involved a military band or orchestra, alternating between choral and
orchestral pieces and closing with all ensembles participating. In 1865 in
the nearby resort Hietzing, Josef Strauss conducted a concert that, though
dominated by *Liedertafel* music, offered a rich variety of vocal and instrumental selections ranging from Meyerbeer to Mendelssohn to Wagner (Ex.
7.8). The program announced that the Strauss-Kapelle and the Hussars
Band would perform between individual numbers.

7.8 *"Summer Liedertafel, by the Vienna Men's Singing Society, Josef Strauss
    with his Orchestra, and the Band of the Royal Hussars-Regiment of the
    King of Prussia, in Die Neue Welt, Hietzing,"* 17 July 1865 [43]
Our Motto: "Be Free and True, in Song and Action"

Band and Orchestra:
Overture, *Rosamunde* (1823)   †Schubert
Excerpts, *Tristan und Isolde* (1859)   Wagner
Lieder ohne Worte, arranged for orchestra   †Mendelssohn
Finale, Act 1, *Die Afrikanerin* (1865)   †Meyerbeer

Singing Society:
Chorus, "Reminiscence and Nostalgia"   †Conradin Kreutzer
"The Parish Picnic"   †Marschner
"Merry Forest Warblers"   Abt
Romance, *Die Afrikanerin*   †Meyerbeer

The Orchestra:
French Polka, *Your Beloved Eyes*   *Josef Strauss*

Singing Society:
Volkslieder from Carinthia   Herbeck
Chorus, "Home is Nearby"   E. S. Engelsberg

---

[43] PA/GMF. See Botstein, "Listening through Reading," pp. 133–4, 145.

Solo Male Quartet, "What Girls do to Logic"	Joseph Koch von Langentreu
Chorus, "Love"	†Kreutzer
Chorus and Declamation, "A Harmless Waltz from a half-gone Era, by a half-dead Fool"	Herbeck
Singing Society and Orchestra: Battle Hymn, "On Romans, to the Altars!"	
Rienzi (1842)	Wagner

All the composers on the 1865 program were German or Austrian, a pattern that was unusual to find before 1848 at a promenade, benefit, or orchestral concert. Here we see how the sense of a German cultural community came alive to a particular extent in *Liedertafel* concerts. That identity did not necessarily have anything to do with contemporary efforts outside Austria to create a unified Germany. Wagner's nationalism was populist and self-interested: he had no use for the Prussian leader Otto von Bismarck either before or after the German Second Empire was established. If anything, nationalism served as an ideological vehicle for the composer to gain prominence for his music in competition with classical music. Just as Wagner was honored to be the final composer on this 1865 program, so he found his way into many other concerts during the 1860s, such as at the promenade concert led by Alfred Mellon. His music encountered very different publics and aesthetic viewpoints when performed in a concert rather than in an opera hall.

The 1865 program also indicates how far apart the Strauss ensemble stood from the world of classical music. Schubert and Mendelssohn did not appear in this context as "classical" composers but rather as contributors to the *Liedertafel* movement, its heroes and its ceremonies. Indeed, by the 1860s the Strauss-Kapelle did not often perform the overtures by Mozart, Beethoven, or Weber that had been standard repertory at its concerts in the 1840s. Yet the operettas of the younger Strauss became so highly respected by the 1890s that classical music orchestras began playing his dance pieces and his father's work in certain contexts, and Richard Strauss led programs combining his music with theirs. *Die Fledermaus* entered the repertory at the Salzburg Festival in the mid-1920s, and the Vienna Philharmonic began playing waltzes at celebration of the New Year in 1929.[44] Few would have thought in 1835 that the fiddler and his players would be honored in terms comparable to those applied to Beethoven.

[44] Strauss-Kapelle Programme, SLBV.

LEIPZIG

Dance music did not always dominate programs at informal concerts. Leipzig illustrates how promenade concerts could be focused on operatic music rather than dance pieces in a small city where an elite society dominated musical life. Informal music events occurred in public houses just outside the city's walls well before 1800. The "occasional" music played at such venues, like that seen happening in 1799 (Ex. 2.6), gave way to repertory initially similar to what was being performed at the Gewandhaus. Elegantly outfitted buildings and gardens were sites for events both indoors and outdoors, the best known being the Küchengarten and the Grossbosischer Garten, near the Grimma Gate, not far from the Gewandhaus.[45] Concerts held outdoors usually offered music arranged for wind instruments, concluding with fireworks. Entrepreneurs carefully balanced Austro-German and French or Italian music and likewise symphonic, operatic, and dance numbers. In 1822 a charity concert offered arrangements for wind instruments of selections from music performed at the subscription concerts, from a Haydn symphony, Mozart's *Don Giovanni*, and Cherubini's *Lodoïska*, along with a potpourri and a set of variations by Rode (Ex. 7.9). Music directors served as soloists and composers: W. Barth, probably related to other musicians of that name in Copenhagen, directed the concerts, performed the Rode solo, and arranged most of the music. C. H. Meyer, who composed a potpourri, held the same position at the Grossbosischer Garten.

7.9 *Concert for Wind Instruments, Küchengarten, Leipzig, to aid the Institute for Poor and Ill Musicians, 25 July 1822*[46]

Symphony no. 100, "Military"	†Haydn/*Barth*
Potpourri	Meyer
Finale, *Don Giovanni*, Act I (1787)	†Mozart/*Barth*
—	
Overture, *Ferdinand Cortez* (1809)	Spontini/Zillmann
Thema con variazioni	Pierre Rode
Terzet and Chorus, *Lodoïska* (1791)	Cherubini/*Barth*
Finale, *Don Giovanni*, Act II	†Mozart/*Barth*
Military Music	

---

[45] *Gemälde von Leipzig und seiner Umgegend für Fremde und Einhimische* (Leipzig: Hinrichsche Buchhandlung, 1823), p. 198; *Lexikon/Enzyklopädie zur Geschichte und Gegenwart der Stadt Leipzig*, http://www.leipzig-lexikon.de/.

[46] Küchengarten, 1816–34, SGML.

An ambitious program at the Küchengarten in 1832, involving an orchestra and a singer, combined symphonic, operatic, and dance pieces with a more equal balance than was common at most promenade concerts at that time (Ex. 7.10). The pieces by Beethoven and Spohr served to introduce the featured operatic numbers by Rossini, Weber, and Meyerbeer, indicating the strong demand existing for international opera in central Germany. Lanner's Bellini medley and the dialect number by Lanner provided a limited component of dance music (see another example of dialect in Ex. 9.3).

7.10 *Concert in the Küchengarten, 11 July 1832* [47]

Symphony no. 7 [? one or two movements]	†Beethoven
For brass:	
Overture, *Fidelio* (1805)	†Beethoven
Notturno	Spohr
Finale, Act II, *Belagerung an Corinth* (1826)	Rossini
—	
For strings:	
Overture, *Oberon* (1826)	†Weber
Ballade, *Robert der Teufel* (1831)	Meyerbeer
"Bekannte Töne der Unbekannten,"	
Waltz on Bellini's *La Straniera* (1829)	Lanner
Siciliano, *Robert der Teufel*	Meyerbeer
Elisens und Katinkens Vereinigung,	
Rutscher und Regtowak [Austrian dialect]	Lanner

The balance in the national origins of pieces heard in Leipzig began to change by the 1840s, as composers from Germany, Austria, and other central European countries were featured more prominently at the city's promenade concerts. Overtures and songs from German opera or operetta, tucked between dance pieces, became the core of the repertory at such events, replacing Parisian cosmopolitanism with music of central European origin. A new pleasure garden, the Tivoli, offered programs of this sort. A concert in 1842 included pieces by Lanner, Strauss, and Labitzky and opera selections by the most important German opera composers – Marschner, Reissiger, Albert Lortzing, and Carl Loewe.[48] None of the opera pieces were over fifteen years old. A concert at a local public house in 1856 went farther in the same direction (Ex. 7.11). The pieces by Rossini and Meyerbeer were far outnumbered by opera excerpts by Reissiger and the Hungarian Ferenc Erkel, dance pieces by Gung'l and Lumbye,

47 Ibid.   48 Concerte in verschiedene Stätten, 1842–72, SGML.

and the Pilgrim's chorus from Wagner's *Tannhäuser*. This repertory tended to be much newer than what Jullien offered in London, comparable to the up-to-date music of the Strauss-Kapelle; all but the overtures by Rossini and Auber dated from 1840. Arranged music began to serve as a unifying framework in promenade concerts, found here in a potpourri composed and performed by the concert's music director, Johann Valentin Hamm. The piece brings to mind the solos performed in Leipzig by C. H. Meyer in 1822 (Ex. 7.9) and the medley played by Thomas Harper in Folkstone (Ex. 7.4).

7.11 *Concert, Auf der Fussel Buen Retiro, Leipzig, 1856*[49]

Constantin-March	Josef Gung'l
Prize-Winning Festival Overture	Vinzenz Lachner
Overture, *Guillaume Tell* (1829)	Rossini
Der Industrielle Walzer	Josef Strauss
Finale, *Schiffbruch der Medusa* (1846)	Carl Reissiger
–	
Overture, *Hunyadi László* (1844)	Ferenc Erkel
Chorus to Bacchus, incidental music to	
Antigone (1841)	†Mendelssohn
Sommernachts-Quadrille	Hans Lumbye
Potpourri for piano, *The Musical Eccentric*	J. H. Hamm
–	
Overture, *Gustave III, ou Le Bal Masqué* (1833)	Auber
Pilgrims' Chorus and Song to the Evening Star,	
Tannhäuser (1845)	Wagner
Coronation March, *Le Prophète* (1849)	Meyerbeer
Kukuks-Polka	Augustus Herzog
Brass Finale	M. Wenck
Fireworks Master	F. C. Schömberg

A promenade concert held in Berlin in 1846 is interesting for having the title, "Concert à la Musard," on a program made up almost entirely of composers from central Europe (Ex. 7.12). The concert at Kroll's Wintergarten blended military band music with dance and opera selections, in this case performed by three different ensembles. Ironically, the program included selections by Gaspare Spontini, who had been ousted as music director at the opera, and Graf Wilhelm von Redern, who had signed that order. A tendency toward a more serious repertory occurred in a concert in

---

[49] Ibid. The *Industrieller Walzer* has been attributed to Gung'l.

memory of the death of Mendelssohn, held at the Wintergarten in February 1848. The orchestra performed Beethoven's "Eroica" Symphony and an arrangement of the *Marcia funebre* in the Sonata Op. 26, as well as a chorus from Mendelssohn's *Antigone* and the wedding ceremony from *Midsummer Nights Dream*. Overtures and military marches comprised the first half.[50]

7.12 *"Concert à la Musard" of 150 Musicians, Wintergarten, Berlin, 11 June 1846*[51]

Overture to *Euryanthe*, Kapelle-Musicians (KM)	†Weber
Finale, Act 1, *Die Vestalin* (1807), Infantry Musicians (IM)	Spontini
Festival March, Cavalry Musicians (CM)	C. L. Oertzen
Austrian Festival March (1846) KM	Strauss, Sen.
Cavatina, *Gemma di Verzy* (1834) IM	Donizetti
Army-March no. 703 CM	Procházka
Overture to *Olimpie* (1819) KM	Spontini
Festival March IM	Albert Leutner
Fantasy on *Robert der Teufel* KM	Meyerbeer/?
March and Ballet, *Der Schützgeist* KM	Jacob Schmitt
Austrian Tattoo IM	
Hunting Quadrille CM	†Lanner
Midsummer Night's Dream Waltz (1845) KM	Mendelssohn/Strauss, Sen.
Tournament March IM	Graf Wilhelm v. Redern
Finale, Symphony no. 5 KM	†Beethoven
Great Feast-March	Spontini
Russian Folk-Hymn	Alexis Lwoff
Parisian Entrance-March	Strauss, Sen.

FROM MISCELLANY TO POPS

The promenade concert successfully established a middle ground between the most formal and informal concerts by the mid-1850s. Opinions about these events varied according to whether the author did or did not defer to the hegemony of classical music. Violinist Joseph Joachim wrote his brother concerning Jullien, "it makes me really angry when the fellow, in his character as conductor introduces his charlatanism into the works

[50] Mahling, "Zum 'Musikbetrieb' Berlins," pp. 178–9.   [51] PA/GMFV.

of Mozart and Beethoven, and this will be inevitable."[52] Yet a reporter in the chatty *Illustrated London News* saw no such problem, saying "badinage apart, Promenade Concerts have been really delightful."[53] Another English observer sought a middle-of-the-road opinion, saying that the secret of the concerts' influence lay in their being "the only kind of entertainment accessible to the general public in which that mighty instrument, a full band, is made the most of."[54] Managers of today's "symphony" orchestras would heartily agree with him.

[52] Joseph Joachim to Heinrich Joachim, January 1857, *Letters from and to Joseph Joachim*, Nora Bickley (trans.) (London: Macmillan, 1914), p. 141.
[53] *Illustrated London News*, 23 December 1843, p. 413.
[54] "Look upon This," *MW*, 2 September 1865, p. 544.

PART III

Founding a new order, 1848–1875

CHAPTER 8

Classical music achieves hegemony

The year 1848 marked a historic watershed in both European music and politics. The revolutions of 1848–1849, paralleled by protest activities in Britain, had long-term consequences despite the failures of revolutionary regimes. "The 1848 revolutions had an agenda-setting function," Jonathan Sperber has argued, "raising issues and posing demands that were not fulfilled at the time, but would determine the direction of future developments."[1] A new political order existed in Europe as a whole by 1871, due in large part to the upheaval. Some form of constitutional and parliamentary government emerged in all countries that formerly had been absolutist, and governments already possessing representative institutions came under pressure to expand voting rights. After 1848 an increasingly larger population participated in political discourse and organizations. Indeed, the upheavals stimulated liberal, nationalist, and socialist movements central to European politics until World War I.

A new order also emerged after 1848 in the musical world: a fragmentation into separate cultural spheres and a redefinition of authority and taste. The growth in the size of the musical public, and the variety of tastes and institutions involved, pushed different types of concerts apart from one another. Musical tastes and institutions became ordered in hierarchical terms, at least in the minds of musical idealists. Concerts based on classics – chamber music and orchestral concerts and the recital – became the high culture of musical life. Indeed, in 1862 a Viennese critic spoke of a pianist aiming to interpret classics as a "revolution in musical taste."[2] Concerts that were defined as commercial entertainment and aimed at a general public appeared in new forms, offering chiefly opera selections and popular songs. The most notable of these were British ballad concerts, French

---

[1] Sperber, *European Revolutions*, p. 251. See also Alex Körner (ed.), *1848: European Revolution?* (Basingstoke, UK: Macmillan, 2000); and Hohendahl, *Building a National Literature.*
[2] "1862," *BTMK*, 1 January 1862, p. 1.

cafés-concerts, German and Austrian *Liedertafel* clubs, and concerts of opera selections and songs in all countries.

Classical music achieved hegemony after 1850, but, as we shall see, its authority was limited in significant ways. By about 1870 the proponents of serious music predominated in musical learning and pedagogy, sacred music, and the most prominent formal concerts. A listener could now hear programs adhering consistently to what was thought to be a "high" learned taste. Classical music also began to be seen as a source of both civic and national pride; tourists began visiting cities with great composers in mind: to Bonn for Beethoven and Leipzig for Bach. Music critics such as Hanslick, Fétis, and Davison were now empowered as authorities on great musical works, defining the social and aesthetic terms in which classics should be understood and performed. The association of "good" music with moral notions became established all over Europe and North America.

A cosmopolitan identity parallel to that of international opera under-pinned the new status of classical music. The hegemony of Italian opera in musical culture began slipping into crisis during the 1840s, complicated by its new links with French opera and challenged by German ideologists and operetta composers. The declining number of new opera productions during the 1850s provided an opening for classical music and its idealistic aesthetics to acquire a stature comparable to that of opera.[3] Classical music spread so widely and with such strong intellectual impact that it acquired a status rivaling that once possessed by Italian opera. A major city was now expected to have a concert series centered on classics that was well known in the international musical world.

Classical music did not, however, achieve hegemony within the worlds of opera or popular song. The classical music world achieved an authority within its own sphere precisely because the musical community became dispersed, with different tastes and repertories going their separate ways. Concerts aimed at a general public built up independent markets signifi-cantly larger than that for classical music. The small singing clubs found in Paris and London during the 1830s were replaced by big, prominent venues such as the Parisian Pavillon de l'Horloge or London's Alhambra Theatre. *Liedertafel* clubs proliferated in German-speaking areas, becom-ing the most common amateur musical activity.[4] Aesthetic hierarchies did

---

[3] On the crisis, see John Rosselli, "Italy, The Decline of a Tradition," *Late Romantic Era from the Mid-Nineteenth Century to World War One*, Jim Samson (ed.) (London: Macmillan, 1991), pp. 126–50; and Matthew Ringel, "Opera in 'The Donizettian Dark Ages': Management, Competition, and Artistic Policy in London, 1861–70," Ph.D. thesis, King's College, University of London (1996).

[4] Heemann, *Männergesangvereine im 19. und frühen 20. Jahrhundert.*

not make much difference to people listening to comic *Liedertafel* songs or watching *vaudeville*-like skits at music halls or *cafés-concerts*.

Concerts oriented toward classical music and those for the general public nonetheless retained some aspects of a common culture. Many of the same publishers put out both popular songs and editions of classics. Concerts oriented toward different tastes might utilize the same halls and offer the same pieces, opera overtures most notably. Some musicians, singers particularly, crossed aesthetic boundaries. Sims Reeves, for example, appeared in opera and ballad concerts, oratorios, and orchestral concerts, and a conservatory would turn out musicians who might either sing *chansonettes* or play quartets. But a nervous, ideologically burdened process of accommodation occurred at the points of contact among the new areas of musical life. The worlds of classics and popular songs spawned publications that treated each other with worried disdain.

The unparalleled upheaval brought by the revolutions of 1848 played a critical role in the formation of a new musical order. As we have seen, idealists propounded an agenda in the 1830s and 1840s to limit opera selections, expel the opera *fantaisie* from programs, and favor classics and well-crafted new works. But *fantaisies* still dominated many virtuoso programs in 1848, and relatively few pianists were offering self-consciously serious programs by that time. The wide-ranging impact of the revolutionary experience affected musical life deeply and forced the musical community to come to grips with its internal crisis. During the 1850s European musical culture entered a new era in the organization of institutions, social values, tastes, and authority.

As a result, musical culture became increasingly politicized, both in musical and ideological terms. Richard Wagner led the way in this regard in his essays of 1848–1851, calling for all authority in the mounting of operas to be vested in the composer-producer. His followers forced a new partisan framework on musical commentary and professional patronage in the ensuing decade. The Wagnerians formed part of the widening of political awareness in the German states, a trend historians take to be forward-looking within Europe as a whole.[5] Adherence to "party" became as fundamental for a musician as for a politician. In 1860 the Viennese composer and journalist Selmar Bagge identified three factions in musical life by using the very terms

[5] Geoff Eley and David Blackbourn, *Peculiarities of German History: Bourgeois Society and Politics in Nineteenth-century Germany* (Oxford: Oxford University Press, 1984); Eley, "How and Where is German History Centered?," in *German History from the Margins*, Neil Gregor, Nils Roemer, and Mark Roseman (eds.) (Bloomington: Indiana University Press, 2006), pp. 268–86.

attached to German and Austrian political factions. He saw "reactionaries" mistrusting all new music, "progressives" dogmatically supporting Wagner's "music of the future," and "liberals" judging new works through classical models.[6] His formulation also applied to most other regions of Europe. A French writer likewise interpreted Jules Pasdeloup's Popular Concerts of Classical Music through his country's revolutionary heritage: "You could say that the nobility and the clergy go only to the Society of Concerts, and that the Third Estate doesn't set foot there." The idea of equality could be applied to concert life: "It is a kind of musical '89 that M. Pasdeloup has just accomplished, proclaiming equality of Frenchmen before the bar of musical justice."[7]

By 1860 commentators in all the major cities were astonished to see how fundamentally musical culture had changed. The new political vocabulary of the time provided the means for making sense of what had happened. Writing in 1852, in the first issue of the Neue Wiener Musik-Zeitung, Eduard Freiherr von Lannoy spoke darkly of the disorder and chaos that had overwhelmed both politics and musical life, arguing that order could only return through adherence to law and musical discipline. "We have come to realize," he declared, "that the constitution of the State is a complicated Artwork that only a few know how to guide, those who possess the knowledge and practical experience to accomplish it." He warned that "those who don't have such wisdom produce conflict and inaction," especially those who "don't recognize how much we benefit from belonging to a large, powerful State."[8]

The most important evidence of a new order, commentators pointed out, was the exclusion of lesser genres from serious concert programs. A pair of tropes became common in the press, either condemning inappropriate genres or announcing that the public had repudiated them. Saying that a musician had offered a "miscellaneous" program functioned as a harsh professional rebuke. The claim that "serious" taste had triumphed over the trivial recalled the process whereby the new order had supplanted the old one. In 1861 L. A. Zellner, editor of the new Blätter für Musik, Theater und Kunst, declared that "[i]n the last ten years Vienna has experienced thorough-going changes in the central aspects of musical life, one of the most extraordinary periods in our music history." He saw opera selections

---

[6] Selmar Bagge, Gedanken und Ansichten über Musik und Musikzustände in einer Reihe gesammelter Aufsätze (Vienna: Wessely, 1860), pp. 133–5.

[7] "Concert populaire de musique classique," RGM, 17 November 1861, p. 361.

[8] Eduard Freiheer von Lannoy, "Was ist die Aufgabe einer musikalsichen Zeitung?" Neue Wiener Musik-Zeitung, 1 January 1852, p. 1.

and opera fantasies disappearing from concerts, concluding that "music that is thoughtless, frivolous, or coquettish is now out of the question [in programs]."⁹ He exulted that the war against virtuosity had been won, now that performers fashionable in the 1840s seemed "silly and hard to believe," like knights in a fairy tale jousting with musical windmills. Even such prominent figures as Servais and Meyer, Zellner claimed, were attracting smaller and less enthusiastic audiences to their concerts.¹⁰ Another commentator was amazed that, as compared to the 1840s, classics had become standard repertory in virtuoso programs, every pianist offering something by Beethoven, and every singer some Schubert.¹¹ In 1857 a correspondent for the *Musical World* said that "things have changed," because "taste for operatic hashes, and airs embedded in arpeggios, is rapidly declining, and a healthier taste is rapidly making a way."¹²

Thus were ideological boundaries established among repertories and types of concerts. The principle of homogeneity arose as a new criterion for designing programs: almost all the pieces on a program were expected to come from related genres and a common level of taste. Whereas classical music concerts excluded lesser genres, music halls and *cafés-concerts* claimed they possessed opera overtures by Mozart and Weber in their own terms. In 1860 a Parisian critic claimed that a process was finally underway for "classifying genres after their intrinsic merit – music of invention and inspiration, music of craft and study, music of the conservatoire, music of the salon, and so on, that would be the start of a new science, and that is the direction in which we need to go."¹³ Still, the tradition of miscellany was adapted to the new situation. Opera selections and virtuoso solos persisted on many orchestral programs, and some musicians continued the old sort of benefit concert.

The acquisition of formal musical learning became the touchstone of idealistic values. Traditionally, listeners were thought to absorb knowledge informally and incrementally in the concert hall. Now, it was said, listeners needed to learn systematically if they were to understand what they heard correctly. This change resulted partly from the extension of concert repertories back into the seventeenth and eighteenth centuries, requiring that musicians help the public learn more about unfamiliar music. But ultimately the new valuation of musical learning sprang from a new

⁹ L. A. Zellner, "1861," *BMTK*, 1 January 1861, p. 1. ¹⁰ *BMTK*, 25 March 1859, pp. 93, 339.
¹¹ "Zehn Jahre aus dem Wiener Musikleben," *Recensionen und Mittheilungen der Monatsschrift für Theater und Musik*, 12 December 1860, pp. 777–80.
¹² "Mazurka de Concert," *MW*, 14 February 1857, p. 99. ¹³ *FM*, 8 April 1860, p. 175.

authority being attributed to such learning. This development sprang from the reform of education on all levels during the second half of the century, as governments tried to deepen trust in state institutions after the upheavals of 1848. "Educating the public" became a key principle in the classical music community such as had not existed in the eighteenth century. Programs began to include notes to help listeners learn more about the pieces to be performed. The musical intelligentsia, from George Grove to correspondents to minor magazines, claimed an intellectual authority the likes of which eighteenth-century authors such as Charles Burney probably did not even imagine. Classical music, now associated with a set of timeless norms, migrated from the scholar's study to public places. By 1870 classical music "no longer appeared as an erudite interest or as a love of the out-of-date," Sophie-Anne Leterrier has written. Quite the contrary, "it defined a canon musicians learned at the Conservatoire; an article of faith in the church; a repertory in the concert hall; and an emblem of nationality on the political front."[14]

Indeed, classical music taste now became a conservative rather than a reforming movement. The idea that "great" music should be the focal point of concert life had begun as a utopian agenda aiming to transform musical culture fundamentally. After 1850 a retrenchment occurred among leading thinkers, who worried that their accomplishments might be washed away by a variety of forces. For one thing, they feared that the classical music repertories, being so new, could not withstand the pressure of tradition to revert back to miscellaneous programs. Second, they saw a new specter, a growing public for popular songs and arias that could overshadow classical music concerts. Their third, most immediate, fear was that followers of Wagner and Liszt (often called the New German School from 1859) would overwhelm classical music by forcing avant-garde pieces onto concert programs. Quite a few commentators had doubts about the progressive styles of Wagner and Liszt or were offended by the faction's tough political posture.

The New German School, which extended its influence well beyond central Germany, arose for practical as well as musical or aesthetic reasons. By 1865 all the major orchestras were performing works by dead composers about three-quarters of the time (Charts 6.1 and 6.2). These numbers indicate the situation that contemporary composers faced – a serious decline in opportunities to have their works performed or recognized professionally. The high canonic status of the great symphonies led to a crisis in the life of

---

[14] Leterrier, *Mélomane et l'historien*, p. 184.

the symphony, Walter Frisch has argued. Although some new works in that genre were performed, the concerts that determined fame and arbitrated canons were all but closed to new compositions.[15]

Ironically, the New German School grew out of the idealism of the 1830s but ended up opposing bitterly the main thinkers who carried it on.[16] If Hanslick or Fétis defined the music of Beethoven as a heritage to be preserved, the followers of Liszt saw radical implications in it that justified their vision of a musical avant-garde.[17] In the process, the notion of New Music arose as a cause, helping composers assert themselves as a professional interest group. The critics Bagge termed progressives made an intense critique of established concerts and opera institutions for failing to perform works by living composers, particularly those following new styles.[18] As one commentator put it in 1852, "given all these complaints that we can't bring back the great classical period, we need to create our own."[19] The progressives even appealed to the traditional value of mixed programming to advance their cause. In 1861 a writer in the Leipzig-based *Signale für die musikalische Welt* declared that "If anybody is going to fill a program just with pieces by Beethoven, Mozart, Schubert, or the like, others will reply, 'that may be very appealing, but it's more than a bit all of one kind of music, and some adjustments have to be made.'"[20] The rallying of listeners to the cause of new music seems to have had some effect, for we shall see that in the 1860s the proportion of pieces by living composers increased by a modest amount after declining precipitously for over a half century. Moreover, by the 1860s many composers secured a solid institutional base as professors in the conservatories that were being established all over Europe. For example, Woldemar Bargiel, whose piano music is admired today, studied at the Leipzig Conservatorium and then taught at the equivalent institution in Cologne.

Composers came to grips with their situation by presenting an increasing number of New Music concerts, a trend we have seen beginning in previous decades. An example of this genre of concert was given in Hannover in 1877 by the Allgemeine Deutsche Musikverein (Ill. 15). Founded by Liszt's followers in 1861, the organization gave an annual "Composer's Meeting"

---

[15] Walter Frisch, *Brahms: The Four Symphonies* (New York: Schirmer, 1996), pp. 18–20; Grotjahn, *Die Sinfonie, passim.*

[16] Weber, "Wagner, Wagnerism and Musical Idealism," *Wagnerism in European Culture and Politics,* pp. 28–71.

[17] Samson, "The Great Composer," p. 271.

[18] Schumann, *Gesammelte Schriften über Musik und Musiker,* 4 vols. (Leipzig: G. Wigand, 1854), vol. 3, pp. 276, 290.

[19] *NZFM,* 1 January 1852, p. 3.   [20] Quoted in Grotjahn, *Die Sinfonie,* p. 148.

(Tonkünstler-Versammlung) that offered several concerts devoted entirely to recent works, often in forward-looking styles. Pieces by five young men and Liszt himself were performed at this concert.[21] Deference to the mainstream of German music is nonetheless evident in the inclusion of Robert Franz (1815–1892), the highly respected lieder composer who did not identify himself with their faction and was not cited as a member of the organization.

Although ideological wars were waged with particular heat in German musical life, similar divisions also appeared in the Paris press in the 1850s. François Fétis and his allies "tried to stem the tides of Romanticism and Wagnerian influence," wrote Katharine Ellis, "to promote instead a *juste milieu* which would take the form of a reinterpretation, through autonomous music, of Beethoven."[22] What was *juste* to one listener, of course, was reactionary to another. What is more, in Paris the performance of piano pieces written in the late eighteenth century stimulated resistance to classical music generally. In 1864 a reviewer complained about "useless exhumations" of pieces from that time. "In the last three months we have been condemned to hear nothing but mouldy music written for the clavecin, because the favored repertory of classical masters for the piano is demanded everywhere." He objected to hearing too many "infantile pianisms of Mozart, trifles by him, Dussek or Steibelt," evoking the authority of cultural tradition by adapting Fontenelle's famous challenge to the sonata as "What's your problem, pianist?" (Pianiste classique, que me veux-tu?)[23] The influence of the Paris Opéra, music publishing, and the persistence of traditional benefit concerts kept this old attitude alive.

Although Britain experienced no revolutionary upheaval in 1848, labor unrest and the Chartist movement had unsteadied the political order, and musical life underwent a set of changes similar to those in Paris or Vienna. In the 1850s the New Philharmonic Society and concerts at the Crystal Palace tried to challenge the hegemony of the Philharmonic Society over orchestral concerts.[24] The aging concert society survived intact but ended up significantly less powerful than its counterparts in the other three cities we are studying. Though classical music programs tended to be more mixed in genre in London than in Vienna or Paris, classical music was viewed in

---

[21] For a list of the programs, see James Deaville, "*Allgemeiner Deutsche Musikverein*," http://www.humanities.mcmaster.ca/~admv/admv.htm; and "The New-German School and the Euterpe Concerts, 1860–1862: A Trojan Horse in Leipzig," *Festschrift Christoph-Hellmut Mahling zum 65. Geburtstag* (Tutzing: Schneider, 1997), pp. 253–70.

[22] Ellis, *Music Criticism*, p. 160. See also Samson, "The Great Composer," pp. 264–5.

[23] Gustave Chouquet, "Clavecinistes et pianistes," *L'Art musical*, 3 March 1864, p. 108.

[24] McVeigh, "Society for British Musicians," *Music and British Culture, 1785–1914*, p. 167.

just as strict terms ideologically. In 1861 William Pole initiated a column on music in *Macmillan's Magazine*, saying that he would limit his attention to "high-class instrumental concerts, i.e., concerts at which music of the first rank and chiefly instrumental, is given," differentiating them from opera, oratorios, or benefit concerts.[25] Pole defined "high-class" concerts as those retaining the best works in repertory, so that they "consist entirely of well-known standard works of the classical composers, such as the symphonies and overtures of Haydn, Mozart, Beethoven, and Spohr, the overtures of Cherubini and Weber, etc."[26] His exclusion of oratorio concerts from his purview indicates that critics such as he regarded them as "middle-brow."

A classical music concert possessed a clearer and more authoritative identity in 1870, as compared with 1840. Two generations had now passed since Beethoven composed his best known orchestral works, twice as long as an old piece had normally survived in the eighteenth century. A wide range of works was now institutionalized, even though a process of recycling still occurred to some extent. Neither "ancient music" in England nor *la musique ancienne* in France had previously achieved such authority.

Around 1850 a new kind of listener emerged in concert life, a listener whose interests lay primarily in musical classics. The poet John Addington Symonds (1840–1893) left a detailed picture of such a person's tastes in letters he wrote from Oxford in the 1860s to his sister, who taught piano in Bristol. Symonds wrote little about contemporary composers or new pieces. When he mentioned opera, he talked about singers rather than works, and he turned to Wagner for theoretical rather than musical matters. He was impressed by Verdi's *Requiem* but thought it relied on "audacious picturesque effects... got cheaply by the composer." He privileged instrumental music of the early nineteenth century: "I think for all instrumental music of the higher kind much longer time than one hearing is required in order to understand it," by which "I make Beethoven triumph in transcendental faith." To him, Beethoven's music seemed a timeless phenomenon. The Fifth Symphony, he wrote, "belongs to the modern world, to the Teutonic mind which made the last cathedrals and to the sense of infinite unfettered Freedom which intoxicates us in this adolescence of the age."[27] A similar devotion to the classics appears to have arisen among German amateurs of Symonds's generation. Authors of

[25] *Macmillan's Magazine* 4 (1861), 449.   [26] Ibid., p. 452.

[27] J. A. Symonds to Henry Dakyns, 29 October 1876, vol 2, p. 437 –8; J. A. to Charlotte Symonds, 12 September 1863, vol. 1, p. 421; J. A. Symonds to Henry Sidgwick, 20 September 1867, vol 1, p. 759 and 7 May 1864, vol.1, p. 470, *Letters of John Addington Symonds*, 3 vols., Herbert M. Schueller and Robert L. Peters (eds.) (Detroit: Wayne State University Press, 1967).

autobiographies born from about 1815 began citing classical music as part of their youth, as their predecessors had rarely done.[28]

For all his devotion to Beethoven, Symonds nonetheless admitted to a "catholicity" of taste, a liking for quite different kinds of music that resisted the new hierarchical assumptions of the time. He outlined the perimeters of his taste when reporting on three sacred works he heard at the 1859 Gloucester Festival: Beethoven's *Christ on the Mount of Olives* (1803/1811), Spohr's *Last Judgment* (*Die letzte Dinge*, 1826), and Rossini's *Stabat Mater* (1832/1841). "The most striking thing in the performance was the difference of style in the three works." He thought that "Beethoven was (comparatively) characterized by *breadth*, Rossini by *pathos*, Spohr by *grace & feeling*."[29] Thus Spohr and Rossini had each earned a distinctive canonic reputation in the mind of a serious listener. That Symonds welcomed their two works to the repertory of good music was ultimately more important than his recognition that they stood on a lesser plane aesthetically than Beethoven and his works. By the same token, Symonds reserved a separate place in his listening for lesser genres, especially overtures and songs he heard at promenade concerts. He stated that "common dance or overture music, if well played, will often rouse in my mind the profoundest yearning," though it be "a few waifs of Meyerbeer and Strauss, with a few brief snatches of Bach and Beethoven."[30] Having referred to a miscellaneous program as having "quantities of the stupidest music I ever heard," he added that "this was relieved by the greatness of the performers and the excellence of some of the pieces," especially an "affected ballad" sung by Sims Reeves.[31]

Significantly, even though Symonds preferred classics to recent works, he remained open to new pieces as a general rule. His taste remained traditional in that he felt obliged to listen to a new piece on its own merits. Although he evaluated it against classical models, he did not distrust new music as such. Indeed, concert repertory was not completely frozen at midcentury, for the music of a few composers – Gounod, Saint-Saëns, Wagner, and Peter Ilych Tchaikovsky – became standard repertory. A much deeper resistance

---

[28] Gramit, "Unremarkable Musical Lives," pp. 159–78.

[29] J. A. to Charlotte Symonds, 16 May 1863, vol. 1, p. 395 and 15 September 1859, vol. 1, p. 203 (emphasis original), *Letters of John Addington Symonds*.

[30] J. A. to Charlotte Symonds, 12 September 1863, vol. 1, p. 421; to Henry Sidgwick, 30 March 1868, vol. 1, p. 799, *Letters of John Addington Symonds*.

[31] Ibid., J. A. to Charlotte Symonds, 12 September 1863, vol. 1, p. 421 and 8 June 1863, vol 1, p. 398–9, *Letters of John Addington Symonds*.

toward contemporary music was to arise at the start of the twentieth century against any new work, whether conservative or avant-garde in style.

By looking in detail at concerts during the 1850s and 1860s, we can see how new program formats emerged from the experimentation done in the previous two decades. The traditional benefit concert broke up into several different formats located in separate musical worlds. First, pianists defined a strict repertory of classics and suitable recent works, borrowing more from programs of Moscheles and Saint-Saëns than from those of Liszt or Marie Pleyel. Concerts by classically focused pianists bound interpretation together with virtuosity as a major new component of music's high culture. Second, concerts made up almost entirely of opera selections and songs – the precedent for the opera "gala" – afforded singers and songwriters a powerful new commercial vehicle. Third, a particular kind of vocal concert emerged in the British ballad concert, whose elegant theatricality captured the mass public for the rest of century. Finally, miscellaneous programs continued to flourish in local events, offering the same genres as before, along with comic acts influenced by the music halls or *cafés-concerts*.[32] We will discuss the last three items in the next chapter. Certain genres nonetheless cut across the barriers between the different worlds emerging in concert life. The opera overture was performed at almost every type of concert that included an orchestra. Moreover, the Viennese Friends of Music offered some popular songs, the Crystal Palace concerts included ballads, and the Gewandhaus presented instrumental solos. A Beethoven piano trio might open a program focused on British songs and glees (Ex. 9.2). Thus a piece from a different realm of taste provided the contrast needed within an otherwise homogeneous program. But in the process that piece was adapted to a different social context.

THE RECITAL, SOLO OR OTHERWISE

Midcentury proved a major turning point for virtuoso concerts. Although a few solo recitals were performed in the 1840s, they were outnumbered by evolving forms of the traditional "miscellaneous" program. During the 1850s virtuosity became linked to interpretation of classics within programs strictly defined in taste, as canonic works replaced *fantaisies* and

[32] Simon McVeigh, "The Benefit Concert in Nineteenth-Century London: From 'Tax on the Nobility' to 'Monstrous Nuisance,'" in *Nineteenth-Century British Music Studies*, Bennett Zon (ed.) (Aldershot, UK: Ashgate, 1999), vol. 1, pp. 242–66.

serious songs pushed out excerpts from recent operas. The solo recital emerged as a major new performing strategy, chiefly in Britain, initially done almost entirely by pianists. Throughout Europe, many concerts involved several musicians, or perhaps even a chamber ensemble with whom the organizer would perform.[33]

The triumph of new musical practice over the old was proclaimed loudly. In London in 1860 Davison observed that Meyer was "doubtless aware that the way of the *virtuose*-proper, and the way of the 'classic' performer (so termed), who gives undivided attention to the old masters, differ entirely."[34] In Vienna in 1862 a critic spoke of the "revolution in musical taste" that had replaced "materialism" with serious artistry while discussing a concert presented by the young pianist Julius Epstein.[35] A traditionally minded listener would not have been impressed, however, to read that, in performing Mozart's little-known Concerto for Two Pianos in E-flat (K. 365), Epstein served as "a teaching musician who reproduced a piece of music rather than a virtuoso, giving a program focused on older classical works."[36] Performers looked to the chamber music concert as a model in designing their programs. Delimitating repertory and focusing on classics posed an idealistic reference point for pianists. As discussed in Chapter 5, there were many options for staging a collaborative concert; it might be led by a pianist and a singer but open with a piano quintet. The sonatas for violin and piano that were unusual at quartet concerts appeared regularly at this kind of concert. In Britain "recital" was often in the title of a program, indicating a seriousness of purpose; the term was still used for instrumentally mixed concerts in London and Paris in 1910.[37]

Arguably, Clara Schumann set the standard of repertory more influentially than any other pianist. Her programs of the 1840s and 1850s defined the range of classical composers thought appropriate to the recital and the formats for the succession of genres. As her husband's health declined in the early 1850s, she turned to other musicians for joint concerts. In 1853, for example, she offered a *soirée* in Leipzig with violinist Joseph Joachim, and they played Beethoven's "Kreutzer" Sonata. She performed pieces by Chopin and by her relative Bargiel, and Joachim played Beethoven's Romance in G and a prelude by Bach, and they offered a piece by her

[33] See also Weber and Ritterman, "Origins of the Piano Recital"; program collections, Salle Pleyel, BOP; and Archive, Wigmore Hall, London.
[34] "Virtuosity of Theodore de Meyer," *MW*, 16 June 1860, p. 382.
[35] "1862," *BTMK*, 1 January 1862, p. 1.
[36] "Concert Julius Epstein," *BTMK*, 16 April 1861, p. 122.   [37] Archive, Wigmore Hall.

husband.[38] The concerts Schumann gave in Paris in 1862 were even more rigorous in their exclusion of recent works and focus on classics, usually opening with a classical piano quintet. In one case violinist Jules Armingaud joined her in Robert's Sonata in A Minor, and a female singer did pieces by Handel, Schubert, and Beethoven (Ill. 7). Yet some critics were skeptical of Clara's subordinating virtuosity to interpretation, implying that she did so because her technique was in decline. A critic declared that she "disdained vulgar success" by performing "in the manner of a professor emeritus who respects the text rather than probing the inner thoughts of the great masters."[39] Some critics did not recognize the interpretive virtuosity inherent in the playing of a new recitalist.

A diverse group of pianists from Germany, Britain, and Russia made London the premier site of the early solo recital in the mid-1850s. They all favored classics to the virtual exclusion of their own music, concentrating on building a repertory appropriate to the revolutionary new concert format. In 1852 the Russian Alexandre Billet presented Concerts of Classical Pianoforte Music, performing alone consistently; in March–April 1856 Clara Schumann, Charles Hallé, and Arabella Goddard all offered similar concerts, using the term *recital* in most cases. The practice spread to Dublin, where Fanny Arthur Robinson, a pupil of Bennett and Thalberg, played alone in the Ancient Concert Rooms.[40] By the late 1860s recitals had become the principal vehicle for pianists favoring classical repertory. One of Schumann's programs illustrates the homogeneity of the new format, seen especially in her performing her husband's pieces in related genres as a group (Ex. 8.1). Opening each half with pieces by Beethoven and Bach nonetheless grew from the traditional practice of beginning with a piece in an old style. Closing the program briskly with a *capriccio scherzando* and a *polonaise* suggests her effort to introduce less severe music at the end. Clara Schumann became a key arbitrator of the canonic standing of composers represented in repertory. In the 1856 concert she juxtaposed pieces by Beethoven and Bach with those by Chopin and Mendelssohn, whose reputations were not yet fully established. She also had an impact on the development of the canon in song literature, because songs by Schubert and her husband remained essential to her repertory.

[38] Dörffel, *Geschichte der Gewandhausconcerte*, vol. 2, pp. 219.
[39] "Concerts: Mme Schumann," *FM*, 30 March 1862, p. 100.
[40] I am indebted to Jennifer O'Connor for this information; see Richard Pine Friam and Charles Acton Friam (eds.), *To Talent Alone: The Royal Irish Academy of Music, 1848–1998* (Dublin: Gill & Macmillan, 1998), p. 500.

8.1 *"Clara Schumann's Pianoforte Recital," Queen's Concert Rooms, Hanover Square, 27 May 1856*[41]

Sonata in C, op. 53	†Beethoven
a) *Schlummerlied*, op. 121	Robert Schumann
b) *Jagdlied*, op. 82	Robert Schumann
c) "Traumeswirren," *Fantasiestücke*, op. 12	Robert Schumann
Prelude and Fugue in A Minor, arranged for piano	†J. S. Bach
Capriccio scherzando in F-sharp Minor	†Mendelssohn
Nocturne in C Minor; Polonaise in A-flat Major	†Chopin

Charles Hallé performed more solo recitals than anyone else between 1855 and 1870. Born in Germany but first established in Paris, he moved to London during the confusion of 1848. Hallé recalled that when he arrived there the Beethoven solo pianoforte sonatas were still regarded as so "abstruse" that John Ella discouraged him from performing any at the Musical Union.[42] He gave solo programs at his rooms on Bryanston Square beginning in 1855 and after 1859 at Willis's Rooms and St. James's Hall. In 1861 Hallé began performing a complete cycle of the Beethoven sonatas at his rooms – seemingly the first pianist to do so – with Schubert songs inserted between individual works.[43] He offered a less specialized program at St. James's: two of Beethoven's best known sonatas, Weber's salon-friendly *Rondo Brilliant*, and elegant pieces by Stephen Heller that Clara Schumann also performed regularly (Ex. 8.2). It was already conventional to offer one or two recent pieces at the end of a program.

8.2 *Charles Hallé, St James's Hall, 5 May 1865*[44]

Sonata in C, op. 2, no. 3	†Beethoven
Partita in B-flat	†J. S. Bach
Rondo Brilliant in E flat, op. 62	†Weber
—	
Sonata in F Minor, op. 57, "Appassionata"	†Beethoven
Impromptu in C Minor, op. 90, no. 1	†Schubert
Prelude in G, op. 81, no. 3	Stephen Heller

[41] Program collection of Janet Ritterman; see her "'Gegensätze, Ecken und scharfe Kanten': Clara Schumanns Besuche in England, 1856–1888," in *Clara Schumann, 1819–1896: Katalog zur Ausstellung*, Ingrid Bodsch and Gerd Nauhaus (eds.) (Bonn, 1996), pp. 235–61.
[42] *Autobiography of Charles Hallé, with Correspondence and Diaries*, Michael Kennedy (ed.) (London: Elek, 1972), p. 116.
[43] *MW*, 17 May 1861, p. 308.
[44] *MW*, 29 April 1865, p. 258; the advertisement discusses his goals in revealing ways.

Nuits Blanches in E, op. 82, no. 9	Stephen Heller
Ballade in A-flat, op. 47	†Chopin

Hans von Bülow was the principal German pianist to perform solo recitals at an early date. Variously a conductor, composer, writer, and pianist, and much favored by Liszt, Bülow put on a series of six *soirées* while teaching in Berlin in the early 1860s. One program illustrates the balance he struck between classical and contemporary music: four pieces each by dead and living composers, including only one of his own (Ex. 8.3). A reviewer was amazed at the novelty of the concert, declaring that Bülow was "determined to captivate his audience without any other person's assistance" and put his own music on a program "so filled with different periods in piano performance."[45] Bülow seems to have given solo recitals more widely than Clara Schumann. He gave a series of six such programs in the Gewandhaus in 1862–1864, each called "An Evening of Old and New Piano Music," and in 1870 he devoted a program strictly to Mendelssohn and Schumann.[46] He eventually made the Beethoven cycle central to his performing career.

8.3 *Hans von Bülow, 3rd Soirée, Saal der Singacademie, Berlin, 3 January 1862*[47]

Sonata in A, op. 101	†Beethoven
Fantasia, op. 17	†Robert Schumann
a) Ballade in C Minor, op. 11	von Bülow
b) Prelude and Fugue, op. 53, no. 1	Anton Rubinstein
c) Chaconne in F	†Handel
Sarabande and Passepied in E Minor	†J. S. Bach
Concert Etudes: *Feux follets*; *Eroica*	Liszt
Bravura Waltz on motives from Gounod's *Faust*	Liszt

Most violinists took a more traditional path than pianists. Though Henry Vieuxtemps led quartets in private gatherings, he clung to miscellaneous programs featuring the opera *fantaisie* throughout his career, often collaborating with cellist Adrien Servais. Camille Sivori, the Genoese student of Paganini, took a more active role in public chamber music. In Vienna in 1867 he led a Haydn quartet and the "Kreutzer" Sonata but also performed pieces by his teacher alongside vocal numbers by Bellini, Berlioz, and the

[45] *NZFM*, 8 January 1862, p. 11.
[46] Vienna, CPH/RCM; Dörffel, *Geschichte der Gewandhausconcerte*, vol. 2, p. 222.
[47] Advertisement, *Neue Berliner Musikzeitung*, 1 January 1862, p. 8. Rudolph Hasert also gave a series of recitals there in 1863; see ibid., 2 December 1863, p. 396.

Canadian François Prume, whose music was becoming fairly well known.[48] Joseph Joachim went the farthest from traditional practice by mapping out a canon for the violin in his concerts, often in conjunction with Johannes Brahms. A concert they performed together in Vienna in 1867 followed a carefully defined repertory of pieces by Bach, Beethoven, Paganini, Spohr, Schubert, and Schumann.[49]

Brahms's collaboration with Joachim suggests a strategy he followed for spreading his name through concerts dominated by classics. Just as Wagner became famous for conducting the Beethoven symphonies, so Brahms established himself as a foremost interpreter of the classical piano repertory. At a concert he gave in 1869 with the singer Julius Stockhausen and a female singer, he performed two pieces by Rameau, music that he and Clara Schumann initiated in the concert hall (Ill. 8). Beethoven's Sonata op. 111 was familiar to the Viennese public by that time, serving to open the program as Beethoven's overture to *Fidelio* had formerly done in benefit concerts. For that matter, Brahms can be credited with helping to establish canons for other instruments thanks to his frequent concerts with Joachim, Stockhausen, and Clara Schumann. Yet he normally limited the amount of his own music on collaborative programs. At the concert with Stockhausen, for example, he played a few of his *Ungarische Tänze* and the Variations, op. 21, no. 2. A Viennese critic remarked about the next concert they did together that a piece by Brahms received well-deserved applause even though listeners did not particularly like his style.[50] Anton Rubinstein tended to offer more of his own music. In an *Abendunterhaltung* he gave at the Gewandhaus in 1867, a program of ten pieces including Beethoven's op. 111, he opened with his Piano Quartet in C and one of his own songs and at the end played several of his pieces for piano.[51]

For his part, Stockhausen was arguably the central figure in the rise of the song recital. His career was quite cosmopolitan, for he was born in Paris to harpist Franz Stockhausen and singer Margarethe Schmuck, major figures at fashionable benefit concerts in London as well as Paris.[52] Some singers had gradually been shifting their careers from opera to concerts, but only after 1850 was it possible to gain international fame singing primarily in the concert hall. Stockhausen gave the first public performance of *Die schöne Müllerin* in Vienna in 1856, joined by the distinguished actor Eduard

[48] 2 March 1867, PA/GMF; see also 1 May 1866, with Alfred Jaell, "Salons Érard," BOP.
[49] 23 November 1867, PA/GMF.   [50] "Berichte: Wien," *AMZ*, 10 March 1869, p. 77.
[51] 21 October 1867, PA/GMFV.
[52] Renate Hofmann (ed.), *Johannes Brahms im Briefwechsel mit Julius Stockhausen* (Tutzing: Schneider, 1993), pp. 9–26.

Devrient to recite the text, and at the Gewandhaus in 1862.[53] Stockhausen was equally interested in folk songs and French music; having sung under contract at the Opéra Comique in the late 1850s, he included an *air* from Boieldieu's *Le Petit Chaperon Rouge* (1818) on this program. Idealistic vocabulary recurs in his letters to Brahms. In 1862, for example, he fumed at the "mode-mad composers" who were selling easy-to-play editions of classics – Saint-Saëns, the latter's teacher Stamaty, violinist Jean-Delphin Alard, and cellist Auguste Franchomme.[54]

Even Sigismond Thalberg, dean of piano virtuosos, gave solo recitals, most prominently in Paris and London in 1862. One program was full of ironies about the new taste for classical music (Ex. 8.4). It included *Spécimen de l'ancien régime*, a witty piece Rossini composed in a series called *Sins of Old Age (Péchés de vieillesse,* 1857–1868).[55] Thalberg bowed to the new canonic ideas when he credited Mozart and Auber on the program for the *fantaisies* on their music which he had composed. Two pieces came from his recent edition of piano pieces, *L'Art du chant appliqué au piano,* op. 70 (1853). By then a major publisher, Léon Escudier praised Thalberg for resisting the "invasion of classical music in piano playing."[56]

8.4 *3rd Concert, Sigismond Thalberg, Salons Érard, 3 May 1862*[57]

"Fenesta vascia" (*L'Art du chant*)	*Thalberg*
Duo, *La Flûte Enchantée* (*L'Art du chant*)	†Mozart [*Thalberg*]
Fantaisie on *Sérénade* and *Menuet, Don Juan*	†Mozart [*Thalberg*]
Deux romances sans paroles	†Mendelssohn
Prelude, *Spécimen de l'ancien régime*	Rossini
Soirées de Pausilippe: hommage à Rossini, op. 75	*Thalberg*
Ballade in G Minor, op. 76	*Thalberg*
Fantaisie on *La Muette de Portici* (1828)	Auber [*Thalberg*]

ORCHESTRAL CONCERTS

Orchestral concert series were more widely known after midcentury and became the central institution of classical music. The revolutionary upheaval motivated orchestras to perform the best known choral-orchestral

[53] Dörffel, *Geschichte der Gewandhausconcerte,* p. 221.
[54] Stockhausen to Brahms, 4 May 1862, *Johannes Brahms im Briefwechsel,* p. 29.
[55] "Rossini," *NGD,* vol. 21, pp. 753–55.
[56] "Seconde séance de S. Thalberg," *FM,* 4 May 1862, p. 138; "The Influence of Thalberg on the Present Generation of Pianists," *Monthly Musical Record,* 1 June 1871, p. 69.
[57] Salle Érard, BOP.

classics to help solidify an unstable social order. Such concerts benefited from the reconstruction of the central city in Vienna, Paris, and Leipzig and were seen as key institutions within a larger national society. New lower-priced concerts built a broad middle-class public that helped legitimate the authority of classical music and indeed that of the elite institutions themselves. Vienna excepted, leaders of elite concerts ended up accepting the new public for the most part. People who had never heard a Beethoven symphony came to know about concerts at the new Musikverein on Vienna's Ring, the Crystal Palace in Sydenham, or the Popular Concerts of Jules Pasdeloup. Similar developments occurred far from the capitals, as concerts proliferated in provincial cities. There they "fed specific local identities, providing a fertile source of civic pride and of empowering myths which allowed a community to view itself against rival towns or regions."[58] Still, music halls and *cafés-concerts* reached far more people than any of these orchestral series.

The dominance of works by dead composers in orchestral programs reached its peak in the early 1860s. Charts 6.1 and 6.2 indicate that the percentage of pieces by dead composers dropped from between seventy-seven and ninety-four percent at the four major series to between seventy-four and eighty-five percent in 1870, the London series now moderately higher than the others. One senses that a tough set of discussions went on between composers and the directing boards of concerts, from which emerged the practice of keeping a slot open for a work by a living composer at some concerts in a series. Composers thus maintained a foothold within classical music concerts, functioning as an interest group in the ongoing renegotiation of the terms of cultural hegemony. Nevertheless, for the rest of the nineteenth century it was unusual for fewer than two-thirds of all pieces performed at an orchestral series to be by dead composers.

All of the major orchestral series came under criticism for neglecting contemporary music. The novelty of performing so much music by deceased composers stimulated a backlash against classical repertory. A French journalist reflected that tendency by remarking that "a certain portion of the public has taken up a taste for 'good' music and made a habit out of it," then asking, "does that not also now raise a question about the fate of living composers?"[59] The issue was sometimes couched as a critique of the upper classes. In 1862 a French writer deplored how "the Conservatoire, in its *petite bonbonnérie*, has for twenty-five years remained closed like a

58 Cyril Ehrlich and Dave Russell, "Victorian Music: A Perspective," *Journal of Victorian Culture* 2 (1998), 117–18.
59 *FM*, 21 January 1855, p. 19.

casserole for a small group of the elect, who have enjoyed the perfumes of beautiful classical pieces."[60] Likewise in Vienna a critic declared in 1860 that "[t]he independent man of taste and musical *propriétaire* will always prefer the ninetieth repetition of a classic that his been on everybody's preferred list for ages, to opening his ears to something that a struggling local composer can offer."[61] The policy of playing one work by a living composer on a program by no means settled this issue.

As the population of the capital cities grew, entrepreneurial conductors set up new orchestral concerts that expanded the size of the classical music public beyond social and intellectual elites. These endeavors challenged the monopoly that the major orchestras in effect held over professional ensembles, attracting listeners who knew the music chiefly from piano transcriptions. The availability of classical programs to a larger public thus paralleled the extension of political rights to the middle classes. The new concert series tended to have larger venues than the elite ones – the Crystal Palace in Sydenham, the Cirque Olympique in Paris, and the Centralhalle in Leipzig. Vienna, the supposed cradle of the classics, did not acquire such a series until 1900, however.

Aesthetic tensions persisted between more or less "pure" formats at orchestral concerts, though the distinction now hinged on the frequency of songs and virtuoso pieces at a concert series. On the one hand, programs offering few songs of virtuoso pieces, suggesting a "higher" aesthetic, were heard the most frequently at the Vienna Philharmonic and the Berlin Court Orchestra. The Society of Concerts in Paris offered a different kind of musical purity because it performed more sacred pieces than anywhere else, usually at two out of three concerts, a practice it maintained until after World War I. On the other hand, the tradition of mixing vocal and instrumental music persisted, though in new formats, at many institutions – at the Leipzig Gewandhaus and Centralhalle and in London at the Philharmonic and the Crystal Palace. Solo pieces were now grouped together at such concerts, most often in the second half of a program. This music was usually more recent than orchestral pieces and thereby lent the programs popular appeal. Equally widespread was the practice of performing opera selections by classical composers with accompaniment by piano rather orchestra, as was done at the Gewandhaus as late as 1910.[62]

The borderline between the programs given at promenade concerts and formal orchestral series remained vague. Concert managers in provincial cities often put on programs focused on a cosmopolitan agenda of opera

---

[60] *Univers musical*, 17 April 1862, p. 173.   [61] *BMTK*, 4 November 1860, p. 114.
[62] Abonnenten-Concerte, SGML.

selections and virtuoso pieces along with classical orchestral pieces, generally without the dance pieces distinctive of the "dance kings." This pattern was particularly common in German spa towns where elite families went regularly to take the waters. In Bad Homburg near Frankfurt, for example, the orchestra in the Kurhaus offered a program in 1856 that included opera selections by Mozart and Verdi and variations on opera tunes by Hummel, Herz, and Paganini.[63] But similar programs were also performed in major cities, for example, in the northwestern port of Bremen, whose Society of Private Concerts (Gesellschaft für Privatkonzerte, founded in 1825) offered symphonic and virtuoso genres with only a few vocal pieces on some occasions, seemingly because the society grew out of the city's official musicians (*Ratmusik*) and the Music-Corps of the Hanseatic Legion.[64] A program in 1851 included the Munich-based pianist Sophie Dulcken and her niece, Isabella, daughter of Louise Dulcken, whose London concerts we have encountered (Ex. 8.5). The latter played two pieces on the concertina, a relative of the accordion – a *fantaisie* by Richard, brother of Henry Blagrove, and a set of variations by her teacher, London guitarist Luigi Regondi. Such was the social fabric among touring musicians in that time. Similar programs were performed at the German Concert Society (Deutsch'sche Konzert-Gesellschaft) in Breslau during the early 1880s.[65]

8.5 *1st Concert, Gesellschaft für Privatconcerte, Bremen, 11 April 1851*[66]

Symphony no. 1 in C	†Beethoven
Arias	†Mozart and †Bellini
Konzert-Stück for piano (Sophie Dulcken)	†Weber
Introduction and Variations on Austrian Lied for Concertina (Isabella Dulcken)	Luigi Regondi
Overture, *Les Abencérages, ou l'étendard de Grenade* (1813)	†Cherubini
Fantaisie on *Cracovienne* (Sophie Dulcken)	Wallace
Fantaisie on motives from Donizetti's *Linda di Chamounix* for concertina (Isabella Dulcken)	Richard Blagrove

[63] Bad Homburg, PC/FUSB
[64] Klaus Blum, *Musikfreunde und Musici: Musikleben in Bremen seit der Aufklärung* (Tutzing: Schneider, 1975), pp. 109–22.
[65] Breslau, PC/FUSB.
[66] Bremen, ibid. The "Cracovienne" refers to Fanny Elssler's Polish dance in the ballet *La Gypsy* (Paris, 1839).

Vienna

The Society of the Friends of Music and the Philharmonic Concerts worked together in 1850s to establish a framework of concerts that would control classical music life in Vienna for the rest of the century. The Society now enlisted professional players, joining forces with the Philharmonic much of the time. In 1860 the Philharmonic went its own way in beginning a series of eight concerts a year, although it designed them in close relationship with the Society. Civic pride now tended to overshadow factional rhetoric when the greatness of classical music life was under discussion. Frances Trollope would have been pleased to see the Viennese upper classes embrace Mozart and Beethoven in the 1850s; classical music was no longer on the cultural periphery. When in 1854 officers of the Philharmonic requested use of the Grosser Redoutensaal from the court, their letter declared that the concerts would be "performances of the world-renowned classical masterpieces of Haydn, Mozart, and Beethoven, for whom Vienna was home, which will help bring the Imperial Opera Orchestra to a new high level of achievement."[67] The Friends of Music became even more central to Viennese life with the building of the Musikverein on the Ring in 1870, a structure housing two concert halls, an archive, and a music store. The reconstitution of the two institutions was related to the productive roles that Austrian liberals played in politics during this period, as historians have recently emphasized. Pieter Judson argued: "Liberals of all varieties, from conservative to radical, may have suffered political defeat in 1848, but their particular notions of public virtue, their myths of community, their visions of economic development gradually came to dominate Austrian public life."[68]

Leaders of the Philharmonic carefully fashioned their programs to be pure but not esoteric. Familiar orchestral pieces dominated at its programs. Sacred music disappeared save for occasional oratorio selections, and opera excerpts became less frequent; vocal music occurred at only one out of three concerts, usually in well-known pieces by Handel, Mozart, or Mendelssohn. A program typically included four works, with one by a living composer, and ended with a symphony, as the Gewandhaus had first done. A program in 1863 illustrates the widening of historical range in the

[67] Hellsberg, *Demokratie der Könige*, p. 107. In 1853 Joseph Hellmesberger directed a series called the Concert Spirituel in the Saal der Musikfreunde, PA/GMF.
[68] Pieter M. Judson, *Exclusive Revolutionaries: Liberal Politics, Social Experience, and National Identity in the Austrian Empire, 1848–1914* (Ann Arbor: University of Michigan Press, 1996), p. 9.

repertory; it offered a piece from four different style periods but did not identify them in pedagogical language (Ex. 8.6). Occasionally a program had only two pieces: Mendelssohn's music to *Midsummer Night's Dream*, for example, combined with a late symphony by Haydn, or Beethoven's music for *Egmont* combined with Robert Schumann's Symphony no. 3, the "Rhenish." But because the directing board offered so few opera selections and included many long works, it made sure most of the pieces were well known to the public, as the pieces cited above indicate.

8.6 *Philharmonische Concerte, Kärtnertor-Theater, Vienna, 22 November 1863* [69]

Overture to *Anacréon*	†Cherubini
Suite for flute and strings [? BWV 1067]	†J. S. Bach
Concert Overture, *Medée*	Woldemar Bargiel
Symphony no. 4 in A, "Italian"	†Mendelssohn

The Viennese orchestra's directing board began holding "trials" of new pieces several times a year, as the Philharmonic Society of London had first done. The practice lasted through at least the 1880s, considerably longer than in London or Paris. The organization's records chronicle meetings where careful choices were made to pieces thought approachable for the subscribers: *Novitäten* by such well-known composers as Franz Lachner, Anton Rubinstein, Robert Volkmann, and Moritz Kässmeyer.[70] The percentage of pieces by dead composers declined modestly from 100 percent in the two concerts given in 1851 and 1854 to around 85 percent in 1855–1864 and 79 percent in 1865–1870.[71] Arguably, the Royal Chapel Orchestra in Berlin adhered to an even purer format than the *Wiener Philharmoniker*. Its director Wilhelm Taubert, the Kapellmeister at the city's opera, offered almost no vocal music and few recent works. A program in 1859 offered two overtures and two major symphonies (Ex. 8.7). As this and the previously cited programs indicate, the music of Cherubini and Méhul remained as central to orchestral concerts in this period as forty years before. Performance of the incidental music to *Athalie* (1845) illustrates how diverse genres of music by Mendelssohn had become central to orchestral concerts in many cities.

[69] Perger, *Festschrift aux Anlass der Feier des fünfzigjährigen ununterbrochenen Bestandes*, p. 58.
[70] Ibid., pp. 56–60; "Protocoll des philharmonischen Comité, Sitzungen, 1870–72," Archive, Vienna Philharmonic Orchestra.
[71] On repertory, see Hellsberg, *Demokratie der Könige*, pp. 136–140.

8.7 *"6te Symphonie-Soirée der Königlichen Capelle, Saal des Königlichen Opernhauses," Berlin, 20 January 1859* [72]

Overture, *Les Abencérages* (1813)	†Cherubini
Symphony in G Minor, K. 550	†Mozart
Overture, incidental music to *Athalie*	†Mendelssohn
Symphony no. 7 in A, op. 92	†Beethoven

The balance of new and old music shifted drastically at the Society Concerts of the Viennese Friends of Music in the 1850s, for by 1860 classics predominated there just as much as at the Philharmonic. The percentage of pieces by dead composers, having never gone above fifty-one percent before 1848, rose to eighty-three percent by 1860–1861. Still, repertory remained newer on the whole in these Viennese concerts than at the London Philharmonic or the Paris Conservatoire concerts. Many works by recently deceased composers such as Mendelssohn, Schubert, and Schumann and a few by composers from before Mozart's time were played. The Society Concerts offered music with a distinctly more popular flavor than the Philharmonic series. As we see in a program from 1863 (Ex. 8.8), the organization's chorus sang part-songs by Schumann and Mendelssohn, music of the same idiom as was sung at the Evening Entertainments in the 1830s (Ex. 4.2) and more recently by Vienna's Men's Singing Society, (Exs. 7.7, 7.8). The program also indicates the canonic status now given some of Robert Schumann's music. Living composers tended to be represented at these concerts chiefly by vocal pieces, as was also the case at many British concerts. The song *Der Hirt* (The Stag), composed by the little-known composer Nathanael Berg, was performed two seasons in a row, probably because Jenny Lind sang it widely. [73]

8.8 *Gesellschafts-Concerte, Saal der Musikfreunde, Vienna 29 November 1863* [74]

Double Chorus, with solos, *98th Psalm*	†Mendelssohn
Chorus, "Griselidis," old Frankish song	[? Carl Reinecke]
Part-song for mixed chorus, "Schön Rohtraut,"	
Romancen und Ballade, op. 67	†R. Schumann

---

[72] *Neue Berliner Musikzeitung*, 19 January 1859, p. 32.
[73] Perger, *Geschichte der k. k. Gesellschaft der Musikfreunde*, p. 301 (14 February 1864; 26 March 1865); "Bin ich in Wold," *Der Hirt, Schwedische Volkslied für Singstimme*, n. d., ÖNB.
[74] Perger, *Geschichte der k. k. Gesellschaft der Musikfreunde*, p. 301. In 1871 Carl Reinecke published *La belle Grisélidis: Improvisata über ein französisches Volkslied aus dem 17. Jahrhundert, für 2 Pianoforte zu 4 Händen*, Op. 94.

Part-song for mixed chorus, "Frühlingsahnung,"
   Sechs Lieder (Im Freien zu singen), op. 48   †Mendelssohn
Dramatic Poem, *Manfred*   †R. Schumann

But no second-level – in effect, middle-class – series emerged in Vienna until 1900. Extreme contrasts between popular and classical music-making had coexisted in the city from the rise of the Strauss-Kapelle and the Concert Spirituel in the 1820s, and the situation after 1850 was not all that different. Although the Philharmonic set a European standard for "pure" programs, neither Johann Strauss the Elder nor the Younger went as far toward classics as other entrepreneur-conductors tended to do. The late date at which professional orchestral concerts emerged in Vienna made it difficult for another series to be established, especially when faced with myriad ensembles imitating the Strauss-Kapelle. For that matter, theatres had a similar static history in Vienna during this period. Fewer new theatres appeared there than in Berlin, Paris, or London, relative to population, especially outside the center of the city.[75] There is strong evidence that the Philharmonic and the Friends of Music stopped a project for a second orchestra led by the concert agent Albert Gutmann in the 1880s.[76] Hofrat Johann von Wörz declared in 1890 that classical music concerts were "reserved for the exclusivity of an infinitesimally small fraction of the Viennese population."[77] The Vienna Philharmonic drew harsh criticism as an isolated, elitist institution. In 1885, the twenty-fifth anniversary of the series, the Vienna City Council voted down a motion to congratulate the orchestra. Strong populist language is evident in a report by the *Vorstadt-Zeitung*:

What does insipid old classical music mean to anyone? A true Viennese is more in tune with popular melodies.... The Philharmonic belongs to music as a form of big-money capitalism and its concerts are attended only by people with fancy outfits. Their lavish coats are unmistakable markers of corruption, and for that reason a self-respecting member of the City Council must not set foot in this institution if he doesn't want to be seen as an enemy of the People.[78]

75 Christophe Charle, "Les théâtres et leurs publics: Paris, Berlin, et Vienne, 1860–1914," *Capitales culturelles/Capitales symboliques: Paris et les expériences européennes XVIIIe–XXe siècles*, C. Charle and Daniel Roche (eds.) (Paris: Publications de la Sorbonne, 2002), pp. 403–20.

76 Albert Gutmann, *Volksconcerte in Wien: Vorschläge zur Bildung eines Concertorchesters* (Vienna: private printing, 1890); Theobald Kretschmann, *Tempi Passati: Aus den Erinnerungen eines Musikanten*, 2 vols. (Vienna: Prohaska, 1913), vol. 2, pp. 55–9; Margaret Notley, " 'Volksconcerte' in Vienna and Late Nineteenth-Century Ideology of the Symphony," *JAMS* 50 (1997), 440; and William Weber "A Myth of Musical Vienna," *Report of the International Musicological Society, 12th Congress, Berkeley, 1977*, Daniel Heartz and Bonnie Blackburn (eds.) (Kassel: Schneider, 1981), pp. 314–18.

77 Quoted in Notley, " 'Volksconcerte' in Vienna"; see also Weber "A Myth of Musical Vienna." Eduard Strauss occasionally performed single movements from classical symphonies by that time with the Strauss-Kapelle.

78 *Vorstadt-Zeitung*, 2 April 1885, p. 2.

Paris

Paris became the most impressive site of classical music orchestral concerts from the early 1860s onward. Separate orchestras were founded by Charles Pasdeloup in 1861, Edouard Colonne in 1873, and Charles Lamoureux in 1881, and the government began to give subsidies to their concerts in the 1870s.[79] In 1866–1867 the Conservatoire concerts began performing each program twice, thus almost doubling the size of the public. The directing board also chose to hold concerts at the Exposition of 1867 and at a celebration of the Ministry of the Marine and the Colonies in 1870. Italian opera selections were performed at the two events that had never appeared at the subscription concerts, including a duo from *Don Pasquale*, the first time the orchestra undertook music by Donizetti. Tourist guides began mentioning the concerts; *Paris illustré* stated that the series offered "the most renowned concerts in Paris ... that provide nothing else but works of the great masters."[80]

The first policy limiting new works at the Conservatoire concerts came immediately after the 1848 revolution. In 1849 the newly elected conductor Narcisse Girard eliminated the system whereby composers could apply for a piece to be "tried" by the orchestra. Too much time was spent, he stated, dealing with the many applications and trying to play mediocre manuscripts. When in 1856 Empress Eugénie remarked to Girard that only one living composer – Rossini – was represented on a program, he replied, "Madame, the repertoire of our society is the Louvre of musical art."[81] In 1861 the directing board nonetheless worked out a procedure to solicit works from a few well-established musicians.[82] This would be done judiciously, the board was told, because some subscribers "get upset when they see the name of a single contemporary composer on the programs, and say loudly that we should only perform pieces by dead composers."[83] The percentage of such pieces did fall significantly, from ninety-four percent in 1864–1865 to seventy-eight percent in 1869–1870. The board took advantage of the new two-performance schedule to present more new

---

[79] Myriam Chimènes, "Le Budget de la musique sous la 3e République," in *La Musique du théorique au politique*, Hugues Dufourt and Joël-Marie Fauquet (eds.) (Paris: Aux amateurs de livres, 1991), pp. 261–312.

[80] Adolphe Joanne, *Paris illustré en 1870 et 1876: Guide de l'étranger et du parisien*, 3rd ed. (Paris: Hachette, 1876), p. 612.

[81] Holoman, *Société des Concerts*, pp. 196–8; see also pp. 176–8, 296–9.

[82] Société des Concerts du Conservatoire, "Procès-verbaux du comité," 2 June 1861, 12 January 1864, Fonds Conservatoire, BNF.

[83] "Compte-rendu de l'exercice 1863–64," ibid.

pieces. In 1869, for example, a violin concerto by Victorin Joncières was played one week and Saint-Saëns performed one of his the next, along with a learned motet by Bach and well-known orchestral pieces (Ex. 8.9).

8.9 *Société des Concerts, Salle du Conservatoire, 12 & 19 December 1869* [84]

Symphony no. 4, in A, "Italian"	†Mendelssohn
Motet for double chorus	†J. S. Bach
Dec. 12: Concerto for violin	Victorin Joncières
Dec. 19: Concerto for Piano, no. 3 in E-flat	*Saint-Saëns*
Overture to *Manfred*	†Schumann
Incidental music, *Ruins of Athens*	†Beethoven

Like the Vienna Philharmonic, the Conservatoire concerts found ways to satisfy conflicting pressures without diverting the programs too far from the essential repertory. The institution could neither go overboard in performing French music, past or present, nor even think of performing a selection from an *opéra-comique*. Yet in 1864, three seasons after Pasdeloup started his series, the Conservatoire concerts went so far as to perform the fabulously popular overture to Ferdinand Hérold's *Zampa, ou La fiancée de marbre* (1831), and on the same day honored the recently deceased Fromental Halévy with his setting of the "Ave verum corpus" (1850). With the *Zampa* performances (two years in a row) the Conservatoire concerts held common company with the city's booming *cafés-concerts*. Hérold, the master of *opéra-comique*, had never been represented on the programs; Halévy had appeared only in 1849, appropriately enough in *Prométhée enchaîné*, a *scène* he set to a text by his brother Léon on the model of Aeschylus. [85]

In 1861 Jules Pasdeloup took up where the Concerts St. Honoré left off in 1840, gambling that a repertory made up of orchestral classical music would pay for itself in a city where vocal music – sacred or secular – seemed to rule. The *cafés-concerts* had limited the growth of promenade concerts, but, he surely suspected, a niche could be found for formal concerts devoted to classical works and virtuoso pieces. He offered by far the most homogeneous programs of orchestral music anywhere in this period, drawing in part from promenade concerts at the Jardin d'Hiver, and he played not much more contemporary music than the Conservatoire concerts; in fact, he put his series at the very same time in the week. A letter sent to subscribers in the early 1880s illustrates how firmly a canonic repertory became established in

[84] Holoman, http://hector.ucdavis.edu/sdc/MainFrame.htm.
[85] Ibid., concerts 16 March 1865 and 18 March 1849.

these concerts: "Classical music will form the basis of the programs, as has been their long tradition."[86] The abandonment of vocal music made Pasdeloup's programs entirely different from those given at the Crystal Palace or by the Euterpe Society. Although Pasdeloup often offered one or two choral programs called "Concerts Spirituel" at Easter, solo songs or opera excerpts almost never appeared on his programs before the 1880s. Many of his programs offered a symphony at the start and near the end of a concert, as we see in a program in 1864 (Ex. 8.10). Thus arose an irony: whereas the elite Society of Concerts felt compelled to keep the tradition of vocal music in play, a middle-class concert series could ignore such music completely, as promenade concerts had already done. Still, Pasdeloup did not simply play what was usually called "classical music" in that time, because most of his concerts included an accompanied solo number of the sort that the Conservatoire concerts abandoned around 1850, and in this respect the concerts resembled promenade concerts. On the 1864 program a solo for horn was performed by Victor Mohr, winner of the first prize for horn at the Conservatory in 1847, who left the Society of Concerts – dismissed for absences – to play both in the opera orchestra and Pasdeloup's ensemble.[87] By the early 1870s Pasdeloup's concerts had established themselves firmly enough that more new pieces were introduced, though rarely more than two of the five usually done at each concert.

8.10 *Concerts Populaires de Musique Classique, Cirque Napoléon, 28 February 1864* [88]

Symphony no. 2 in D	†Beethoven
Boléro, Solo for horn	Victor Mohr
Overture, *The Hebrides (Fingal's Cave)*	†Mendelssohn
Symphony in B-flat [?K. 319]	†Mozart
Invitation to the Waltz	†Weber

Musicians in Brussels imitated Pasdeloup's series closely in their Popular Concerts of Classical Music begun in 1864. Single movements were common in these sprawling orchestral programs that involved almost no vocal music. One in 1868 offered listeners a hefty musical meal – the first movement of Beethoven's Ninth Symphony, overtures by Julius Rietz and Michael Glinka, and Schumann's Concerto for Piano in A Minor.[89] The

---

[86] J. Pasdeloup to subscribers, 25 September 1883, Program Collection, BHVP.
[87] Holoman, http://hector.ucdavis.edu/sdc/MainFrame.htm.
[88] Program Collection, BHVP.   [89] Brussels, PC/FUSB.

Andante from a symphony by Schubert (one of the two in B-Flat) illustrates a major expansion in the range of his music performed. Concerts in the French city of Angers nonetheless resisted the shift to classical repertory significantly. The Association Artistique d'Angers, begun in 1877 in the western end of the Loire Valley, offered adventurous – though on a certain plane conservative – programs with more recent music than any of the Parisian series. Here, as in Paris, new genres were replacing the symphony at many concerts. Victorin de Joncière conducted numerous suites and operatic entr'actes, for example, a suite from Jules Massenet's incidental music for the Greek tragedy *Les Erinnyes*. A practice evolved of performing several pieces by a living composer together, as was rarely done by any major orchestra.[90]

Leipzig

Leipzig was not a major site of revolution in March 1848, but it was deeply disturbed by the uprisings and even more by the one in Dresden in May 1849. The programs at the Gewandhaus during the crisis were aimed to bolster public order, rather as was done in 1806–1807.[91] The most revered celebratory works were chosen: Beethoven's Ninth Symphony and Padre Giovanni Martini's setting of the 85th Psalm, and on New Year's Day, 1850, cantatas by Bach and Mendelssohn (Ex. 8.11). Classics now came to dominate the programs as rarely before.

8.11 *Abonnenten-Concerte, Gewandhaus, 1 January 1850* [92]

Cantata, *Ein' feste Burg ist unser Gott*	†J. S. Bach
95th Psalm, soloists, chorus and orchestra	†Mendelssohn
Overture, *Consecration of the House*, op. 124	†Beethoven
—	
Symphony no. 41 in C, K.551	†Mozart

Memorials to major composers, done first for Mozart in the late 1820s, were now regular events at the Gewandhaus. Several pieces by a composer

90 Centre de Musique Baroque de Versailles, Philidor-Évènement: Concerts en Angers, http://www.cmbv.com and Yannick Simon, *L'Association artistique d'Angers (1877–1893)* (Paris: Société Française de Musicologie, 2007), pp. 275, 278–9.
91 Nösselt, *Gewandhausorchester*, pp. 161–73; Dörffel, *Geschichte der Gewandhausconcerte*, vol. 1, pp. 149, 153. On performance of Beethoven's Ninth Symphony, see *NZFM*, 8 April 1870, p. 143.
92 Abonnenten-Concerte, SGML.

would be performed at a concert not long after his death – piano concertos of Ignaz Moscheles, the famous (some thought turgid) oratorios of Friedrich Schneider, and vocal pieces written by Peter Lindpaintner and Conradin Kreutzer variously for opera or *Liedertafel* contexts.[93] When Spohr died in 1859 he was quickly honored by performance of the overtures and extensive excerpts from *Jessonda* and *Faust*, the much-favored Concerto in G Minor, and also the iconic "Eroica" Symphony. Honors were also extended to the foreigners Gaspare Spontini and George Onslow; indeed, a concert was occasionally focused on Italian or French works. Historically defined programs similar to the one done in 1847 (Ex. 6.2) were also offered occasionally. In the process the traditional sequence of genres broke down almost completely, as programs became different from one another from concert to concert, but unified by broader principles of programming.

Financial needs also took programs in new directions. The 1848 revolution brought to a head long-standing tension between the orchestra and the *Direktorium* regarding pay, pensions, and diverse duties at the opera, the Thomaskirche, and the Gewandhaus. Those issues and the cost of expanding the size of the orchestra led to fund-raising events where repertory often contrasted with that at the subscription concerts. Though some of these programs involved well-known choral-orchestral classics, others resembled miscellaneous benefit concerts. A concert to help the pension fund in 1868 included five recent virtuoso pieces in the first half, and in the second *Harold in Italy* by Berlioz, a composer who was rarely represented at the subscription concerts (Ex. 8.12).

8.12 *Concert for Orchestral Pension Fund, Gewandhaus, 27 February 1868*[94]

Overture, *King Manfred* (1867)	Carl Reinecke
Concerto for Cello no. 2 (1865)	*Carl Davidoff*
Stücke für Pianoforte	*Carl Tausig*
Fantaisie for cello	*Davidoff*
Fantaisie for cello	†Servais
Réminiscences de Don Juan	Liszt
—	
Harold en Italie	Berlioz

[93] Dörffel, *Geschichte der Gewandhausconcerte*, vol. 1, pp. 149–50, 168–72.
[94] Abonnenten-Concerte, SGML. Berlioz's *Roman Carnival Overture* was done at another pension fund concert on 10 February 1870.

The subscription concerts at the Gewandhaus still accommodated a variety of tastes, for most programs included several vocal or instrumental solos. During the 1869–1870 season, for example, sixteen of the twenty concerts included at least one solo vocal number or instrumental solo, the latter now sometimes unaccompanied. One program was almost a mixed recital, including two canonic opera selections, two recent songs, and fairly old violin solos by Spohr and David (Ex. 8.13). This music did not resemble the opera *fantaisie*, however, and instrumental soloists (unlike at the pension fund concert) usually did not play their own music. Just as David's piece had a classical reference point, Mozart's song *An Cloe*, the lieder grew out of the new Schubertian tradition. Songs by relatively little-known composers sometimes gained performance at this august series, probably by choice of the vocalists; Theodor Kirchner was an organist in Zürich, sympathetic to the Brahmsian faction, but little is known of Johann Heuchemer save a few published songs. The survival of virtuosos in the concerts was a source of continuing debate. In his 1884 centennial book on the Leipzig orchestra, Alfred Dörffel complained that a lot of people wanted solos more than orchestral works.[95] Sixty years later, Andreas-Joachim Nösselt observed that "the expectation that soloists appear on almost every evening maintained the virtuoso in a role that has to be called traditional."[96] Public interest in the opera selections, primarily by classical composers, was focused on major singers from outside the city. Although in the 1830s one or two singers had been contracted for a season, rail transport now enabled the directing board to bring in a visitor every week or two.

8.13 *Abonnenten-Concerte, Gewandhaus, 17 February 1870* [97]

Overture, *Manfred* (1849)	†Schumann
Recitative/Aria, "Armida! Dispietata!"/	
"Lascia ch'io pianga," *Rinaldo* (1711)	†Handel
Adagio for violin	†Spohr
Recitative/Aria, "Weh mir! es ist geschehen!"/	
"Ach, ich habe sie verloren," *Orpheus* (1762/1774)	†Gluck
Introduction and Variations for violin on	
theme from Mozart's song *An Cloe* (K.524), op. 11	Ferdinand David
—	
Lied/piano, "Des Morgens in dem Thaue"	Johann Heuchemer
Lied/piano, "Du wundersüsses Kind"	Theodore Kirchner
Symphony no. 2 in D, op. 36	†Beethoven

95 Dörffel, *Geschichte der Gewandhausconcerte*, vol. 1, pp. 164.
96 Nösselt, *Gewandhausorchester*, pp. 167–8.　97 *NZFM*, 15 February 1870, p. 85.

Ideological divisions affected concert programming in Leipzig to a particular extent. Although the Gewandhaus offered little music by Wagner, Liszt, or members of the New German School, the Euterpe Society – by 1860 a professional ensemble – regularly performed music advocated by that camp. Classical repertory nonetheless dominated the Euterpe repertory, as we see in a program that balanced pieces by Liszt and Berlioz with works by Haydn and Beethoven. Here, too, lieder were performed with piano accompaniment (Ex. 8.14).

8.14 *Euterpe-Verein, Buchhändler-Börse, 15 January 1861* [98]

Symphony in C Minor	†Haydn
Aria, "Höre Israel, höre des Herrn Stimme!" *Elias*	†Mendelssohn
Overture, *Coriolanus*	†Beethoven
–	
Symphonic Poem, *Tasso: lamento e trionfo*	Liszt
Lieder:	
a) "Auf dem Wasser zu singen" D774	†Schubert
b) "Frühlingslied"	†Mendelssohn
Overture, *Benvenuto Cellini* (1838)	Berlioz

Support for musical progressives came as well from a concert series focused on Baroque music, founded by the choral director Carl Riedel in 1854. The concerts grew out of unhappiness that the Gewandhaus was favoring Catholic over Protestant church music and neglecting composers before Bach's time. But Riedel also offered pieces by followers of Liszt and Wagner and indeed served as president of the Allgemeine Deutsche Musikverein for twenty years. A Riedel program in 1870, for example, mingled pieces by Wagnerians Peter Cornelius and Joachim Raff with choruses supposedly derived from music of the late medieval Hussites (Ex. 8.15). Thus could a musician patch together different genres and causes, enabling the series to last until World War I.

8.15 *Riedel'scher-Verein, Thomaskirche, 2 October 1870* [99]

Chorale Prelude for organ	†Bach
Choral Lieder from Hussite Taborites	L. Zwonart

[98] Euterpe-Concerte, SGML; Deaville, "The New German School and the Euterpe Concerts, 1860–1862: A Trojan Horse in Leipzig," *Festschrift Christoph-Hellmut Mahling zum 65. Geburtstag* (Tutzing: Schneider, 1997), pp. 253–270.
[99] Alberg Göhler, *Der Riedel-Verein zu Leipzig: Eine Denkschrift zur Feier seines fünfzigjährigen Bestehens* (Leipzig: Riedel-Verein, 1904), pp. 81–82.

Andante, Sonata for Violin in A Minor, unaccomp.	†Bach
Adagio, Sonata for violin and piano	†Bach
Lieder, "Mitten wir im Leben"; "Pilgers Ruhethal"	Peter Cornelius
Aria, "Erbarme dich mein, O Herre Gott,"	
alto and violin	†Bach
"Ich harre dein, O Herr," *De profundis*, for	
soprano, women's chorus, orchestra	Joachim Raff
"Ich weiss, dass mein Erlöser lebt," *Messiah*	†Handel
Andante for violin	†Tartini
Chorus, "Fürchte dich nicht," *Elias*	†Mendelssohn
Abendlied for violin and organ	†Schumann
Chorus, "Wie lieblich sind die Boten,"	
Paulus	†Mendelssohn

London

A certain egalitarianism governed London's classical music life in the 1850s, because the leading orchestra in that city was less powerful than elsewhere. As the Philharmonic Society continued to face issues of legitimacy, low-priced chamber music concerts competed effectively with the aristocratic Musical Union. What is more, no overarching differences emerged between programming in and out of the capital city. Contrasting ways of mixing vocal and instrumental pieces were followed at orchestral series in London and in such cities as Birmingham, Manchester, and Liverpool. Almost all of their repertories mingled orchestral classics, British vocal pieces, and Italian opera selections.

The Philharmonic Society continued to offer an unusual number of opera selections, some of fairly recent vintage. At its concerts one could hear a great variety of excerpts by Donizetti, Paër, Meyerbeer, Pacini, and Verdi, and indeed Auber, Hérold, and Gounod. Moreover, songs that had been written for the salon and then inserted into operas ended up in Philharmonic programs. Both kinds of music, by Mercadante and Benedict, can be seen on an 1861 program, along with an aria by the twenty-three-year-old Pacini (Ex. 8.16). The programs now offered somewhat fewer pieces than before but, preserving the traditional link between vocal and instrumental virtuosity, stuck closely to the traditional sequence of genres for the most part. Austro-German classics predominated at some Philharmonic concerts; by 1860 one might hear almost no music composed after 1820. The rival New Philharmonic Society – "truly a replacement Parliament,"

Simon McVeigh suggested – offered somewhat less from opera and more by British composers, but within a similar format.[100]

8.16 *Philharmonic Society, Hanover Square Rooms, 18 March 1861* [101]

Dead March, *Saul* (memorial for Duchess of Kent)	†Handel
Symphony in D, no. 2	†Beethoven
Aria, "Lungi del caro bene," *La Sposa Fidele* (1819)	Pacini
Romanza, *Il sogno di Torquato Tasso*	Mercadante
Overture, *Euryanthe* (1823)	†Weber
–	
Symphony in A Minor, no. 3, "Scotch"	†Mendelssohn
Duet, *I Montanari, on Styrian Melodies*, op. 48 (1853)	Julius Benedict
Overture, *Guillaume Tell* (1829)	Rossini

The interdependence of vocal and instrumental music survived in different form at the Crystal Palace concerts led by August Manns. To be sure, the series brought classical instrumental music to the middling classes, a major contribution to British musical life.[102] But its programs also included much vocal music – opera, operetta, oratorio, and song, both British and foreign. After being transplanted to Sydenham, the various spaces in the Crystal Palace offered a wide range of entertainments, some verging on the music hall, and Manns's mixed programs shared in that mood. A program in 1870 intertwined Beethoven's Second Symphony and a piece from Haydn's *Creation* with arias by Mercadante and Meyerbeer and a lullaby from Arthur Sullivan's early *Cox and Box; Or, the Long-Lost Brothers* (1866), a one-act burlesque about a landlord renting the same room to two men (Ex. 8.17). An overture by Bennett and a religious scene by the song writer Luigi Bordèse were set between familiar overtures by Rossini and Mendelssohn. This mingling of genres and nationalities reminds one of what was offered by the Evening Entertainments in Vienna. But there were distinct limits to inclusiveness at the Crystal Palace. Although Manns offered an artful ballad from time to time, he excluded the glee, a genre that survived in local concerts but had dropped out of concerts assumed to be cosmopolitan in taste. Interestingly enough, Beethoven's Second Symphony was often performed in this period (Exs. 8.10 and 8.13), perhaps offering contrast with the richer textures more recently employed.

---

[100] McVeigh, "Society of British Musicians," p. 167; St. Martin's Hall, CPH/RCM.
[101] Foster, *History of the Philharmonic Society*, p. 264.
[102] Michael Musgrave, *Musical Life of the Crystal Palace* (Cambridge: Cambridge University Press, 1995).

8.17 *Crystal Palace Concerts, Sydenham, 7 October 1870*[103]

Overture, *Siège de Corinthe* (1826)	†Rossini
Scene, *David Singing before Saul* (1869)	Luigi Bordèse
Aria, "In native worth," *Creation*	†Haydn
Symphony no. 2, op. 36	†Beethoven
Aria, "Ah! Rammento," *Leonora* (1844)	Mercadante
Aria, "The Monk," *Margherita d'Anjou* (1820)	†Meyerbeer
Fantasia-Overture, *Paradise and the Peri* (1862)	Bennett
Lullaby, "Birds in the Night," *Cox and Box; or, the Long-Lost Brothers* (1866)	*Sullivan*
Song, "When other Lips," *Bohemian Girl* (1843)	Balfe
Overture, *Midsummer Night's Dream*	†Mendelssohn

The orchestras founded in industrial Manchester and Liverpool became considerably more central to musical life in those cities than the new or old Philharmonic was in London.[104] If anything, Hallé, who built both provincial orchestras, used the model of the Crystal Palace more than that of the Philharmonic Society because he regularly offered "indigenous" music, as the ideologists had begun to call British music by that the time.[105] Instrumental solos were central to his programs, along with opera numbers and the better sort of parlor songs. A concert in 1862 (Ex. 8.18) alternated genres and national origins in traditional fashion, offering piano solos in the second half, as was done with violin pieces at the Gewandhaus (Ex. 8.13). Performing Bishop's *Home! Sweet Home!*, the most widely sung of all ballads, carried populist as well as nationalist implications. In the 1860s one or two British songs might appear on a program in Manchester or Liverpool, most often by Arne, Balfe, or William Vincent Wallace. *Liedertafel* songs by Julius Otto or Friedrich Kücken, some as sung by Vienna's Men's Singing Society, were common as well, in effect replacing the glee. The songs by Arditi and Bishop and the overture by Auber were all done at music halls by then.

8.18 *Hallé Concerts, Free Trade Hall, Manchester, 13 February 1862*[106]

Symphony in E-flat [?no. 38, K. 543]	†Mozart
Scene, "Wie nahte mir," *Der Freischütz* (1821)	†Weber

103 Crystal Palace, CPH/RCM.
104 Simon Gunn, "The Sublime and the Vulgar: The Hallé Concerts and the Constitution of 'High Culture' in Manchester, c.1850–1880," *Journal of Victorian Culture* 2 (1997), 208–28.
105 George Macfarren, "The National Music of our Native Land," *Musical Times* 1 July (1870), 519.
106 *Sir Charles Hallé's Concerts in Manchester . . . 1858 to 1895*, Thomas Batley (ed.) (Manchester: Charles Sever, 1895), p. 95.

Concerto for Piano no. 3 in C Minor, op. 37	†Beethoven
Ballad, *Home! Sweet Home!*, originally in	
Clari, or The Maid of Milan (1823)	†Bishop
Overture, *Les Abencérages* (1813)	†Cherubini

–

Overture to *Fernand Cortez* (1809)	†Spontini
Cavatina, "Casta diva," *Norma* (1831)	†Bellini
Scherzo, Nocturne, and Wedding March,	
Midsummer Night's Dream	†Mendelssohn
Solos for piano, Charles Hallé:	
a) Gavottes and Musettes	†J. S. Bach
b) "Pièce de clavecin" in D	†Scarlatti
Waltz Song, *La Stella* (1861)	Luigi Arditi
Overture, *Zanetta* (1840)	Auber

The Boston Symphony Orchestra offered programs at its founding in 1881 not unlike those of the Gewandhaus we have discussed. Vocal music loomed larger at this time than in the 1840s. A program in the first season offered a pair of recent songs, framed by overtures composed a year apart by Méhul and Cherubini (Ex. 8.19). The convention of adding an obligato, such as we see here, gave a new aspect to the interdependence of vocal and instrumental virtuosity. For that matter, the symmetry of this program takes one back to eighteenth-century practice.

8.19 *Boston Symphony Orchestra, Music Hall, 18/19 November 1881* [107]

Overture, *Joseph and His Brethren* (1807)	†Méhul
Recitative/Air for tenor, *Joseph*	†Méhul
Symphony no. 3, "Eroica"	†Beethoven
Songs with piano:	
a) "The Dream" (Der Traum) *10 Lieder*,	
op. 83, no. 10 (1869)	Rubinstein
b) *Gipsy Serenade* (Zigeunerisches Ständchen),	
vio. oblig. (1877)	George Henschel
Overture, *Faniska* (1806)	†Cherubini

Performance of excerpts from Wagner's operas by orchestras did not face the aesthetic critique that Italian opera selections had long received. His

---

[107] Transcript and analysis of programs of the Boston Symphony Orchestra, Robert D. King (ed.), typescript, Harvard University Library.

music entered the province of classical music on the highest possible level because from the start the excerpts were paired with Beethoven's overtures and symphonies, yielding a Promethean experience in contrasting new and old styles. Wagnerites helped visiting conductor Hans Richter organize a series of concerts in 1877 that became central to musical life for some time. At first the programs included several vocal selections, but in time that gave way in part to strictly orchestral programs such as Pasdeloup offered in Paris. A concert given in 1879 included two pieces with voice and two without, accompanied by familiar works by Mozart and Schumann (Ex. 8.20). Audiences soon could not get enough of the Beethoven–Wagner mix, and impresarios found that endless repetition of Wagnerian repertory helped keep their concerts in the black.

8.20 *Richter Concerts, St. James's Hall, 5 May 1879* [108]

Wagner:
Kaisermarsch
"Blick' ich umher in diesem edlen Kreise," *Tannhäuser*
Introduction to Act 3, *Die Meistersänger*
Duet, "Wie aus der Ferne," *Fliegände Holländer*
Aria, *Entführung aus dem Serail*   †Mozart
Overture, *Manfred*   †Schumann
–
Symphony no. 7   †Beethoven

    Chamber music concerts in London continued to draw a larger and more diversified public than could be found in any other major city. In 1859 the publishers Thomas and Samuel Arthur Chappell began a weekly series, the Monday Popular Concerts (on Saturday as well from 1865 to 1876). The title was intended to indicate that the repertory did not follow as "pure" a format as learned meetings like those of the Beethoven Quartet Society. Every concert included several vocal or instrumental pieces, in some cases overshadowing the genres that had been the main concern of Schuppanzigh and Baillot. The programs resembled the balanced format that Bennett achieved among chamber, vocal, and solo instrumental pieces at his concerts in the 1840s and 1850s. A program in 1861 opened with an octet and closed with a quartet, framing piano sonatas and vocal pieces by Clementi, Mendelssohn, and the widely known Henry Smart (Ex. 8.21); pairing *notturnos* by Blangini and Paër was a nice touch. Music by Mendelssohn served as a binding-agent in these concerts. Because he wrote so fluently for

[108] St. James's Hall, CPH/RCM.

different publics, his Octet set forth a common ground for more or less serious genres, and as well among older and newer styles. John Ella offered similar programs at the Musical Union, though focused more on instrumental than vocal solos.

8.21 *Monday Popular Concerts, St. James's Hall, 28 January 1861* [109]

Octet in E-flat, op. 20	†Mendelssohn
Aria, "O cara imagine," *Don Giovanni*	†Mozart
"On music's softest pinions," *Sechs Gesänge:*	
Auf Flügeln des Gesanges, op. 34, no. 2	†Mendelssohn
Notturno, "Per vali, per boschi" [1830s]	†Felice Blangini
Sonata in D for piano	†Clementi
—	
Sonata in A for violin and piano [K. 331?]	†Mozart
Song, *Estelle* (1861)	Henry Smart
Duet, "Puro ciel tranquilla notte," *Three Italian*	
Notturnos for Two Voices (London, 1820), no. 2	†Paër
Quartet in G, op. 18, no. 2	†Beethoven

Chamber music by British composers were rarely performed at the Monday Popular Concerts. But a remarkable number of chamber pieces by Britons and by women composers were performed at the concerts of the New Philharmonic Society in the mid-1860s. The financial challenge posed by the orchestral series led the Society's leaders to offer instead a mixture of solo and chamber pieces, both vocal and instrumental. In 1864 a concert included the Trio in G by Alice Mary Smith, who subsequently became an associate member of the Philharmonic Society. The focus on music by women composers was related to the early movement for women's suffrage active in that decade, aided by John Stuart Mill and other liberals.[110] Once again we find a close link between efforts for musical and political change.

A NEW SERIOUSNESS

By 1870 a new culture of musical seriousness encompassed the European classical music world. Eighteenth-century listeners had exemplified that quality in the craft-based critique of singers that Sir Horace Walpole

---

[109] Popular Concerts, BL.
[110] St. James's Hall, CPH/RCM; *British Musical Biography*, p. 379; Philippa Levine, *Victorian Feminism, 1850–1900* (Gainesville, Fla.: University Press of Florida, 1994), pp. 65, 74, 76; Deborah Rohr, "Women and the Music Profession in Victorian England: Royal Society of Female Musicians, 1839–1866," *Journal of Musicological Research* 18 (1999), 307–46; materials given by Simon McVeigh.

practiced as talent scout for the King's Theatre in Italy. Seriousness was also part of the eighteenth-century search for the sublime in choral-orchestral works, led, for example, by musicians directing the Parisian Concert Spirituel and Vienna's oratorio concerts. Nineteenth-century musical culture called for a loftier kind of seriousness than its predecessor, searching for an idealistic, and in some contexts spiritual, dimension of taste that Walpole would have found presumptuous. Taste was now founded on a body of classical works and invested with the status of truth based on systematic knowledge. It is impressive how successfully the quartet concert, the recital, and classical music orchestras established a world true to the new values, due to the certainty they communicated ideologically. We have, of course, seen that most orchestral programs still included operatic and virtuosic pieces right to the end of the century; the "culture of performance," as Joseph Horowitz calls it, remained central to classical music culture.[III] Thanks to the compromise struck between virtuosity and interpretation, concert-goers flocked to hear Clara Schumann, Joseph Joachim, and Julius Stockhausen in search of higher musical meaning.

III Horowitz, *Classical Music in America*, Part One.

CHAPTER 9

Vocal music for the general public

Publisher William Boosey mapped out succinctly the landscape of musical taste in the late nineteenth century when he stated in his memoir that "we shall discuss grand operas, light operas, concerts, serious and otherwise, [and] publishing and performing rights in music."[1] Boosey used the word *otherwise* because he had no word at his disposal to encompass the diverse concerts outside the classical music world that he dealt with after joining the press in 1880. Admittedly, in Britain the term *popular song* was commonly used by the 1860s, and the broader concept of *popular music* occasionally appeared in print.[2] We can therefore identify this period as the starting point of the cultural structure presently identified as popular music. Yet the term *popular music* was used widely only in Britain, and even there writers were wary of grouping the new kinds of commercial concerts together. That is why I find it productive to speak of this area of musical life instead as one attracting a "general public," with its own subdivisions, that enjoyed the most widely known music, different from the more specialized classical music world. This chapter examines the audiences, repertories, and programs typical of three types of events: the early opera "gala," found in all four of our major cities; the ballad concert in London; and, comparably, the London music hall and the Paris *café-concert*. The order we follow among them is not chronological but is gauged by the increasing independence of the concerts from the classical music world.

"The general public in search of amusement will always find a sure guide in our publication," stated a lead article in a music hall periodical in 1867 that employed the term central to our discussion.[3] Vocal music usually reached a wider public than instrumental music, utilizing a text to portray, act, and emote. The three types of concerts each had an instrumental component,

[1] William Boosey, *Fifty Years of Music* (London: Ernest Benn, 1931), p. 9.
[2] Richard Middleton, "Popular Music," *NGG*, vol. 20, pp. 128–30.
[3] "Address to our Readers," *Weekly Theatrical and Music Hall Review*, 14 December 1867, p. 1, first issue.

273

but all of them were focused on solo singers, most of whom performed in theatrical as well as in musical terms. Most commonly the performer portrayed a traditional social type, adapting it to his or her personal style. Much of this music grew out of conventions of street theatre or *vaudeville*, as new musical settings replaced traditional tunes, what the French call *timbres*.

All three kinds of concerts were fundamentally commercial, being linked to publishing companies or theatre speculators. The commercial aspect lent a theatrical quality to performances, much as was the case in benefit concerts. The excitement of following reports – and by the end of the century charts – about high-selling songs became deeply intermingled with delight in hearing the songs. Knowing genres, singing styles, and reputations seemed essential to enjoying this entertainment even though systematic learning was not expected. Around each type of concert there developed a critical discourse that established its own standards, expectations, and manner of speaking, even though the commentators were less empowered than those for classical music. The common culture of operatic music provided a larger reference point for all these events but the ballad concerts. An overture almost always opened the night at a music hall or a *café-concert*, and a set of duos would often close it. The overtures, chiefly by Weber, Rossini, and Auber, linked music halls and *cafés-concerts* with traditions of musical sociability and thereby helped firm up the events' standing in society. Because the music business made sure almost everyone heard operatic music, in the home or on the street, the mass public now "possessed" it to a significant extent. It was not limited to the elite publics whose theatres produced it.

The three kinds of vocal music concerts vastly expanded both the number of concert-goers and their range as to social class. Music halls and *cafés-concerts* went the farthest in both regards, developing publics among prosperous artisans, small shopkeepers, and clerks and to some extent their wives and families. The most prominent venues drew broadly from the middle classes and were even visited by adventurous members of the cities' elites. The English ballad concerts attracted a broad middle-class public, though a few venues were oriented toward working-class listeners. The early opera galas drew some wealthy patrons of opera singers, and local galas drew a lower-middle-class public. In any case, people who went to all these concerts were by no means new to music, having enjoyed it often in the home, the tavern, or the theatre.

In Britain and to some extent in France the word *popular* all but replaced "favorite" in music editions during the nineteenth century, gradually acquiring a complicated set of meanings.[4] At first the word was ideologically

---

4 Scott, *Singing Bourgeois*, p. 208; Scott, "Music and Social Class," pp. 545–46.

neutral, simply indicating that a piece was widely admired. The broader, more conceptual term *popular music* began appearing after midcentury, used most often by British and occasionally by French musicians or publishers. Thus Duff and Stewart of Oxford Street offered a monthly collection of songs called the *Magazine of Popular Music*, one issue including "The Goodbye at the Door" and "Old Friends and Other Days."[5] By then the term *popular* could carry a social meaning, an aesthetic meaning, or both, indicating either that the music was aimed at the middle classes or that it was intended for the general public rather than specialists. Both meanings could be read into the titles of London's "Popular Monday Concerts" (chamber music) and the Parisian "Popular Concerts of Classical Music" (orchestral concerts). But the aesthetic meaning became more significant in the long run, generally carrying a negative connotation. In 1862 the canon-building *Musical World* published a letter, "Classical v. Popular Music," complaining that many of "our *eminent* professors" seemed to feel "*obliged* to be of a money-grasping nature."[6] In 1881 a reviewer felt so uneasy about calling the chamber music concerts "popular" that he put the word in quotes and assured his readers that he had gone to a "concert spirituel" more sophisticated than a ballad concert.[7] Representatives of different kinds of music used the aesthetic meaning to compete with one another. For example, a magazine hawking opera medleys accused the music halls of fostering the "popular music mania" that was ruining good taste.[8] The overtures and selections from which music for the medleys came, however, were not considered to be "popular" in the generic sense, because they and the early opera "galas" were a focal point for opera connoisseurs.

A neutral posture nonetheless did develop regarding popular songs. In 1871 an advertisement for a series of *Favourite Pianoforte Compositions*, mostly opera medleys, stated that "[w]hen a piece has reached its third edition, all we can do is to quote Johnson's remark upon Gray's 'Elegy' – 'It is vain to blame and useless to praise it.'"[9] All told, the harsh dispute over matters of musical taste in the British Isles may explain why the word *popular* took on a much more important role there linguistically than in France or Germany. A similar differentiation between tastes developed in all these countries, but with contrasting styles of discourse.

---

[5] "New Music," *Society: Literary, Scientific, Political, Fashionable, Musical, Theatrical, Artistic, & General*, 23 June 1875, p. 134.
[6] *MW*, 13 September 1862, p. 587.
[7] "Concerts," *Monthly Musical Record*, 1 December 1881, p. 237.
[8] "Metropolitan Music-Halls," *Musical Monthly and Repertoire of Literature, the Drama, & the Arts*, 1 March 1864, p. 34.
[9] "Sydney Smith's *Favourite Pianoforte Compositions*," *Monthly Musical Record*, 1 February 1871, p. 24.

The crisis in international opera at the middle of the century kept works on stage to a far greater extent than had been the case previously. As composers and publishers achieved tighter control over premières, impresarios found it increasingly difficult to mount new productions and therefore fell back on established works that drew steady audiences. Opera halls continued staging works composed between about 1810 and 1850, chiefly operas by Donizetti, Bellini, and Meyerbeer, and also Rossini's *Barbiere di Siviglia* and Mozart's *Don Giovanni* and *Nozze di Figaro*. Fewer new works or composers drew public acclaim as compared with the decades before 1850. Although around 1840 one could easily count a dozen opera composers often discussed in the press, by 1870 that happened to few other than Verdi, Gounod, and Wagner. Musicologists have only begun to investigate these developments or to determine how far the opera world went toward building a canon around the older works that were performed. John Rosselli suggested that neither impresarios nor critics went very far in conceiving of an operatic canon until the end of the century, and Matthew Ringel found little effort to canonize or historicize old works in the two London theatres. Katharine Ellis has nonetheless argued convincingly that the Théâtre Lyrique in Paris built a substantial canonic repertory in the 1860s.[10] Thus because the operas involved in different countries and halls differed so much in genre, regional origin, and reception, only a tenuous sense of canonic framework emerged among them all internationally for some time. The intellectual apparatus that surrounded symphonic works remained incompatible with that of the greatest operas. Yet for all that, the very survival of *Don Giovanni*, *Barbiere di Siviglia*, *Lucia di Lammermoor*, and *Norma* betokened a canonic identity for each one that was independent of classical instrumental music.

A wide array of old opera pieces persisted in the concerts that arose after 1850. If the "gala" was devoted to international opera since Mozart, and ballad concerts portrayed the history of English opera, both *cafés-concerts* and music halls were rooted in the overture and the vocal selection. For example, a program at the Parisian Pavillon de l'Horloge in 1850 (Ex. 9.8) opened with Boieldieu's *Voitures versées* (1808) and ended with Henri Berton's *Le Délire, ou les Suites d'une Erreur* (1799). By the same token, British ballad concerts often included pieces by Dibdin and Bishop

[10] Katharine Ellis, "Systems Failure in Operatic Paris: The Acid Test of the Théâtre-Lyrique," in *Stage Music and Cultural Transfer: Paris, 1830–1914*, Mark Everist and Annegret Fauser (eds.) (Chicago: University of Chicago Press, forthcoming); Jutta Toelle, "Venice and its Opera House: Hope and Despair at the Teatro la Fenice, 1866–1897," *Journal of Musicological Research* 26 (2007), 33–54; Rosselli, "Italy, The Decline of a Tradition"; Ringel, "Opera in 'The Donizettian Dark Ages'"; Poriss, "A Madwoman's Choice: Aria Substitution in *Lucia di Lammermoor*," pp. 3–5.

(Ex. 9.5), and in 1869 a Leipzig concert called "Singspiel-Halle (Salon Variété)" offered the *air* of the Seneschal from Boieldieu's *Jean de Paris* (Ill. 22). These pieces suggest that there existed a learned segment within the public for popular songs, listeners who had particularly deep knowledge of the repertory. These pieces acquired different kinds of canonic identity in the various contexts where they were performed; the overture to *Nozze di Figaro*, for example, was performed in Paris at the Society of Concerts, the *café-concert* Morel, and the promenade concerts at the Jardin d'Hiver. We will find disputes breaking out over which kind of concert "possessed" such a piece.

A collection of opera potpourris for piano published in the 1860s demonstrates a canon of opera composers from a German perspective (Ill. 26). Designed by Henri Cramer – a musician born in Frankfurt who published hundreds of potpourris and piano pieces – the edition included twenty-nine composers, among whom only Auber, Verdi, Wagner, and Friedrich Flotow were still producing operas in the 1860s.[11] Cramer's scheme favors Germans and Austrians on the left and Italians on the right, but involves French composers on both lists, significantly enough. The left-hand column tends to predominate. Not only is it surprising to find Meyerbeer absent (Cramer had issued several editions of his music), but also to see relatively few Italian names as compared with the diverse German and Austrian ones. Mozart and Beethoven parallel Cherubini and Rossini as the canonic pinnacles on each side. The left-hand column follows with three early figures – Weber, Méhul, and Spohr – and then Lortzing, Lindpaintner, Marschner, and Conradin Kreutzer, with Boieldieu among them. The list concludes with pairs of French and Austrian composers from contrasting generations: Auber/Thomas, and Joseph Weigl/Heinrich Esser. The right-hand column mingles French and Italian composers to a particular extent – after Verdi, Halévy, and Adam, it looks back to Spontini and Mercadante and the giants Donizetti and Bellini. The column ends with an interesting group: Flotow, Lachner, and Hérold, with Wagner last but by no means least. The only surprise here is finding a little-known Belgian, Armand Limnander de Nieuwenhove, who was based in Paris.

Just as we see in this edition, a national definition of repertory became more common somewhat after 1850. As we saw with promenade concerts, a national musical identity grew in large part from a reaction against the

---

[11] Fétis located Cramer in Paris in 1843 and stated that some thought he was related to J.-B. Cramer, which seems unlikely: François Fétis, *Biographie universelle des musiciens et bibliographie générale de la musique*, 8 vols. (Paris: Didot, 1863–70), 2:384–86. A well-constructed operatic *ballade* by Cramer is included in *The Nineteenth-Century Piano Ballade: An Anthology*, James Parakilas (ed.) (Madison, WI: A-R Editions, 1990), pp. ix–x, 8–11.

world of the cosmopolitan upper classes for enforcing values offensive to
a region or a social class. Paris was seen as the capital of that cultural
empire, and *grand opéra* as its main musical influence. Attacks on international opera exemplified movements that Benedict Anderson defined as
"antimetropolitan": reaction against a dominating power or social class and
efforts to stimulate new social and political identities.[12] Most impressively,
journalists promoting the British music halls viciously derided the aristocracy and those fawning on it for ignoring the nation's music. In 1868 a
music hall periodical paraphrased words of composer George Macfarren
in saying that "our aristocracy, lay and clerical, of blood and wealth, 'took
to ignoring everything Anglican' in music." Favoring Italian music since
the time of Queen Anne meant that "[t]he multitude were cheated out of
the means of improving their own music," making everyone think of England "being unmusical and having no national music."[13] Robert Schumann
and Richard Wagner spoke to a similar issue when they used nationalistic
themes to condemn a decadent elite culture based in Paris.

  Yet the concerts of vocal music took on cosmopolitan identities in their
own right. Managers of music halls and *cafés-concerts* borrowed repertory
from one another just as conductors of promenade concerts did. The *can-
can* migrated from Paris to London in the late 1860s, one observer com-
menting that it satisfied dandies more than did tedious old opera numbers.[14] Conversely, English ventriloquists crossed the Channel to Parisian
cafés-concerts, along with acrobats and other kinds of nonmusical entertain-
ers. All three types of vocal concerts under study here welcomed a slick new
group of song composers from various countries – Blumenthal, Wallace,
Kücken, and Pinsuti, for example – who had their songs performed variously in salons, the opera, the home, and the new vocal concerts (see
Exs. 4.5, 5.8, 7.4, 8.5).

THE EARLY OPERA "GALA"

Devoting concerts almost entirely to opera selections represented a major
change in concert tradition. The "opera gala," as it was called in the twentieth century, weakened the long equality and interdependence of vocal and

[12] Benedict Anderson, *Imagined Communities: Reflections on the Origin and Spread of Nationalism*, 2nd ed. (London: Verso, 1991), pp. 47–65.
[13] "Music and the Multitude," *MHG*, 12 December, 1868, p. 286; George Macfarren, "'The English Are Not a Musical People,'" *Cornhill Magazine* 18 (1868), 357–63. See also "English Music," *MHG*, 1 April 1868, p. 13, and "Modern English Music," *The Players: A Dramatic, Musical and Literary Journal*, 13 April 1861, p. 322.
[14] "*Almées* of the Alhambra," *The Mask*, April 1868, p. 82.

instrumental virtuosity in the concert hall. An early form of such concerts grew out of the tradition of private music making in courts and upper-class homes. As the miscellaneous benefit concert came under increasing fire, salon concerts assumed a new prominence in fashionable life, as has been studied in interesting ways in Paris and Toronto, Canada.[15] Such events then spawned public concerts designed partly on their model (Ex. 9.1, Ills. 24, 25). The early opera gala offered from ten to twenty pieces, songs as well as opera selections, with a few instrumental numbers included for contrast, all usually performed to piano accompaniment. The repertory included many canonic selections but did not present what was termed a "classical" repertory. As such the opera gala differed substantially from what Brahms and Stockhausen put on together in 1869 (Ill. 8). By the 1880s major singers gave an increasing number of opera galas in big halls with orchestral accompaniment. In 1886, for example, the diva Adelina Patti scheduled three concerts close together in Paris at the Théâtre Eden and then four in London at the Royal Albert Hall, a premier venue for such events.[16]

Opera galas were particularly numerous in Paris, offered both by singers and singing teachers. As fewer popular new operas came on stage, a widening variety of old opera selections remained in concert use, even though few of the works were still performed on stage. An early example of this kind of concert was given in Paris 1851 by the bass singer C. G. Nérini, who was then singing at La Scala (Ex. 9.1). Nérini's choices were fairly recent: he drew from *Marino Faliero* (1835), the first opera Donizetti composed for Paris; from *Bravo* (1839), one of Mercadante's biggest triumphs; and from Verdi's immensely popular *Ernani* (1844). A piece with an idiosyncratic canonic status appears in the song *Plaisir d'amour* (1784), by the Paris-based composer Jean-Paul-Égide Martini, which had long been inserted into operas and performed in concerts.

9.1 *Singer C. G. Nérini, Salle Herz, 20 February 1851*[17]

Air, *Bravo* (1839)	Mercadante
Romance	†Donizetti

[15] David Tunley, *Salons, Singers, and Songs: A Background to Romantic French Song, 1830–1870* (Aldershot, UK: Ashgate, 2002); and Kristina Marie Guiguet, *The Ideal World of Mrs. Widder's Soirée Musical: Social Identities and Musical life in Nineteenth-Century Ontario* (Gatineau, Quebec: Canadian Museum of Civilization, 2004).
[16] John Frederick Cone, *Adelina Patti: Queen of Hearts* (Boulder, Colo., 2001), pp. 172, 369.
[17] Salle Herz, BOP.

Solo for violin	* * *
Cavatina of Figaro, *Barbiere di Siviglia* (1816)	Rossini
Trio, *Ernani* (1844)	Verdi

–

Air, *Lucia di Lammermoor* (1835)	†Donizetti
Romance, *Plaisir d'amour ne dure qu'un moment*	†J.-P.-E. Martini
Solo for flute on Verdi's *Battiglia di Legnano* (1849)	*Emanuel Krakamp*
Romance, *Prière à la Madone*	Luigi Gordigiani
Air, *La Favorita* (1840)	†Donizetti
Duo, *Marino Faliero* (1835)	†Donizetti

A concert given in Paris by Mme Ronzi, née Scalese, a singer from a prominent musical family, illustrates how firmly a canonic repertory of opera selections was established in concerts by 1869 (Ill. 25). Mme Ronzi, said a reviewer, was "an artist *de la bonne école*" possessing "exquisite taste," whose concerts were always popular.[18] Verdi and Gounod were the only living composers on a program dominated by Rossini, Donizetti, and Bellini. Ronzi did not sing only well known music; here she drew pieces from *Beatrice di Tenda* (1833), *Italiana in Algieri* (1813), and *Maria de Rudenz* (1838), none of which had not been produced for at least fifteen years at the influential Théâtre Italien.[19] Her program also included three leading song composers – Blumenthal, Giovanni Lucantoni, and Adolphe Fumagalli – whose music became closely linked to opera selections. That the prosperous Franco-Italian opera composer Jules Alary provided accompaniment suggests that the concert drew a prestigious audience. For his part, Alary mingled cosmopolitan opera selections with popular songs at a concert he presented in 1873. Offering standard selections by Mozart, Cimarosa, Rossini, Auber, and Verdi, he closed each half with a piece by Edmond Lhuillier, a leading *chansonnier* of the *cafés-concerts*. Charles Gounod also wrote for such venues, for he was represented on the program not only by a duo from the opera *Roméo et Juliette* but also by a *mélodie* published in a collection of pieces sung at the *cafés-concerts*.[20]

Some composers aimed at the aristocracy in writing songs for salons, concerts, and inclusion in operas. Blumenthal presented a concert – listing

[18] "Auditions musicales," *RGM*, 7 May 1865, pp. 146–47; "Ronzi," François-Joseph Fétis, *Biographie universelle des musiciens et bibliographie général de la musique*, 8 vols., 2nd ed. (Paris: Didot, 1863–70), vol. 7, p. 307. Possibly a daughter of baritone Raffaelo Scalese, she seems to have married a nephew of the great Mme Guiseppina Ronzi, née de Bégnis, who at her death in 1853 was described as "one of the first actresses who graced the Italian lyric stage," *Musical World and Times* (New York), 6 August 1853, p. 213.
[19] Fold-out chart, Albert Soubise, *Le Théâtre Italien de 1801 à 1913* (Paris: Fischbacher, 1913).
[20] Salle Herz, BOP; "Sérénade," *Album des Théâtres et Concerts* (Paris: Le Bailly, 1869).

twenty-five titled patrons on his program – that illustrates the taste upper-class listeners considered to be "general" to them all (Ill. 24). Although Blumenthal offered several of his own pieces, his main concern was to represent a broad range of opera and song composers: he drew from recent pieces by Donizetti and Verdi and canonic selections by Boieldieu and Martin y Soler (the latter coming from *La scuola dei maritati* of 1795). As we saw in the program of Mme Ronzi, London salons heard songs composed for that context by Francesco Masini, Emanuele Biletta, and Paul Henrion. Both public and private concerts like this were numerous in London during the 1850s, often organized by the singer Giacinta Puzzi, *née* Toso. After an unpromising start at the King's Theatre Mme Puzzi did a thriving business in the concert world, working with her husband, the horn player Giovanni Puzzi.[21] Although opera halls were becoming less important to the social life of the upper classes, opera selections stayed central to their musical taste. A Beethoven trio might open a concert, but the world of classical music had little to do with these events, which presumed that listeners had heard music by a wide range of Italian and French composers and song writers. Donizetti was emerging as the key canonic figure in this musical sphere.

The same types of people heard a lot of British music at concerts near their country homes. Pieces by British composers dominated an 1859 concert patronized by a long list of nobles and gentry in the assembly rooms of the Borough of Hastings and St. Leonard's on the southeast coast (Ex. 9.2). Pieces from the classical and British canons came at the start of the concert – Beethoven and Gluck versus Callcott and Bishop – but ten pieces by living British composers were the core of the program. The glee lived on in such contexts, in this case one by rising balladeer John Hatton, set to words by John Donne. The *fantaisie* found a permanent home in such concerts, including one by the famous trumpeter Thomas Harper on Arne's iconic song, "The Soldier Tir'd," and another for the concertina by Richard Blagrove, brother of the leader of quartet concerts. Similar programs were also given to middle-class audiences in London. Choral conductor Henry Leslie put on a series of choral programs with songs by Hook and Lord Mornington that were regularly mentioned in *The Era*, a leading publication for the music halls.[22] Thus British vocal music continued to command a large and diverse set of publics.

---

[21] Mme Puzzi, CHP/RCM; E. Bradley Strauchen-Scherer, "Lost Luggage: Giovanni Puzzi and the Management of Giovanni Rubini's Farewell Tour of 1842," in *Music in the British Provinces 1690–1914*, Rachel Cowgill and Peter Holman (eds.) (Aldershot, UK: Ashgate, forthcoming).

[22] "Mr Henry Leslie's Choir," *The Era*, 12 January 1862, p. 11; "Store Street Concert Hall," *The Era*, 21 May 1871, p. 3.

9.2 *"Miscellaneous Concert," Borough of Hastings and St. Leonard's, Music Hall, 12 January 1859*[23]

String Trio in G, op. 9, no. 1	†Beethoven
Song, "When Midnight's darkest Veil"	Franz or Vinzenz Lachner
Aria, "Che faro," *Orphée et Eurydice* (1762/1774)	†Gluck
Fantaisie for cello	Servais
Song, "Friend of the Brave" (1814)	†Callcott
Song, "Lo! here the gentle Lark," violin obligato	†Bishop
Duet, "The exile's Home"	†Antoine Romagnesi
Fantaisie-caprice for violin, op. 11	Henry Vieuxtemps
Song, "The Village Blacksmith" (1855)	Willoughby Weiss
Glee, "Come, Live with me"	John Hatton
—	
Duet for concertina and violin	Henry Blagrove
New Ballad, "True Love never Dies"	Edward Hime
Song, "The Guard Ship"	Samuel Lover
Fantasia for trumpet on "The Soldier Tired"	†Arne/ *Thomas Harper*
Song, "My old Friend John," on melody from reign of James II	Edward Land
Solo for concertina, on *Guillaume Tell*	Rossini/ *Richard Blagrove*
Glee, "All among the Barley"	Elizabeth Stirling
Song, "Nothing more"	William Winn
Finale, "God save the Queen"	†John Bull

Concerts by *Liedertafel* choruses in Germany offered music even more homogeneous in genre and national origin. In 1850 the Leipzig opera chorus performed a program in the Centralhalle where every composer was German or Austrian, as had not often happened at the Gewandhaus (Ex. 9.3). Although the eminent Ferdinand David was featured, lieder and choral songs dominated the program, most prominently pieces by Mendelssohn similar to those we have seen done in the Viennese Evening Entertainments (Ex. 4.2). The piece from Beethoven's *Fidelio* must have seemed like a *Liedertafel* number in this context, and two comic recitations made the occasion similar in conviviality to the *café-concert*. Demand for cosmopolitan repertory by no means died in Leipzig, however. A concert

---

[23] Thomas Harper, CPH/RCM. See Allan Atlas, "The Victorian Concertina," *NCMR* 3 (2006), 33–62.

put on in the Centralhalle by the concert agent Bernard Ullman in 1874 combined numerous virtuoso pieces, only one by a German, with selections by Rossini, Donizetti, and Meyerbeer.[24]

9.3 *Leipzig Opera Chorus, Centralhalle, 17 June 1850*[25]

Song for male chorus	†Mendelssohn
Song, "Die Welt ist so schön"	C. L. Fischer
Andante und Scherzo capriccioso for violin, op. 16	*Ferdinand David*
Song	Franz or Vinzenz Lachner
Two lieder	David
Recitation, "The Old Comedian"	*Anastasius Grün*
Sonntagslied	Kücken
—	
Chorus and solos of the Prisoners, Act I, *Fidelio*	†Beethoven
Caprice for violin, op. 20	*David*
Lied, "Die Elfen"	Julius Rietz
Lieder	†Schubert
Humorous Recitation, "I'm a proud Berliner"	*Grün*
Male Chorus, "Es ist Bestimmt von Gottes Rath," *Gesänge*, op. 47	†Mendelssohn

Viennese musicians offered a good deal more music by German composers after 1850 than previously, but usually joined by some Italian selections. A concert at the store of a leading Viennese piano manufacturer, for example, featured pieces by Heinrich Esser and Heinrich Proch and a lied in Austrian dialect (as in Ex. 7.10) but also included excerpts by Donizetti and Rossini (Ex. 9.4). Private concerts now also mixed Austrian song with Italian opera, so different from the repertory Frances Trollope heard at aristocratic salons in 1835. Proch arranged a private concert at the home of the Prince Coburg-Cohary in 1856 that mingled songs by Esser and Schubert with pieces by Donizetti and Luigi Gordigiani.[26]

9.4 *Singer Caroline Dziwientnik, Salon of Court Fortepiano-Maker Herr J. B. Streicher, Vienna, 18 March 1860*[27]

Aria, *Dom Sebastian, King of Portugal* (1838)	†Donizetti
Fantasy for violin	Vieuxtemps

---

[24] Regional history collection, SBL.   [25] Verschiedene Concerte, 1850–70, SGML.
[26] *Konzert bei Prinz Coburg-Cohary*, March 1856, PA/GMF.   [27] PA/GMF.

Lied in Austrian dialect	
Two lieder for male voice	Esser
Lied, "Die stille Wasserose"	Proch
Declamation by male speaker	
Konzertstück for Piano	
Aria, *Il Barbiere di Siviglia* (1816)	†Rossini

THE BALLAD CONCERT

Concerts built around the ballad broke more decisively from the cosmopolitan operatic tradition than any other musical event in this period save the *Liedertafel*. If Italian opera was traditionally linked with the nobility, the parlor song held a distinctively bourgeois identity, thanks to the sentimental nature of the texts and the commercialism that pervaded its performances. The term *popular music* can therefore appropriately be applied to the ballad concerts.[28] We have seen that the ballad and related kinds of songs gradually dominated Anglo-American programs: combined with opera selections at the Pantheon in 1786 and Boston in 1799 (Exs. 2.8, 2.9), made independent of Italian texts in Hull in 1834 (Ill. 21), featured in Birmingham in 1844 (Ex. 5.8), and put into a canonic framework in Kent in 1859 (Ex. 9.2). This development culminated in John Boosey's founding of the London Ballad Concerts in 1867, where British ballads, songs, and glees became a repertory in their own right, lasting until 1936. Under his careful management, the series soon controlled the song market throughout Britain. Many listeners took little heed of idealists who condemned publishers for paying singers to perform "royalty" ballads. Commercialism added emotive and dramatic elements to ballad concerts as also happened in virtuoso concerts.

Boosey's series became a major alternative to the Philharmonic Society and the Monday Popular Concerts, both of which also had links with music publishing. Performances occurred once or twice a week, October through June, in a hall holding 2,000 people, and even more went to similar events at the Crystal Palace and other venues. As many as 8,601 people were reported at a ballad concert in the Transept of the Palace in July 1866 and 17,000 at another one in August. One commentator declared that "[t]here are thousands who would never go to St. James's Hall to hear a quartet or a sonata, that can thoroughly appreciate a 'good old song'; and for this numerous class the Ballad Concerts supply exactly what they like."[29]

[28] Scott, *Singing Bourgeois*, pp. viii–xii and *passim*.
[29] *TL*, 30 July 1866, p. 7; *TL*, 8 August 1866, p. 11; "Ballad Concerts," *Monthly Musical Record*, 1 February 1871, p. 24; Scott, *Singing Bourgeois*, pp. 122–23.

Because some of his public was quite well heeled, in the early 1870s Boosey began holding "morning" concerts at 2 P.M. on Mondays.

The Boosey concerts maintained a highly homogeneous repertory and self-conscious national identity (Ex. 9.5). Italian opera selections were rare at the series; the only music by Rossini came from his sacred works. The great majority of the twenty to twenty-five pieces on a program were by British composers, except for a few songs by foreigners such as Blumenthal or Pinsuti. Three or four instrumental pieces punctuated a Boosey program, usually solos for piano, violin, or cello, sometimes by Thalberg or Liszt. Arabella Goddard played the piano pieces most often in the 1870s. Three vocal genres alternated on the programs: the solo ballad, the glee for three or four voices, and the part-song for a medium-sized chorus. A piece for multiple voices usually opened and closed each half. A highly skilled accompanist served as director of the proceedings, and an organlike harmonium or a string ensemble occasionally supported the choral pieces.

A regular visitor to the ballad concerts would get to know a British canon of songs since the late seventeenth century, that "epoch of our great national music," as was said about "Westminster Drollery," supposedly composed in 1672. Pieces by Carey, Arne, Shield, Dibdin, Webbe, and Bishop emerged as something of a Pantheon in this area of musical life.[30] During their first several seasons the programs included so many old pieces that the concerts began taking on an antiquarian air. Boosey soon brought the concerts back to the mainstream of taste, offering only two or three old pieces at each concert. The 1870 concert booklets stated the policy bluntly: "The Programmes will consist almost entirely of Modern Music and include some NEW SONGS and BALLADS by POPULAR COMPOSERS, Written expressly for these Concerts." Boosey's publications were naturally advertised on the covers of the program booklets.

The order of pieces at a concert was governed chiefly by the specialties of a concert's five to seven soloists. A young corps of singers began their careers with the Boosey series, which can be seen in the program of 1870 where all five soloists were between twenty-eight and thirty-eight years old (Ex. 9.5). The singers went on to varied careers, singing opera or oratorio, often in distinguished capacities. Helen Lemens-Sherington and W. H. Cummings became professors at the Royal Academy of Music, Cummings contributing significantly to the study of English music.

---

[30] "Ballad Concert," *TL*, 24 June 1878, p. 10; *Popular Music of the Olden Time; a Collection of Ancient Songs, Ballads and Dance Tunes, Illustrative of the National Music of England* (London: Chappell, 1855–1859).

9.5 Final Concert, London Ballad Concerts, St. James's Hall, 21 May 1870[31]

Part-song, *O Hush Thee, my Babie*	Arthur Sullivan
Song, *In Sheltered Vale*	Carl Formes
Song, *The Mother's Dream*	Sullivan
New song, *Always Alone*	Henriette
New song, *Ladye Fair*	Mrs. Alfred Phillips
Song, "Birds in the Night," *Cox and Box*;	
The Long Lost Brothers (1866)	Sullivan
Piano solo: *Fantaisie* on *Les Huguenots*, op. 20	Thalberg
Glee, "Fox Jumped over the Parson's Gate,"	
Guy Mannering (1816, with Thomas Attwood)	†Bishop
Song, *Rose of Erin* (words by Claribel)	Benedict
New song, *Lillie's Good Night*	Elizabeth Philp

—

Part-song, *Ever True*	*John Hatton*
New Song, *Corisande* (words by Gilbert)	James Molloy
Song, *A Bridal Song*	Charlotte Sainton-Dolby
Duet, *Evening Song*	Virginia Gabriel
Piano solo: *Home! Sweet Home!*	
with variations (1859)	Thalberg
Song, "Love has eyes," *The Farmer's Wife* (1815)	†Bishop
Song, *Since Long Ago*	Mrs. Philips
Song, *Somebody*	Walter Macfarren
New song, *Marching Along*	Molloy
Ballad, *Poor Tom Bowling, or the Sailor's*	†Dibdin
Epitaph (1790)	
Part-song, "Remembrance," *Vier Lieder* (1844)	†Mendelssohn

It was common to find five women composers on a program, as in this instance. Composing songs had become quite respectable for women, an activity more open to them than writing instrumental music.[32] Mrs Alfred Phillips, who also wrote such theatre pieces as *An Organic Affection* (1852), was represented twice. Charlotte Sainton-Dolby, renowned for singing at

---

[31] Boosey Concerts, CPH/RCM.

[32] Paula Gillett, *Musical Women in England, 1870–1914: 'Encroaching on All Man's Privileges'* (New York: St. Martin's Press, 2000) and "Entrepreneurial Women Musicians in Britain: From the 1790s to the Early 1900s," in Weber (ed.), *Musician as Entrepreneur*, pp. 198–220; Weber, "From Miscellany to Homogeneity: Concert Programs at the Royal Academy and Royal College of Music in the 1880s," *Music and British Culture*, pp. 299–320.

oratorio concerts, had been Boosey's main adviser for designing the series. Virginia Gabriel, who had studied in Paris, wrote sophisticated pieces for piano and best-selling ballads such as *Evening Song*. Other contributors were Mary Alice Smith (well known for her chamber works) and the cultlike poet Claribel (Charlotte Barnard). Pieces by Helen Selina, Countess Gifford, were sung long after her death in 1867.

Male composers represented at the ballad concerts were for the most part specialists in the idiom who did not often compose for classical music concerts. John Hatton (1809–1886), director of the 1870 concert, influenced the evolution of the ballad to a particular extent. Music director at the Princess Theatre, Hatton wrote incidental music for Shakespearean plays and published close to 150 songs. The Irishman James Lyman Molloy (1837–1909) moved the ballad away from its long-standing Italian lyric style, although he later became private chamberlain to Pope Leo XIII.[33] Arthur Sullivan (1852–1900) today is associated with his famous operettas, but in the 1870s most knew him for his ballads, which were performed frequently at the Boosey concerts. Sullivan's colleagues in the classical music world had seen him as the hope of British music but soon wrote him off as their "lost leader."[34] Nevertheless, a few composers who participated in the classical music world also wrote songs for the Boosey concerts. Walter Macfarren (1826–1905), brother of George Macfarren and professor at the Royal Academy of Music, wrote widely in the idiom and trained many of the best known women song composers.[35]

Although the Boosey concerts included a few composers we associate with classical music, in most cases the pieces were composed for convivial contexts and for that reason were not part of classical music repertories at that time. The four-part song by Mendelssohn that ended the 1870 concert typified this practice, having a long performing history outside classical music concerts, similar to the Viennese Evening Entertainments (Exs. 4.2, 5.11). More classical pieces were performed at the concerts by the mid-1880s, including one of Beethoven's early piano sonatas and a violin solo by the eighteenth-century Jean-Marie Leclair. At the same time, the number of pieces by women composers declined significantly, for the commercial success of the ballad drew more men to the field. At the same time, ballad concerts were started for a working-class clientele in music halls, sharing

---

[33] Scott, *Singing Bourgeois*, pp. 125, 130, 152–3.
[34] Meirion Hughes, *English Musical Renaissance and the Press: 1850–1914: Watchmen of Music* (Aldershot, UK: Ashgate, 2002), p. 107.
[35] Weber, "From Miscellany to Homogeneity," *Music and British Culture*, pp. 312–23, 318–19.

the stage with circus acts. The temperance movement subsidized "music for the people" at the Royal Victoria Hall on Waterloo Street, which later became the Old Vic. Leaders of temperance organizations – aristocratic as well as middle-class – sometimes attended the concerts.[36] Opera excerpts and instrumental numbers were as numerous as ballads in this context.

Like promenade concerts, ballad concerts were not recognized by critics as part of serious musical life. In 1878 a reviewer in *The Times* complained that the distinguished songs of the eighteenth century were giving way to "ditties" and demanded that Boosey "raise the level of his performance" because "the line ought to be drawn at the ordinary sentimental drawing-room song, without artistic merit or originality."[37] The massive market for ballads induced musicians specializing in classical music to appear at Boosey's concerts but only at their peril. *The Times* chastised Arabella Goddard, the respected interpreter of Beethoven, for offering "a silly *pièce-de-salon*" by Julius Schulhoff, whose playing Liszt greatly admired.[38] The authoritative *Academy and Literature*, reporting on a student concert at the Royal Academy of Music, derided a song by Alice Heathcote, "Why, lovely charmer," because it "belongs to a style of composition which should not be encouraged at the Academy."[39] But ballad concerts did have defenders in the press. Another *Times* critic suggested grounds for accommodation between ballads and classics when he argued that the Boosey concerts had earned a "legitimate acceptation" by many people, however different the events might be from the chamber music performances held in the same hall. Songs were one of four main types of taste, he declared, for "as there are people who like oratorios or operas, and people who like symphonies, quartets, sonatas, etc., so there are people who like genuine songs and ballads, old and new."[40]

THE MUSIC HALL IN LONDON

We can begin speaking of "popular music" with particular confidence when we turn to the subject of music halls and *cafés-concerts* in the 1850s and 1860s. I hazard to say that music halls grew faster and on a larger scale than the *cafés-concerts*, but the latter ended up enjoying greater intellectual independence from classical music life. We will inquire here into the interaction of songs

[36] "Royal Victoria Hall," *LT*, 5 November 1881, p. 6; 17 December 1991, p. 9; 24 April 1882, p. 10.
[37] "Ballad Concert," *LT*, 24 June 1878, p. 10.   [38] Ibid.; Hamilton, *After the Golden Age*, Ch. 5.
[39] "Concerts," *Academy and Literature*, 1 March 1879, p. 202.
[40] "London Ballad Concerts," *LT*, 15 April 1873, p. 8.

and opera selections in music hall programs. The common culture of opera played a central role in this kind of entertainment, linking a self-consciously "popular" institution to long-standing musical traditions.

The traditional singing of ballads in British taverns and clubs led to organized concerts in taverns and the more up-scale "song-and-supper" rooms in the 1820s, and then to the much bigger music halls in the late 1840s. The song-and-supper room, usually in a wing of a public house, was "determinedly anti-feminist," noted Harold Scott, in a time when women were taking increasingly central roles in musical life.[41] The most prominent one was a Covent Garden venue called Evans's, where a variety of amateur and professional singers would perform before a paid audience that could eat or drink. A "chairman" or "conductor" supervised the interaction of performers and the audience, sometimes providing the piano accompaniment. The rooms were linked closely to the musical theatre and the literary world. Charles Dickens noted in *Boz* in 1839 that "the more musical portion of the play-going community" went afterwards to a "harmonic meeting," where eighty to a hundred people, overwhelmingly men, interacted closely with the music by banging their pewter cups when they liked a song or a singer.[42] Thackeray stated that such rooms drew "low shop-boys and attorney's clerks," more generally "young rakish-looking lads with a dubious sprinkling of middle-aged youth and stalwart red-faced fellows from the country."[43]

Diaries written in 1840 and 1850 by Charles Rice, a courier for the British Museum who sang at the better known rooms, give us a glimpse into the interplay between singer and listener at the "Grapes" in Southwark on 9 March 1840:

Room crowded, 211 paying at doors; Singing went off flatly at first, but loudly applauded afterwards. Myers sang "The Old House at Home," very well; but some of his efforts were much hissed during the evening; – and on his walking up to sing once or twice, the audience called for me, and some bother ensued, before peace was obtained, and he received some more "Goose" for his pains. Ryan . . . attempted "Jolly Nose" (in character) but the effort was dreadfully faint. . . . Mrs Ryan does not appear to be much liked here, as she was not encored all the Evening. I sang this evening "Ballooning," "Jackdaw of Rheims," "Billy Taylor," "St. Anthony,"

[41] Harold Scott, *Early Doors: Origins of the Music Hall* (London: Nicholson & Watson, 1946), p. 116.
[42] Charles Dickens, *Sketches by "Boz": Illustrative of Every-day-life and Every-day-people* (London: Chapman and Hall, 1839), pp. 363, 64–65.
[43] William Thackeray, *Miscellanies, Prose and Verse*, 4 vols. (London: Bradbury & Evans, 1855–1860), vol. 2, p. 356.

"Billy Crow," "Tom Noddy," and others, which were continually encored . . . Room closed at 1/2 12.[44]

Two of the songs were written by music directors at major theatres: "Jolly nose" by George Rodwell (Covent Garden Theatre) and "Old house at home," from *Francis the First* (1838), by Edward James Loder (Princess Theatre). Rice's chronology includes a fairly wide selection of pieces from early English opera, similar to that at the Boosey Ballad Concerts. The earliest mentioned was *Sally in our Alley* by Henry Carey, first performed at Drury Lane in 1717. Pieces by Henry Purcell and Thomas Arne were probably also sung at the rooms, though none crops up in Rice's chronology. Many pieces dated from between 1770 and 1800, particularly songs that Dibdin performed in one-man shows such as *The Wags* and *The Oddities*, called "table entertainments" for a small theatre. Aristocratic patronage of song writing appears in a glee cited fifteen times, "To all you ladies now at land," that J. W. Callcott set to words by the Earl of Dorset. Similarly, Rice noted that a group of singers turned up at a place called Yorkshire Stingo to sing some "highly sacred Concert Music," probably from Handel's oratorios.[45]

International opera was represented prominently in the repertory. The earliest piece Rice cited was quite unusual, "Revenge he cries and the traitor dies," set to a march from Antonio Salieri's *Tarare* (1788). He also reported hearing a translation of "Das klinget so herrlich" from Mozart's *Die Zauberflöte* (1791) and an aria from Spohr's *Zemire und Azor* (1819). The "domestification" of Italian opera is indicated by the performance of "As I view these scenes so charming," from Henry Bishop's adaptation of Bellini's *Sonnambula* (1831), mentioned eight times in the diaries. Further evidence for the wide public appreciation of Auber appears in the five times pieces were drawn from *Gustavus III*, *La Muette de Portici*, or *Fra Diavolo* (1828–1833). Thus did the cosmopolitan and the mundane come together at the song-and-supper rooms, described by Harold Scott as "Rossini and refreshment tickets, Auber and alcohol, Bellini and bottled beer."[46] British specialists in popular song nonetheless dominated the song-and-supper rooms. William Wilson's "Tom Noddy" and "Billy Taylor" turned up almost fifty times each. Henry Bishop also loomed large in this context, his songs occurring at least fifteen times, mostly from *Guy Mannering, or The Gipsy's*

44 *Tavern Singing in Early Victorian London: Diaries of Charles Rice for 1840 and 1850*, Laurence Senelick (ed.) (London: Society for Theatre Research, 1997), p. 55; Scott, *Early Doors*, pp. 55, 117; Peter Bailey (ed.), *Music Hall: Business of Pleasure* (Milton Keynes, UK: Open University Press, 1986).
45 *Tavern Singing*, p. 163.   46 Scott, *Early Doors*, p. 79.

Prophecy (1816). "The Chough and the crow to roost have gone to roost" from that work rivaled *Home! Sweet Home!* in frequency of performance for a long time.

In the 1840s music halls opened up the tradition of convivial music-making to a far larger public by expanding the range of entertainments framed by an orchestra and welcoming women both as singers and listeners. Male dominance of song culture declined significantly; although men might still be more numerous in the audience, women immediately came to the fore as singers. Music halls drew a more noticeably working-class public than any other type of European concert. The music hall in Shoreditch, a poor community north of the City of London, reportedly welcomed 20,000 customers a year by 1872.[47] A well-off public was attracted to the leading London halls by special seating and occasional "morning" concerts during the week. Indeed, Derek Scott argues that the cockney character at the halls derived in large part from middle-class culture.[48] By 1866 there were thirty music halls in the metropolis that could hold more than 1,500 people and many more in a few cases. In the West End, the Royal Alhambra Palace – a "promenade" theatre, a step up from conventional music halls – offered twenty-five singers, an orchestra of sixty, and a ballet of a 150. Most music halls had no more than ten players, however, and so were far smaller than the ensembles at promenade concerts.[49]

Opera thrived in this context, used by theatre managers to demonstrate the respectability and musical ambitions of their enterprises. The opera selections performed in music halls tended to be consistently well known, as compared with those done in song-and-supper rooms. The eighteenth-century was represented by little more than Mozart, and certainly nothing as unusual as the Salieri piece sung at the "Grapes." That led the *Musical World* to come down from on high to declare that the music halls were "rapidly degenerating" from the musical standards of the song-and-supper rooms and becoming "a great public 'social evil.'"[50] Weston's Music Hall in Holborn advertised that it would offer "Mozart's great works," a Rossini medley, a piece from Auber's *Gustavus III* (1833), and, interestingly enough, a medley for four instruments based on music by Mendelssohn and Wallace. The Oxford Music Hall tended to announce selections just from major operas

[47] "Alhambra, Shoreditch," *The Era*, 7 January 1872, p. 13.
[48] Scott, *Sounds of the Metropolis*, Ch. 7.
[49] Dagmar Kift, *Victorian Music Hall: Culture, Class and Conflict*, Roy Kift (trans.) (Cambridge: Cambridge University Press, 1996), pp. 2, 17–21; "Tasmanian Intelligence," *MHG*, 11 April 1868, p. 5; Scott, *Sounds of the Metropolis*, p.?.
[50] "London Music Halls," *MW*, 9 August 1862, p. 502.

such as Donizetti's *Lucrezia Borgia* (1833), Verdi's *Simon Boccanegra* (1857), and Auber's *La Circassienne* (1861).[51] For that matter, in 1859 Canterbury Hall, located in Lambeth across the river from Westminster, presented the first British rendition of Gounod's *Faust*, in concert style. Still, the core of the repertory was British songs, which persisted from the song-and-supper rooms and were supplemented with new pieces by many specialists composing for the halls.

Nonmusical entertainment became increasingly important in music halls in the mid-1850s, earlier than in Paris's *cafés-concerts*. Music halls that possessed a substantial orchestra offered dance acts on topical themes and traditional pantomime done on a large scale, all dancers wearing costumes. Gymnasts, acrobats, and ventriloquists became standard repertory at the larger halls, and trained animals became common as well. A report on what was done at Canterbury Hall was typical for 1868 (Ex. 9.6):

9.6 *Programme of the Amusements, Canterbury Hall, Lambeth, London, 1 April 1868*[52]

- Mr A. Coombs, singing "Look out for a rainy day"
- Mr Daniel, "a nigger of high order," instrumentalist, vocalist & dancer
- Miss Louie Sherrington, serio-comique, "Upper Ten [Thousand]"
- Mr Harry Liston, "a public favorite," singing "Ginger" and "Nobody's Child"
- Mr Vance, humorous impersonations, "Chickalcary Cove"
- Signor Ethardo, acrobat, on the Spiral Staircase
- Mr Hamilton, baritone from Evans's
- Watteau Ballet, 3 women, 1 man, "Parisian Carnival Quadrille" and a Can-can
- Comic pantomime ballet, 3 men, 1 woman
- "Revels of the Athletes," 40 dancers
- Orchestra under Mr Alfred Lee, "best known for 'Champagne Charlie'"

Some venues already offered "variety" shows that deemphasized songs. An 1870 bill for the Boston Music Hall, for example, listed only one vocalist and a "flutina" solo among the many acts of the Adelphi Theatre Comique Star Company.[53]

As we have seen with the English promenade concerts, tension arose over who "possessed" the repertory common to music halls and classical music

[51] "London Music Halls," *Era*, 9 February 1862, p. 16; "The Oxford," *Era*, 16 February 1862, p. 14.
[52] "Canterbury Hall," 1 April 1868, p. 13.   [53] Music Hall, Boston, 26 March 1870, AAS.

concerts. The *Music Halls' Gazette* did acknowledge links between the two worlds, stating that a vocal music concert at the Crystal Palace drew many music hall singers, who were fond of "hearing good music well sung."[54] But another writer, probably the publisher Richard Allerton, averred that music by Meyerbeer, Offenbach, Verdi, Auber, or Strauss "is not 'classical' . . . [it is instead] proven by its popularity . . . and, for our own part, we are very glad that it is not."[55] The terms "classical" and "popular" had indeed become cultural opposites in the press. Music halls "alone have had the foresight to discover in what direction popular taste was tending," this writer declared; he told "the *habitués* of the Temples of High Art in St. James's" not to force on others "a deliciously incomprehensible quartett by Beethoven, or a sublime sonata by Schubert." By contrast, a report on a night at the upscale Oxford music hall did borrow vocabulary from the other musical world, asking "have not Champagne Charlie" and "Walking in the Zoo" "become almost classical?"[56]

Thus did the world of classical music music draw particular scorn in Britain for presumptuous claims to knowledge and high taste. Peter Bailey has suggested how a different kind of knowledge, or "knowingness," functioned in the music halls. A major feature of music hall singing was a conceit, a wink of the eye, that conveyed a "knowing" discernment by the artiste, with which the audience also participated while interpreting verbal and musical allusions. "Knowingness might be defined as what everybody knows," wrote Bailey, "but some know better than others."[57] Musical knowledge did not bring as high an empowerment in the music hall as in the classical music world, either to performers or critics. Indeed, a singer might well have to struggle to keep the audience's attention.

THE *CAFÉ-CONCERT* IN PARIS

During the 1850s and 1860s the Parisian *café-concert* resembled the London music hall in many respects. Both featured performers singing "in character" for audiences who could eat, drink, talk, or interact with what happened on stage. Opera selections linked popular songs to the common culture of musical theatre. Acrobats, jugglers, and ventriloquists added an element of *variété*. But the *cafés-concerts* drew more people from the middle classes

---

[54] "Musical Performances," *MHG*, 11 April 1868, p. 3.
[55] Lead editorial, *MHG*, 5 September 1868, p. 172.
[56] "London Music Halls," *Era*, 5 March 1871, p. 12.
[57] Peter Bailey, *Popular Culture and Performance in the Victorian City* (Cambridge: Cambridge University Press, 1998), p. 128.

than did music halls, and their venues were not as numerous or as large in scale. The *café-concert* emerged from a breakdown in legal restrictions on entertainments just before the Revolution of 1848, followed by a loosening of rules that brought productions in costume by the late 1860s. The new freedom opened up vast new opportunities for show people to put on circuses and horse shows as well as concerts. The *café-concert* thus emerged from a cathartic interaction between entertainment and politics, bringing a certain kind of democratization to French leisure activities.[58]

Like the music hall, the *café-concert* grew out of a long tradition of song clubs dominated by men. The gender bias not only derived from social etiquette but also from the banning of women from the learned craft of writing *chansons* in Le Caveau. During the 1830s and 1840s women were thought foreign to the *cafés-chantants* and *goguettes* where *chansons* were performed to *airs du couplet*; the context was in effect more private than the London song-and-supper rooms. The *cafés-concerts* thus brought major change to public life when they introduced women into song culture. During the mid-1840s a few entrepreneurs began putting on concerts in the open air on the Champs Elysées: a half dozen men and women would perform alone or in pairs with an orchestra of ten or twelve players. When the 1848 revolution made entertainment monopolies ineffective, Isaac Strauss began directing promenade concerts with pieces of *opéra*, *opéra-bouffe*, and *vaudeville*, along with revolutionary choruses, as we see in a program from the summer of 1848 (Ex. 9.7). From the start *cafés-concerts* offered more music from domestic opera than was done in Britain. The *parodie burlesque* of Meyerbeer's *Robert-le-Diable* cited here was in a genre that went back some 200 years, and the *scène bouffe* grew from the tradition of the increasingly serious *opéra comique*.

9.7 *Concert directed by Isaac Strauss, Jardin d'Hiver [1848]*[59]

Valse, *Le Baise-Main*	*Strauss*
Chant national, *La Françoise*, sung by Les Enfants de Paris	Marc Leprévost
Air, *Straniera* (1829)	†Bellini
Fantaisie on themes from *Moïse* for piano & melodium	Rossini/?

58 Concetta Condemi, *Les Cafés-concerts: Histoire d'un divertissement (1849–1914)* (Paris: Quai Voltaire, 1992), p. 60 and *passim*; Marc-Constantin, *Histoire des cafés-concerts et des cafés de Paris*, 2nd ed. (Paris: Renauld, 1872); E. A. D., *Les Cafés-concerts en 1866* (Paris: Charles Egrot, 1866); "Les Cafés-concerts," *Gazette de Paris*, 30 August 1857, pp. 3–4.
59 Jardin d'Hiver, BOP. "Jenny" is found in Music Collection, GRI; the Weber concerto was published as *Le Croisé* under the influence of Liszt.

Air, *Sonnambula* (1831)	†Bellini
Air, *La Gazza Ladra* (1817)	Rossini
Fantaisie for violin on themes from Donizetti's	
La Favorita	*Bernardin*
Air, *La Dame Blanche* (1825)	†Boieldieu
Polka, *Des Lampions*, chorus & orchestra	*Strauss*
—	
Concert-Stück, orchestrated, titled *Le Croisé*	†Weber
Air, "Il canto di Calabre"	Ercole Mécatti
Mélodie, Le Bengalis	†Hippolyte Monpou
Mélodie, Jenny l'ouvrière	J.-G. Arnauld
L'Andalouse	†Monpou
Waltz, *Il n'y a qu'un l'avis*	*Strauss*
Turkish Polka, *Souvenir du Bosphore*	*Strauss*
Air, *Cheval de Bronze* (1835)	Auber
Romance dramatique, Marguerite et Marie	Delatour
Chorus, *La Marche Républicaine*, sung	
by Les Enfants de Paris	
Scène bouffe, *Je suis enrhumé du cerveau*	
(1845)	Victor Parizot
Parodie burlesque, *Titi à la représentation de*	
Robert-le-Diable (Meyerbeer, 1831)	Ernest Déjazet

At least five prominent *cafés-concerts* were operating on the Champs-Elysée or near the Palais-Royal by the summer of 1850. Patrons were required to purchase food or drink but not a ticket; smoking was permitted, and beer as well as wine was served, changes that drew complaints in the press. The patrons were fairly prosperous. A skeptical observer described the public in 1853 as "people from the middling classes of small shopkeepers, lesser *rentiers* of the Marais, young clerks and bailiff assistants, . . . who for want of anything better to do hear a *chansonette* over coffee, a *couplet* while downing a beer."[60] A comment fifteen years later indicates the importance of *cafés-concerts* to a locality: "businessmen and their employees and workers, chiefly from that *quartier*, go there once their work is done, with no attempt to dress up or to pay attention to the hour."[61] By that time gentlemen, and even some prosperous women, had begun going to famous halls such as the Eldorado. In 1889 a journalist looked back to the 1860s, when "both male

[60] *Almanach de l'illustration* (Paris, 1853), p. 32.
[61] E. de Biéville in *Le Siècle*, quoted in *l'Eldorado et la question des cafés-concerts* (Paris: L. Hugonis, 1875), p. 20. See also *Mémoires de Thérésa écrits par elle-même* (Paris: E. Dentu, 1865), pp. 231–32.

and female singers sat near the stage, drinking and humming the tunes, taking their turn in collegial fashion." He loved the "serious repertory of which the public can never get enough, . . . that is, as long as the music does not begin to bore."[62]

Daily programs announced in periodicals in 1850–1851 provide a detailed picture of repertory at the early *cafés-concerts*. The Pavillon d'Horloge appeared on the Champs-Elysées as early as 1844; owned by Mlle Anna Picolo, a singer as well as *limonadière* and *directrice*, it eventually moved indoors, near the new Palais d'Industrie, in a hall whose main floor seated 500 people.[63] A program given there in 1850 alternated between male and female voices and between opera selections and *vaudeville*-like numbers (Ex. 9.8). Although no more than two singers could perform at once, the skits of one or two people were focused on character types that sprang directly from the *vaudeville* tradition, alternating between comic and romantic themes. Costumes like those standard at music halls were not allowed in Paris until 1867, but performers drew from the long French tradition of mimicry. Even though the old *timbres* had largely disappeared, as late as 1869 a commentator remarked that a singer at the Alhambra "interprets *vaudeville* perfectly," though the *chansonette* "Le Pifferaro" seemed beyond her ken.[64] The program offered "The Old Corporal," the drunken "Jolly Lajoie," and diverse Normans, a region long associated with *vaudeville*. Sexual allusion was rife, as in "The Real Joan of Arc" (Jeanne d'Arc, *inédit*) and "Little Norman Pin-Ups" (Les petites affiches Normandes) on another program. The canonic repertory of overtures by Boieldieu, Isouard, and Berton suggests the presence of song connoisseurs comparable to those in London's song-and-supper clubs, though in neither case did such a group achieve an authority comparable to those in classical music world. A commentator articulated how ordinary people now "possessed" the operatic repertory: "Ah, poor Rossini! If you only knew! The unfortunate Meyerbeer! How badly you are all treated!"[65]

---

[62] André Chadourne, *Les Cafés-concerts* (Paris: Dentu, 1889), pp. 86, 99.

[63] *Gazette de Paris*, 13 September 1857, pp. 5–6. Also cited were the Café Morel, Pavillon des Ambassadeurs, Café-Concert du Luxembourg, and Chateau des Fleurs. See program of the Café Morel in *l'Argus: Journal-programme des spectacles et des concerts*, 25 May 1850, p. 3. An estimated 300 *cafés-concerts* existed in Paris by 1890, two decades later than in London; see Condemi, *Les Cafés-concerts*, p. 60.

[64] "L'Alhambra," *Le Théâtre-concert: Revue critique des théâtres, concerts et curiosités de Paris*, 6 November 1869, p. 1. See "Airs de vaudeville," *RGM*, 2 June 1839, pp. 201–2. Henry Gidel, *Le vaudeville* (Paris: Presse Universitaire, 1986).

[65] Joseph Lassouquère, *Cafés-concerts, moralité, extrait du Courrier du Gers* (Auch: Foix, 1865), p. 4.

9.8 *Pavillon de l'Horloge, Champs-Elysées, 15 May 1850*[66]

Overture	†Boieldieu, *Les Voitures Versées* (Carriages Upended, 1808)
Zélie	"The Shepherdess"
Charles Constant	"Jolly Lajoie"
Mme Devillers	"The Warbler's Mate"
Martin	*Zaira* [†Bellini, 1831 or Mercadante, 1829]
Mlle Bouvard	"Daniel"
Magne	"The Stranger"
Dubouchet	"John the Norman"
Mlle Carmen	Rossini, *La Gazza Ladra* (1817)
Orchestra	"Quadrille and Polka of Boltico"
—	
Orchestra	"The Siege of Misolodghy"
Mme Carmen	"Sweet Marjolam"
Constant	"The Grosbeak"
Mlle Zélie	"A Gracious Sorceress"
Magne	"The Old Corporal"
Mlle Adrienne	"The Real Joan of Arc"
Dubouchet	†Donizetti, *Lucia di Lammermoor* (1835)
Magne	†Weber, *Robin des Bois* (*Der Freischütz*, 1824)
Constant	"Jolly Lajoie"
The Orchestra	Polka
Martin	Rossini, *La Gazza Ladra*
Devillers	†Nicolo Isouard, *Jeannot and Colin* (1814)
Overture	†Berton, *Le Délire, ou les Suites d'une Erreur* (1799)

During the 1860s *cafés-concerts* developed a greater variety of entertainments, as we see in a program at the Grand Casino de Paris, near the Place de la Bastille (Ill. 23). Nine singers each did one to three songs, followed by a ballet pantomime ("The Millers"), several acrobatic acts, and finally a series of eighteen operatic duets, as was conventional at the end of a *café-concert*. Six pieces were in *vaudeville*, *opéra-bouffe*, or *saynète* (skit); four were from *opéra-comique*; and three came from full-length *opéras*. The oldest was a *vaudeville – Monsieur et Madame Dénis, ou La Veille de la Saint-Jean* (1808) – and the newest were George Bizet's *La Jolie Fille de Perth* and a

---

[66] *La Caricature: Programme illustré des théâtres*, 15 May 1850, p. 3. See Eugène Héros, "Le Pavillon de l'Horloge et le Jardin de Paris," article [c.1890], BNF.

parody on Offenbach called *Le beau Paris* (1867). Such luminaries as Halévy, Hérold, and Adam were also represented on the program.

Parisian entrepreneurs turned to the British music hall for models when they began offering large spectacles and other entertainments in the 1870s. A night at the Pavillon de l'Horloge in 1878 included performers formerly in Britain such as a ventriloquist called Sir Vaughan, singers in the operetta *Gascon Young Blood*, and acrobats of the Troupe Jackley, all accompanied by an orchestra of fifty.[67] Yet songs remained a focal point even in theatres featuring big shows. A program at the Folies-Bergères in 1868 offered songs by six men and four women; *La Fille de Pierrot*, an operetta in one act with music by the prominent Frédéric Barbier; and a *saynète* called *The Monkey and the Married Woman*.[68]

French opera and *chansonettes* were not promoted in nationalistic terms, as was done for British song, because cosmopolitan and national music shared the limelight more equally in France. But the growing focus on French overtures displays a national focus not apparent in classical music programs during the middle of the century. We can see this tendency in a list of the orchestral pieces performed at the Eldorado in the last three months of 1882; the only overture by a foreign composer was Balfe's *La Bohémienne*.[69] The overtures were fairly old, composed mostly between 1830 and 1850 (by Auber, Hérold, and Meyerbeer) and in 1850–1870 (by Thomas, Gounod, Adam, and Maillart). The only pieces less than a decade old were Ambroise Thomas's *Gilles et Gillotin* (1874) and Robert Planquette's *Les Chevaux-légers* (1882). The schedule included eight overtures by Auber and five by Thomas, indicating how familiar their music remained among the general public. Instrumental solos were as popular at these venues as at promenade concerts, and were apparently composed and performed by members of the orchestra. Nevertheless, most of the dance pieces were by the central Europeans dominant in promenade concerts – Gung'l, Strauss the Younger, and the Viennese Philipp Fahrbach.

Events similar to those at music halls or *café-concerts* also occurred in German cities. In December 1866 the Hôtel de Saxe offered an evening called "Singspiel-Halle (Salon Variété)" (Ill. 22). Although *The Sleep Walker* (1824) was identified as a *Singspiel*, most were called a "Comic

[67] Advertisement, "Concert de l'Horloge," *Revue théâtrale illustrée*, August 1878, BNF.

[68] Program, Folies-Bergères, and piece clipped from *Album des théâtres*, February 1868, BNF.

[69] *Eldorado, 25e Année, Programme des morceaux d'orchestre executés du 20 Septembre au 31 Décembre 1882*, BNF. On the hall, see *L'Eldorado et la question des cafés-concerts* (Paris: L. Hugonis, 1875); and Paulus, *Trente ans de café-concert: Souvenirs*, Octave Pradels (ed.) (Paris: Société d'édition et de Publications, 1908).

Scene with Song": "Peter the Mute," "The Orphan Child," "Narcissus in Tails," "A Political Houseboy," and "A Cook's Confession of Love." The skit about the orphan came from a song composed by Clara Röhmeyer, whose family directed a conservatory in the Baden city of Pforzheim.[70] One wonders what kinds of jokes were made about the "political houseboy" just after Prussia's crushing defeat of Austria, particularly because of the populist, perhaps *grossdeutsch*, point of view in the Austrian Lied in dialect. International opera was nonetheless represented by Mozart and Boieldieu, along with a piece by the rising piano virtuoso Ernst Pauer.

The French *café-concert* was recognized artistically in remarkably strong terms by the late 1860s. The tradition of writing and setting songs had greater continuity, and a firmer intellectual basis, between 1750 and 1850 in France, as compared with Britain, and that put the songs of the *café-concert* on a firm basis among the intelligentsia. As early as 1857 a commentator in the *Gazette de Paris* praised those halls for reinvigorating the *chanson* and derided Le Caveau as a bunch of out-of-date old men.[71] In 1867 a critic attributed a strong aesthetic legitimacy to the *café-concert* when, praising a performance of the leading singer Thérésa (Emma Valadon), he invoked the model of Corneille:

Of which art do we speak in this context? Of the choreography, of the music, of the librettos, of the theatre design, of the statues within it? . . . First we hear the coarse cries of Mlle Thérésa; then we encounter a Corneille-like tirade, artfully done; tomorrow the art will be something else. It is necessary to take art as it comes, and accept modes for what they do at any one moment.[72]

THE GENESIS OF POPULAR MUSIC

The whole idea of "popular music" was just as much a novelty in 1850 as "classical music" had been in 1810. That is why one has to be impressed with the prominence, scale, and professionalism achieved by music halls, *cafés-concerts*, and ballad concerts in their early decades. Although these events grew out of strong traditions of music-making, what emerged by 1870 affected a far wider range of social classes and stood proudly independent from elite institutions, but nonetheless linked with mainstream culture. "Popular music" designed for the general public thus began in the 1850s and

---

[70] Clara Röhmeyer, music, and Theodor Storm, words, *Waisenkind* (Pforzheim: Theodor Röhmeyer, n. d.), in *From the Women Composers Collection, University of Michigan* (Woodbridge, Conn.: Research Publications, 1998).

[71] "Une visite au Caveau," *Gazette de Paris*, 20 September 1857, pp. 1–2.

[72] Claimed to have been written by Edmond Texier in 1867, quoted in *L'Eldorado*, pp. 25–26.

1860s. If the British music halls achieved the largest scale of entertainment, and ballad concerts the most distinctive national taste, French *cafés-concerts* acquired what Bernard Gendron called a "cultural empowerment of popular music," taking on an authority parallel to the Conservatoire concerts.[73] Particularly significant divisions occurred over matters of taste in Britain, as we have seen in quarrels over who "possessed" opera selections in music halls. The city with the freest market in musical life was thus the most fragmented in taste. But the early opera galas stood apart from popular music. Opera was identified with neither classics nor with popular songs, and it could thereby contribute a common culture to musical life as a whole.

[73] Bernard Gendron, *Between Montmartre and the Mudd Club: Popular Music and the Avant-garde* (Chicago, Ill.: University of Chicago Press, 2002), p. 5.

EPILOGUE

The state of the musical community in 1914

In 1909, when the young music critic Sydney Grew looked back in time, he saw a major discontinuity between his age and that of his grandparents:

The music that we produce or listen to now has scarcely any relation with that of a hundred years ago; in no way are our ideas like those of our grandparents. What they wanted (and had) was something pleasant, graceful, elegant, and eminently musicianly; it was . . . empty of all that makes art valuable – the impetus to thought. It must have been listened to with the careless ease once accorded to the old Italian opera. It could have been no more than the merest relaxation. Much of it became so widely popular that it still retains a regrettably firm hold upon unthinking people.[1]

Grew portrayed accurately, if with considerable snobbery, the deep division in taste that had emerged between pieces that were "pleasant" and "musicianly" and those derived from an "impetus to thought." Yet he saw the old taste persisting, presumably at opera galas and music halls, among "unthinking people" who wanted "the merest relaxation."

This epilogue will assess the state of the musical community just after 1900, reviewing the divisions that we have been tracing since the late eighteenth century, between contemporary and classical music and between light and serious music. I have argued that listeners might expect both relaxation and thought in eighteenth-century musical life. Different kinds of music cohabited in the same programs, making room for one another through a process of accommodation. That structure nonetheless remained at some distance from songs of the salon, tavern, and the popular theatre. The growing popularity of songs and opera medleys, in some quarters, and the demand for more serious programming, in others, led to a breakdown of the old musical order after 1800, a change related to crises in national and international politics during the ensuing decades. Powerful new kinds of music impelled this process – the promethean symphonies of

[1] Sydney Grew, "English and Modern Ideas of Music," *MOTR*, November 1909, p. 89. He published such books as *Bach* (1947) and *Our Favourite Musicians, from Stanford to Holbrooke* (1922).

301

Beethoven, the sumptuous vocalism of Donizetti, and the elegant virtuosity of Thalberg. The widely disseminated songs of Heinrich Proch, Louis Niedermeyer, and Henry Bishop played powerful parts in this process, too. The whole nature of programming was thus transformed within about two generations. The traditional interdependence of solo voices and instruments – the *bel canto* of the concert – became much weaker. The "miscellany" of genres gave way to musical homogeneity in some concerts, accompanied by an unprecedented diversity in historical periods represented. Even though traces of the "miscellany" remained after 1875, that usually amounted to specialized programming by 1914.

The organization of concert life expanded in new directions after 1800, breaking up the old social order that had governed it. String quartets cast aside tradition by driving vocal music completely from their programs. Orchestral societies set up lofty new goals for themselves and the musical community as a whole and began giving concerts focused on music by deceased "great" composers. Virtuosos and singers experimented in various ways. Some tried to rival the brilliant inventiveness of opera singing, indeed its commercial returns, and others narrowed their repertory strictly to serious works; a few gave "recitals" alone. A set of compromises were worked out over these grand ideals at midcentury. Instrumentalists defined a new kind of virtuosity in the interpretation of classical sonatas and concertos, and orchestras kept traditionalists satisfied by bringing in star soloists. Composers made some progress in pressuring for a slot to be kept open for a new work on classical programs. The development largest in scale came in the 1850s, when concerts sometimes called "popular music" got off to a quick start in the British music hall, the French *café-concert*, and concerts of the Strauss-Kapelle. Entrepreneur-conductors succeeded in establishing the promenade concert as a middle ground between these venues and classical music concerts. Thus did divisions open up along a spectrum of music deemed from light to serious. The world of opera, indeed the opera "gala," served as an intermediary among these spheres, providing a common culture of overtures and vocal selections with a canonic repertory of its own.

Different countries contributed to the transformation of musical taste in diverse ways. Pairs of cities or countries tended to invent new kinds of concerts: quartet concerts arose in Vienna and Paris, playing a symphony alone after intermission was first done in Leipzig and London, and musician-led orchestral societies were initiated in London and Paris. On a broader plane, popular music concerts evolved with particular prominence in North America and Britain. Patterns also cut across one another. For example, a free market developed in the musical world earliest in London and Vienna, as compared with the more monopolistic Paris and Leipzig. Catholicism and court tradition differentiated musical culture in Paris and Vienna from that in London and Leipzig. Therefore one does not find a unified Germanic musical culture looming here. Vienna and Leipzig shared relatively little in their musical institutions aside from the classical repertory usually seen as Germanic.[2] Nor did capital and provincial cities always differ significantly, and the latter sometimes led the way in concert programming.

The social and cultural institutions established in musical life in the 1850s remained in place in 1914. "Symphony" orchestras, *cafés-concerts*, opera galas, and recitalists were willing to cultivate their respective musical gardens in a time when populations were increasing and cultural opportunities expanding. By 1910 the division between "concerts, serious and otherwise," as William Boosey put it, had become clearer and firmer, with less interaction between them. Classical music still dominated music criticism and pedagogy, although events aimed at the general public overshadowed those of orchestras and quartets on sales charts and at the box-office. Fewer composers attached to the classical music world wrote much for the general public, as Schubert and Mendelssohn had done quite actively. Indeed, writing a commercially successful song no longer seemed proper for such composers; Frederick Cowen, for example, lamented that he had to apologize to colleagues for doing that. Women composers known in large part for popular songs, Maude Valérie White most prominent among them, saw their reputations decline for this reason at the turn of the century.[3] A reporter in the London *Musical Opinion and Music Trade Review* stated the issue politely, "To my thinking, the more sober-minded musician is too prone to underrate the work of the popular class song composer."[4] But Edward Lloyd defended his eclectic repertory in blunt terms:

Why not popular songs? The people like them, and if the words have a good tone and the music is pleasing to the audience, why should I not sing them? If I sing at a classical concert I sing a classical song with pleasure; but it seems to me that those who call out about my singing of popular songs are just those who do not pay for admission to concerts but want the tickets given to them![5]

Ironically, the division between popular and serious music, now sharpened ideologically, helped bring unity to the disparate parts of the classical

[2] Wyn Jones, *Symphony in Beethoven's Vienna*, pp. 8–10, 32–33, 190–91.
[3] Frederic Cowen, *My Art and My Friends* (London: Arnold, 1904), pp. 104–6.
[4] D'Auverge Barnard, "Popular Song Composers," *MOTR*, December 1909, p. 172.
[5] Quoted from *MT*, January 1899, in Percy A. Scholes, *Mirror of Music, 1844–1944: A Century of Musical Life in Britain* (London: Novello, 1947), p. 293.

music world. Orchestral concerts and recitals enjoyed a premier place in
urban life during this period. The "golden age" for classical music grew
from the compromise between virtuosity and idealism that allowed virtuosos "performative" independence under the imprimatur of the classics.
Pianists, playing what they called "the instrument of the immortals," gave
their canon popular appeal by performing in a "grand manner" with flex-
ibility in rhythm and dynamics. "Preluding," a personal introduction to
a work, was still conventional.[6] Virtuosos on the whole played their own
music more widely than had Hallé, Joachim, or Clara Schumann, though
they did not often venture outside of solo genres for their particular instruments. Larger and grander halls constructed in the late nineteenth century
added to the luster of many concerts. The leading orchestral series distinguished themselves more consistently from other ensembles by adhering
to a "pure" format of three to five works, with few instrumental solos; the
Gewandhaus now followed that practice, as did the newly founded Berlin
Philharmonic (1882) and London Symphony Orchestra (1904). Orchestras
in the next professional tier, joined by the Wiener Concertverein (1900) and
London's Queen's Hall Concerts (1893), became significantly more prominent socially and artistically than they had been in 1875. Although vocal
pieces remained common in this second tier of orchestral concerts, fewer
short pieces were offered than had been the case in the 1860s.

The repertories of promenade concerts likewise grew closer to those
performed at more formal events. Less flashy or entrepreneurial conductors
arose who deemphasized dance pieces in favor of overtures, opera medleys,
marches, and short classical pieces, rather like what German orchestral
concerts had been in the 1850s (Exs. 7.12, 8.5).[7] The seven or eight pieces at
Henry Wood's reshaped Promenade Concerts in 1895 were not unlike what
was presented at the Kurhaus in Bad Nauheim north of Frankfurt. Such
repertories now tended to be cosmopolitan, linked to the musical theatre
although usually offering no vocal music.[8]

By 1910 opera repertories were increasingly dominated by the music of
deceased composers, but the opera canon was still intellectually underde-
veloped. The "work concept" had become accepted for the most respected
older operas by 1900, whether they were in or out of repertory. Yet an aesthetic gap remained between the canons in opera and the concert hall, the
former having thus far failed to acquire the overarching truth and certainty

[6] Hamilton, *After the Golden Age*, Ch. 5.   [7] Spitzer, "Entrepreneur-Conductors."
[8] Promenades, CPH/RCM; Bad Nauheim, FUSB; *The Proms: A New History*, Jenny Doctor and David
Wright (eds.) (London: Thames and Hudson, 2007). See the massive collection of programs from
Germany and few other places, 1900–1914, *Concert-Programme-Austausch*, pp. 1946.ad., BL.

attributed to the latter. One senses such an intellectual insecurity regarding the canonic operas to a particular extent in Britain. An article on "popular songs" published in 1896 included famous opera tunes under that heading, the author suggesting that it was hard to determine why some operas became so famous.[9] Indeed, an English society novel published in 1896 portrayed a countess saying that, "If we could keep Gounod's melodies now, and get them reharmonized by Saint-Saëns or [Louis-Charles] Bruneau, it would certainly be charming."[10] Such aesthetic problems hardly mattered to much of the public, for by this time opera galas were among the most fashionable events in concert life. In London a diva such as Nellie Melba would book a concert in the Royal Albert Hall to perform numbers by Mozart, Weber, Mercadante, Verdi, Gounod, Arditi, and Giacomo Puccini.

The grandeur of the golden age of classical music was deeply shaken by a crisis that erupted over new music in the decade prior to World War I. We have seen that around 1865 a compromise was worked out in the major orchestras, allowing a few new works to be performed, after which the traditional recycling of old music for new continued, if on a much smaller scale than before. But by 1900 yet another generation lay between new works and the core classical repertory. The popularity of music written between 1850 and 1880 by Wagner, Liszt, Gounod, Saint-Saëns, Tchaikovsky, and Bedřich Smetana continued to dominate orchestral programs to the disadvantage of new works. Moreover, as playing a solo recital from memory became the premier vehicle for virtuosos, their repertories became smaller and included even fewer recent pieces. Singers began historicizing their programs, arranging them in chronological order. For that matter, early music ensembles and modern dance companies diverted the intelligentsia from new music concerts.

The addition of new works to canons failed to produce judgments as absolute as those achieved during the early nineteenth century. No composer was received with unanimous approval: Wagner was thought undisciplined, Gounod and Tchaikovsky popularizing, and Brahms obscure. As *Le Ménestrel* said of Brahms in 1911, "In that so extensive *oeuvre* of music one will regularly find many dull, dense, or repetitious passages that must exclude him from our present-day musical Pantheon."[11] Critics asked

---

[9] "Popular Songs," *Cornhill Magazine* 26 (1896), 405–11. See Poriss, "A Madwoman's Choice: Aria Substitution in *Lucia di Lammermoor*," pp. 3–5 and *Changing the Score: Aria Insertions, Opera Singers, and the Authority of Performance*, in progress. Poriss reports that four or five pieces – a short concert – were often inserted at one point, most notably in the lesson scene of Rossini's *Il Barbiere di Siviglia*.
[10] Robert Hichens, *The Green Carnation* (London: Heinemann, 1896), p. 14; Solie, *Music in Other Words*, pp. 187–218.
[11] See "Revue des grands concerts et semaine musicale: Colonne," *Ménestrel*, 2 December 1911, p. 380.

whether the whole process of canonization was unreliable. After hearing Edward Elgar's *Cockaigne Overture* in 1910, John Runciman declared, "Is Elgar still a classic, I wonder, or has he outlived the burst of cheap immediate fame that followed *Gerontius?*" Critics had jumped the gun, said Runciman, by immortalizing Gounod, Puccini, Antonin Dvořák, Pietro Mascagni, and Ruggero Leoncavallo "after a single hearing," creating a problem for Dvořák most of all in the long run.[12]

After 1900 a suspicion of new music emerged among the classical music public that was far more categorical than what was expressed around 1870. A recurrent theme in many parts of Europe was the warning that the public found new works an insufferable burden. The standard repertory of classics had become so well known that almost anything unfamiliar was treated with suspicion, quite different from the taste of John Addington Symonds in the 1860s. Listeners ceased to be attracted by a première at a concert; critics began making a sweeping denunciation of new music in and of itself. Most significantly, such criticism was aimed at pieces written in conservative as well as in advanced styles. For example, a Leipzig magazine for amateur choral societies – whose music was rarely "progressive" – declared in 1913: "So you want even more modern music? Haven't we had enough already? Isn't it clear that as soon as a conductor brings on a new piece, the hall empties out immediately, and that is the best way to scare people off?"[13] Reports on the English choral festivals said much the same. The annual events had been drawing smaller audiences, and new oratorios were often blamed for the problem. One writer said that "serious modern composers and their works never appeal to our people; and their music is always so difficult and costs much more money."[14]

German composers faced a particularly difficult situation because their country was identified so closely with the classical music tradition. A British critic saw the crisis among German composers as prototypical of Europe as a whole:

Germany is living on its past: a great and glorious past it is true, but one that from the very nature of things cannot prolong itself far into the future ... Nor are the other great European schools of music in much better case. A kind of dry rot in matters musical seems to be spreading all over the continent; a lethargy succeeding the overexertion and the strenuous energy of the past.[15]

12 John F. Runciman, "National Composers at Queen's Hall," *MOTR*, February 1910, p. 337.
13 Richard Oehmichen, "Mehr moderne Musik fürs moderne tägliche Leben," *Deutsche Sängerbundeszeitung*, 7 June 1913, p. 374.
14 "Weird Opinions: First & Second Cathedral Organist," *MOTR*, September 1910, p. 842.
15 C. Elvey Cope, "The Future of Music, and the Final Aim of Art," *MOTR*, June 1910, p. 621.

Proponents of contemporary music fought back by elevating performance of new music as a high virtue in a way that would have seemed strange in 1830. "What is going to happen to young composers?" became a refrain in the new music world. A lead article in a Leipzig music magazine declared in 1910 that "Schubert, Schumann, Brahms, Wolf, R. Strauss – anything else is regarded as a nuisance. It is so difficult to get anything new and good in front of the public. And so what is going to happen to young composers? Singers say they've done all they need to do in that department by offering pieces by Wolf and Strauss."[16]

By 1910 the New Music concert had become a major component of musical life. Concerts like the one held in Hanover in 1877 (Ill. 15) became common throughout Europe and North America, usually drawing a specialized public of composers, their students, and patrons. Private patronage persisted, sometimes helping to attract a broader public, as can be seen in the concerts of Thomas Beecham in London and countess Elizabeth Greffulhe, née La Rochefoucauld, in Paris.[17] Programs composed entirely of recent works tended to make critics unhappy. A program given by the Munich New String Quartet in Leipzig led the critic from the Social Democratic *Leipziger Volkszeitung* to regret that "the four gentlemen attended us with an entirely modern program." One work appalled him because the composer, Jan Ingehoven, "fritters away what musical talent he does possess by going too far in the contemporary direction."[18] Although recent works were heard unusually often in Paris in the late nineteenth century, by 1910 orchestral conductors who drew subsidies from the government repeated a few popular pieces several times a year to fulfill the requirement that they leave room for new music by French composers.[19]

The heightened suspicion of contemporary music was not triggered by the extravagances of an avant-garde. Admittedly, early tendencies toward modernism – an "ambivalent" form, as Walter Frisch sees it – can be traced to the 1870s, especially in the music of Richard Strauss.[20] But neither

[16] *Musikalisches Wochenblatt*, 29 September 1910, p. 1.
[17] "Concerts of Thomas Beecham: 1909–45," BL; Jann Pasler, "Countess Greffulhe as Entrepreneur," *Musician as Entrepreneur*, pp. 221–55.
[18] "Musik," *Leipziger Volkszeitung*, 3 February 1913, p. 14.
[19] Jann Pasler, *Writing through Music: Essays on Music, Culture, and Politics* (New York: Oxford University Press, forthcoming), Ch. 12, "Concert Programs and their Narratives as Emblems of Ideology," and Ch. 13, "Material Culture and Postmodern Positivism: Rethinking the 'Popular' in Late-Nineteenth-Century French Music."; Jane F. Fulcher, *French Cultural Politics & Music: From the Dreyfus Affair to the First World War* (New York: Oxford University Press, 1999), pp. 214–26; Chimènes, "Le Budget de la musique sous la 3e République."
[20] Walter Frisch, *German Modernism: Music and the Ideas* (Berkeley: University of California Press, 2005), pp. 7–35.

Arnold Schoenberg nor Igor Stravinsky broke fundamentally from traditional practices until almost 1910, and that music was not well known until the *causes célèbres* over *Rite of Spring* and *Pierrot Lunaire* in the year 1913.[21] If anything, the heightened hostility to contemporary works began driving composers into extreme directions. We must therefore look back at the history of concert repertories if we are to explain the crisis in new music that arose by 1914. The hegemony of classical music achieved during the 1850s put composers in an increasingly problematic situation. Richard Strauss achieved far greater prominence than any other composer, but that made some jealous enough to attack him for deserting the ideals of their profession. Ironically, it was the aged *Wagnerianer*, Felix Draeseke, who opened a dispute over him in 1906, decrying "Die Confusion in der Musik."[22]

A rigid dichotomy thus emerged between classical and contemporary works such as has not occurred in the fine arts. Painting and sculpture had traditionally maintained a stable balance, more or less, between canon and creativity since the sixteenth century. In retrospect, one can argue that such a practice could not last long in nineteenth-century musical culture. Canons came relatively late to music, awkwardly close to the time when aspects of mass culture transformed the arts in contrasting ways, bringing an unusually severe alienation of composers from the general public. The growing distance between the classical music world and *cafés-concerts* and music halls limited composers' options for writing for different publics.

We have seen that the transformation of musical life in the nineteenth century can be seen as a kind of political process. The movement to reform taste and repertories formed part of the reconstitution of political authority in Europe as a whole, and new concerts for the general public came with the rise of mass politics. Conflict among tastes and interest groups brought about a segmentation of musical life, on the broadest plane that between classical and popular music. For all the success of the "golden age" in classical music during the early twentieth century, the compromises inherent in the new framework remained problematic on a long-term basis. People who listened only to classics might naively hope that such music would become a universal taste. Propagandists for popular songs struggled to find aesthetic legitimacy for their music in their own intellectual terms.

---

[21] Thrun, *Neue Musik*, 93–220; Esteban Buch, *Le cas Schönberg: Naissance de l'avant-garde musicale* (Paris: Editions Gallimard, 2006), pp. 235–58.

[22] Susanne Shigihara (ed.), *"Die Konfusion in der Musik": Felix Draesekes Kampfschrift von 1906 und ihre Folgen* (Bonn: Schröder, 1990).

Composers of avant-garde music sometimes gave up writing for anyone but themselves. The contrasting insecurities in the worlds of classical, popular, and avant-garde music that began around 1850 still exist today to a considerable extent.

Yet idealism and business sense have managed since then to work in tandem toward the common good in the classical music world. Wealthy patrons or governments kept challenging kinds of music-making in existence, supporting soloists, quartets, or new music groups whose concerts usually drew small audiences. Profits from sales of music by Verdi, Massenet, or the Beatles allowed publishers to put out pieces or recordings of music by Debussy, Schoenberg, and Elliott Carter. That happened in part because the rhetoric separating popular, classical, and avant-garde music proved politically malleable. Deep-seated conflicts can bring vitality to a cultural world; people have enjoyed arguing about Schoenberg and Elvis Presley. The lines between musical spheres changed in the twentieth century because of exploitation of the phonograph and the radio, opening up new publics for both popular and classical music. Then composers and performing groups began cutting across boundaries, as hip culture disseminated "minimalist" music to a wide public and the Kronos Quartet played music by Thelonius Monk as well as Bela Bartók. It is particularly impressive how widely classical music has moved all around the world, as Asian musicians have brought new insights to performing classics. That is why I look back in admiration at the musicians who devised the first programs of classical or popular music, and why I like to savor the ideological disputes which gave this history such intellectual vitality.

Selected bibliography

PRINCIPAL ARCHIVES OF CONCERT PROGRAMS

Austria

ÖNB	Österreichische Nationalbibliothek, Vienna
PA/GMFV	Program Archive, Gesellschaft der Musikfreunde, Vienna
SLBV	Stadt- und Landesbibliothek, Vienna
UMDK	Universität für Musik und Darstellende Kunst, Vienna

France

BNF	Bibliothèque Nationale, Paris
BOP	Bibliothèque de l'Opéra, Paris
MB	Musée de Bordeaux
BHVP	Musée de l'Histoire de la Ville de Paris
MM	Musée de Montmartre, Paris

Germany

DSB	Deutsche Staatsbibliothek, Berlin
PA/FUSB	Program Archive Universitäts- und Stadtsbibliothek, Frankfurt
UBG	Universitätsbibliothek, Göttingen
SBL	Stadtbibliothek Leipzig
SGML	Stadtgeschichtliches Museum, Leipzig

Great Britain

BCL	Birmingham Central Library
BL	British Library, London
BLO	Bodleian Library, Oxford
BLO/JJ	Bodleian Library, John Johnson Collection of Ephemera
CUL	Cambridge University Library
CPH/RCM	Centre for Performance History, Royal College of Music, London

Selected bibliography

United States

BPL	Boston Public Library
GRI	Getty Research Institute, Los Angeles
HMLA	Harvard Musical Association Library, Boston
AAS	American Antiquarian Society, Worcester, MA

Abbreviations of Sources

AMA	*Allgemeiner musikalische Anzeiger* (Vienna)
AMZ	*Allgemeine musikalische Zeitung* (Leipzig)
AMZK	*Allgemeine musikalische Zeitung, mit besonderer Rücksicht auf den österreichischen Kaiserstaat* (Vienna)
ATH	*Athenaeum*
AWMZ	*Allgemeine Wiener Musik-Zeitung*
BMTK	*Blätter für Musik, Theater und Kunst*
COKE	Unpublished letters of Lady Mary Coke, 1775–1791, collection of the Hon. Caroline Douglas-Home, Coldstream, Scotland, photocopies at Lewis Walpole Library, Farmington, CT; see below for those of 1759–1774.
CORR	*Correspondance des amateurs musiciens, rédigée par le Cit. Cocatrix, Amateur*
FM	*France Musicale*
JAMS	*Journal of the American Musicological Society*
JLM	*Journal des Luxus und der Moden*
MC	*Morning Chronicle*
MHG	*Music Halls' Gazette*
MOTR	*Musical Opinion and Music Trade Review*
MW	*Musical World*
NCM	*19th Century Music*
NCMR	*Nineteenth-Century Music Review*
NGD	*New Grove Dictionary of Music and Musicians*, eds. Stanley Sadie and John Tyrrell, 30 vols., London: Macmillan, 2001
NZfM	*Neue Zeitschrift für Musik*
QMMR	*Quarterly Musical Magazine and Review*
RGM	*Revue et Gazette musicale*
SMW	*Signale für die musikalische Welt*
TL	*The Times*, London
TZ	*Theaterzeitung*, Vienna

PRIMARY PRINTED SOURCES

Boosey, William, *Fifty Years of Music*, London: Ernest Benn, 1931.
Cler, Albert, *Physiologie du musicien*, Paris: Aubert, 1843.

Coke, Lady Mary, *The Letters and Journals of Lady Mary Coke* (ed. J. A. Home), 4 vols., Edinburgh, D. Douglas, 1889–1896. (See above, COKE, for letters 1775–1791).

Dialogue entre Lulli, Rameau et Orphée, dans les Champs Elisées, Amsterdam, 1774.

[Dibdin, Charles], *Bystander, or, Universal Weekly Expositor, by a Literary Association*, London, 1790.

Guynemer, Charles, *Essay on Chamber Classical Music*, London: The Author, 1846.

Hanslick, Eduard, *Geschichte des Concertwesens in Wien*, Vienna, 1869.

Hawkins, John, *A General History of the Science and Practice of Music*, 2 vols., London: Novello, 1875; New York: Dover, 1963.

Hofmann, Rudolf, *Der Wiener Männergesangverein: Chronik der Jahre 1843 bis 1893*, Vienna: Verlag des Wiener Männergesangvereines, 1893.

Macfarren, George, "'The English are Not a Musical People,'" *Cornhill Magazine* 18 (1868), pp. 344–63.

Rivière, Jules, *My Musical Life and Recollections*, London: Sampson, 1893.

Stolle, Friedrich, *Die sächsische Revolution oder Dresden und Leipzig in den Jahren 1830 und 1831*, Leipzig: Otto Wigand, 1835.

———, *Das neue Leipzig nebst einer Kreuzthurminspiration über Dresden, Leipzig*: Otto Wigand, 1834.

Symonds, J. A., *Letters of John Addington Symonds*, 3 vols., Herbert M. Schueller and Robert L. Peters (eds.), Detroit: Wayne State University Press, 1967.

Trollope, Frances, *Vienna and the Austrians; with Some Account of a Journey through Swabia, Bavaria, the Tyrol, and the Salzbourg*, 2 vols., London: Richard Bentley, 1838.

Unser Planet: Blätter für Unterhaltung, Zeitgeschichte, Literatur, Kunst und Theater.

Gustave Vapereau, *Dictionnaire universel des contemporains*, 2 vols., 2nd ed., Paris: Hachette, 1861.

Volksfreund: Freiheit, Gleichheit, Brüderlichkeit!, Leipzig: C. V. Weller. 1848.

Worgan, T. D., *The Musical Reformer*, London: S. Maunder, 1829.

SECONDARY SOURCES

Applegate, Celia, *Bach in Berlin: A Cultural History of Mendelssohn's Revival of the St. Matthew Passion*, Ithaca, N.Y.: Cornell University Press, 2005.

———, "How German Is It? Nationalism and the Idea of Serious Music in the Early Nineteenth Century, *19th Century Music* 21 (1998), 274–296.

Bailey, Peter, *Popular Culture and Performance in the Victorian City*, Cambridge: Cambridge University Press, 1998.

Bashford, Christina, "The Late Beethoven Quartets and the London Press, 1836-ca. 1850," *Musical Quarterly* 84 (2000), 84–122.

Beachy, Robert, *The Soul of Commerce: Credit, Property and Politics in Leipzig, 1750–1840*, Leiden: Brill, 2005.

Biba, Otto, "Beobachtungen zur Österreichischen Musikszene des 18. Jahrhunderts," *Österreichische Musik/Musik in Österreich: Theophil Antonicek zum 60. Geburtstag*, Elisabeth Hilscher (ed.), Tutzing: Schneider, 1998, pp. 213–30.

_____, "Franz Schubert in den musikalischen Abendunterhaltungen der Gesellschaft der Musikfreunde," in *Schubert-Studien: Festgabe zum Schubert-Jahr 1978*, Franz Grasberger and Othmar Wessely (eds.), Vienna: Österreichisches Akademie der Wissenschaft, 1978, 7–31.

_____, "Grundzüge des Konzertwesens in Wien zu Mozarts Zeit," *Mozart-Jahrbuch* 26 (1978–1979), 132–43.

Blanning, T. C. W., *Culture of Power and the Power of Culture: Old Regime Europe, 1660–1789*, Oxford: Oxford University Press, 2002.

_____, *The French Revolution in Germany: Occupation and Resistance in the Rhineland, 1792–1802*, New York: Oxford University Press, 1983.

Bonds, Mark Evan, "Idealism and the Aesthetics of Instrumental Music at the Turn of the Nineteenth Century," *JAMS* 50 (1997), 387–420.

_____, *Instrumental Ideas: Listening to the Symphony in the Age of Beethoven*, Princeton, N.J.: Princeton University Press, 2006.

Botstein, Leon, "Listening through Reading: Musical Literacy and the Concert Audience," *NCM* 16 (1992), 129–45.

Bourdieu, Pierre, *Distinction: A Social Critique of the Judgment of Taste*, Richard Nice (trans.), Cambridge: Harvard University Press, 1984.

Brewer, John, *Pleasures of the Imagination: English Culture in the Eighteenth Century*, New York: Farrar Straus Giroux, 1997.

British Musical Biography: A Dictionary of Musical Artists, Authors and Composers Born in Britain and its Colonies, James D. Brown and Stephen S. Stratton (eds.), New York: Da Capo, 1971.

Broyles, Michael, *"Music of the Highest Class": Elitism and Populism in Antebellum Boston*, New Haven, Conn.: Yale University Press, 1992.

Brown, Bruce, *Gluck and the French Theatre in Vienna*, Oxford: Clarendon Press, 1991.

Buch, Esteban, *Beethoven's Ninth: A Political History* Richard Miller (trans.) (Chicago, Ill.: University of Chicago Press, 1999).

Burchell, Jenny, *Polite or Commercial Concerts? Concert Management and Orchestral Repertoire in Edinburgh, Bath, Oxford, Manchester, and Newcastle, 1730–1799*, New York: Garland, 1996.

Citron, Marcia J., *Gender and Musical Canon*, Cambridge: Cambridge University Press, 2003.

Condemi, Concetta, *Les Cafés-concerts: Histoire d'un divertissement, 1849–1914*, Paris: Quai Voltaire, 1992.

Cooper, Victoria, *House of Novello: Practice and Policy of a Victorian Music Publisher, 1829–1866*, Aldershot, UK: Ashgate, 2003.

Dahlhaus, Carl, *Nineteenth-Century Music*, J. Bradford Robinson (trans.), Berkeley: University of California Press, 1989.

Dean, Jeffrey, "The Evolution of a Canon at the Papal Chapel: The Importance of Old Music in the Fifteenth and Sixteenth Centuries," in *Papal Music and*

Musicians in Late Medieval and Renaissance Rome, Oxford: Clarendon Press, 1998, pp. 138–166.

Didi-Huberman, Georges, "Artistic Survival: Panofsky vs. Warburg and the Exorcism of Impure Time," *Common Knowledge* 9 (2003), 273–85.

Dörffel, Alfred, *Geschichte der Gewandhausconcerte zu Leipzig vom 25. November 1781 bis 25. November 1881*, 2 vols., Leipzig: Breitkopf & Härtel, 1881–84.

Ehrlich, Cyril, *First Philharmonic: A History of the Royal Philharmonic Society*, Oxford: Oxford University Press, 1995.

Eitner, Robert (ed.), *Biographisch-Bibliographisches Quellen-Lexicon der Musiker und Musikgelehrter*, 11 vols., 2nd. ed., Leipzig, 1900–1904; Graz: Akademisches Druck- und Verlangsanstalt, 1959.

Ellis, Katharine, *Interpreting the Musical Past: Early Music in Nineteenth-Century France*, Oxford: Clarendon Press, 2005.

———, *Music Criticism in Nineteenth-Century France: La Revue et Gazette musicale de Paris, 1834–1880*, Cambridge: Cambridge University Press, 1995.

Fauquet, Joël-Marie (ed.), *Dictionnaire de la musique en France aux XIXe siècle*, Paris: Fayard, 2003.

———, *Les sociétés de musique de chambre à Paris de la Restauration à 1870*, Paris: Aux Amateurs de Livres, 1986.

Ferris, David, "Public Performance and Private Understanding: Clara Wieck's Concerts in Berlin," *JAMS* 56 (2003), 351–408.

Finscher, Ludwig. "Zum Begriff der Klassik in der Musik," *Deutsche Jahrbuch für Musik* 11 (1966), 9–34.

Foster, Myles Birket, *The History of the Philharmonic Society of London: 1813–1912*, London: John Lane, 1912.

Franklin, R. W., *Nineteenth-Century Churches: The History of a New Catholicism in Württemberg, England, and France*, New York: Garland, 1987.

Garratt, James, *Palestrina and the German Romantic Imagination: Interpreting Historicism in Nineteenth-Century Music*, Cambridge: Cambridge University Press, 2002.

Gibbs, Christopher H., "Schubert in deutschsprachigen Lexica nach 1830," *Schubert durch die Brille* 13 (1994), 70–78.

———, *Cambridge Companion to Schubert*, Christopher H. Gibbs (ed.), Cambridge: Cambridge University Press, 1997.

Gibbs, Christopher and Dana Gooley (eds.), *Franz Liszt and His World*, Princeton: Princeton University Press, 2006.

Goehr, Lydia, *The Imaginary Museum of Musical Works: An Essay in the Philosophy of Music*, Oxford: Clarendon Press, 1992.

Gooley, Dana, *The Virtuoso Liszt*, Cambridge: Cambridge University Press, 2004.

Gramit, David, *Cultivating Music: The Aspirations, Interests, and Limits of German Musical Culture, 1770–1848*, Berkeley: University of California Press, 2002.

———, "Unremarkable Musical Lives: Autobiographical Narratives, Music, and the Shaping of the Self," in *Musical Biography: Towards New Paradigms*, Jolanta T. Pekacz (ed.), Aldershot, UK: Ashgate, 2006, pp.159–78.

Grotjahn, Rebecca, *Die Sinfonie im deutschen Kulturgebeit 1850 bis 1875*, Sinzig: Studio, 1998.

Hall-Witt, Jennifer, *Fashionable Acts: Opera and Elite Culture in London, 1780–1880*, Lebanon, N.H.: University of New Hampshire Press, 2007.

Hamilton, Kenneth, *After the Golden Age: The Decline of Romantic Pianism and the Dawn of Modern Performance*, Oxford: Oxford University Press, 2007.

Handlos, Martha, "Die Wiener Concerts Spirituels (1819–1848)," in *Österreichische Musik/Musik in Österreich: Beiträge zur Musikgeschichte Mitteleuropas, Theophil Antonicek zum 60. Geburtstag*, Elisabeth Hilscher (ed.), Tutzing: Hans Schneider, 1998, pp. 283–319.

Hanson, Alice M., *Musical Life in Biedermeier Vienna*, Cambridge: Cambridge University Press, 1985.

Heartz, Daniel, *Music in European Capitals: The Galant Style, 1720–1780*, New York: W. W. Norton, 2000.

Heemann, Annegret, *Männergesangvereine im 19. und frühen 20. Jahrhundert: Ein Beitrag zur städtischen Musikgeschichte Münsters*, Frankfurt am Main: Peter Lang, 1992.

Hellsberg, Clemens, *Demokratie der Könige: Die Geschichte der Wiener Philharmoniker*, Zürich: Schweizer Verlagshaus, 1993.

Holoman, D. Kern, *The Société des Concerts du Conservatoire, 1828–1967*, Berkeley: University of California Press, 2004.

_____, *Société des Concerts du Conservatoire*, http://hector.ucdavis.edu/sdc/MainFrame.htm.

Horowitz, Joseph, *Classical Music in America: A History of its Rise and Fall*, New York: W. W. Norton, 2005.

Irving, Howard, *Ancients and Moderns: William Crotch and the Development of Classical Music*, Aldershot: Ashgate, 1999.

Johnson, James H., *Listening in Paris: A Cultural History*, Berkeley: University of California Press, 1995.

Judson, Pieter, *Exclusive Revolutionaries: Liberal Politics, Social Experience, and National Identity in the Austrian Empire, 1848–1914*, Ann Arbor: University of Michigan Press, 1996.

Kerman, Joseph, "A Few Canonic Variations," in *Canons*, Robert von Hallberg (ed.), Chicago, Ill.: University of Chicago Press, 1984, 177–96.

_____, "Beethoven Quartet Audiences: Actual, Potential, Ideal," *Beethoven Quartet Companion*, Robert Winter and Robert Martin (eds.), Berkeley: University of California Press, 1994, pp. 7–28.

Kraus, Beate Angelika, *Beethoven-Rezeption in Frankreich: Von ihren Angangen bis zum Untergang des Second Empire*, Bonn: Beethoven-Haus, 2001.

Leterrier, Sophie-Anne, *Le mélomane et l'historien*, Paris: Armand Colin, 2005.

Linke, Norbert, *Musik erobert die Welt; oder wie die Wiener Familie Strauss die "Unterhaltungsmusik" revolutionirte*, Vienna: Herold, 1987.

Mahling, Christoph Helmut, "Zum Musikbetrieb Berlins und seinen Institutionen in der ersten Hälfte des 19. Jahrhunderts." *Studien zur Musikgeschichte Berlins im früen 19. Jahrhundert*, Carl Dahlhaus (ed.), Regensburg: Bosse, 1980, pp. 27–284.

Mangum, John, "Apollo and the German Muses: Opera and the Articulation of Class, Politics and Society in Prussia, 1740–1806," unpublished Ph.D. dissertation, University of California, Los Angeles (2002).

McVeigh, Simon, *Concert Life in London from Mozart to Haydn*, Cambridge: Cambridge University Press, 1993.

Melton, James Van Horn, "School, Stage, Salon: Musical Cultures in Haydn's Vienna," *Journal of Modern History* 76 (2004), 251–79.

Menninger, Margaret, "The Serious Matter of True Joy: Music and Cultural Philanthropy in Leipzig, 1781–1933," in Thomas Adam (ed.), *Philanthropy, Patronage and Civil Society: Lessons from Germany, the United States, Britain and Canada*, Bloomington: Indiana University Press, 2004, pp. 120–37.

Morrow, Mary Sue, *Concert Life in Haydn's Vienna: Aspects of a Developing Musical and Social Institution*, Stuyvesant, N.Y.: Pendragon, 1989.

———, *German Music Criticism in the Late Eighteenth Century: Aesthetic Issues in Instrumental Music*, Cambridge: Cambridge University Press, 1997.

Music and British Culture, 1785–1914: Essays in Honour of Cyril Ehrlich, Leanne Langley and Christina Bashford (eds.), Oxford: Oxford University Press, 2000.

Le musicien et ses voyages: Pratiques, réseaux et représentations, Christian Meyer (ed.), Berlin: Berliner Wissenschafts-Verlag, 2003.

Noiray, Michel, *Vocabulaire de la musique de l'époque classique*, Paris: Minerve, 2005.

Nösselt, Hans-Joachim, *Das Gewandhausorchester: Entstehung und Entwicklung eines Orchesters*, Leipzig: Köhler & Amelang, 1943.

Perger, Richard von, *Denkschrift aus Anlass der Feier des fünfzigjährigen ununterbrochenen Bestandes des Philharmonischen Konzerte in Wien, 1860–1910*, Vienna: Fromme, 1910.

Piano in Nineteenth-Century British Culture: Essays on Instruments, Performers and Repertoire, Susan Wollenberg and Therese Ellsworth (eds.), Aldershot, UK: Ashgate, 2007,

Pierre, Constant, *Le Conservatoire national de musique et de declamation: Documents administratifs recueillis ou reconstitués*, Paris: Imprimérie Nationale, 1900.

———, *Histoire du Concert Spirituel (1725–1790)*, Paris: Société Française du Musicologie, 1975.

Pohl, C. F., *Denkschrift aus Anlass des hundertjährigen Bestehens der Tonkünstler-Societät*, Vienna: Tonkünstler-Societät, 1871.

Pomeroy, Elizabeth, *Elizabethan Miscellanies: Their Development and Conventions*, Berkeley: University of California Press, 1973.

Poriss, Hilary, "A Madwoman's Choice: Aria Substitution in *Lucia di Lammermoor*," *Cambridge Opera Journal* 13 (2001), 1–28

———, "Making Their Way through the World: Italian One-Hit Wonders," *19th Century Music* 24 (2001), 197–224.

Reimer, Erich, "Repertoirebildung und Kanonisierung: Zur Vorgeschichte des Klassikbegriffs (1800–1835)," *Archiv für Musikwissenschaft* 43 (1986), 241–60.

Rice, John A., *Empress Marie Therese and Music at the Viennese Court, 1792–1807*, Cambridge: Cambridge University Press, 2003.

Riley, Matthew, *Musical Listening in the German Enlightenment: Attention, Wonder and Astonishment*, Aldershot, UK: Ashgate, 2004.

Robins, Brian, *Catch and Glee Culture in Eighteenth-Century England*, Woodbridge, UK: Boydell, 2006.

Rosselli, John, "Italy, The Decline of a Tradition," *The Late Romantic Era from the Mid-Nineteenth Century to World War One*, Jim Samson (ed.), London: Macmillan, 1991, pp. 126–50.

Samson, Jim (ed.), *Cambridge History of Nineteenth-Century Music* (Cambridge: Cambridge University Press, 1992).

Schering, Arnold, "Aus den Jugendjahren der musikalischen Neuromantik," *Peters Jahrbuch* 24 (1917), 45–63.

Schering, Arnold, and Rudolf Wustmann, *Musikgeschichte Leipzigs*, 3 vols., Leipzig: Merseburger, 1974.

Scott, Derek, "Music and Social Class," *Cambridge History of the Nineteenth Century*, Jim Samson (ed.), Cambridge: Cambridge University Press, pp. 544–67.

———, *Singing Bourgeois: Songs of the Victorian Drawing Room and Parlour*, 2nd ed., Aldershot, UK: Ashgate, 2001.

———, *Sounds of the Metropolis: The 19th-Century Popular Music Revolution in London, New York, Paris and Vienna*, New York: Oxford University Press, 2008.

Scott, Harold, *Early Doors: Origins of the Music Hall*, London: Nicholson & Watson, 1946.

Sheehan, James, *German History, 1770–1866*, Oxford: Oxford University Press, 1989.

Sociétés de concert en Europe, 1700–1920: Structures, pratiques musicales et sociabilités, Hans-Erich Bödeker and Patrice Veit (eds.), Berlin: Berliner Wissenschaftsverlag, 2007.

Solie, Ruth, *Music in Other Words: Victorian Conversations*, Berkeley: University of California Press, 2004.

Sperber, Jonathan, *European Revolutions, 1848–1851*, Cambridge: Cambridge University Press, 1994.

Spitzer, John, and Neal Zaslaw, *Birth of the Orchestra: History of an Institution, 1650–1815*, Oxford: Oxford University Press, 2004.

Thrun, Martin, *Neue Musik im deutschen Musikleben bis 1933*, Bonn: Orpheus-Verlag, 1995.

Weber, William, "Canonicity and Collegiality: 'Other' Composers, 1790–1850," *Common Knowledge* 14 (2008), 105–23.

———, "Did People Listen in the Eighteenth Century?" *Early Music* 25 (1997), 678–91.

———, "L'Institution et son public: l'opéra à Paris et à Londres au XVIIIe siècle," *Annales E.S.C.* 48 (1993), 1519–40.

———, "Mentalité, tradition, et origines du canon musical en France et en Angleterre au XVIIIe siècle," *Annales E.S.C.* 42 (1989), 849–75.

———, *Music and the Middle Class: The Social Structure Concert Life in London, Paris, and Vienna, 1830–1848*, 2nd ed., Aldershot, UK: Ashgate, 2003.

———, *Musician as Entrepreneur and Opportunist, 1700–1914: Managers, Charlatans and Idealists*, W. Weber (ed.), Bloomington: Indiana University Press, 2004.

———, "*La musique ancienne* in the Waning of the Ancien Régime," *Journal of Modern History* 56 (1984), 58–88.

———, *Rise of Musical Classics in Eighteenth-Century England*, Oxford: Clarendon Press, 1992.

Wustmann, Gustav, "Die Gewandhausconcerte," *Aus Leipzigs Vergangenheit: Gesammelte Schriften*, 3 vols., Leipzig: F. W. Grunow, 1885–1909, vol. 2, pp. 458–88.

Wyn Jones, David, *The Symphony in Beethoven's Vienna*, Cambridge: Cambridge University Press, 2006.

Index

Abel, C.-F., 47, 70
Abendunterhaltung, title for chamber music
    concerts, 134
Abendunterhaltungen (Evening
    Entertainments), Vienna, 128, 129, 142,
    197–8, 224
Abt, Franz, 224
Académie Royale de Musique (Paris). *See* Opéra,
    Paris
Academy of Ancient Music, 32, 60, 68, 69, 70,
    71, 178
Academy of Music, Boston, 190
Accademia Filarmonica, Bologna, 32
Adam, Adolphe, 223, 277
Alary, Jules, 280
Albertini, Gioacchino, 55
Albrechtsberger, Johann, 56, 201
Alhambra Palace, London, 218, 236
Alhambra, Paris, 296
Alkan, Charles, 162
Allegri, Gregorio, 202
Allgemeine Deutsche Musikverein, 8, 138, 241,
    265, Ill. 15
Allgemeine musikalische Anzeiger, 106
Allgemeine musikalische Zeitung, 78, 96, 105, 106,
    108, 110, 115, 180, 201, 207
Allgemeine Wiener Musik-Zeitung, 118
Almaviva, Count, 55
Alsager, Thomas, 136
Amiens, 17
Ancient Concert Rooms, Dublin, 247
ancient music, 29, 68, 80–1, 91
    Britain, 68–72
    France, 72–5
    Germany, 75–8
Anderson, Benedict, 278
Angers. *See* Association Artistique d'Angers
Applegate, Celia, 96, 213
Arban, J.-B., 219
Arditi, Luigi, 268, 305
ariette, 29

aristocracy. *See* nobility
Armingaud, Jules, 247
Arne, Thomas, 28, 58–61, 64, 71, 72, 157, 158, 185,
    186, 189, 190, 219, 268, 281, 285, 290
Arnold, Samuel, 64, 156, 157
Arteaga, Esteban de, 33
Ashley, John, 64
Asioli, Bonifazio, 201
Association Artistique d'Angers, 262
Attwood, Thomas, 185
Auber, D.-F.-E., 91, 144, 154, 157, 158, 189, 190,
    195, 215, 251, 266, 277, 280, 298
    critical commentary, 97, 109, 110
    music halls, 274, 290, 291
    overtures, 186, 190, 215, 218, 268
    promenade concerts, 220–2, 229,
    295
Augarten, Vienna, 57
Avison, Charles, 28, 33, 63, 68

Bach, C.-P.-E., 105, 176, 201
Bach, J. C., 28, 47, 52, 70, 96
Bach, J.-S., 33, 37, 38, 78–9, 96, 107, 162, 163,
    164, 179, 197, 213, 244, 246, 247, 249, 256,
    260, 262, 265, 269
    Adolf Hesse, 163
    Brandenburg Concertos, 123
    Gewandhaus, 183
    quartet concerts, 138
    Saint-Saëns, 162
Bad Homburg, 254
Bad Nauheim, 304
Bagge, Selmar, 237, 241
Bailey, Peter, 293
Baillot, Pierre, 7, 91, 118, 119, 123, 124, 130, 132,
    133, 140, 190, 193, 270
Balfe, Michael, 150, 186, 190, 217, 268, 298
ballad, 2, 25, 28, 64, 165
    ballad opera, 62
    eighteenth century, 60
    nineteenth century, 156

321

Index